Current Issues
in Cognitive Processes

The Tulane Flowerree
Symposium on Cognition

Current Issues in Cognitive Processes

The Tulane Flowerree Symposium on Cognition

Edited by
Chizuko Izawa
Tulane University

LEA LAWRENCE ERLBAUM ASSOCIATES, PUBLISHERS
1989   Hillsdale, New Jersey   Hove and London

Lawrence Erlbaum Associates, Inc., Publishers
365 Broadway
Hillsdale, New Jersey 07642

Library of Congress Cataloging-in-Publication Data
Tulane Flowerree Symposium on Cognition (1987 : New Orleans, La.)
    Current issues in cognitive processes : the Tulane Flowerree
Symposium on Cognition, [held on February 23-24, 1987, at Tulane
University, New Orleans, Louisiana] / edited by Chizuko Izawa.
        p.   cm.
    Includes index.
    ISBN 0-8058-0144-8   ISBN 0-8058-0669-5 (pbk.)
    1. Cognition—Congresses. 2. Memory—Congresses. I. Izawa,
Chizuko. II. Tulane University.
    BF311.T78 1987
    153—dc19   88-22597

Printed in the United States of America
10 9 8 7 6 5 4 3 2 1

Contents

List of Contributors

Paul C. Amrhein
University of Wisconsin, Madison

Robert A. Bjork
University of California, Los Angeles

Jerome R. Busemeyer
Purdue University

Bradford R. Challis
Purdue University

William K. Estes
Harvard University

Scott Gronlund
Northwestern University

Robert G. Hayden
Tulane University

Chizuko Izawa
Tulane University

Bennet B. Murdock, Jr.
University of Toronto

Kevin Murnane
Indiana University

Douglas L. Nelson
University of South Florida

Dean J. Patterson
Tulane University

Alan Richardson-Klavehn
University of California, Los Angeles

Henry L. Roediger, III
Rice University

Marc Roth
Indiana University

Richard M. Shiffrin
Indiana University

Joan Gay Snodgrass
New York University

Robert L. Solso
University of Nevada, Reno

John Theios
University of Wisconsin, Madison

James T. Townsend
Purdue University

Preface

This volume presents the proceedings of the 1987 Flowerree Mardi Gras Symposium on Cognition held on February 23 and 24, 1987 at Tulane University in New Orleans. The symposium was made possible by a generous endowment from Robert E. Flowerree of Portland, Oregon, a graduate of the psychology department in 1942. The symposium is an annual event and may deal with any topic in psychology: The 1987 symposium was the third and the focus was cognitive psychology. This volume represents the first book-length publication of any of the Flowerree Symposia. Through it, we seek to share with readers and colleagues the excitement occasioned by the presentation at the symposium of new developments in cognition.

As the organizer and convener of this symposium, this editor's first task was to determine the desired coverage and the most suitable participants. My primary concern in discharging the responsibilities was excellence; there is no substitute for quality. One approach often utilized is to focus on a narrowly defined specific topic. Although this type can be very meaningful to the specialists in that field and effective at professional meetings, it may have somewhat limited appeal and utility in a university community where a substantial proportion of the audience are students not yet with sufficient expertise, or patience to profit from 2 full days of presentations on narrow topics.

An alternative approach, considering the type of audience anticipated, along with promoting the educational thrust of the symposium, would be to select a broad topic, allowing diversity to provide spice through variety. Variety does, indeed, characterize the current state of affairs in cognitive psychology. Accordingly, the best course of action was to make the symposium's fare varied and excellent.

Consequently, we sought out the most accomplished scholars whose contributions were state of the art in cognition, and as many of them as possible for a 2-day conference.

The payoff for that strategy proved satisfying and stimulating. The symposium audience had the privilege to witness trendsetters in action, firing the scientific imagination of both students and professionals. An enduring increment of interest in the mechanisms of cognition and in questions still to be answered constituted a major effect of the symposium, especially for students.

The topics covered by our speakers are all under active pursuit in laboratories across the nation: Many of the speeches represent the latest frontiers; some courageously explore important but less cultivated domains; and others still challenge significant but neglected issues of the past and persevere in their resolve to illuminate problems left unsolved for decades, because of their inherent difficulty or lack of trendiness. New advances, new theories, novel approaches, and methodological innovations are welcome and essential in facilitating the advancement of our science. Such improvements, however, do not always come from solely focusing on the most popular trends in a field.

Brave souls are needed to tackle unpopular or unappreciated frontiers. New discoveries and ideas often originate in unexpected, and at times, solitary quarters, where unpopular issues are often dealt with, by those out of step with the fashions of the time (although the latter are usually the most tempting and safest topics). At this Flowerree Symposium on Cognition, we endeavored to sample some of these unpopular topics, which on the basis of their excellence, contributed to the advance of knowledge.

Consequently, the symposium did accommodate topics and types of presentations from a very wide spectrum. They have one thing in common, however; all presentations excelled in contributing significantly to advancing cognitive psychology. Every chapter contains salient findings, the result of many years of intense effort and devotion by first-rate investigators.

This editor has one regret: Only a small fraction of the important issues in cognitive processes could be accommodated in a 2-day symposium, or in one volume. The larger part of the iceberg remains to be discussed and presented. Fortunately, however, the Flowerree Symposium is an annual event, and the topic of cognition will be explored here again, when its turn comes around in a few short years. Let us look forward to our future Flowerree Symposia on Cognition to reach then the currently unreachable.

Chapter 1 provides a brief history of the Symposium and a Mardi Gras style introduction of the contributors. The first chapter is based, in part, on the oral presentations made during the 1987 Flowerree Symposium, of February 23 and 24, 1987. We seek in this way to convey the positive mood of excitement and interest of both participants and audience. As for the rest, the readers are left in the hands of some of the best talent in cognition, our authors.

Chizuko Izawa

1

Introduction to the Tulane Flowerree Symposium on Cognition

Chizuko Izawa
Tulane University

Robert E. Flowerree of Portland, Oregon, a psychology major and a 1942 graduate of Tulane University, generously endowed the University's Department of Psychology to promote the advancement of scientific psychology at Tulane. The department utilizes part of the endowment for an annual 2-day symposium on varied topics during each Mardi Gras season.

The first one was organized by then departmental chairperson Dr. Edgar O'Neal and dealt with "Conflict in the Family"; the second was organized by his predecessor as chairperson, Dr. Arnold Gerall, and focused on "Sex Differences: Hormonal and Experiential Influences Throughout Life."

The current Flowerree Mardi Gras Symposium on Cognition, the third such symposium, was organized by this editor, and took place on February 23 and 24, 1987. This particular symposium was historic both in the sense that it produced the first book-length publication and that it was honored by the presence of Mr. and Mrs. Robert E. Flowerree!

Tulane University is a private, nonsectarian research university established by Paul Tulane in 1834, initially as a medical school; other disciplines followed incrementally—today there are 11 colleges and schools involving approximately 10,300 students from all 50 states and 60 foreign countries; 6,400 undergraduates and 3,900 graduate students, taught by 830 full-time faculty members. Nine colleges and schools are located on the park-like 110 acre uptown campus, next to the beautiful Audubon Park and Zoo, thrice the size of the campus. Both are 5 miles from New Orleans' central business district. Tulane's uptown facilities are housed in 66 buildings and are still growing. The School of Medicine and the School of Public Health and Tropical Medicine, as well as Tulane Hospital and Clinic, are located in the Medical Center occupying several blocks in central New Orleans.

1

1834 was not only the year this university was founded, it also marked the publication, at the University of Leipzig, of Ernst Heinrich Weber's (1795-1878) seminal *De tactu: annotationes anatomicae et physiologiae* [On touch: From the perspectives of anatomy and physiology]. This was the beginning of modern research on the sense of touch, from which he developed Weber's law. In that year also, Gustav Theordor Fechner (1801-1887) was appointed professor of physics at Leipzig. That was 2 years after Wilhelm Wundt (1832-1920), the founder of experimental psychology, was born in the suburb of Mannheim and 51 years before Hermann Ebbinghaus wrote his epoch-making book, *Ueber das Gedaechtnis* [On memory] in 1885.

We were most fortunate to have 11 nationally and internationally recognized contributors from a variety of laboratories, including the one at Tulane, for the 1987 Flowerree Symposium on Cognition. They came here from all over North America. They were men and women of science, of both majority and minority populations. They included current and former editors of major experimental and cognitive psychology journals such as the *Psychological Review*, the *Journal of Experimental Psychology*, the *Journal of Comparative and Physiological Psychology*, the *Journal of Mathematical Psychology*, and *Memory & Cognition*. Their presence on this campus added considerably to the visibility of this excellent institution and department, and set a new high standard of excellence for future Flowerree Symposia.

Each of our contributors is among the most accomplished figures in his or her field. It is they who have shaped contemporary cognitive psychology. All have published prolifically. It would have taken the majority of each speaker's allotted time of the symposium just to enunciate all the titles of his or her publications. In fact, if we were to add together all the pages of their publications, we would be dealing with many hundreds of thousands of pages! And we will have added several hundred more pages when the 1987 Flowerree Symposium appears in print.

It is our fervent ambition that this symposium will enhance the annual tradition of excellence in the Flowerree Symposium by at least a quantum jump. There is every reason for such heady optimism. This organizer has already received unsolicited inquiries and expressions of interest from those wishing to be considered as future participants. Let us also hope that the Psychology Department's recognition of cognitive psychology is also being reaffirmed today. A reaffirmation made manifest soon one hopes by palpable enhancements of resources that will raise the visibility and status of cognitive psychology, and thus enhance its scope and productivity.

In what follows, the contributors are introduced in the order in which they spoke at the 1987 Symposium (not the order in which their contributions appear in this volume). The place is New Orleans and the time is Mardi Gras. It is therefore referred to as the Flowerree Mardi Gras Symposium. Accordingly, the introductory chapter is somewhat unorthodox by design, but it conveys to a degree the atmosphere in which this highly sophisticated scientific discourse was conducted. We hope that many of our readers will venture to New Orleans in spring to enjoy future Mardi Gras Symposia at Tulane.

The following introductions of the contributors are based on this editor's direct, empirical observations, suitable to the occasion. More comprehensive and detailed summaries of their considerable achievements are easily available elsewhere.

DAY ONE
(in order of their appearance)

Henry L. Roediger, III:

It is difficult to think of anyone better than Roddy Roediger to lead the parade for our 1987 Flowerree Mardi Gras Cognitive Krewe. He gives the symposium the desired high tone. Our first speaker is the current editor of a core journal, the *Journal of Experimental Psychology: Learning, Memory, and Cognition*. His research interests and those of this editor overlap strongly in such areas as test trials and retrieval phenomena.

Professor Roediger received his PhD from Yale in 1973 and is now Professor of Psychology at Purdue. He is a first-class researcher, as well as a master teacher as evidenced by his large Introductory Psychology classes, which are graced by his and his associates' text *Psychology* (Roediger, Rushton, Capaldi, & Paris, 1987) in its second edition. Today, he discusses "Hypermnesia: Improvements in Recall With Repeated Testing"; it appears as chapter 7 (with Challis) in this volume and it provides an excellent review of the literature, the empirical facts, and gives theoretical insight into the intriguing phenomena of reminiscence and hypermnesia, as well as the different processing of pictures and words.

Douglas L. Nelson:

Douglas L. Nelson represents the South as full professor from the University of South Florida in Tampa. His doctorate in experimental psychology is from the University of Wisconsin in 1967. Dr. Nelson has been extremely active in verbal learning and cognitive psychology, and very prolific throughout. His enthusiasm for psychology is really fantastic.

Today, his presentation centers on "Implicitly Activated Knowledge and Memory," which appears in chapter 11. Doug discusses how implicitly activated concepts influence one's memory in respect to encoded information. Discussed also are empirical findings obtained over the past decade concerning both cue and target-size effects and the sensory-semantic model.

Richard M. Shiffrin:

The next speaker, Richard M. Shiffrin from Indiana University, requires no introduction. This is his second visit with us in 6 years. Rich Shiffrin is the past editor of the *Journal of Experimental Psychology: Learning, Memory, and Cognition*. He also coedited a volume on *Cognitive Theory* (Restle, Shiffrin, Castellan, Lindman, & Pisoni, 1975) and authored numerous articles and book chapters for a variety of publications.

Many of this editor's classmates from both the University of Tokyo and Stanford have achieved distinction, and Rich Shiffrin is an outstanding example of this. Although he and I overlapped by only 1 year as students at Stanford, his creative potential was clearly evident at that early stage.

His 1968 dissertation was revolutionary and was published with his dissertation mentor, Richard Atkinson, a recent director of the National Science Foundation (NSF) and currently Chancellor of the University of California at San Diego. Rich Shiffrin has continued to display his abundant talents through his work on short-term memory, the automatic and search processes, and in many other domains critical to theory and experimentation.

Professor Shiffrin shares with us the newest developments from his laboratory. Shiffrin's written version of this presentation, "On Units of Storage and Retrieval" is coauthored with Murnane, Gronlund, and Roth, and constitutes our chapter 3. Shiffrin et al. sought to determine what memory units are involved in storing and retrieving. They tested the idea that only low-level units such as words form the units of memory that are then interconnected associatively. Their evidence overwhelmingly favors storage of a higher level, that is, a sentence unit for sentence study.

It appears to this editor that such a unit may in some ways conform to the largest coherent good form, or *Gestalt* that is meaningful to the subject. A good Gestalt may be important for the survival of the memory unit and its resistance to erosion imposed by other competing items, or by the mere passage of time, or both, depending on the theoretical orientation one may espouse. That good Gestalt may be provided by the experimenter in the case of the sentence conditions, but a good Gestalt is unlikely to be available in the scrambled sentence study. Thus, the subjects may have no alternative but to resort to generate their own makeshift Gestalt as best as they can (inclusive of inventing idiosyncratic meanings) to make the input subjectively meaningful, even if that input has no formal meaning (in cases of scrambled sentences, anomalous or nonsense items). That memory unit would necessarily be smaller than the scrambled sentence that makes no sense. Breaking the sentence into segments seems, therefore, unavoidable.

Independent of such speculations, Shiffrin et al. present an incisive and comprehensive evaluation of alternative models, in their search for a model that accounts for their data. Their own theoretical approach is brilliant and profound. Characteristically, Shiffrin and his associates have made a highly substantive, perhaps pace setting, contribution to this volume.

(Lunch Break)

John Theios:

Professor John Theios is another of the Stanford PhDs this editor has had the good fortune to know. He was completing his dissertation just as this editor was starting graduate work at Stanford in 1961. In addition to his excellent work in both human and animal cognition and in mathematical psychology, he is remarkably versatile and has one of the sharpest analytical instincts. His thinking tends to reflect the cutting edge of scientific psychology in evolution.

Being a Californian, he also has what the editor considers to be one of the better qualities of Californians, namely, the guts to question tradition-bound vices. Professor Theios was among the very first of the friends and colleagues of this editor to encourage her in overcoming male-chauvinistic obstacles—unfortunately too prevalent among us in academia as well as in our own profession.

John Theios is a full professor at the University of Wisconsin. This afternoon, we look forward to his presentation of the "Theory of Perceptual and Cognitive Processing of Pictures and Words." His written version with Paul Amrhein appears in chapter 12, "The Role of Spatial Frequency and Visual Details in the Recognition of Patterns and Words," a fitting high point on which to conclude this volume.

Chizuko Izawa:

The editor was introduced to the symposium audience by William K. Estes. She graduated from the University of Tokyo, came to Stanford, did her dissertation with Estes, and in 1965 was his first PhD at Stanford. His influence on my thinking, although transmuted since, remains. The printed version of the presentation appears as chapter 8. There, the efficacy of study-test and anticipation methods are addressed. The identity model, formulated to account for varied and diverse results, was shown to hold for visual, auditory, and tactual modalities and for various verbal and nonverbal materials. The issues dealt with in chapter 8 have potential implications and applicability for educational and applied psychology, as well as cross-cultural issues in this domain.

Robert Solso:

Fresh from Moscow, in the Soviet Union that is, and not Idaho, Bob Solso will bring Day 1 of the 1987 Flowerree Symposium on Cognition to a gratifying conclusion. He is an accomplished administrator and an excellent psychologist, as well as the chairperson of these departments. Until 1983, Bob Solso was Chairperson of Psychology at the University of Idaho and is now at the University of Nevada at Reno.

Professor Solso received his PhD at St. Louis University in 1967 and has written several books—one of which is the eminently well regarded text, *Cognitive Psychology* (2nd edition, 1988). Bob Solso has agreed to provide us this afternoon, with an exposition of the latest research from his laboratory, "Prototypes, Schemata and the Form of Human Knowledge: The Cognition of Abstraction," entered as chapter 10 in this volume. He offers a provocative hypothesis in a noble attempt to establish a mega-theory of cognition. He makes a plea that we address the real issues of real people. Are you ready for such a mega-theory? It is you, the reading audience, who needs to answer this question.

DAY TWO
(in order of their appearance)

Joan Gay Snodgrass:

First among the distinguished speakers of the second day is a lady for whom this author has a lot of respect. Gay Snodgrass is a University of Pennsylvania PhD (1966), and has published extensively on the processing of picture information. She coauthored the text *Human Experimental Psychology* (Snodgrass, Levy-Berger, & Hayden, 1985). It was our intention to show the book, but someone stole it from this editor's bookshelf recently. Thieves know what's best!

Professor Snodgrass shares with us her research on "How Many Memory Systems Are There Really?: Some Evidence From the Fragmented Picture Task." It appears as chapter 6 in this volume. After introducing an excellent review on both Tulving's (1985) memory system and picture fragment studies in their connection to implicit memory issues, Snodgrass tested the separate memories hypothesis. A most revealing discussion is given on activation, processing differences or similarities between encoding and test, and separate memory systems.

Bennet B. Murdock, Jr.:

It is our good fortune to have another among the most creative minds in cognition. His intense dedication to the science of psychology is truly remarkable. Bennet Murdock is the only one, among my friends, who can boast of having known Clark L. Hull personally. He was at Yale just after Hull retired from active teaching. Yale awarded Ben his doctorate in 1951.

Being a skier, Professor Murdock preferred colder climates and moved to the University of Vermont and thereafter, the University of Missouri. However, in 1965, he went to the University of Toronto and has graced that institution ever since. Ben's short-term memory studies, modality effects among others, are now well known classics. This editor, among many others, have used his book *Human Memory Theory and Data* (Murdock, 1974) to advantage. He has been working on a distributed memory model for the past 10 years. "Learning in a Distributed Memory Model" is his subject at this symposium. That discussion appears in chapter 4 of this volume.

Murdock made an extraordinary effort to accommodate learning phenomena in paired-associate learning within the distributed memory model. In view of the fact that human associative learning is by no means simple, he favors development of a fairly complex model with multiple (five in this case) mechanisms. Then, some of the mechanisms in the multiprocess model may be eliminated if they turn out to be unneeded. His coverage is comprehensive; it represents much hard work, and rightly commands the attention of readers.

William K. Estes:

Now, after much waiting, time has come to present our keynote speaker, or in the Mardi Gras jargon, the king of the 1987 Flowerree Mardi Gras Krewe. We are honored to have one of the most eminent psychologists in America today. William K. Estes received his PhD from the University of Minnesota in 1943 with B. F. Skinner serving as chairman of his dissertation committee. After being on the faculties of Indiana, Stanford, and Rockefeller Universities, he moved to Harvard in 1979, an institution better known hereabouts as the "Tulane of the North." Incidentally, he conducts his research at William James Hall during the daytime and returns to the former home of its namesake each evening—an appealing continuity.

Bill Estes is perhaps best known as a founding father of modern mathematical psychology. Of all the theories he has proposed so far, this writer's favorite is his stimulus fluctuation construct. It is one of the most elegant models extant; its basic concepts are still utilized in important segments of our research.

Bill Estes was one of the early winners of APA's Awards for Distinguished Scientific Contributions, and is a former President of APA's Division of Experimental Psychology. He has also served as Chairman of the Psychonomic Society.

Beginning with an Associate Editorship of the *Journal of Experimental Psychology* very early in his career, he later edited the *Journal of Comparative and Physiological Psychology* and most recently, the *Psychological Review*. He has been on the editorial boards of nearly all the major journals of experimental and cognitive psychology. Bill Estes has authored and coauthored countless volumes and hundreds of journal articles. Most recently, he edited the six volume series, *Handbook of Learning and Cognitive Processes* (Estes 1975a, 1975b, 1976a, 1976b, 1978a, 1978b).

Of course, his work has been known internationally for some time now. Here is the Japanese rendition of *Learning Theory and Mental Development* (Estes, 1985), produced with some minor assistance from his translator. As in other domains of science and modern life, the output of psychological research by Japan has risen qualitatively and quantitatively to a point of parity with occidental efforts. Unquestionably, Japanese influence on psychology will become increasingly evident, not only in the cross-cultural domain, but also in all the other areas of scientific psychology. Here again, Bill is a step ahead of the crowd.

Professor Estes will now enlighten us about "Information and Value in Cognitive Learning Theory." The lead chapter for the scientific portion of this volume is the published version of this keynote speech, namely chapter 2, "Early and Late Memory Processing in Models for Category Learning." As is characteristic of his work, that chapter presents an incisive and decisive study. It assesses the prototype versus the exemplar–memory models, and puts forth a number of shrewd suggestions, in respect to the future direction of profitable research in this field. No one should miss his chapter.

A Short Time After William K. Estes' Keynote Speech

There is something more to tell about the keynote speaker, Bill Estes. A real revelation! He once considered joining Tulane—but it was not to be. Had we succeeded in tempting him, Tulane would have become the Harvard of the South much earlier! As it is, we must continue to struggle. But, rather than dwelling on the past, we wanted him to remember his role as the keynote speaker at the 1987 Flowerree Symposium. "Bill, please accept this token and be sure to wear it for your next round of golf in Cambridge! Will you please open it and let it all hang out!" (What he had was a school shirt with large block letters to cover the entire front, that read: HARVARD, THE TULANE OF THE NORTH.)

(Lunch Break)

James T. Townsend:

Our next speaker, James T. Townsend, is the current editor of the *Journal of Mathematical Psychology* and the coauthor of *Stochastic Modeling of Elementary Psychological Processes* (Townsend & Ashby, 1986). His beautiful volume has always been on my desk within easy reach, to be shown this afternoon. Very unfortunately, however, some time ago, my office suffered a lot of water damage from spillage in the biology lab above my office—a frog blocked a sink drain—the book was ruined and its replacement has not arrived. We are very sorry; it is hoped the book will arrive before the next Flowerree Mardi Gras Symposium on Cognition. In any event, Jim Townsend is full professor of Psychology at Purdue as well as a former classmate of this writer at Stanford.

Professor Townsend was on right after Bill Estes, a tough act to follow—but on the other hand, he had the benefit of a good example! He presented a discussion on "Constructing a Mathematical Theory of Approach-Avoidance Dynamics." His written version (with Busemeyer) appears as chapter 4 and is titled "Approach-Avoidance: Return to Dynamic Decision Behavior."

It is refreshing to find authors with sufficient verve to attack an important yet largely forgotten research problem, avoided by most other convention-bound investigators, whose focus appears to be limited largely to maximize the number of publications. A process abetted by many journal editors' preference for safe, fashionable topics. The fallout from that vicious cycle is that difficult problems requiring inordinate amounts of ingenuity, effort, and time tend to remain unresolved, becoming more and more "out-of-date" and thus, continue to be pushed even further into the background and in the process, even less publishable in the eyes of authors.

Scientific inquiries need be geared to the development of new knowledge, irrespective of topic, or how "fashionable" it is thought to be by the scientific "establishment." It is in that spirit that this editor extends a wholehearted welcome to the Townsend and Busemeyer's paper. It succeeded in a novel restructuring of Kurt Lewin's old field theory!

Robert A. Bjork:

We have now reached the grand finale of the 1987 Flowerree Mardi Gras Symposium on Cognition. As in the world of Kabuki, a delicate combination of song, dance, and drama, the most accomplished performer, the only one allowed to continue the centuries old traditional master's name, always appears last. That is a major reason for asking Robert A. Bjork of UCLA, past editor of *Memory & Cognition*, to do this most difficult job of bringing the symposium to a successful and satisfying conclusion.

As a graduate student at Stanford, Bob Bjork and two fellow students published a book, *Problems in Mathematical Learning Theory With Solutions to Accompany an Introduction to Mathematical Learning Theory by Atkinson, Bower and Crothers* (Batchelder, Bjork, & Yellot, 1966). He and this editor had more classes and seminars together than anyone else at this symposium and both did dissertations under Bill Estes. Here, however, quite apart from his penchant to bring tasks to a successful conclusion, he was one of the few persons who benefits from the *recency effect*!

Bob Bjork and Alan Richardson-Klavehn, his student, addressed the topic "On the Puzzling Relationship Between Environmental Context and Human

Memory." Their's is chapter 9 in this volume. Much of their efforts revolves around convincing us that the environmental context is central to a proper understanding of human memory. In that task, they succeed admirably. They focus on the effects of one type of context (incidental, extra-item) on one type of performance (recall), but they then interpret those effects within the framework of a new three-dimensional taxonomy of context effects, the dimension being type of context (intra-item vs. extra-item), context-target relationship (integral vs. influential vs. incidental), and type of processing (data-driven vs. conceptually driven). Interesting!

REFERENCES

Batchelder, W. H., Bjork, R. A., & Yellot, J. I., Jr. (1966). *Problems in mathematical learning theory with solutions to accompany an introduction to mathematical learning theory by Atkinson, Bower and Crothers.* New York: Wiley.

Estes, W. K. (Ed.). (1975a). *Handbook of learning and cognitive processes, Vol. 1, Introduction to concepts and issues.* Hillsdale, NJ: Lawrence Erlbaum Associates.

Estes, W. K. (Ed.). (1975b). *Handbook of learning and cognitive processes, Vol. 2, Conditioning and behavior theory.* Hillsdale, NJ: Lawrence Erlbaum Associates.

Estes, W. K. (Ed.). (1976a). *Handbook of learning and cognitive processes, Vol. 3, Approaches to human learning and motivation.* Hillsdale, NJ: Lawrence Erlbaum Associates.

Estes, W. K. (Ed.). (1976b). *Handbook of learning and cognitive processes, Vol. 4, Attention and memory.* Hillsdale, NJ: Lawrence Erlbaum Associates.

Estes, W. K. (Ed.). (1978a). *Handbook of learning and cognitive processes, Vol. 5, Human information processing.* Hillsdale, NJ: Lawrence Erlbaum Associates.

Estes, W. K. (Ed.). (1978b). *Handbook of learning and cognitive processes, Vol. 6, Linguistic functions in cognitive theory.* Hillsdale, NJ: Lawrence Erlbaum Associates.

Estes, W. K. (1985). *Learning theory and mental development* (J. Komaki, Japanese Trans.). Kyoto, Japan: Nakanishiya. (Original work published 1970).

Murdock, B. B., Jr. (1974). *Human memory: Theory and data.* Hillsdale, NJ: Lawrence Erlbaum Associates.

Restle, F., Shiffrin, R. M., Castellan, N. J., Lindman, H. R., & Pisoni, D. B. (Eds.). (1975). *Cognitive theory. Vol. 1.* Hillsdale, NJ: Lawrence Erlbaum Associates.

Roediger, H. L., Rushton, J. P., Capaldi, E. D., & Paris, S. G. (1987). *Psychology.* (2nd ed.). Glenview, IL: Scott Foresman.

Snodgrass, J. G., Levy-Berger, G., & Hayden, M. (1985). *Human experimental psychology.* Oxford: Oxford University Press.

Solso, R. L. (1988). *Cognitive psychology* (2nd ed.). Boston: Allyn & Bacon.

Townsend, J. T., & Ashby, F. G. (1986). *Stochastic modeling of elementary psychological processes.* Cambridge, England: Cambridge University Press.

Tulving, E. (1985). How many memory systems are there? *American Psychologist, 40,* 385–398.

2

Early and Late
Memory Processing in Models
for Category Learning

W. K. Estes
Harvard University

Its appearance bracketed by the widely celebrated centennial of the publication of Ebbinghaus' monograph on memory, and the forthcoming centennial of the publication of William James' *The Principles of Psychology* (1890), this volume combines the experimental and theoretical motifs that have flowed over a century from those two epoch-making works. In experimental psychology the most notable developments over the century have perhaps been in methodology—advances in standards of control, power of statistical analyses, and relevance of experimental work to theories. Insights gained from decades of experimental research on memory that followed Ebbinghaus pointed up the need for controlling such factors as sequential and contextual effects by counterbalancing or like measures; inputs from the concurrently expanding field of statistics led to appreciation of the potentialities of factorial design, blocking, and statistical control of variables in cases where experimental control is not feasible; and the advances in design in turn enabled more powerful statistical analyses of data. These developments, however, only set the stage for progress in understanding phenomena, for which the key is interaction between experimental research and theory. The use of experiments to test theoretical ideas was appreciated well enough at the turn of the century, but the use of theories, in particular quantitative theories, to structure and interpret research was slower to develop. Progress has occurred, and perhaps with an accelerating trend, prime examples being the increasing widespread applications of signal detectability theory and semantic network models in research on perception and memory (reviewed by Murdock, 1974, and Baddeley, 1976, respectively and illustrated by many of the chapters in this volume). We are beginning to see models that enable us to address issues that resist purely empirical approaches.

The power of present day models is greatly augmented by the availability of digital computers, which have evolved from the calculating machine conceived by Charles Babbage some 150 years ago to general information processors that provide an important metaphor for cognitive theories.

All of these motifs are well represented in this volume. In this chapter, I concentrate on the conjunction of the lines of research flowing from James and Babbage and seek to illustrate some important lines of work in current models of learning and memory. Though I am primarily concerned with a pervasive theoretical issue in the information-processing approach to cognition, I also highlight two problems of method. One is that of fostering a continuing interplay between the development of general theoretical frameworks and the realization of aspects of them in specific testable models. The second problem is identifiability—the question of when different models or assumptions actually have different testable implications. Both the interplay of general and specific theory and considerations of identifiability are seen in this effort.

For illustrative empirical material, I draw on the currently active line of research having to do with human category learning, in particular, new work on the problems of distinguishing empirically between models based on storage and retrieval of memories of specific category exemplars and models based on the abstraction of prototypes.

EARLY VERSUS LATE MEMORY PROCESSING

The general theoretical issue on which I focus has arisen in many different contexts in cognitive psychology. In research on selective attention this issue is known as the question of early versus late selection in information processing, the classical early selection view being associated with Broadbent's original filter model (Broadbent, 1958) and late selection with a number of subsequent theories including Deutsch and Deutsch (1963) and Shiffrin (1976). In that context, the question is whether a great part of the flood of information coming into the sensory systems is discarded as a result of selective filtering at an early stage or whether a great part of the information is processed and encoded, even up to semantic levels, with selection being imposed at a relatively late stage in response to task demands. In semantic memory research, the same issue has appeared as the question of computation versus prestorage (Smith, 1978). A familiar instance of the prestorage type is the semantic network model of Collins and Quillian (1969), in which it is assumed that the information specifying the meaning of concept is stored at the appropriate node in a semantic network and need only be accessed at the time when a judgment concerning meaning is called for. In the semantic network model, not only are properties or other attributes of a concept stored at specific points in the network, but also relations between a given concept

Value

Symptom	High	Low
Temp.	1	0
White cells	1	0

Learning sequence

Disease:	A	B	B	A	B	A	A	B
Symptoms:	10	01	00	10	10	11	01	01

FIG. 2.1.   Illustrative sequence of trials in a problem involving categorization of hypothetical patients into disease categories on the basis of symptom patterns. In each designated pattern, the first digit is the value of temp. and the second digit is the value of white cells.

and others, as for example those representing superordinate or subordinate categories, are directly represented by links in the network. In contrast, in some feature models, information is stored in feature lists or the equivalent and computations of relationships between words or concepts have to be accomplished at the time when judgments are called for. In human categorization and classification learning, the early–late distinction can be illustrated in terms of a contrast between prototype and exemplar–memory models.

PROTOTYPE VERSUS EXEMPLAR–MEMORY MODELS

The distinction between these two types of models can be discussed conveniently in terms of a type of task employed in many researches reported by Medin and his associates (Medin, Altom, & Murphy, 1984; Medin & Schaffer, 1978; Medin & Smith, 1981) and in a recent study of my own (Estes, 1986b). The experimental task is presented to subjects as a simulation of the problem faced by a physician learning from experience with patients to classify them into disease categories on the basis of symptom patterns. A highly simplified illustrative example is shown in Fig. 2.1. We consider a case in which the problem is to distinguish between two disease categories, A and B, on the basis of values of two symptoms. As shown in the upper part of the figure, the two symptoms, one having to do with temperature and one with white cell count, are represented as binary valued attributes, a high value being designated by 1 and a low value by 0. In the lower part of the figure we illustrate a possible sequence of learning experiences on each of which a particular symptom pattern has been presented to the learner and accompanied by feedback indicating the disease category. On the first occasion, for example,

Representation

Memory Array		Prototype			
A	B	A		B	
11	01	.75	.75	.25	.50
10	00				
11	10				
01	01				

FIG. 2.2. Memory array and category prototypes generated by the learning sequence in Fig. 2.1.

the symptom pattern is a high value for temperature and a low value for white cells and the disease category is indicated to be A.

The symptoms individually are imperfectly correlated with the disease categories, but nonetheless attention to the patterns provides a basis for some differentiation as illustrated in Fig. 2.2. The left side of the figure represents the memory array that would be built up in a model of the type introduced by Medin and Schaffer (1978) and further developed by Nosofsky (1984) and Estes (1986a, 1986b). Each of the patterns that appeared in the trial sequence shown at the bottom of Fig. 2.1 has been entered in the appropriate memory array. If, following the sequence, the individual were presented with pattern 11 we would expect it to be classified as an A because the test pattern perfectly matches some memory representations that appear in the A but none in the B category. A test with pattern 01 would provide more of a problem because that pattern appears in both A and B memory vectors but we might expect some preference for category B. In the class of exemplar–memory models I am considering, the process assumed is one of mentally computing the similarity of the test exemplar to each of the stored instances in the category A vector to generate a total index of similarity of the test pattern to category A, then doing the same with respect to the stored exemplars of category B. Finally the ratio of the A similarity to the sum of the A and B similarities is computed as an estimate of the probability that the test exemplar came from category A and the test exemplar is assigned to category A with that probability.

Represented on the right side of Fig. 2.2 are the average prototypes of the two categories that would result from the same learning experience. The prototype for each category is a vector having two cells, one including the average value of the temperature symptom in that category and the second the average relative frequency of the white cell symptom in that category. It can be readily verified that the values entered for the average prototypes of the two categories are indeed average relative frequencies of value 1 for the two symptoms in each of the two categories. In the prototype model it is assumed that

when a test pattern is presented for categorization, the process is one of judging the distance in a mental similarity space between the test pattern and the
prototype of each category and then assigning the exemplar to the category
for which the distance is smaller.

Clearly the exemplar–memory model is an example of late selection,
because full information concerning the attributes of all previously experienced
exemplars is stored in memory and the entire memory array is consulted at
the time when a judgment is required for a new pattern. The prototype model
is a similarly clear example of early selection as the memory representation
retains only average feature values, all other details of the specific learning
experience having been discarded. Each of these types of models has its advantages and disadvantages as a basis for cognitive activities pertaining to
categorization. Considerations of efficiency would seem to favor the prototype
models, because incoming information need be processed only once (to up-
date the relevant prototype) and at the time when a categorization judgment
is called for the individual need only compare a test pattern to the relevant
prototypes unencumbered by the problem of dealing with an accumulation
in memory of other information about the learning experiences. The other
side of the coin is that the price of early selection and compression of highly
filtered information into a prototype is that some of the discarded information might, if retained, prove useful in response to future task demands. Also,
if environmental conditions change (e.g., as in the shifting patterns of symptoms characteristic of influenza between or even within seasons), a learner
who makes categorizations on the basis of accumulated exemplar memories
might be in a position to respond more quickly to changed conditions. The
costs is that categorization judgments would presumably be slower if an extensive memory array had to be consulted on each occasion than if only prototypes had to be consulted.

Because the forms of the memory representations and the processes assumed to be operating on them are quite different in the exemplar–memory
and prototype models, it has generally been assumed that they should be easy
to distinguish experimentally. Thus, it came as a surprise, once sufficiently
formalized versions of both types of models had become available for comparison, to find that many of the predictions assumed to be peculiar to prototype models were actually implied also by exemplar–memory models (Smith
& Medin, 1981).

The problems faced in distinguishing between exemplar–memory and prototype models were clarified somewhat by analytical work demonstrating that
for the major class of categorization problems in which category exemplars
are generated from independent (that is uncorrelated) features, models that
differ only with respect to the exemplar–memory versus prototype distinction are asymptotically equivalent (Estes, 1986a). By asymptotically equivalent,
we mean that if a learner is given a sufficiently long series of category exemplars with feedback, then predictions from the two models concerning the

levels of accuracy reached, and even the detailed pattern of fluctuations of performance from trial to trial in response to particular exemplars that are relatively easy or relatively difficult to classify, become indistinguishable. If the independence assumption is not satisfied, that is if features are correlated, then the two models are not equivalent. In general, for correlated features, the exemplar–memory model predicts higher levels of performance than a matched prototype model and has even been shown to account for the course of learning in a situation where learning could not have been predicted at all from a prototype model (Estes, 1986b, Experiment 2). Does this result suggest that the early–late issue is resolved, with the exemplar–memory representative of the late-processing class of models remaining triumphantly in possession of the field? That conclusion would be much too hasty. For one thing, it is still possible on the evidence discussed so far that a prototype model for independent feature situations could be distinguished from exemplar–memory models on pre-asymptotic data and might prove superior. Also, one should note that weakening the case for prototype models does not automatically strengthen the case for exemplar–memory models. The assumptions of these models need more direct support. I follow up both of these thoughts in the following discussion.

First, let us consider the possibility that the two classes of models might be distinguishable on the basis of data obtained early in learning. The issue is not readily amenable to mathematical analysis, so I exhibit some relevant evidence by generating computer simulations of the two types of models and comparing them with each other and, in each case, with empirical data. One appropriate set of data is available in Experiment 1 of Estes (1986b). For these data the procedure described in Estes (1986a) was followed to produce comparable models of the two types. For the principal comparisons presented, it was assumed that, in the prototype model, distance between perceived exemplars and prototypes is judged in a city-block metric and that in the corresponding exemplar–memory model the same metric is employed for representations of similarities between perceived and remembered exemplar

TABLE 2.1
Comparison of City-Block Distance Models

Group	Exemplar		Prototype	
Labels	ss	r	ss	r
	—	-	—	-
1	.061	.80	.093	.57
2	.106	.56	.133	.43
No Labels				
1	.062	.77	.101	.55
2	.108	.83	.054	.54

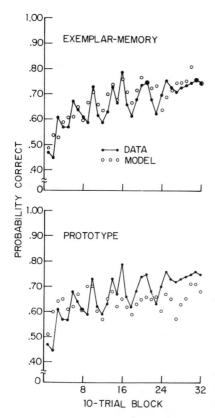

FIG. 2.3. Fits of the exemplar–memory and prototype models to the learning function of a subset of data (Experiment 1, Group 1) reported in Estes (1986b).

patterns. Each of the models had two free parameters: A parameter p denotes the probability that the exemplar pattern presented on a trial is effectively stored in memory, in the case of the exemplar–memory model, or effectively entered into adjustment of the current prototype representation, in the case of the prototype model; the other parameter in each case is a scaling constant reflecting the efficiency with which the learner distinguishes distances in the city-block metric. Each model was fitted to the data from each of the four experimental groups of the experiment by means of a hill-climbing program with a least-squares criterion and the results are summarized in Table 2.1.

On the sum of squares measure, the two types of models do not differ greatly, though there is a small but relatively consistent advantage for the exemplar–memory model. On the other hand if we look at the correlations between observed and predicted values, we note a consistent and rather large advantage for the exemplar–memory over the prototype model. The reason, in part, is that the prototype model predicts too little variability in performance, as may be seen in Fig. 2.3, which presents a comparison of the two models applied to one of the sets of data from Estes (1986b). Thus, although

TABLE 2.2
Percentages of Correct Categorization by 80-Trial Block
for More Frequently (A) and Less Frequently (B) Sampled Categories

	Data		Standard Exemplar Model		Pure Similarity Model	
Block	A	B	A	B	A	B
1	68	42	68	44	57	57
2	79	58	80	54	71	73
3	78	55	86	52	78	76

the differences are not great, the exemplar–memory model seems to represent the grain of the learning data better than does the prototype model, a conclusion supported also by results of Nosofsky (1984, 1986).

A different kind of information bearing on exemplar–memory versus prototype models is available from experiments in which category frequencies are unequal. If more exemplars are sampled from one category than from another during a learning series, then the memory array will contain more representations from the former category. In an exemplar–memory model, when a test exemplar is presented for categorization, its summed similarity will, other things equal, be greater to the category that has the larger number of representations in memory. In a prototype model, however, the prototype representations of categories formed in memory are a function of the average values of features in the categories and there is no necessary relationship between the similarity of a test exemplar to a category prototype and the frequency with which exemplars of the category have been sampled.

An unpublished experiment conducted in my laboratory with the same general design and procedures as those described in Estes (1986b) involved the categorization of bar charts that simulated symptom patterns into categories corresponding to diseases. For one group of 12 subjects, categories A and B were sampled in a ratio of 3:1 during a series of learning trials and, as shown in the far left section of Table 2.2, proportions of current categorizations were uniformly higher and increased more steeply over learning blocks for the more frequent category. The values in the middle section of Table 2.2 are predictions from the standard exemplar–memory model (Estes, 1986b) and will be seen to describe the observed trends quite well. In the right hand section of Table 2.2, predictions are given for a "pure similarity" version of the exemplar model, virtually the equivalent of a prototype model (Estes, 1986a), and these predictions fail entirely to capture the pattern of differences between category A and B performance in the observed data. A prototype model that used some other measure (e.g., modal rather than mean feature values) would have the same difficulty. These results, again tend to support the idea that categorizations are based on judgments of similarity between perceived and remembered exemplar patterns rather than on judgments of distance between perceived patterns and prototypes.

I do not mean to suggest that prototypic representations are pure fiction, only that they are not automatically formed and used as a basis for categorization under the usual conditions of category learning. With special instructions, individuals doubtless can be induced to form some kind of prototypic representation (Busemeyer, 1987) but it is quite possible that these are formed at the time of a test on the basis of information in the memory array rather than being generated trial by trial in the manner assumed in prototype learning models.

EVIDENCE ON MEMORY SEARCH

Several kinds of evidence offer possibilities of checking more directly on the idea that categorization judgments are based on search of an array of exemplar representations. Some limited positive evidence comes from recognition data. Estes (1986b) found that recognition was facilitated by the incorporation of unique cues into exemplar patterns but only for recognition judgments on old exemplars that had occurred within about 10 trials of the current test trial, that is, within the range of short-term memory. The same study also yielded a lag effect (*lag* denotes the interval between a test trial and the most recent previous occurrence of the same exemplar pattern) for categorization. The probability of current categorization of old exemplars decreased as a function of lag from a maximum at a lag of 2 to an apparently asymptotic value for lags of 10 or more. As pointed out by Medin (1986), there is a possible confounding in that analysis in that items tested at long lags might on the average be more difficult than those tested at short lags. However, two recent, as yet unpublished, studies in my laboratory allow similar analyses but with the additional control that comparisons are made only on exemplar patterns that occur at all of the lags tested. In one study, dealing with categorization of letter strings representing words of a hypothetical language into categories representing parts of speech, percentage correct declined from 78% at lags of 2-5 to 73% at lags of 10 and higher, but the decrease was not statistically reliable. A possible complication here is that the letter strings (e.g., FEKNAJTO or DCIGOJAF) might have been particularly difficult to remember in comparison with bar charts. In another study in which the stimulus patterns were triangles varying in height and width, percentage correct declined from a maximum of 69% at lag 3 to a level of 60% at lags of 10 and higher, this difference being significant ($t = 3.25$, $p < .02$).

Another recent study in my laboratory was designed to examine possible evidence for an intertial effect that would be predicted by an exemplar-

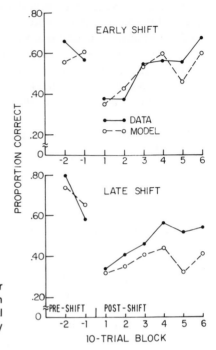

FIG. 2.4. Correct response proportions for blocks preceding and following shifts in category assignments together with theoretical values computed from the exemplar–memory model.

memory model. The critical manipulation was to give two groups of subjects a series of categorization learning trials in a three category problem, and at either an early or a late point in the series shift the feedback conditions for two of the categories. The task was to learn how to assign artificial words to grammatical categories, labeled here A,B, and C for convenience. Conditions for Category A were constant throughout a 240-trial learning series for both groups. For the early shift group, Categories B and C were switched after trial 60 in the sense that, following the switch, exemplar patterns that would have been called instances of Category B before the switch were now labeled as correct for C and exemplars that would have been correct for C were now labeled as correct for B, so that the subjects had to undo their previous learning on those two categories and learn the new assignments. For the late shift group, a similar shift occurred after trial 180.

According to the exemplar–memory model, speed of relearning following the switch should be slower for the late than for the early shift condition. The reason is that the exemplar patterns that have been stored in the memory array for Category B, say, prior to the switch all have to be sampled and relearned with new Category C labels following the switch; and the greater the number of patterns stored prior to the shift the longer it necessarily takes to sample and reassign them all following the shift.

Figure 2.4 shows the relevant data for relearning following an early or a late shift, presented in the upper and lower panels respectively. For the observed data, the steepness of the learning curves over the six 10-trial blocks following the shift appears to be very similar for the early and late shift conditions, and this similarity of trends is confirmed by an analysis of variance showing that the interaction of post shift blocks with early–late shift is entirely nonsignificant ($F = .03$). On the other hand, the plots of predicted functions from the exemplar–memory model, also shown in Fig. 2.4, illustrate the relationship predicted by the model—relatively rapid learning following an early shift and much slower relearning following a late shift. Thus, these results do not support the idea that categorization judgments are based on search of a full cumulative memory array as assumed in the exemplar–memory model. The generality of this result deserves emphasis. The qualitative prediction of the exemplar–memory model regarding slower relearning after a late shift is shared by all models in which category judgments depend on cumulative contents of memory (including, for example, the ACT model of Anderson, 1983, the pattern–storage model of Hayes-Roth and Hayes-Roth, 1977, and feature-frequency models such as those described by Reed, 1972). An adequate model must have the property that when conditions change during the course of learning, efficient adjustment occurs following the shift so that responses quickly come to be made on the basis of memory only for the recent past.

Still another source of evidence is available in reaction time data. Assuming that retrieval and comparison of a pattern from memory takes measurable time, as assumed, for example, in the memory scanning models of Sternberg (1966) and others, it would be predicted that, other things equal, reaction time for categorization judgments on old exemplars should increase over the course of learning as the size of the memory array that must be searched on each test increases. Mean reaction times, shown in Table 2.3 for data from the study of letter-string categorization previously cited, lend no support to the implication from the exemplar–memory model, the trend in reaction times over blocks being actually downward and very similar for old and new exemplars. This last finding needs to be followed up with designs that permit examination of reaction time as a function of size of the memory array independently of practice effects. However, it does not seem that additional data are needed to warrant the conclusion that the assumption of categorization based on search of a memory array holds only within the range of short-term memory.

TABLE 2.3
Mean Correct Reaction Times (in sec) For Categorization Responses

Exemplar	Block			
	1	2	3	4
New	2.48	2.03	1.97	1.75
Old	2.06	2.00	1.71	1.62

CONCLUSION

Where do we go from here? Comparisons of late versus early memory-processing models of categorization, exemplified by the exemplar–memory and the prototype models, respectively, have uniformly resulted in support for the late-processing model. However, attempts to find direct evidence for search of the cumulative memory array at the time of each categorization judgment have yielded negative results except when the comparisons between perceived and remembered exemplars fall within the span of short-term memory.

It seems hard to avoid the conclusion that an adequate model must represent a combination of early and late processing, with a number of recently experienced exemplars being held in a temporary buffer. Within the buffer, processing may occur in accord with the assumptions of the exemplar–memory model, but exemplar representations no longer in the temporary buffer must be processed into a form in which similarity judgments can be made without recourse to item by item searches (Estes, 1986a). Performance in a typical categorization learning experiment would, then, represent a mixture of a responses based on search of the short-term memory buffer and responses based on the long-term representation. The overall system would thus retain the advantages of late-processing models in that shifts of conditions could readily be detected in consequence of the suddenly changed contents of the short-term buffer, but performance would not need to become slower and more error prone over a lengthy learning series since, except for occasions when responses could be based on the buffer, judgments would be derived from the long-term representation in a way not requiring extended search. Fresh ideas are needed, and these may come from the recent surge of research on connectionist models. A specific proposal for the long-term process, based on the idea that parallel distributed processing of the items passing through the short-term buffer generates a long-term representation that does not require serial search, is sketched in Estes (1988).

However the details of implementation work out, it appears that a combined model may be able to combine the advantages of early and late memory processing. Beyond the earliest stage of learning in any new situation, decisions about categorization could be based on the results of mental computations accomplished prior to a given test trial, but following any shift in conditions, quick reestablishment of efficient performance could be facilitated by the possibility of making judgments on the basis of the contents of short-term memory until enough new data have been processed to enable new computations on the basis of a revised long-term memory store. The urgent need now is for new experimentation directed explicitly at the assessment of the separate contributions of short-and long-term processes to categorization performance.

ACKNOWLEDGMENTS

Research reported in this chapter was supported in part by Grants BNS 86-09232 from the National Science Foundation and MH 37208 from the National Institute of Mental Health. Jane Campbell, Joshua Hurwitz, and Nicholas Hatsopoulos assisted with the experimental work and the model-fitting computations.

REFERENCES

Anderson, J. R. (1983). *The architecture of cognition.* Cambridge, MA: Harvard University Press.

Baddeley, A. D. (1976). *The psychology of memory.* New York: Basic Books.

Broadbent, D. E. (1958). *Perception and communication.* New York: Pergamon Press.

Busemeyer, J. R. (1987, August). *A new method for investigating prototype learning.* Paper presented at the meeting of the Society for Mathematical Psychology, University of California, Berkeley.

Collins, A. M., & Quillian, M. R. (1969). Retrieval time for semantic memory. *Journal of Verbal Learning and Verbal Behavior, 8,* 240–247.

Deutsch, J. A., & Deutsch, D. (1963). Attention: Some theoretical considerations. *Psychological Review, 70,* 80–90.

Estes, W. K. (1986a). Array models for category learning. *Cognitive Psychology, 18,* 500–549.

Estes, W. K. (1986b). Memory storage and retrieval processes in category learning. *Journal of Experimental Psychology: General, 115,* 155–174.

Estes, W. K. (1988). Toward a framework for combining connectionist and symbol-processing models. *Journal of Memory and Language, 27,* 196–212.

Hayes-Roth, B., & Hayes-Roth, F. (1977). Concept learning and the recognition and classification of exemplars. *Journal of Verbal Learning and Verbal Behavior, 16,* 321–338.

James, W. (1890). *The principles of psychology.* New York: Holt.

Medin, D. L. (1986). Comment on "Memory storage and retrieval processes in category learning." *Journal of Experimental Psychology: General, 115,* 373–381.

Medin, D. L., Altom, M. W., & Murphy, T. D. (1984). Given versus induced category representations: Use of prototype and exemplar information in classification. *Journal of Experimental Psychology: Learning, Memory, and Cognition, 10,* 333–352.

Medin, D. L, & Schaffer, M. M. (1978). Context theory of classification learning. *Psychological Review, 85,* 207–238.

Medin, D. L., & Smith, E. E. (1981). Strategies and classification learning. *Journal of Experimental Psychology: Human Learning and Memory, 7,* 241–253.

Murdock, B. B., Jr. (1974). *Human memory: Theory and data.* Hillsdale, NJ: Lawrence Erlbaum Associates.

Nosofsky, R. M. (1984). Choice, similarity, and the context theory of classification. *Journal of Experimental Psychology: Learning, Memory, and Cognition, 10,* 104–114.

Nosofsky, R. M. (1986). Attention, similarity, and the identification–categorization relationship. *Journal of Experimental Psychology: General, 115,* 39–57.

Reed, S. K. (1972). Pattern recognition and categorization. *Cognitive Psychology, 3,* 382–407.

Shiffrin, R. M. (1976). Capacity limitations in information processing, attention, and memory. In W. K. Estes (Ed.), *Handbook of learning and cognitive processes: Attention and memory* (Vol. 4, pp. 177–236). Hillsdale, NJ: Lawrence Erlbaum Associates.

Smith, E. E. (1978). Theories of semantic memory. In W. K. Estes (Ed.), *Handbook of learning* and cognitive processes: Linguistic functions in cognitive theory (Vol. 6, pp. 1–56). Hillsdale, NJ: Lawrence Erlbaum Associates.

Smith, E. E., & Medin, D. L. (1981). *Categories and concepts.* Cambridge, MA: Harvard University Press.

Sternberg, S. (1966). High-speed scanning in human memory. *Science, 153*, 652–654.

3

On Units of Storage and Retrieval

Richard M. Shiffrin
Kevin Murnane
Indiana University

Scott Gronlund
Northwestern University

Marc Roth
Indiana University

Theorists of memory must decide what kinds of units are to be entered into memory, used to probe memory, and recovered from memory. For example, should a word be stored as a set of associated letters, a lexical entry, a concept, some combination of all of these, or something else? Should a paragraph be stored as letters, words, propositions, sentences, a single paragraph unit, some combination of these, or other things? In this chapter we are concerned specifically with sentences. Is a sentence best considered as a collection of interconnected units like words? Jones' fragment model (1984) is of this form. Or is a sentence best considered as a single unit with words or sentence fragments as part of that unit's structure, as in the model proposed by Kintsch (1974). In this chapter we begin an examination of this issue, and attempt to winnow some of the many alternatives.

Our primary goal is to pit models that posit individual units for each word in a sentence against models that posit a single unit for the entire sentence. Questions concerning the relationships among word-level units, or the internal structure of a sentence-level unit, are beyond the scope of this chapter.

There are two related questions to consider. First, what are the units that are stored in memory? For example, if sentences are studied, are word- or sentence-level units stored? Second, what are the units that are used to probe memory at retrieval? For example, if some of the words from a studied sentence are given as retrieval cues, are they used individually to probe memory or are they combined into a single retrieval cue?

An answer to these questions is best obtained within the context of a memory theory. In this chapter, the Search of Associative Memory (SAM) model of Raaijmakers and Shiffrin (1980, 1981) provides that context, but we also consider some alternative classes of models. In order to focus the preliminary discussion, it is useful to consider the experimental task that is the basis of the studies presented later. Suppose five-item sentences are studied in which all words in all sentences are unique. At test, some subset of the words from each sentence are presented as retrieval cues. The subject is asked to recall either a particular target word from the sentence or all of the remaining words in the sentence.

First, consider the level of the storage units. During study of each sentence, it is presumed that various elaborative encoding processes are directed toward individual words, sentences, or both (we will ignore between-sentence encoding processes). After encoding, is a group of associatively connected word units placed in memory, as in the left panel of Fig. 3.1, is a single sentence unit stored in memory as in the right panel of Fig. 3.1, or are both stored?

One way in which these two approaches differ becomes clear in the context of models, like SAM, that assume recall operates as a search process with separate sampling and recovery mechanisms. Suppose that memory units are sampled one at a time on a probabilistic basis. If the units are sentences, then sampling a sentence gives access to all of the words in the sentence without the need for further sampling. If the units are individual words, then each word must be sampled in turn (those samples probably separated by samples of words in other sentences) for the whole sentence to be recalled. Furthermore, once a word unit has been sampled, it may be sampled again later in the search, thereby slowing the process of recall. In contrast to the sentence-unit approach, each successive word tends to take longer to be recalled.

Consider next the level of the units used in retrieval. Retrieval is accomplished through the use of a retrieval probe that consists of cues provided by the experimenter, extracted from the environmental context, or generated by the subject. What is the level of the probe units?

We consider three possibilities for the experimental situation sketched previously. First, if the provided cues are used at the word level, the cue words could be used individually, in an order chosen by the subject, in separate, successive retrieval attempts. We term this the *successive word* retrieval strategy. Second, the words could be used simultaneously as a group of concurrent cues acting as a single retrieval unit. We term this the *concurrent word* strategy. Finally, the provided words could be encoded together as a higher order unit, as an incomplete, partial sentence cue. Memory would then be probed with this single unit. We term this the *sentence unit* strategy.

Thus, working within the SAM model, we consider the following model types: The units stored in memory will be either (a) lower level (e.g., single word units) or (b) higher level (e.g., sentence units). The retrieval units will be either (a) lower level (e.g., single word units), associated with either the successive word or concurrent retrieval strategies or (b) higher level (e.g., sentence units, or partial sentence units). Issues similar to these arise in models other than SAM, but discussion is deferred to a later point in the chapter,

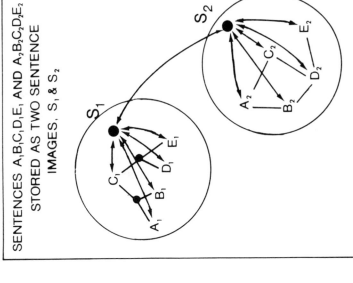

SENTENCES $A_1B_1C_1D_1E_1$ AND $A_2B_2C_2D_2E_2$ STORED AS TWO SENTENCE IMAGES, S_1 & S_2

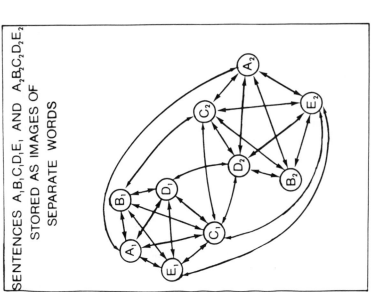

SENTENCES $A_1B_1C_1D_1E_1$ AND $A_2B_2C_2D_2E_2$ STORED AS IMAGES OF SEPARATE WORDS

FIG. 3.1. Illustration of two methods of storing two 5-word sentences in memory. Left panel: separate storage of each word, with pairwise associations. Right panel: storage of each sentence, each containing the constituent words among the internal structure.

27

because the precise characterization of the issue depends on each model. We turn next to a description of the SAM model.

THE SAM MODEL FOR WORD RETRIEVAL

We begin by describing the SAM model as it was developed to handle free and cued recall of lists of unrelated words. When trying to retrieve from memory, the subject generates a set of cues, called the probe set, which is used to probe memory on a particular cycle of memory search. Each probe of memory results in activation of the units stored in memory; the amount of activation of a given unit is determined by the associative connection between the set of probe cues and that unit. For recognition, the unit activations are summed together and the recognition decision is based on the sum (for details see Gillund & Shiffrin, 1984). For free or cued recall, one unit is *sampled* with a probability proportional to its activation (the probability of sampling is the ratio of the particular unit's activation to the summed activation of all of the units). Once a unit is sampled, a *recovery* process is carried out that results in some portion of the information encoded in that unit being made available to the subject. If the subject decides to continue the search, a new set of probe cues is selected (possibly the same as the previous set), and another probe of memory is carried out. Sampling of units is always done with replacement.

The stored memory units in SAM are called *images*, though use of this term is not intended to imply that the information in an image is limited to visual or sensory properties. A given image is a complex collection of information. For example, even when something as simple as a single visually presented word is stored, the image may contain sensory, lexical, syntactic and semantic information, as well as subject generated episodic and associative information.

Even though these images or units may be quite complex, they form a partition of memory in the following senses:

1. An image is unitized so that the information in any one that is sampled is potentially recoverable without the need for further sampling.
2. The information in nonsampled units does not contribute to the recovery process for a sampled unit.
3. The information in unit A does not contain information sufficient to allow effective recovery of the core information in some other unit, B, without unit B's being sampled.

Thus, if word images have been stored, sampling of a unit would allow recovery of information (e.g., the name of the word) contained in that unit only. Recovery of the name of any other word would require sampling of that unit.

This last assumption is, of course, critical for the present theoretical development. If sampling of one unit could result in recovery of another unit without additional sampling, then the unit would in effect be a multiword unit. Previous applications of the SAM model to recall tasks assumed that the sampling of an image can, at best, result in recovery of the word encoded in that image. For example, in Raaijmakers and Shiffrin (1981), pairs of items were studied. When one member of a pair was used as a retrieval cue, sampling of an image of a word from an irrelevant pair could of course occur. If a word image from the cued pair was sampled, it could be the cue image itself or the target word image. If the cue image was sampled, recovery of the target word image was assumed not to be possible. Instead, it was assumed that sampling must continue until the image of the target word was sampled.

Having said this, it must be admitted that nowhere in the development of the SAM model is the nature of images restricted. For example, in Gillund and Shiffrin (1981) images of complex pictures such as scenes, and images of words were both posited to exist in memory, although any one image could encode only one picture or one word. If sentences were studied it would presumably be possible to have images which encode whole sentences, within sentence propositions, words, or all three simultaneously. In this chapter we try to present evidence that would allow at least some of the many possibilities to be eliminated. In particular, for situations in which sentences are studied, we want to test a set of models in which only word-level images are encoded. Researchers who have worked on psycholinguistic topics have usually assumed word-level-only hypotheses to be unworkable. However, an associative network among word-level images provides a surprisingly powerful tool for dealing with sentence memory, and some models of this type have been proposed (e.g., Jones, 1984; Ross & Bower, 1981). The word-level hypothesis, as implausible as it may seem to some theorists, is far from trivial to rule out, either for studied sentences or for studied word pairs. For example, Mandler, Rabinowitz, and Simon (1981) argued that the word-level hypothesis for word pairs could be ruled out. However, their analysis was predicated upon certain assumptions not true in SAM. We have found the word-level version of SAM to be quite capable of handling their data. For a careful discussion of the difficulties of distinguishing these classes of approaches in paradigms using very small groups of items (e.g., 2 or 3 at most), see Bain and Humphreys (1988) and Humphreys, Pike, Bain, and Tehan (in press).

Just as SAM imposes no restrictions on the level of stored units, it imposes no restrictions on the nature of the cues in the probe set. In the case of recall of a studied list of unrelated words, the cues that have been utilized in previous applications include the *context* cue, (a pointer to words on the studied list), and some of the words from the list itself (the ones already recalled or those provided as cues by the experimenter). In cases where the lists are categorized, category cues have been posited. In Gronlund and Shiffrin

(1986), alphabetic and size cues were also considered in situations where subjects were instructed to use particular retrieval strategies.

In the SAM framework, each cue, Q_i, in a probe set, Q_1, Q_2, ... Q_n, is given a weight W_i. This weight represents something like the salience of a particular cue or the attention given to that cue. It is crucial that these weights are constrained to some maximum (usually 1.0) (see Gronlund & Shiffrin, 1986). In this way, retrieval is made a limited capacity process. Adding additional cues must take attention away from other potentially useful cues. That is, there is a cost incurred by the addition of retrieval cues.

To see how cue weighting makes retrieval a limited capacity process, define the activation of image I_i given cues Q_1, Q_2, ..., Q_m and weights W_1, W_2, ..., W_m as $A(I_i|Q_1, W_1, Q_2, W_2, ..., Q_m, W_m)$ or, more simply, $A(I_i)$. Let the retrieval strength of cue Q_j to image I_j be $S(Q_j, I_j)$. Then

$$A(I_i) = \prod_{j=1}^{m} S(Q_j, I_i)^{W_j} \tag{1}$$

$$\sum_{j=1}^{m} W_j = 1.0 \tag{1a}$$

Equation 1 has the following important properties.

1. The higher the strength between a cue and an image, the higher the activation. (As is indicated shortly, higher activation translates into increased sampling probability and increased recovery probability if sampled.)

2. Assigning higher weights to stronger cues increases activation.

3. Adding relatively weak cues to a probe set lowers activation because the weights assigned to the new cues lower the weight available to be assigned to the remaining stronger cues.

4. If the probe set consists of the strongest cue for an image, then adding other cues can only decrease activation.

5. If all strengths are equal, then activation is independent of the number of cues in the probe set.

To see how activation values affect performance we must specify how these values are used in recall. We also briefly consider how activation values are used in recognition. (Although we are concerned with recall tasks in this chapter, some alternative models use assumptions for recall that are like the SAM assumptions for recognition, so that a brief description facilitates comparisons.)

For recognition the old–new decision is based simply on total activation. If there are N images in memory,

$$A = \sum_{j=1}^{N} A(I_j) \tag{2}$$

This total activation value, A, is simply the sum of the activations of all images in memory caused by the probe set. It has been termed familiarity in previous articles, and a decision is made by comparing it to a criterion value.

For recall, the probability of sampling image I_i is simply the activation of that image by the probe set divided by the total activation:

$$P_s(I_i) = \frac{A(I_i)}{\sum_{j=1}^{N} A(I_j)} \tag{3}$$

In cases where the image contains words (not groups of words), recovery is straightforward. Once an image has been sampled, the probability that enough information will be retrieved from it to report the name of the encoded word is an exponential function of the sum of the weighted strengths of the probe set to the sampled image:

$$P_R(I_i) = 1 - \exp\left\{ - \sum_{j=1}^{m} W_j S(Q_j, I_i) \right\} \tag{4}$$

The recovery process when images and cues consist of higher order units such as sentences has been considered by Gronlund (1986). He proposed that each component word in a higher order unit is given a chance at recovery in turn. An exponential function governed each recovery probability as in Equation 4 but with a different parameter.

When the currently sampled image has been sampled earlier in the search, special rules apply to recovery (independence of successive recovery attempts has not proved workable because a sufficiently long search would always result in successful recall). It has been assumed that only the part of the activation due to cues that have not been used previously to sample that image contributes to recovery. For example, if a set of cues is used to sample a given image and recovery fails, and if later in the search that same cue set is used to sample that same image, then the recovery probability would be zero.

In SAM, learning can occur during retrieval as well as during study. Whenever a successful recovery occurs, learning will take place (called "incremenating" in previous work), such that the associative connections between the cues used and the image sampled are strengthened. As a result, a subsequent use of the same cues would produce a larger activation value for the previously recovered image and thereby increase its probability of being sampled again. This tends to produce a form of retrieval inhibition (Roediger

& Neely, 1982), as other images in memory will have a reduced chance of being sampled later in the search.

After any cycle of the search the subject must decide whether to continue the search, and, if continuing, which cues to use on the next cycle. These cues may be the same as those used on the previous cycle or they may differ. What strategy will be most efficient will depend on the task in question, the particular storage processes that took place during study, and the course of retrieval thus far. In free recall tasks we have assumed that subjects sometimes only use a context cue and sometimes use both the context cue and an item that has been recently recalled. In cued recall tasks we have assumed that the subject uses context plus the provided test words as cues.

Finally, we have considered various rules for terminating the search process. These include reaching a time limit, accumulating some criterion number of unsuccessful searches, accumulating a criterion number of successive unsuccessful searches, and successfully recalling the desired information.

In this chapter we carefully examine the time to recall as well as the accuracy of recall. In SAM, the time to recall is assumed to be a linear function of the number of search cycles undertaken. That is, the mean time for each cycle of the search is assumed to be constant.

A PROTOTYPE STUDY AND PREDICTIONS FROM SOME SIMPLIFIED MODELS

Working within the SAM framework as just outlined, Gronlund (1986) carried out several studies addressing the question of units in storage and retrieval. A variant carried out by K. Murnane provides the starting point for the experiments described in this chapter. We begin by describing a simplified version of this study and by pointing out the predictions from several classes of models making different assumptions about units.

The prototypical study employs a sentence memory paradigm. The subject studies M five-word sentences (ignoring function words), these $5M$ words being unique. At test, the subject is given as cues one, two, three, or four words from a studied sentence and asked to recall some particular word not presented as a cue (the target). We are concerned with the probability of target recall, and the average time to output the target, as a function of the number of cues.

In order to derive predictions we make certain simplifying assumptions about the storage processes. (These assumptions will be relaxed later.) If the stored images and the retrieval cues are in word-level units, we assume that the strength between the context cue and any word in any sentence is a constant value, a. The strength between any word used as a cue and the image of any word in the sentence that contains that word (including the cue word itself) is a constant, b. The strength between a word cue and any word in some other sentence is a constant, d.

Model 1: Word-Level Storage and Retrieval Units, Concurrent Retrieval Strategy

Assume that context is used as one cue and given a weight of 0.5; assume that the provided test words are also used as cues and share weights that sum to 0.5. Assume also that this probe set is used over and over during the response period until time runs out (i.e., a fixed number of search cycles).

The probability of sampling the target-word image is given by Equation 3. This probability does not depend on the number of word cues provided or the weights assigned to the word cues. Furthermore, the probability will not change during the course of the search (as learning during retrieval cannot take place until the target is retrieved successfully). The reason why the probability does not vary lies in Equation 1. All of the word to word strengths for a given image are constant, so that their product is just the constant raised to a power equal to the sum of the weights assigned to each. By assumption the sum of the weights is 0.5. The recovery probability is similarly constant as is evident from an inspection of Equation 4.

The implications of these observations are straightforward. The accuracy of recall and the average time until recall are constant as a function of increasing numbers of cues. These predictions are illustrated in the left panels of Fig. 3.2.

Model 2: Word-Level Storage and Retrieval Units, Sequential Retrieval Strategy

Assume that each probe set consists of the context cue with a weight of 0.5 and one of the word cues with a weight of 0.5. Assume that each word cue is used for some number of search cycles before a switch is made to the next cue. If time remains when all cues have been used, the cues are reused in sequence.

According to this model, probability of recall will rise with the number of cues because the extra cues provide extra chances for recovery. That is, the sampling and recovery probabilities will remain unchanged during the search except for the case where the target image is sampled more than once. On these subsequent samples, recovery probability will be above zero only when the cue word is different than it was for the previous samples (which resulted in unsuccessful recovery). Obviously, this will happen more often when more cues are provided.

On the other hand, the latency for correct recall will increase with more cues. On the average, recall will be early in the sampling period for a given cue. When there are many cues, the average recall time tends to be later because the use of new cues later in the recall period allows extra late recalls to occur. Recovery would have been impossible on resamples if only one word cue had been available. In effect, the successive use of different cues tends to spread

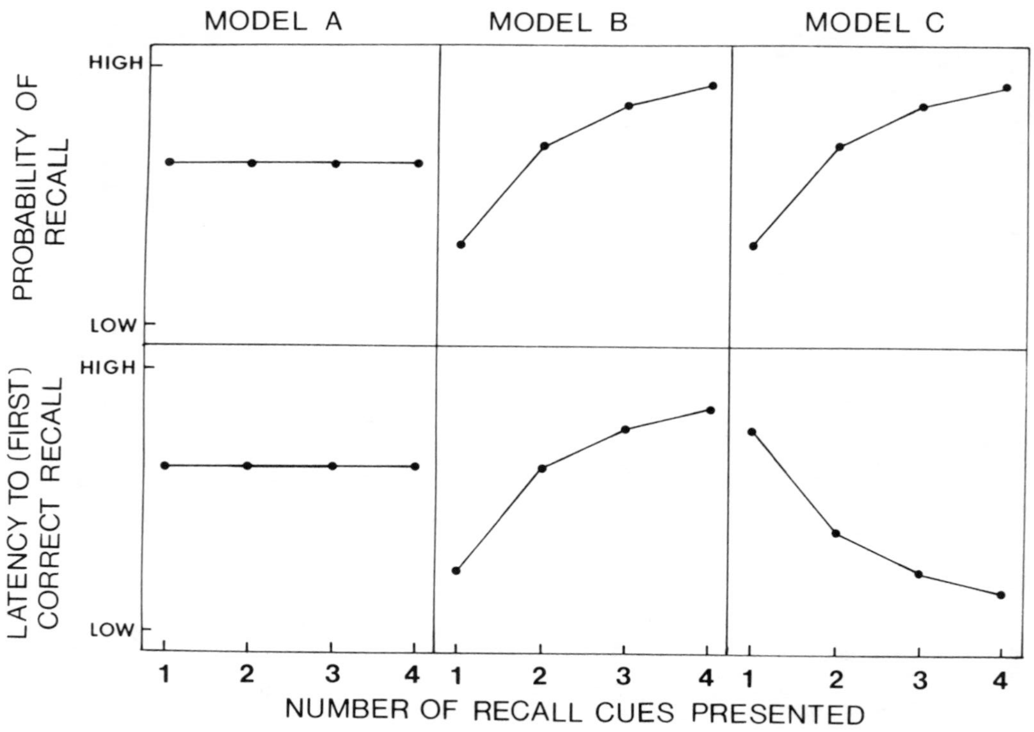

FIG. 3.2. Qualitative predictions of accuracy (top) and latency (bottom) of cued recall as the number of cues from a five-item sentence is varied, for several classes of models specifiable within the SAM framework. Left panels: concurrent use of word-level cues for either word-level or sentence-level storage. Middle Panels: sequential use of word-level cues, for either word-level or sentence-level storage. Right panels: sentence-level storage and partial-sentence-level cuing.

recall more uniformly through the recall period, thereby lengthening the average latency. These predictions are illustrated in the middle panels of Fig. 3.2.

Model 3: Sentence-Level Storage and Retrieval

Assume that storage takes place with sentence units. The context cue has a strength a to each sentence image. The word cues are formed into a group and form a single partial sentence cue. This cue has a strength to each other sentence of d, but the strength to the image of its own sentence depends on the match of the cue to the sentence. The match, and hence the strength, will be higher the more word cues are provided. Let the strengths be $b(1) < b(2) < b(3) < b(4)$ for 1, 2, 3, and 4 cues respectively. It is assumed that the probe cue is used continuously until the recall time expires.

Because of the strength differences due to degree of match, it is evident that both sampling and recovery will be better when more cues are provided. As a result, accuracy will rise and latency will fall as the number of cues is increased. These predictions are illustrated in the right panels of Fig. 3.2.

Model 4: Sentence-Level Storage; Word-Level Retrieval, Concurrent Strategy

Other than the fact that there are only one fifth as many images stored, this model is analogous to Model 1. Because of the cue weighting property, accuracy and latency are predicted to be flat, as in the left hand panels of Fig. 3.2.

Model 5: Sentence-Level Storage; Word-Level Retrieval, Sequential Strategy

This model is analogous to Model 2: The extra cues will improve accuracy due to extra recovery chances, but they will also distribute recall more evenly through the recall period, slowing latency. The predictions are illustrated in the central panels of Fig. 3.2.

The rather different patterns of predictions in panels A, B, and C of Fig. 3.2 provide the impetus for the series of studies reported in this chapter. We begin by describing the studies carried out by Murnane.

EXPERIMENT 1

Experiment 1a was a straightforward examination of cued recall of words from a sentence. Experiment 1b was a variant of Experiment 1a in which the cues given at test were presented in scrambled locations relative to their proper positions in the studied sentence. Experiment 1c presented the sentences of

Experiment 1a repeatedly over 8 days of training to assess the effects of learning.

In Experiment 1a, subjects were given sentences at study that were all of the form "The adjective noun verb the adjective noun." At test, a sentence frame was presented that was composed of some of the words from the studied sentence in their proper sentence locations combined with blanks for missing words. One of these blanks contained question marks indicating which word was the target. The subjects' task was to recall the target word. For example, a test with 3 cues would appear as follows:

Study: The alert boy found the magic sword
Test: The alert _____ found the <u>? ? ?</u> sword

The correct response in the above example would be "magic." Sentences were presented in 5 blocks of 20 for a total of 100 sentences. All 500 words (exclusive of "the") were unique. Each block began with the presentation of each of the 20 sentences for 10 seconds of study. Following a 30-second addition task, the test cues were presented with a 12-second recall period for each

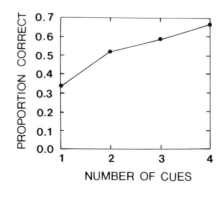

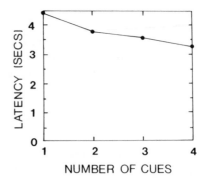

FIG. 3.3. Accuracy and latency of cued recall as a function of number of cues for Experiment 1a (sentence-order testing).

sentence. Presentation of the next test sentence occurred after all subjects had responded, or after 12 seconds, whichever came first. A series of 10 practice trials was given before data collection began.

The position of the target and the number of cues were systematically manipulated in a factorial design so that all 20 possible combinations of the 5 target locations by 1 through 4 possible cues appeared in each block. The order in which each of these 20 possible combinations appeared was randomized over subjects and over blocks for each subject. Recall accuracy was measured as the proportion of correct responses. Latency was given by the time to initial keypress of a correct response. All responses other than the target or an unambiguous spelling variant were counted as errors. Fifty-three subjects ran in groups of 1 to 6.

The results of Experiment 1a are shown in Fig. 3.3. All findings mentioned are statistically significant at least at the 0.01 level unless otherwise stipulated. As is readily apparent, accuracy increased with increasing number of cues (top panel) and latency decreased with increasing number of cues (bottom panel). This pattern is consistent with the model that posits sentence-level units at both storage and retrieval and is inconsistent with the various models positing word-level units at storage or retrieval.

Our data show that increasing the number of cues from a sentence increases the likelihood of recalling a target word from that sentence. However, in a great many situations extra cues actually harm recall; the effect is termed the "part-list cuing effect" (e.g., Slamecka, 1968, 1969; for a review and extended discussion within the SAM framework see Raaijmakers & Shiffrin, 1981). The situations in which the part-list cuing effect hold seem to be ones in which the group of items to be recalled are not all integrated into a single unit (e.g., a long list of unrelated words). An increasing accuracy function is found in situations in which the items to be recalled are likely to be integrated into a unit (e.g., Jones, 1984; Park, 1980; Ross & Bower, 1981). In fact, Park (1980) was able to change a negative part-list cuing effect into one of increasing accuracy by instructing subjects to encode a small group of items together using interactive imagery. This line of reasoning may suggest that the observation of increasing accuracy provides further evidence in favor of sentence-level storage units. This argument does not quite hold up within the SAM framework because, as we have argued (see Fig. 3.2), a memory structure based on word images that are highly and strongly interconnected combined with a sequential strategy of cue utilization can also predict increasing accuracy. The latency results are, therefore, crucial to rule out such a model, because contrary to the findings of Experiment 1a, it predicts increasing latency with increased number of cues.

If the degree of match between the retrieval probe and the stored unit is the key to the latency decrease when sentence units are employed at both storage and retrieval, then lessening the match ought to cause the decrease to lessen, or even disappear. We attempted to manipulate the degree of match

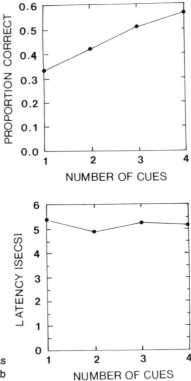

FIG. 3.4. Accuracy and latency of cued recall as a function of number of cues for Experiment 1b (scrambled-order testing).

by giving subjects test cues that contained words in scrambled locations relative to their positions in the originally studied sentences. We reasoned that this would disrupt the match between the stored sentence unit and the retrieval unit in at least two ways: (a) order information would be lost at the word level and (b) coherence and meaningfulness would be lost at the semantic level. Experiment 1b was designed as a test of these ideas.

The procedure of Experiment 1b was identical to that of Experiment 1a except that the cues presented at test were in scrambled locations relative to their studied sentence position. The task was to type in the word that had originally appeared in the position indicated by question marks. For example, the subject might see a study-test sequence such as the following:

Study: The alert boy found the magic sword
Test: _____ sword the alert ? ? ? found

Again, the correct response would be "magic." The same sentences were used as in Experiment 1a. Presentation time at study was shortened to 8 seconds and the recall period was lengthened to 15 seconds. There were 49 subjects, 24 of whom had also taken part in Experiment 1a.

The results of Experiment 1b are shown in Fig. 3.4. The subjects who had taken part in Experiment 1a showed slightly higher accuracy and lower latencies, but the pattern of results was identical to that for the new subjects. We have therefore combined the results. Accuracy rose with increasing number of cues, but not as sharply as in Experiment 1a (a rise of .34 to .67 in 1a, and .33 to .57 in 1b). On the other hand, the latency function was essentially flat across number of cues. The flattening of the latency function in this study is consistent with the prediction of the sentence unit model, assuming that the scrambling at test removes the matching advantage of additional cues.

Although the latency results of Experiment 1b are consistent with a sentence-level model that posits degree of overall match as the key to sampling, the pattern of the accuracy and latency results is different from any of the patterns illustrated in Fig. 3.2. Why should accuracy increase whereas latency is flat? We propose a disassociation of the sampling and recovery processes in SAM. Specifically, we propose that the disorder introduced by scrambling the locations of the test cues reduces the cue-to-image match, offsetting the advantage due to the extra cues, and thereby leaving the efficiency of sampling roughly constant as cue numbers increase. Thus the time to first sample the relevant image should be roughly constant. However, once the relevant image is sampled, it is proposed that the order of cues is less important than their number. Recovery is assumed to be a read-out process that is facilitated by more cues, no matter the order in which these cues appear. Thus, increasing the number of cues produces increasing accuracy (regardless of the scrambling of cues) as long as there is a high probability that the relevant image is eventually sampled.

We are thus proposing that the latency decrease in the sentence study–sentence test condition is due to sampling rather than recovery. Evidence concerning this hypothesis may be available if sentences are very well learned. In this case, recovery should become so efficient and automatic for any number of cues that no significant latency difference should occur. On the other hand, the efficiency of sampling should improve with practice less readily, because one of the cues is context and *all* items will have strong context associations after training. Thus, if the latency decrease resides wholly in the recovery process, it should largely be obliterated after extended learning of the sentences, but if the decrease lies in sampling, extended training might reduce the latency decrease only slightly. Such reasoning led to the design of Experiment 1c.

Experiment 1c

Eight subjects who had been in the upper half of the performance distribution in both Experiments 1a and 1b were selected to take part in Experiment 1c. Each session was basically a replication of Experiment 1a (sentence study–sentence order test). Subjects participated in one session per day for 8 days.

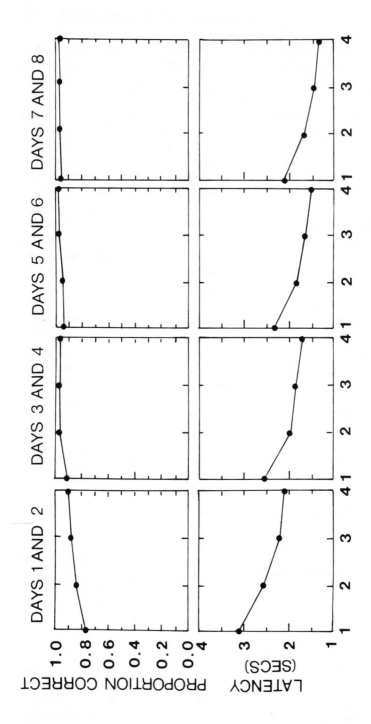

FIG. 3.5. Accuracy and latency of cued recall as a function of number of cues, for each 2 days of training with the same sentences, for Experiment 1c (sentence-order testing).

40

Each day the same 100 sentences were studied in a new random order. The tests for a given sentence were randomized across days so that for each sentence the number and sentence position of cues varied between sessions. The study times per sentence were lessened as training proceeded. Other procedural details were identical to those in Experiment 1a.

The results, averaged across each successive group of 2 sessions are depicted in Fig. 3.5. As expected, accuracy climbed rapidly toward ceiling as training proceeded. The latency functions continued to decrease as training continued. Most interesting, the decrease in the latencies was only slightly (albeit significantly) lowered by training. Because recovery from a sampled image is likely to be fast and effortless after training, this result supports the view that the sampling process underlies the latency decrease with number of cues.[1]

If a sentence-unit model is assumed, it is reasonable to expect that training continually increases the strength of connection between cue words and the sentence image. As each individual word cue becomes more strongly connected to the sentence image the existence of floor effects ought to result in a lessening of the latency decrease with increasing numbers of cues. The data show this lessening of the latency decrease but it is surprisingly small given the extent of training. This suggests that the overall degree of match between the probe unit and the sentence image is still a prime determinant of sampling even when each word in the sentence provides a good retrieval cue.

The subjects in Experiment 1c were given a free recall task on their last day of participation in the experiment. The recall period lasted either 30 or 40 minutes for different subjects. All subjects reported that they were still actively recalling sentences when their recall period was over. Of a total of 800 possible sentence recalls, subjects recalled 557 sentences. With 7 exceptions, all of these recalls were of complete sentences. All 7 exceptions were cases where one word was missing from the recalled sentence. These results support the view that subjects are sampling and retrieving from sentence-level units. Some sentences are not sampled in the recall period, but once sampled, each sentence is recovered perfectly. If sampling of word images were occurring, words from different sentences would have been interleaved in recall. Also, recall from a sentence, given that at least one word is recalled from that sentence, would not have been complete: If sampling failures are needed to explain why sentences are missed, sampling failures should also have caused words within a sentence to be missed.

EXPERIMENT 2

The predictions illustrated in Fig. 3.2 are based on certain restrictive assumptions. If these assumptions are relaxed, we must reconsider whether a word-

---

[1]A ninth session was run with a scrambled test order. Unfortunately, the data were later lost due to equipment failure.

level model might be capable of handling the present results. In particular, suppose the strengths stored are not all equal, and suppose that the subject can assign higher weights to the stronger cues. For example, suppose that items are stored in a sequential chain, one word to the next, with all strengths other than those between words in sequence being low. Knowing this at test, the subject chooses to assign as much weight as possible to the test word preceding the target word if it is available. The more test cues are provided, the more likely that the word preceding the target position will be provided as a cue. Hence, additional cues would improve accuracy while simultaneously lowering latency.

This explanation rests on the increased probability of finding a valuable cue as the number of cues increases. However, if the subject were asked to recall any, or all, of the remaining words from a cued sentence, rather than a particular word, the advantage of having more cues would disappear or even reverse. This is because an equally strong cue-target connection would probably exist whether the subject was presented with one or four cues. When four test words are given, the subject is limited to recalling the one missing word but may choose the best available cue to do so. When one test word is given, the subject is initially limited to this single cue but is free to recall the word to which it is most strongly connected.

In fact, there are a number of reasons to think that the unequal strength word-level model should predict poorer accuracy and slower latency with more cues, when the task is to recall as many of the missing words as possible. For one thing, one provided cue tends quickly and automatically to sample a strong image, whereas sampling based on more than one cue may be hindered by the subject's not knowing which of the provided cues is the best to use. It may require valuable time to consider the set of provided cues and pick the best one out. Perhaps the most important factor acting to depress performance with more cues is that the more cues are provided, the more likely that the image of one of the cues themselves would be sampled at any point in time. The fewer the available cues, the more images would be available to be sampled and output. These considerations point to the response latency for the first word recalled as a highly discriminating datum; if this latency decreases with increasing number of cues, the sentence-level model would be given considerable support.

Experiment 2 attempts to take advantage of this line of reasoning by asking subjects to respond as quickly as possible with as many words as possible from the cued sentence. (It is based on one condition in Experiment 3 in Gronlund, 1986.) It was run as two closely related studies. The only difference was in the test format. In Experiment 2a the target items to be recalled were represented as dashes. The number of dashes indicated the number of letters in the to-be-recalled word. In Experiment 2b the word length of targets was not provided; each target word was represented by 12 dashes regardless of

TABLE 3.1
Study and Test Conditions for Experiment 2

Study	Test
Sentence Order $A_1N_1VA_2N_2$	Sentence Order $A_1\text{-} VA_2\text{-}$
Sentence Order $A_1N_1VA_2N_2$	Scrambled Order $V\text{-}A_2\text{-}A_1$
Scrambled Order Sentence $VA_1N_2N_1A_2$	Sentence Order $A_1\text{-} VA_2\text{-}$
Scrambled Order Sentence $VA_1N_2N_1A_2$	Same Scrambled Order $VA_1\text{-}\text{-} A_2$
Scrambled Order Sentence $VA_1N_2N_1A_2$	Different Scrambled Order $\text{-}\text{-} A_2VA_1$
Nonsense Sentence $A_1N_1VA_2N_2$	Nonsense Sentence Order $A_1\text{-} VA_2\text{-}$
Nonsense Sentence $A_1N_1VA_2N_2$	Scrambled Order $V\text{-}A_2\text{-} A_1$

word length. The results from these studies did not differ so they have been combined and will be discussed jointly.

The sentences in Experiment 2 were of the same form as those used in Experiment 1, "The Adjective1 Noun1 Verbed the Adjective2 Noun2." In some conditions, one of two scrambled permutations of the 5 elements was studied ("the" always preceded an adjective). These permutations were: (a) "Verb the Adjective1 Noun2 Noun1 the Adjective2" and (b) "Noun1 Noun2 the Adjective2 Verb the Adjective1." We denote the adjectives and nouns with numbers indicating the original sentence position because most sentences had a natural order that could not be altered without producing syntactic or semantic violations or distortions. For example, the sentence "The happy fox ate the green lettuce" would not form a good sentence in any of the other possible permutations fitting the experimental frame. In a final set of conditions the form of the sentence remained "The Adjective1 Noun1 Verbed the Adjective2 Noun2," but the words did not make semantic sense (e.g., "The perplexed basket spanked the eager computer"). We term these nonsense sentences.

For each of these types of studied 5-tuples there were several test conditions. These are summarized in Table 3.1. For the 5-tuples studied in sentence order, tests could be in study order (sentence–sentence) or either of the two scrambled orders (sentence–scrambled). For the nonsense sentences, tests could be in study order (nonsense–nonsense) or either of the two scrambled orders (nonsense–scrambled). For the scrambled study sentences, tests could be either in the studied order (scrambled–same scrambled), in the other scrambled order (scrambled–different scrambled), or in sentence order (scrambled–sentence). For any of these study-test types the number of provided cues was one, two, three, or four. Nonpresented words were replace by dashes in the appropriate locations.

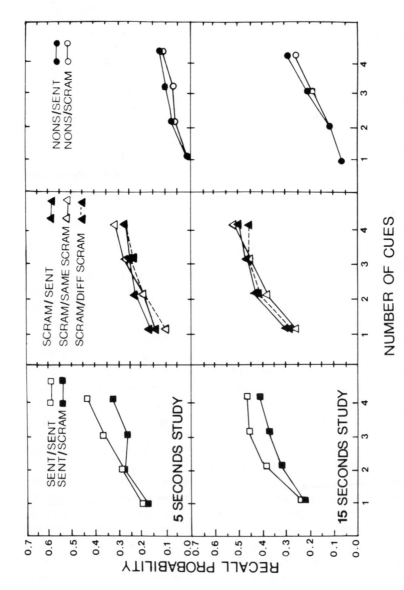

FIG. 3.6. Average probability of recall of a given word, as a function of the number of cues, for the seven conditions of Experiment 2, for 5 and 15 seconds of study time per sentence.

Two study times were used: 5 seconds and 15 seconds per 5-tuple. A block of study trials consisted of 14 five-tuples, two each of the seven study-test types in Table 3.1. All study times in a block were constant. A period of 30 seconds of arithmetic was used to clear short-term memory after study and prior to test. Each study-test type was then tested twice, in random order, one test per studied 5-tuple, with the number of cues consisting of two different choices from the set of four. Over two different blocks at one study time, all four set sizes would be tested once for each condition.

Subjects were instructed to recall as many of the missing words as possible as quickly as possible in any order. A 45-second recall period was provided for each test sentence. Responses were typed at a computer keyboard and answers appeared on a CRT screen.

The experiment began with a practice block of trials to familiarize the subject with the procedure and then proceeded through eight blocks, four at each study time, in random order. There were 171 subjects in all, 108 in Experiment 2a and 63 in Experiment 2b.

Results

The probability of correct recall for a particular item, averaged across target items, is shown for 5 and 15 seconds in Fig. 3.6. The probability that at least one item is recalled is shown for 5 and 15 seconds in Fig. 3.7. The latency to first correct recall for 5 and 15 seconds is given in Fig. 3.8. The results discussed are significant at the 0.01 level unless otherwise specified.

The accuracy results in Fig. 3.6 replicate and extend those seen in Experiment 1. All of the curves show a monotonic increase in recall with increasing number of cues. For the scrambled study or nonsense sentence study conditions, test type did not matter. However, sentence study was significantly better when tested in sentence order. Nonsense sentence study always produced much lower accuracy than any of the other conditions. Interestingly, scrambled study was worse than sentence study only for the 5-second study condition. For the 15-second study condition, scrambled study actually produced slightly higher accuracy than the sentence study-sentence test condition ($p = .06$). Presumably, 5 seconds was not enough time for effective encoding of scrambled sentences. Fifteen seconds of study not only allowed time for encoding, but the more difficult act of encoding the scrambled 5-tuple appears to have improved performance beyond the level for sentence study (see Graf, 1980, 1981; Slamecka & Graf, 1978).

The accuracy results in Fig. 3.7 show a U-shaped pattern, clearly indicating two processes at work: (a) As the number of cues increases there are fewer targets available for recall, tending to produce a lower probability that at least one would be recalled; (b) Fewer cues produce poorer access to memory. These data do not allow us to specify whether the deficit with fewer cues is due to a failure of sampling or a failure of recovery following sampling. However,

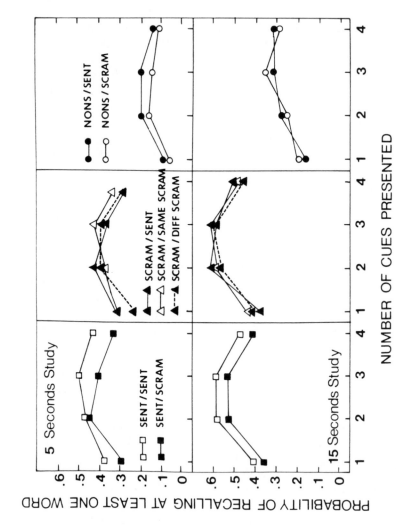

FIG. 3.7. Probability of recalling at least one word, as a function of the number of cues, for the seven conditions of Experiment 2, for 5 and 15 seconds of study time per sentence.

46

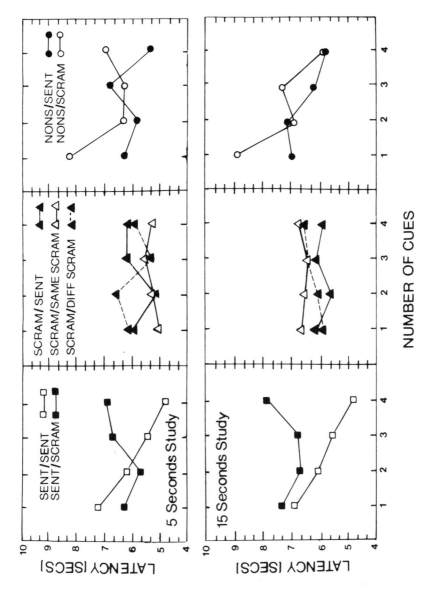

FIG. 3.8. Latency to begin the first correct recall, as a function of the number of cues, for the seven conditions of Experiment 2, for 5 and 15 seconds of study time per sentence.

47

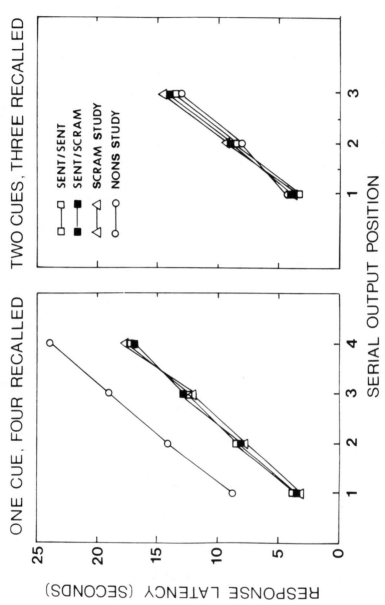

FIG. 3.9. Latency to begin recall of successive words in Experiment 2, when one cue is used and four words are recalled correctly (left panel), or two cues are used and three words are recalled correctly (right panel). (The elevated function in the left panel is probably due to an extremely small number of observations.)

because only 14 sentences were studied, we suspect the 45-second recall period was long enough for sampling of most of the relevant images most of the time. If so, the recall failure with few cues is probably due to an inability to recover the names of items once the images containing them have been sampled.

As in the earlier studies, the latency results are highly informative (see Fig. 3.8). (Due to low numbers of observations, we will not discuss the nonsense sentence latencies.) Confirming the results of Experiment 1a, the sentence–sentence condition was the only condition exhibiting a strongly decreasing pattern of latencies; the decrease for this condition suggests an increasing match between a partial sentence cue and a stored sentence image. The sentence study–scrambled test conditions exhibited a slightly U-shaped pattern ($p = .04$). The latencies for the scrambled study conditions exhibited highly individual patterns but little consistency; averaged together they exhibited a largely flat pattern, perhaps increasing slightly for both 5 and 15 seconds of study.

The latencies for words recalled beyond the first provide evidence concerning serial processes. The relevant data are shown in Fig. 3.9 for the one and two cue conditions in which all the target items were recalled correctly. All of these functions are linear, with the two cue functions having slightly larger slopes ($p = .02$). The fact that all of these functions are similar suggests that the reason may be the same in each case; recall may be the result of a readout from an image that contains all the words in the presented 5-tuple. These results argue against the view that recall in some of the conditions is based upon sampling of single word images. It may be that the requirement that all target words be recalled tends to select out those cases in which a high level code has been stored. Perhaps cases in which single word images are stored tend to produce imperfect recall. This reasoning suggests examination of the distribution of the number of correct recalls for various conditions.

There are various ways to look at the distributions of particular numbers of recalls. For summary purposes, it seems best to normalize each distribution so that it sums to 1.0, so the patterns, rather than the absolute recall levels, can be compared. The appropriate data are shown in Fig. 3.10 for one, two, and three cues, for each condition (summing over the scrambled conditions and the nonsense sentence conditions). The overall recall level for a condition is given to the left of each curve.

It should be noted that there is an overall tendency for the "slope" of the distribution function to be related to the overall recall level for that condition, a finding that would be predicted by most models. Thus, it seems best to compare different conditions only when their overall recall levels do not much differ. The data in Fig. 3.10 show that the slopes of the distribution functions are similar when the overall recall level is similar (with one exception: There is a small tendency for greater recalls of both remaining items when three cues are used in the sentence–sentence condition). All in all, the

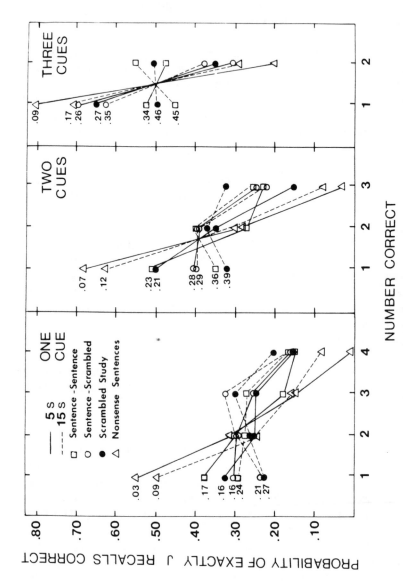

FIG. 3.10. Normalized probability of recalling exactly j items correctly, as a function of j for the one cue (left panel), two cue (center panel), and three cue (right panel) conditions of Experiment 2. To the left of each function is the average recall probability for that condition.

TABLE 3.2

a) 1 Cue: Probability All Four Recalls in Sentence Order Given 4 Recalls, 5 and 15 Seconds Combined:

Study	Test		
	Sentence	Same Scrambled	Different Scrambled
Sentence	.79	—	.68
Scrambled	.47	.38	.37

b) 1 Cue: Probability Both Recalled in Sentence Order Given Exactly Two Recalled:

5 Seconds:	Sentence	Same Scrambled	Different Scrambled
Sentence	.68	—	.63
Scrambled	.54	.55	.50

15 Seconds:			
Sentence	.79	—	.77
Scrambled	.70	.62	.61

c) 3 Cues: Probability Both Recalled in Sentence Order Given Both Recalled:

5 Seconds:	Sentence	Same Scrambled	Different Scrambled
Sentence	.73	—	.76
Scrambled	.69	.69	.62

15 Seconds:	Sentence	Same Scrambled	Different Scrambled
Sentence	.76	—	.72
Scrambled	.64	.65	.70

distribution data provide little evidence for different storage and retrieval processes in the different conditions. As a first approximation to a model, then, we will assume that sentence-level storage and retrieval operates in all conditions.

Finally, if it is the case that a sentence image is contacted in memory and that a readout process occurs, it would be natural to expect that the words would be recalled in sentence order. There are many ways to look at output order; we examined many approaches and all are consistent. We report just a few simple, typical results. First, consider those cases in which one cue was used and all four of the remaining words were recalled correctly. We ask how often all four items are recalled in the order of the "originating" sentence. For studied sentences, the method of analysis is obvious. For scrambled study, we found that subjects did *not* tend to recall in the scrambled study order. We therefore report how often the recall order matches the order of the original sentence from which the scrambled sentence was obtained. The probabilities of ordering recall in the originating sentence order are given in Table 3.2a. In cases where one cue is used and exactly two (of four) items are recalled, the probability that these are recalled in originating sentence order is given in Table 3.2b. In cases where three cues are used and both remaining items are recalled, the probability that these are recalled in originating sentence order is given in Table 3.2c.

The sentence study conditions with recall of four items exhibit a remarkable tendency for items to be output in sentence order. The scrambled study cases exhibit a lower but strong tendency as well. A finer analysis of the data revealed a much stronger tendency to output items in originating sentence order than is revealed even by Table 3.2a. Failures were usually off by just one item or by a switch from active to passive tense. Furthermore, many recall attempts that did not produce four correctly recalled words failed because one of the original words was replaced by a semantically related word, but with recall still in the originating sentence order. Tables 3.2b and 3.2c show that two recalled words also tend to be output in originating sentence order, but the effect is not as strong. In fact, in scrambled study cases, when only two of four items are recalled, and when there is only 5 seconds of study time, output order is near chance levels. Perhaps this analysis selects out the few cases in which stored codes are not sentences. As far as the other conditions in Table 3.2b and 3.2c are concerned, it must be noted that subjects may not choose to output items in sentence order even if storage had occurred in sentence order. Conversely, however, it is hard to see why output would be in originating sentence order if storage of the originating sentence had not taken place.

All in all, the output order findings tend to suggest that sentences frequently tend to be stored as images in memory. In cases involving scrambled study, the subjects apparently attempt to unscramble the words to make a sentence, succeeding quite often when there are 15 seconds of study time, but succeeding less often when there are only 5 seconds of study time. The implication nonetheless is that sentence images tend to be stored even in the scrambled study conditions. This point is important enough that we report one additional analysis of the order data. When one cue is used, and all four target words are recalled, we can tabulate the number of times that the word in the *i*-th position (excluding the cue position) in the originating sentence is reported in the *j*-th output position, for *i* and *j* ranging from 1 to 4. The results are given for the sentence study and scrambled study conditions (not enough cases are available for the nonsense conditions) in Table 3.3. A tendency to recall in originating sentence position is seen as a tendency for large entries in the upper left to lower right diagonal of each 4 x 4 table. The important point to note here is the strong tendency for such output in the scrambled study cases, regardless of the type of test, and despite the fact that the scrambled

TABLE 3.3
Number of Times that Word in Originating Sentence Position i is
Output in Position j Given One Cue and Four Items Recalled

	5 Seconds					15 Seconds				
i	1	2	3	4		1	2	3	4	j
Sentence/Sentence	19	0	0	0		17	2	2	2	1
	0	18	1	0		2	17	2	2	2
	0	0	18	1		2	3	17	1	3
	0	1	0	18		2	1	2	18	4
Sentence/Scrambled	13	2	0	1		19	0	1	2	1
	0	9	6	1		1	17	2	2	2
	2	1	9	4		2	2	17	1	3
	1	4	1	10		0	3	2	17	4
Scrambled/Sentence	17	2	2	2		18	5	7	4	1
	2	16	4	1		7	16	4	7	2
	3	1	14	5		5	9	14	6	3
	1	4	3	15		4	4	9	17	4
Scrambled/Same	9	0	0	0		13	5	2	12	1
	0	7	1	1		7	12	10	3	2
	0	2	7	0		7	6	15	4	3
	0	0	1	8		5	9	5	13	4
Scrambled/Different	6	2	4	1		20	5	3	10	1
	3	5	3	2		4	19	11	4	2
	1	4	3	5		9	5	19	5	3
	3	2	3	5		5	9	5	19	4

(continued)

TABLE 3.3
(continued)

	5 Seconds				*i*	15 Seconds				
	1	2	3	4		1	2	3	4	
	32	4	6	3		51	15	12	26	1
All Scrambled	5	28	8	4		18	47	25	14	2
	4	7	24	10		21	20	48	15	3
	4	6	7	28		14	22	19	49	4
										j
	5	2	2	0		6	11	7	8	1
Sentence/Same	1	4	2	2		10	9	10	3	2
	1	3	1	4		12	5	5	10	3
	2	0	4	3		4	7	10	11	4

Note: *i* = Study position
        j = Output position

study sentences can sometimes be unscrambled in several ways to make plausible sentences. We think these data strongly suggest that subjects are storing sentence-level units whenever possible, and in most cases in the conditions of our study.

Up to this point we have pointed out the ability of a sentence-level model within the SAM framework to handle the various findings, and have pointed out the difficulties for certain simple word-level models. However, it is important to consider more sophisticated versions of word-level models, as well as models combining word-level and sentence-level mechanisms. For instance, the flat latency function and rising accuracy function seen in sentence study–scrambled test conditions could result from a mixture of two processes. The word-level sequential model in panel B of Fig. 3.2 could apply on some trials and the sentence-level model in panel C of Fig. 3.2 could apply on the remaining trials. Presumably the latencies are about equal for one cue and diverge as the number of cues increases. Such a mixture could account for the observed patterns of accuracy and mean reaction time, but it predicts an increase in the variance of the reaction times as cue numbers increase. The standard deviations of the latencies, calculated for each subject and then averaged are shown in panels A and B of Fig. 3.11 for Experiments 1a and 1b and in Fig. 3.12 for Experiment 2. Clearly the standard deviations are not increasing in the scrambled condition, casting doubt on the mixture hypothesis.

We have argued that the results of Experiment 2 rule out a word-level model

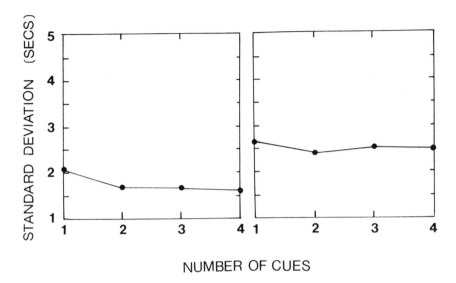

FIG. 3.11. Standard deviation of the response latency as a function of the number of cues for Experiment 1a (left panel) and Experiment 1b (right panel).

based on unequal storage strengths between cues and images coupled with a sophisticated choice of cue items, but there is another version of such models that could be considered. Suppose there is an asymmetric relationship between any two words such that the retrieval strength is determined mostly by the cue rather than the image. Thus, cue item A could strongly activate image B without cue item B strongly activating image A. If the main variation in strengths occurred among cue items rather than images, and if the subject could choose the best cue from several provided cues to use as a memory probe, then at least some of the results of Experiment 2 might be predicted. For example, if one particular word was a strong cue for all images of words from its sentence and all other words were weak cues for all other images (including the image of the strong word cue), then providing extra cues would increase the probability that the good cue would be available. Having a good cue would speed up sampling of the relevant target image. If this effect were large enough it could overcome the tendency for more cues to slow up recall because of the sampling of the cues themselves. There are many other similar model variants of this general type. Although they may be able to provide an account of the latency decrease with increasing numbers of cues, they do not do so well with other aspects of the data. For example, such models provide no good reason why the scrambling at test in Experiment 2 produces a different pattern of results from that observed in the sentence–sentence condition. Also, these model types do not suggest a basis for the linearly increasing output times seen in Fig. 3.9.

Finally, we can try to examine the hypothesis that certain items are good cues, but not good targets. To do so, we table how often a given word is output in response to some other word as a cue. In order to sum over different cue numbers, a weighting scheme was used: If word i was recalled in response to cue j, the count in the (i, j) cell would be increased by $1/k$ where k was the number of cues used on that trial. These numbers were then divided by the maximum possible score in a cell to produce probabilities and these are given in Table 3.4. The key datum to note is that there are some large differences in the table, but in the wrong direction for the hypothesis under consideration. That is, the verb is recalled less often than other items, but is fairly close to the other items as a cue. This data does not provide support for the asymmetric word-level model in question.

In summary, we have not been able to find a word-level model that provides an adequate account of the results from our studies. This conclusion

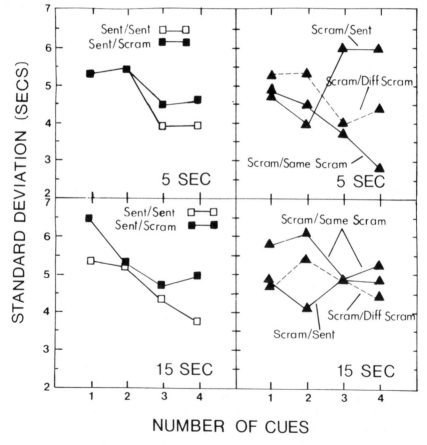

FIG. 3.12.   Standard deviation of the latency to first correct recall as a function of the number of cues for various conditions of Experiment 2.

TABLE 3.4
Probability of Recall of Target j to Cue i

		A_1	N_1	V	A_2	N_2
	A_1	—	.75	.46	.58	.72
	N_1	.70	—	.47	.65	.74
Sentence/Sentence	V	.63	.67	—	.61	.70
	A_2	.57	.63	.35	—	.74
	N_2	.73	.80	.49	.72	—
Cue Word						
	A_1	—	.63	.38	.53	.61
	N_1	.67	—	.39	.61	.67
Sentence/Scrambled	V	.52	.59	—	.51	.61
	A_2	.59	.71	.39	—	.68
	N_2	.63	.64	.36	.56	—

Target Word

is based on the use of the SAM theoretical framework, but probably holds more generally, because the SAM word-level model is quite powerful, with a number of alternative encoding the retrieval mechanisms and strategies. Thus, we think it reasonable to rule out word-level images and cues as the sole basis for performance. The patterns of accuracy and latency as cue numbers vary, the linear latency function for successive words recalled, the distributional analyses, and the tendency to recall in sentence order all confirm this conclusion.

Having ruled out word-level models it is tempting to accept sentence-level models as an alternative. However, not all sentence-level models can adequately handle the findings. The fact that subjects, even in the scrambled study conditions, tend to report items in the originating sentence order suggests that the subjects are attempting to reorganize the scrambled words into a sentence unit of the typical type for this experiment. If they succeed in doing so, then a test in the originating sentence order ought to match increasingly well as the number of cues increases. However, the latency results (Fig. 3.8, middle panels) do not support such a conclusion. Alternately, if on some trials the scrambled study sentence is stored in its presented order, then a same scrambled test should have matched better with more cues on those trials. Again, the latency findings do not support this hypothesis. The latency results for sentence–order, same–scrambled, and different–scrambled test are essentially indistinguishable.

We would like to propose a solution to this dilemma based on the hypothesis that subjects store not only the final encoded sentence but also the encoding operations by which the presented 5-tuple is turned into that final sentence (see Kolers, 1973, 1975; Kolers & Ostry, 1974; Kolers & Roediger, 1984). The benefits of increasing cue numbers are seen, according to this view, only when *both* the order of the cue words and the reorganization operations match those stored in the memory image. Tests in the sentence–sentence condition would clearly satisfy this criterion. Tests in the scrambled–study, sentence–test condition clearly would not because the presented cues would not contain the reorganization encoding contained in the image. One might think that the scrambled–study, same–scrambled test condition would satisfy the criterion, but it must be remembered that reorganization of the *cues* into sentence form surely takes a good deal of time (suggested by the poor performance in the scrambled–study conditions at 5 seconds of study time). If so, any gains in latency due to increased matching would surely be wiped out by the time needed to reorganize the cues. In fact, due to the time needed for such operations, the subject may *begin* search of memory by probing with the cue items in their presented order.

TOWARD A MULTILEVEL MODEL OF STORAGE AND RETRIEVAL

We begin by describing a new variant of the SAM model appropriate to handle the data presented in this chapter.

Storage and Encoding

Especially for recall tasks, the research literature makes it clear that storage is crucially dependent on the nature of the effortful encoding and rehearsal processes carried out by the subject at and shortly after presentation. To put is simply, what gets stored is what is encoded and rehearsed in short-term memory at study (Shiffrin, 1975). Applying this principle to the present paradigms is straightforward. Groups of five items, either in sentence format or otherwise, are presented in anticipation of cued recall tests. These circumstances lead the subject to encode these 5-tuples as connected, organized units; rehearsal is not dedicated either to encoding of isolated items or to encoding of groupings composed of words from different presentation sets. (Some automatic encoding of individual words to context might occur simply as a result of reading the presented 5-tuple. If so, and if such encoding could be considered independent of the higher level encoding that is assumed to be occupying the subject's attention, the contribution of such low-level encoding is assumed to be negligible for cued recall tests.)

As a result of these encoding operations, a relatively well integrated set of information is stored about the presented 5-tuple. This set of information contains the individual words as constituents along with a good deal of extra information having to do with between-word relationships. It may also contain information about the encoding operations themselves, especially if these operations required effort and elaboration. The integrated result is what we have been calling a higher level unit or image. For the case of sentence presentation, the encoding is assumed to result in a sentence unit that fairly well matches the order of presentation and the syntax and meaning intended by the experimenter. Furthermore, such encoding is assumed to be relatively easy, not requiring much time or effort. Thus, extra rehearsal time beyond 5 seconds produces relatively little recall advantage due to encoding factors. For the case of scrambled sentence presentation, time consuming, elaborative processing is necessary. Thus, extra study time is very helpful and produces a large recall benefit (see Fig. 3.6, panel B).

Making semantic sense of the nonsense sentences is so difficult that even extra study time is not efficacious in producing high-level units composed of a set of words that cohere together. In these conditions, word units and pair units may be stored more often than higher level units. These conclusions are suggested by the accuracy data (Fig. 3.6 and 3.7) and by the distributional accuracy data (Fig. 3.10).

In summary, what gets stored for each 5-tuple is an integrated set of information at as high a level as the encoding conditions allow. Thus, for sentence study, a sentence unit integrating all five words will often be stored, even when only 5 seconds are allowed for study. In contrast, units consisting of smaller groups of words will sometimes be stored when scrambled sentences are studied for 5 seconds, and the unit size may tend to be smaller yet when nonsense 5-tuples are studied. We have not found much support for the view that the storage of low-level images (e.g., of individual words) contributes in important ways to the performance observed in our studies, but more sophisticated research would be necessary to assess the degree to which low-level images might be stored.

Retrieval: Sampling

We assume that the subject forms a probe set from the context cue and the provided cue words. Let us assume that the context cue is always given a fixed weight, say 0.5. Use of the remaining weight depends on which of several possible strategies is employed. We have discussed three possible retrieval modes:

1. The provided cues are used individually in separate, sequential retrieval attempts. This model is certainly not consistent with the sentence–sentence latency results of Experiments 1 and 2. To the degree that this strategy pro-

duces an increasing latency function, it is inconsistent with the other conditions as well. We do not argue that this strategy is impossible. It remains a viable approach that might be employed if the experimental paradigm provided the proper inducement to do so.

2. The provided words are used as individual items in a group of concurrent cues in the probe set; the items are weighted so that their sum equals 0.5. This model tends to predict flat accuracy and latency functions. The accuracy predictions are in conflict with all of the data presented in this chapter. As for latency, if we assume that recovery operates on a different basis from sampling, then only the predictions of latency to first recall are relevant. In this case, only the sentence–sentence results would not be consistent with strategy 2. Strategy 2 could not be used in the scrambled study–sentence test conditions since the cuing conditions must determine the retrieval strategy. Strategy 2 could have potentially been used in any of the other conditions.

In the scrambled test conditions a higher level cue may be difficult to form quickly. In such cases, memory may be probed, at least at first, with individual words, weighted appropriately, according to strategy 2. As search proceeds, reorganization of the cue words may lead to the development of a partial higher order cue and strategy 3 below may be involved. Note, however, that the latency to first response will probably not be speeded since the time needed to reorganize the cues and form a partial sentence cue would offset any gains due to improved matching as numbers of cues increase. Nonsense sentences in any test form may prove difficult to encode into partial higher level cues and as a result strategy 2 may be used in this condition as well.

3. The provided words are combined into a single probe cue that acts as an incomplete higher order unit. This single unit is assigned a weight of 0.5. The match of the probe unit to the stored image determines the retrieval strength that governs sampling. We assume that degree of match in this case refers not to the words and their order alone, but to a combination of the words, their stored order, the encoding operations used to produce the final stored image, and any other features of the final stored image. Clearly, this strategy will produce an increasing match, and hence a decreasing latency, as the number of cues grows in the sentence–sentence condition. However, in the scrambled study–sentence test case the degree of match will not improve as cues increase because the operations used to produce the final stored image will not be part of the probe cue. In the scrambled study–scrambled test conditions, strategy 3 will not be followed, at least initially, because a higher order image is not formable without rearrangement of the words and rearrangement is a relatively slow process. In these cases, strategy 2 is probably used.

How might these various assumptions be incorporated into SAM in a quantitative fashion? Not many parameters are needed. The strength of the context cue to a stored higher order image probably varies with study time, and also with the type of 5-tuple studied. If strategy 2 is followed, the strength of each word to the higher order image containing that word can be assumed at a first approximation to be a constant value. This constant value would be higher than the strength of the word cue to any other higher order image that does not contain the word. As argued in the introduction, the fact that the weights sum to 0.5 regardless of number of cues will produce the same sampling probability for the relevant image regardless of number of cues. Hence, time to first recall will be flat.

If strategy 3 is followed and there is a mismatch of order of words or type of encoding operation between cue and image, then the strength between the partial higher order cue and the relevant image will be a constant value regardless of the number of cues, a value higher than the strength to any other image. When there is a match, which occurs in the sentence–sentence conditions, the strength to the relevant stored image will increase as number of cues increases, producing an increasing sampling probability and decreasing latency to first recall.

All of these predictions would of course hold true whether subjects are asked to recall all items (as in Experiment 2) or just one specified item (as in Experiment 1), because in both cases the same higher order image would have to be sampled on the basis of the same cue information.

Retrieval: Recovery

Once a higher order image has been sampled, recovery cannot be based on the same strength value that governs sampling. If recovery and sampling were based on the same strength values, then recall accuracy would tend to be flat whenever the latency functions were flat, a prediction inconsistent with our data. Thus we must assume that extra cues improve recovery even when the match strength underlying sampling does not rise with extra cues. Previous applications of SAM have always involved recovery and sampling based on the same strength values; however, the issue has never really been addressed because previous versions of SAM always assumed word-level images as the storage units. Functional separation of roles seems fairly natural in the present setting where sampling is based on degree of overall match and recovery is posited as a readout process. Scrambling the cue set can sufficiently disrupt the degree of match so that the difference between one and four cues has little or no effect on sampling. The same scrambling would not disrupt recovery because reading out a word from an already sampled image would be facilitated by the presence of a cue word anywhere in the cue set. Thus increasing the number of cues in a scrambled condition would provide a recovery advantage even when it did not provide a sampling advantage.

Probably the easiest way to quantify these notions within an amended SAM framework would be to assume that recovery depends on the strengths of the individual words to the image and the number of words in the cue that are also in the image, but not on the order of the words. This would be consistent with our data, but any testing or further elaboration of this notion would have to await further experimentation.

Considerations of Storage at Multiple Levels

The present data leave little doubt concerning the storage and use of sentence-level units. Are elements of sentences stored simultaneously at several different levels? Although our results can be accounted for without such an assumption, there is relatively little direct evidence concerning this point. Conceptually and logically, the view that makes the most sense to us would involve linking the type of images stored to the nature of the encoding processes in short-term memory. Thus, if the subject rehearses and encodes a sentence in short-term memory as an integrated whole, then a single higher level unit might result, having the words as component parts. On the other hand, if several different encodings were carried out, perhaps at different times, one involving sentence level encoding and separate ones involving coding aimed at individual words, then several different images might be stored at different levels.

A second rationale for the storage of two or more images at different levels for the same sentence lies in the possibility of incidental or automatic storage. For example, even if no effort is expended on rehearsal of an individual word in isolation, its presentation might automatically lead to at least some storage of a low-level image. Similarly, a meaning of a word that is different from the meaning fitting the sentence context could conceivably be stored as a different, low-level image, due to automatic activation at presentation. Even if such processes and storage occur, evidence and intuition both suggest that such incidental images would be very weak, almost certainly too weak for observable effects to appear in recall tasks. It may be that evidence for such storage could be found in certain kinds of recognition paradigms, or paradigms involving indirect measures of memory.

Consequences of the Amendments to the SAM Model

The alterations in the SAM framework proposed in this chapter have been induced by data from sentence paradigms. However, the changes have implications for model applications in the simpler domains of word and paired associate storage. For example, pairs of items have been treated in prior work as two separate images linked by an association; the present approach would probably lead to treating storage in such cases as a single higher level image of a pair. Perhaps pair images would be stored most often when there is time at presentation for elaborative encoding to take place and when the words making up the pair have some natural relationship (semantic or otherwise). A similar argument could be made in the case of storage of lists of individual words, as in free recall tasks, since it is generally assumed that the various words are rehearsed together in various combinations during study. It is reasonable to suppose that such rehearsal produces higher level images at least some of the time depending on factors such as study time and the types of relationships existing among the words on the list.

It is clear that such an extended model applied to free recall of isolated words in lists, or cued recall in paired associate paradigms, would be more complicated and would involve a greater number of parameters and assumptions. This extra power may not be needed to handle data from such paradigms. Also, within such paradigms, it may be difficult to find a critical test distinguishing between a model that assumes separate images linked by associations and a model that assumes pair storage. It may prove acceptable, therefore, to continue to apply the simpler version of SAM to the simpler paradigms, reserving the more complex version we are now proposing for paradigms involving sentences, textual material, and the like.

One consequence of the shift to paradigms involving sentences has been the necessity to consider in more detail than heretofore the nature of the stored representation. Although we have intentionally tried to remain neutral regarding particular representations for sentences (other than to assume some unitized image), it has proven, and will continue to prove necessary to begin to consider some aspects of the image structure in order to predict order of output effects, differential cuing effectiveness and other aspects of the data. For example, it was found necessary to assume that the image included the set of encoding operations used to unscramble a sentence as well as the sentence in its final form. As we continue to extend SAM to more complex domains, we expect the trend toward needing particular assumptions about storage representations to continue. In the process SAM will shift from a "retrieval theory" to a more balanced "storage and retrieval theory."

IMPLICATIONS FOR OTHER MODELS

As a starting point we might consider two models developed for cued recall of stored n-tuples of words. Although some of the paradigms did not use sentences (the words were either unrelated or related by a theme), the models are simple and easily applied to our present experiments. Jones (1976, 1984) put forth a fragment model in which the n-tuple of stored words is represented by a subset of the complete set of pairwise associations between all presented words. When any cue word is presented, recall succeeds for any target word for which a pathway of links from the cue word to the target exists at the moment of test. Ross and Bower (1981) considered a schema model in which each word is linked to a central "schema node" but not directly to each other. Any word presented as a cue has some probability of accessing the schema; if the schema is accessed, then there is another probability that independently determines the recallability of each target word. Previous research suggested that the pattern of recalls in response to one or two cues argued for the fragment model for unrelated words and for the schema model for related words (see Jones, 1984). Jones (1980; Jones & Payne, 1982) also argued that the fragment model provides a good account of cued recall from stored sentences.

Without considerable augmentation, neither of these models seems likely to be able to handle our sentence findings. Certainly, the tendency to output in sentence order would not be predicted. Although the fragment and schema models do not provide latency predictions, one can imagine adding a latency mechanism. However this is done, it is hard to see how either model could predict a decreasing latency function only for the sentence–sentence condition. For example, why should scrambled testing make a difference? Something related to the sentence structure seems to be essential to handle our findings. Jones (1984) commented that much of sentence memory can be understood without making special assumptions about the stored representations of sentences (as opposed to word groups). In a sense, we have been testing this assumption in the context of the SAM model. Our data do seem to suggest something special about stored sentence units.

Next consider some of the alternatives to SAM that have been suggested for cued recall in recent years. We should say at the outset that any model that allows for storage of a higher order sentence unit is likely to be able to predict increasing accuracy and decreasing latency as the number of cues increases. This is the result we observed in the sentence–sentence condition. Whether such models could predict the other results is another matter entirely. The models we shall consider could conceivably encode a sentence unit, but this has not yet been done.

Consider first a model by Murdock (1982), known as TODAM, and a similar model by Metcalfe (1982, 1985), known as CHARM. Each word is represented by a long vector of features. Encoding of two words together is accomplished by convolving the two vectors to produce a single (convolution) vector. The convolution vectors representing all such encoded pairs are summed together to form memory. When memory is probed with a cue word, the cue vector is correlated with memory producing a noisy vector that tends to be similar to the word that had been convolved with the cue word. In these models the essential process that relates items is the act of convolution. A stored sentence could be represented by a series of pairwise convolutions. In this sense such a model would be similar to the previous approach used by SAM: The sentence is represented by pairwise associations. Neither Murdock nor Metcalfe specified how sentences are encoded but Murdock (1983) dealt with serial order recall using a chain of pairwise associations. Will such a model suffice for the present data? Retrieval would have to be based on probing memory with one of the cue words. It is hard to see why latency to first output would fall with increasing cue numbers. It is especially hard to see why scrambling the test words would make any difference. Finally, it is hard to see why the various scrambled study conditions should produce similar results given that the model is somehow made to produce different results for different test types in the sentence study conditions. Based on such considerations we think rather a good case could be made for encoding a sentence as a single unit. In these models, that would have to be accomplished by forming some sort of five-fold convolution, or simply treating a sentence as a new vector of features, somewhat independent of the features making up each constituent word. Further speculation concerning these models would lead us far afield, but the main point is that something like a higher order sentence unit would be required within the context of these models.

A distributed model by Pike (1984) also assumes words are represented by vectors of features. An association is stored by taking the product of the two vectors. The resultant matrix is added to the matrices representing all other associative pairs to form memory. Retrieval occurs when memory is probed with a word cue by premultiplying the memory matrix by the row vector for the word cue. Output will be a noisy vector similar to the word stored with the cue. If storage is limited to pairwise associations, essentially the same arguments applied to Murdock's and Metcalfe's models could be repeated. We would conclude that a higher order sentence unit needs to be stored. Pike briefly discusses this possibility. A five word sentence could be stored as a five dimensional matrix representing the product of the individual word vectors, or alternatively as a new vector of features different than those making up the constituent words. Either version of the model would probably need extensive modifications to handle the present data. Other distributed memory models share some of the features of the models by Murdock, Metcalfe, and Pike, and might require similar assumptions to handle the present results. These include the neural network models of James Anderson (1973; Anderson, Silverstein, Ritz, & Jones, 1977), Grossberg and Stone (1986), and McClelland and Rumelhart (1985).

The MINERVA2 model of Hintzman (1984) shares many features of the distributed models, but assumes separate storage of the vectors representing the memory items. In this model, a group of items is stored as a long vector consisting of the item vectors lined up end-to-front. A probe item activates each stored vector, and these are summed to form the retrieval vector. This model would have little difficulty handling the sentence–sentence results taken by themselves, but would have difficulty with the results obtained in the other conditions. In this model, also, a decision would have to be made concerning whether to treat a sentence as one long vector consisting of the individual word vectors, or as a single new vector with features different than those in the individual words.

Anderson and Bower's HAM model (1973) assumes higher order sentence units are stored. Although there are separate concept nodes stored for each word, these are connected by a stored structure of links in a tree. Furthermore, access to the sentence is all-or-none; the concept nodes do not have to be sampled or accessed one at a time. Whatever words are available in the sentence are recalled together. This model would have relatively little difficulty handling the sentence–sentence results (with appropriate amendments). It is less clear how the results of the various other conditions would be handled, and that question would have to be left to further research.

FINAL REMARKS

Our investigation of cued recall of sentences has convinced us that the units of memory in this case must include high level entities like sentences, and not just images of individual words linked by associations. We also concluded that the cues that are used to probe memory must include similar higher order units, in cases where it is possible to form them (such as a test group consisting of several items from a sentence in correct order). These conclusions were reached within the context of the SAM model for recall, but a review of some other memory models suggested that a similar conclusion might be necessary in those contexts as well. Having established this point, we intend in the future to explore models of sentence memory, paragraph memory, and so forth, using as a starting point the amended SAM model presented in this chapter. In particular we will test further the hypotheses that sampling and recovery might be based on different values, and that encoding operations are stored and help determine the match between retrieval cues and stored images.

REFERENCES

Anderson, J. A. (1973). A theory of recognition of items from short memorized lists. *Psychological Review, 80,* 417–438.

Anderson, J. A., Silverstein, J. W., Ritz, S. A., & Jones, R. S. (1977). Distinctive features, categorical perception, and probability learning: Some applications of a neural model. *Psychological Review, 84,* 413–451.

Anderson, J. R., & Bower, G. H. (1973). *Human associative memory.* Hillsdale, NJ: Lawrence Erlbaum Associates.

Bain, J. D., & Humphreys, M. S. (1988). Relational context: Independent cues, meaning, or configurations? In G. M. Davies & D. M. Thomson (Eds.), *Memory in context: Context in memory.* New York: Wiley.

Gillund, G., & Shiffrin, R. M. (1981). Free recall of complex pictures and abstract words. *Journal of Verbal Learning and Verbal Behavior, 20,* 575–592.

Graf, P. (1980). Two consequences of generating: Increased inter- and intraword organization of sentences. *Journal of Verbal Learning and Verbal Behavior, 19,* 316–327.

Graf, P. (1981). Reading and generating normal and transformed sentences. *Canadian Journal of Psychology, 33,* 293–308.

Gronlund, S. D. (1986). *Multi-level storage and retrieval: An empirical investigation and theoretical analysis.* Unpublished doctoral dissertation, Department of Psychology, Indiana University, Bloomington, IN.

Gronlund, S. D., & Shiffrin, R. M. (1986). Retrieval strategies in recall of natural categories and categorized lists. *Journal of Experimental Psychology: Learning, Memory, and Cognition, 12,* 550–561.

Grossberg, S., & Stone, G. (1986). Neural dynamics of word recognition and recall: Attentional priming, learning, and resonance. *Psychological Review, 93,* 46–74.

Hintzman, D. L. (1984). Minerva 2: A simulation of human memory. *Behavior Research Methods, Instrumentation and Computers, 26,* 96–101.

Humphreys, M. S., Pike, R., Bain, J. D., & Tehan, G. (in press). Global matching: A comparison of the SAM, Minerva II, Matrix, and TODAM models. *Journal of Mathematical Psychology.*

Jones, G. V. (1976). A fragmentation hypothesis of memory: Cued recall of pictures and of sequential position. *Journal of Experimental Psychology: General, 105,* 277–293.

Jones, G. V. (1980). Interaction of intrinsic and extrinsic knowledge in sentence recall. In R. S. Nickerson (Ed.), *Attention and performance VIII* (pp. 637–649). Hillsdale, NJ: Lawrence Erlbaum Associates.

Jones, G. V. (1984). Fragment and schema models for recall. *Memory & Cognition, 12,* 250–263.

Jones, G. V., & Payne, M. S. (1982). Recall and the flexibility of linguistic processing. In A. Flammer & W. Kintsch (Eds.), *Discourse processing* (pp. 314–324). New York: North-Holland.

Kintsch, W. (1974). *The representation of meaning in memory.* Hillsdale, NJ: Lawrence Erlbaum Associates.

Kolers, P. A. (1973). Remembering operations. *Memory & Cognition, 1,* 347–355.

Kolers, P. A. (1975). Specificity of operations in sentence recognition. *Cognitive Psychology, 7,* 289–306.

Kolers, P. A., & Ostry, D. J. (1974). Time course of loss of information regarding pattern analyzing operations. *Journal of Verbal Learning and Verbal Behavior, 13,* 599–612.

Kolers, P. A., & Roediger, H. L. (1984). Procedures of mind. *Journal of Verbal Learning and Verbal Behavior, 23,* 425–449.

Mandler, G., Rabinowitz, J. C., & Simon, R. A. (1981). Coordinate organization: The holistic representation of word pairs. *American Journal of Psychology, 94,* 209–222.

McClelland, J. L., & Rumelhart, D. E. (1985). Distributed memory and the representation of general and specific information. *Journal of Experimental Psychology: General, 114,* 159–188.

Metcalfe, J. (1982). A composite holographic associative recall model. *Psychological Review, 89,* 627–661.

Metcalfe, J. (1985). Levels of processing, encoding specificity, elaboration, and CHARM. *Psychological Review, 92,* 1–38.

Murdock, B. B., Jr. (1982). A theory for the storage and retrieval of item and associative information. *Psychological Review, 89,* 609–626.

Murdock, B. B., Jr. (1983). A distributed memory model for serial-order information. *Psychological Review, 90,* 316–338.

Park, N. W. (1980). *Superadditivity of retrieval cues as a function of encoding conditions.* Unpublished doctoral dissertation, Department of Psychology, University of Toronto.

Pike, R. (1984). Comparison of convolution and matrix distributed memory systems for associative recall and recognition. *Psychological Review, 91,* 281–294.

Raaijmakers, J. G. W., & Shiffrin, R. M. (1980). SAM: A theory of probabilistic search of associative memory. In G. Bower (Ed.), *The psychology of learning and motivation* (Vol. 14, pp. 207–262). New York: Academic Press.

Raaijmakers, J. G. W., & Shiffrin, R. M. (1981). Search of associative memory. *Psychological Review, 88,* 93–134.

Roediger, H. L, & Neely, J. H. (1982). Retrieval blocks in episodic and semantic memory. *Canadian Journal of Psychology, 36,* 213–242.

Ross, B. H., & Bower, G. H. (1981). Comparisons of models of associative recall. *Memory & Cognition, 9*, 1–16.

Shiffrin, R. M. (1975). Short-term store: The basis for a memory system. In F. Restle, R. M. Shiffrin, N. J. Castellan, H. Lindman, & D. B. Pisoni (Eds.), *Cognitive theory* (Vol. 1). Hillsdale, NJ: Lawrence Erlbaum Associates.

Slamecka, N. J. (1968). An examination of trace storage in free recall. *Journal of Experimental Psychology, 76*, 504–513.

Slamecka, N. J. (1969). Testing for associative storage in multitrial free recall. *Journal of Experimental Psychology, 81*, 557–560.

Slamecka, N. J., & Graf, P. (1978). The generation effect: Delineation of a phenomenon. *Journal of Experimental Psychology: Human Learning and Memory, 4*, 592–604.

4

Learning in a Distributed Memory Model

Bennet B. Murdock, Jr.
University of Toronto

In this chapter I discuss the question of how learning is handled in a distributed-memory model. By "learning" I mean the standard definition; namely, the improvement in performance with repeated presentations. Learning occurs in recognition memory, paired-associate tasks, and serial-order tasks, but I shall only consider the first two here. Serial-order learning has been discussed elsewhere (Lewandowsky & Murdock, in press).

Learning in recognition memory is discussed in terms of the matched-filter model of Anderson (1973), whereas paired-associate learning is discussed in terms of TODAM (Murdock, 1982). The matched-filter model is an early distributed-memory model for item recognition. TODAM is an acronym for a Theory of Distributed Associative Memory, and it is a distributed memory model for recall and recognition.

Why should we single out learning for special attention? Not only is learning a classic problem in the cognitive area but it can be a real problem for distributed-memory models. At least in some distributed-memory models performance does not improve with repetition so no learning occurs under standard conditions. That is, performance can be good, bad, or indifferent after a single presentation so *memory* occurs, but it does not get better with repetition. This problem along with several possible solutions was discussed in Murdock and Lamon (1988), but we will carry the analysis further here.

For recognition learning, the basic mechanism to be proposed is probabilistic encoding. It is assumed that, on each presentation of an item, each "feature" of the item is encoded with some probability p where this probability may be less than 1. This notion of probabilistic encoding is not new; it was suggested by Estes (1959) in his stimulus sampling theory and has been used by many others (e.g., Bower, 1972; Hintzman, 1986; Kohonen, 1977). Another modification is to represent similarity in the model. Similarity is defined in terms of the theoretical correlation coefficient ϱ of the bivariate normal distribution. We shall present the derivations necessary to compute a d' measure in terms of the parameters of the model, and discuss a few applications to data.

The situation is somewhat more complicated for paired-associate learning. We shall suggest a number of factors that may be at work there; these include probabilistic encoding, attentional shifts, a decrease in response competition, more efficient deblurring, and a decrease in similarity over trials. Unfortunately we have not yet been able to work out all the necessary derivations for similarity in the paired-associate case, so that part will be rather sketchy.

THE MATCHED-FILTER MODEL

Description

The matched-filter model of Anderson (1973) makes two basic assumptions about the representation of information in memory. The first assumption is that items or events can be represented as N-dimensional random vectors. That is, an item or event can be represented as an N-dimensional vector whose elements are independent random variables. The second assumption is that the feature distribution from which these elements are sampled is a normal distribution with mean zero and variance P/N, where P is the power of the vector. Generally $P = 1$ so in effect the variance of the feature distribution is simply $1/N$.

It should be appreciated that these features are abstract entities and not to be confused with real-life properties of the stimuli. Undoubtedly there is some correspondence, but to get on with the model we shall not consider this matter further. They are abstract entities just as the elements in the stimulus sampling theory of Estes (1950) were abstract entities. To try to emphasize this point, generally we shall use the term "elements" not "features."

For recognition, one needs to specify what the storage equation is and what the nature of the comparison process is, and then interface the memory model with a decision model in order to predict performance. Taking some liberties with the original formulation of the matched-filter model let me represent the storage equation as

$$\mathbf{M}_i = \alpha \mathbf{M}_{i-1} + p(t)f_i \tag{1}$$

where $\mathbf{M}$ is the memory vector, f is the item vector, α is a forgetting parameter that generates a serial-position effect, and $p(t)$ is the parameter mentioned above for probabilisitic encoding. (This notion was not part of the original model but I am introducing it here to facilitate exposition.)

What this equation says is that the memory vector after the l-th item has been presented is the sum of two components: The memory vector, before it was presented, decremented by α (where $0 \leq \alpha \leq 1.0$) and the l-th item probabilistically encoded. From a process point of view, think of a single memory vector $\mathbf{M}$ that is constantly being updated. As each new item comes along it is added to $\mathbf{M}$, except that $\mathbf{M}$ is decremented first.

It seems rather obvious that the encoding probability should be a function of the presentation duration so I have used $p(t)$ to denote this dependence. If we assume feature encoding to be a Poisson process (e.g., Luce, 1986), then we can parameterize this process as

$$p(t) = 1 - e^{-b(t-t_0)} \tag{2}$$

where b is the rate constant and t_0 is the "functional" time zero. Encoding does not start instantaneously, and it must be offset from stimulus onset by some small amount. We consider this the encoding "lag" and specify it as t_0. For simplicity, I generally use p rather than $p(t)$ except where the presentation duration is directly manipulated, but this dependence on t is always assumed.

In any distributed-memory model all information is stored in a common pool and in the matched-filter model this common pool is $\mathbf{M}$. Unlike node-and-link models, there is no separate or discrete storage of information; everything is added together in a common memory. The advantage of such a system is that it is a direct-access system; no search is required. The disadvantage is that it is noisy. However, one can calculate exactly how noisy it is, and in principle one can always reduce the noise level to an acceptable level by increasing the dimensionality of the space.

Direct access works for both cued recall and recognition, but the matched-filter model only applies to recognition. This necessitates a comparison process that can be represented as

$$\mathbf{f} \cdot \mathbf{M} = s \tag{3}$$

where s is a scalar quantity denoting strength. The comparison operation is the dot product; that is, when the probe item is presented, it is dotted with the memory vector and the result is the strength or familiarity of the probe. It is this strength value s that then forms the input to the decision system and an observable response ensues.

One possible view of the decision system (from Hockley & Murdock, 1987) is shown in Fig. 4.1. It is similar but not identical to the decision component of the original matched-filter model, and it can handle the basic findings on accuracy and latency from most of the standard recognition-memory paradigms. For purposes of the present chapter we do not need all the power of this model, but what we do need are the strength distributions shown at the bottom of the figure. These two distributions are the familiar old- and new-item distributions of signal-detection theory, and their moments can be

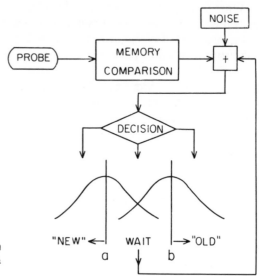

FIG. 4.1.   A model for the decision system. (Figure 1 from Hockley & Murdock, 1987.)

derived from the assumptions given above. Thus, these distributions are not ad hoc but result as a natural consequence of the assumptions of the model. We turn to these derivations later.

Here, then, are the basic aspects of the matched-filter model, a simple and powerful model for recognition memory. Although this model has problems (see Murdock & Lamon, 1988), one should perhaps also appreciate what it can do. With only a few basic assumptions one can derive a number of results that are in good agreement with empirical results on recognition memory. It is perhaps the simplest of all distributed memory models yet it behaves in quite a reasonable fashion.

Learning

The reason the matched-filter model does not learn is that under standard conditions both the mean and the variance increase with repetition. That is, the mean and variances of the strength distributions shown at the bottom of Fig. 4.1 both increase, and do so in a way that leaves d' unchanged. A proof of this statement has been given in Murdock and Lamon (1988), and will not be repeated here.

One alternative to probabilisitic encoding was considered in this same paper, and that was a closed-loop model. A closed-loop model is one in which the information stored in memory depends upon the information already in memory at the time of presentation. It uses negative feedback in the sense that the stronger the current information the less new information is added. Whereas this seems eminently reasonable, and is a standard learning mechanism in many connectionist memory models (see, e.g., McClelland & Rumelhart, 1985), it was clearly contradicted by the repetition effect.

Using an RRSP (Reverse Rock Substitution Procedure) wherein items correctly recognized on the test phase of one trial were replaced with different items on the next study phase, Murdock and Lamon (1988) found that repetition was more important than item difficulty. That is, one could compare difficult (i.e., unrecognized) items that had two presentations with standard items having only a single presentation, and the advantage of repetition clearly overcame the disadvantage of item difficulty. This was a very robust finding across three experiments, and we tried to simulate it with a closed-loop model. Despite many attempts we were completely unsuccessful. Unlike the data, in the simulations the two conditions (difficult repeated items and standard once-presented items) were always about equal in recognition performance. A cursory simulation of the open-loop model gave qualitatively the right results, so we consider probabilistic encoding a more fruitful alternative to explore.

In the next section we discuss the derivations for the model. In addition to probabilistic encoding, we also include a similarity parameter ϱ. In this way we can quantify interitem similarity. Like the elements in the item vectors, the similarity notion is abstract; it does not specify what the basis of the similarity is. However, there is a very large body of research showing that similarity is an important variable in paired-associate learning, and it seems reasonable to include it in recognition learning as well.

Derivations

Assume we have a list of L items presented R times in a fixed presentation order. (Experimenters generally use a randomized presentation order, but the assumption of a fixed order makes the derivations easier. The consequences of violating this assumption are probably not too serious.) Each item is represented as an N-dimensional random vector. Assume the interitem similarity is given by ϱ where ϱ is the theoretical correlation coefficient of the bivariate normal distribution. The similarity is across items not within items; that is, the similarity between the i-th element of any two items is ϱ, but the similarity between the i-th and j-th element of any one item is zero.

For recognition we need the old- and the new-item mean and variance that results when the probe item is compared to the memory vector. Call these μ_k, μ_N, σ_k^2, and σ_N^2 respectively where the subscript k denotes the serial position in the range 1–L and N as a subscript denotes "new." The new-item mean is not necessarily zero, and in general the old-item variance is slightly larger than the new-item variance. We use d' as our dependent variable where

$$d' \equiv \frac{\mu_k - \mu_N}{\sqrt{.5\sigma_N^2 + .5\sigma_k^2}} \tag{4}$$

TABLE 4.1
Means and Variances for Recognition

Old-Item Probes

$$\mu_k = pD(A + \varrho(B-A))$$

$$\sigma_k{}^2 = \frac{1}{N}\{(p^2D^2 + pqE)(3A^2 + (1+2\varrho^2)(C-A^2)) +$$

$$p^2D^2(6\varrho A(B-A) + (B^2 - C - 2A(B-A))(\varrho + 2\varrho^2)) - \mu_k{}^2\}$$

Similar New-Item Probe

$$\mu_N = pD\varrho B$$

$$\sigma_N{}^2 = \frac{1}{N}\{(p^2D^2 + pqE)(1+2\varrho^2)C + p^2D^2(B^2 - C)(\varrho + 2\varrho^2) - \mu_N{}^2\}$$

Dissimilar New-Item Probe

$$\mu_N = 0$$

$$\sigma_N{}^2 = \frac{1}{N}\{(p^2D^2 + pqE)C + p^2D^2(B^2 - C)\varrho\}$$

Symbols

$$A \equiv a_k = \alpha^{L-k}$$

$$B \equiv \sum_l a_l = \frac{1-\alpha^L}{1-\alpha}$$

$$C \equiv \sum_l a_l{}^2 = \frac{1-\alpha^{2L}}{1-\alpha^2}$$

$$D \equiv \sum_r b_r{}^2 = \frac{1-\alpha^{RL}}{1-\alpha^L}$$

$$E \equiv \sum_r b_r{}^2 = \frac{1-\alpha^{2RL}}{1-\alpha^{2L}}$$

The detailed derivations for the old-item mean and variance are given in Appendix 1. A summary of the derivations is shown in Table 4.1. It gives the means and variances for old-item probes, similar new-item probes, and dissimilar new-item probes. These are all one needs to compute a value of d' according to the expression given at the beginning of this section.

All the items are assumed to be similar to one another. Conceptually, think of a prototypical item to which all list items are similar. Say we have a bivariate distribution in x and y; let a sample from x be the prototype and then L random samples are drawn from y, in all cases y given x. If the theoretical correlation coefficient between x and y is ϱ^*, then the expected intercorrelation between any two samples from y is $(\varrho^*)^2$. So, what I am calling ϱ is the correlation coefficient between any two samples, and the correlation between any sample and the prototype is $\varrho^* = \sqrt{\varrho}$.[1]

This analysis suggests how one could simulate the model. To set up a list of any desired degree of similarity, construct a prototype and then derive all

---

[1] I thank Elke Weber for helping me on this point.

list items from it where the prototype is x and the items are the y's. More specifically, one must do this N times, once for each element in the vectors. So, as previously noted, similarity is across items but not within items.

Given the expressions for the mean and variance of the old-item probe that are derived in Appendix 1, comparable expressions for similar and dissimilar new-item probes can almost be obtained by inspection. A similar new-item probe is one that is assumed to be related to the prototype just like the list items were. With categorized lists, this would be a member of the same category. A dissimilar new-item probe is not related to the prototype ($\varrho = 0$). With categorized lists, this would be a different-category probe. (These are sometimes called internal and external negatives; see, e.g., Johns, 1985.) To obtain the similar new-item expressions from the old-item expressions simply drop the A term (i.e., a_k) and sum over the whole list. To obtain the dissimilar from the similar new-item expressions the correlation between the probe and the list items is zero but there is still a covariance component left. So, the fact that the list items are similar still matters with an external negative probe.

It is immediately apparent that the new-item variance for an external negative probe will be larger for a categorized list than for a noncategorized list. One might be tempted to infer that performance on external negatives should be slower or less accurate with categorized lists than with noncategorized lists, and this seems rather unlikely. However, one must consider both old- and new-item probes and use d', not the new-item variance, as the appropriate measure of performance. We shall return to this point shortly.

APPLICATIONS

We now have an augmented version of the matched-filter model that incorporates parameters for presentation duration, encoding probability, similarity, forgetting, and the dimensionality of the space. With the explicit expressions we have obtained one can easily derive predictions or fit the model to accuracy data from experiments on recognition memory. One could also interface this memory model with a decision model such as the Memory Interrogation Model (MIM) described in Hockley and Murdock (1987). Then we could fit the combined model to accuracy and latency data from many experiments on recognition memory. However, this will be a major undertaking, and we have not started on this yet. What we can do, however, is illustrate some sample applications of the model to accuracy data by showing the effects the various parameters have on d'.

Probabilistic Encoding

Because the claim is that probabilistic encoding allows learning to occur, this will be documented first. Illustrative results are shown in Table 4.2. For sample

TABLE 4.2
d' for Sample Parameter Values for Four Different Values of p

		Serial Position				
p	R	1	2	3	4	5
.05	1	0.379	0.417	0.458	0.502	0.549
	2	0.497	0.548	0.602	0.660	0.722
	3	0.563	0.620	0.682	0.748	0.818
.2	1	0.702	0.774	0.852	0.935	1.025
	2	0.841	0.928	1.022	1.124	1.233
	3	0.903	0.997	1.098	1.209	1.328
.6	1	1.036	1.145	1.263	1.392	1.533
	2	1.099	1.214	1.341	1.479	1.630
	3	1.120	1.238	1.367	1.509	1.663
1.0	1	1.185	1.311	1.449	1.601	1.767
	2	1.185	1.311	1.449	1.601	1.767
	3	1.185	1.311	1.449	1.601	1.767

Note: $L = 5$, $N = 64$, $\alpha = .9$, $\varrho = .3$

parameter value ($N = 64$, $\alpha = .9$, and $\varrho = .3$), we give the d' values for four different values of p (.05, 0.2, 0.6, and 1.0). We are assuming three trials on a five-item list, and we give the d' value computed according to Equation 4 for each serial position on trial. As can be seen, increasing p affects both the starting value and the slope of the learning curve. As p increases the starting value increases but the slope decreases and, when $p = 1.0$, the learning curve is flat. Thus, without probabilistic encoding, learning would not occur.[2]

Presentation Duration

Because p is really p(t), what is the effect of presentation duration on d'? To find out, all we need to do is specify the value of b, the rate constant for the Poisson process, and t_0, the encoding lag, and these two parameters will then determine the value of p(t). The suggested relationship is given in Equation 2. Then all we have to do is select values for our independent variable t and, by turning the crank, we will get our values for d'. The end result is illustrated in Table 4.2, and variations in presentation duration could be a reason why p might vary.

There is some pertinent data by Loftus (1974) showing the effect of presentation duration on recognition memory for words. He used a variety of durations, and showed the results for individual subjects. As might be ex-

---

[2]It goes without saying that there are other learning schemes than probabilistic encoding. All we mean is that the matched filter model will not learn if $p = 1.0$, and this holds true regardless of ϱ.

pected, as presentation duration increased from 25 msec to 500 msec there was a sizable increase in d'. The model is qualitatively in agreement with these results. When I tried to fit the model quantitatively the fit was not too good, but the reason could be output interference. Loftus used a study-test procedure, and we have found abundant evidence for output interference in our experiments on recognition memory (see, e.g., Murdock & Anderson, 1975). By "output interference" I mean the effect of testing some items on the memory for others, and this is not yet represented in the model.[3]

Forgetting

The data in Table 4.2 also illustrate the effect of α on d'. Regardless of the value of p there is a monotonic recency effect, and this is produced by the forgetting parameter. We have extensive evidence for such a recency effect in recognition memory (Murdock & Anderson, 1975), so at least qualitatively the model is in good accord with the data. The recency gradient becomes flatter as α increases; illustrative results are shown in Table 4.3 for values of α of 0.9, 0.95, and 0.98. Note that, for the last serial position or two, d' is *inversely* related to α. The reason, presumably, is that the reduction in variance (noise from earlier items) more than offsets the decreased mean value resulting from the lower α values.

Similarity

As similarity increases, performance decreases. This is illustrated in Table 4.4 for the same parameter values with ϱ values of .0, .15, and .30. I should stress

TABLE 4.3
d' for Sample Parameter Values for Three Different Values of α

α	R	Serial Position				
		1	2	3	4	5
.90	1	1.036	1.145	1.263	1.392	1.533
	2	1.099	1.214	1.341	1.479	1.630
	3	1.120	1.238	1.367	1.509	1.663
.95	1	1.161	1.218	1.277	1.340	1.404
	2	1.235	1.296	1.360	1.426	1.496
	3	1.262	1.325	1.390	1.459	1.530
.98	1	1.234	1.257	1.281	1.305	1.330
	2	1.314	1.339	1.365	1.391	1.417
	3	1.344	1.370	1.396	1.423	1.450

Note: $L = 5$, $N = 64$, $\varrho = .3$, $p = .6$

---

[3]For another approach to fitting the Loftus data see Weber (1988).

TABLE 4.4
d' for Sample Parameter Values for Three Different Values of ϱ

ϱ	R	Serial Position				
		1	2	3	4	5
.00	1	2.105	2.317	2.546	2.790	3.050
	2	2.344	2.582	2.840	3.116	3.411
	3	2.434	2.683	2.951	3.240	3.549
.15	1	1.489	1.642	1.808	1.997	2.180
	2	1.606	1.771	1.951	2.147	2.359
	3	1.646	1.816	2.002	2.205	2.423
.30	1	1.036	1.145	1.263	1.392	1.533
	2	1.099	1.214	1.341	1.479	1.630
	3	1.120	1.238	1.367	1.509	1.663

Note: $L = 5$, $N = 64$, $\alpha = .9$, $p = .6$

that this result assumes that all items in the list are similar to one another and that the lures are "internal negatives" (i.e., they too are similar in the same way). Thus, there is a common prototype for all items, old and new, and the interitem similarity is ϱ for all items.

Supporting evidence for this effect was found in a study that was run as part of a class project here at Toronto by Brian Fitzsimmons. He used lists that met the necessary condition, and I report his results here very briefly.

There were four subjects each tested twice under each condition. Under the high-similarity condition all items, old and new, were from a single category of the Toronto Categorized Word Pool (Murdock, 1976). Under the low-similarity condition all items, old and new, were random samples from the pool. There were 18 items in the study list and 36 items in the test list, the presentation rate was 1 item/sec, and the order of conditions was counterbalanced across subjects. The mean percent correct was 74.7% and 83.8% for the high- and low-similarity condition, respectively. Thus, the results came out as predicted; performance on the high-similar list was worse than performance on the low-similar list.[4]

Internal and External Negatives

The effects of similarity depend on whether internal or external negatives are used. If internal negatives are used, increasing similarity has a detrimental effect on accuracy (i.e., d' decreases). If external negatives are used, increasing similarity has a facilitative effect on accuracy (i.e., d' increases). Illustrative results with these same parameter values are shown in Table 4.5.

---

[4]I am assuming that randomly selected words have an interitem similarity of zero, and that is probably not true. But they are surely less similar than words all selected from the same category.

With categorized lists, external negatives are clearly faster than internal negatives (e.g., Johns, 1985; Okada & Burrows, 1973). I do not know of any evidence on the complete interaction, but there may be some. Because the distinction between internal and external negatives does not make sense with uncategorized (or unrelated) lists, what is needed is data from experiments with high and low similarity crossed with internal and external negatives. It would be interesting to see if the predictions of the model were confirmed.

In general this augmented version of the matched filter model seems to do the right things. It learns, it forgets, it is responsive to presentation duration and similarity, and it shows the right kind of recency effect. Whether is can account for more fine-grained effects such as the mixed-versus pure-list results reported by Shiffrin (1988) remains to be seen.

The results given in the preceding tables were illustrative, and the parameter values were selected to illustrate as simply as possible the experimental effect under consideration. Somewhat more reasonable parameter values are illustrated in Table 4.6, where $N = 512$, $\alpha = .98$, $p = .05$, and $\varrho = .1$. The d' values for five trials on an eight-item list are probably somewhat too low, but perhaps they are located in a more realistic part of the parameter space.

Similarity Reduction

The suggested learning mechanism is based on probabilistic encoding. As documented above, learning does not occur if $p = 1.0$ but increases as p decreases. Another possibility (beside the closed-loop version) should be considered; namely, a reduction in similarity. Learning could occur if similarity decreased over trials, and this is not an unreasonable possibility.

To be specific, assume a geometric decrease in the similarity parameter over trials; in particular, let

$$\varrho_r = \varrho_1 s^{r-1} \qquad (2)$$

where ϱ_1 is the value of ϱ on Trial 1 and s is the rate constant. The results of a simulation with a four-item list with $\alpha = .9$, $N = 1$, $p = 1.0$, $\varrho_1 = .4$, and $s = .4$ are shown in Table 4.7. As can be seen, d' increased over trials in a negatively-accelerated fashion.

In this simulation the old items stay the same over trials whereas it was the new items whose similarity decreases over trials. As is customary in experiments using the study-test procedure, we drew a new sample of lures on each trial and it was the similarity of the lures to the prototype that decreased. This may seem the wrong way to go about it; one might argue that the intraitem similarity of the old items should decrease. However, such a decrease necessitates changing the old items on each trial, and this seems even more problematical.

In any event, it should be noted that probabilistic encoding is not the only way that learning could occur; similarity reduction is another. Probabilistic

TABLE 4.5
d' for Sample Parameter Values for Internal and External Netatives with
High and Low Similarity

			Serial Position				
Negatives	ϱ	R	1	2	3	4	5
Internal	.0	1	2.105	2.317	2.546	2.790	3.050
		2	2.344	2.582	2.840	3.116	3.411
		3	2.434	2.683	2.951	3.240	3.549
Internal	.3	1	1.036	1.145	1.263	1.392	1.533
		2	1.099	1.214	1.341	1.479	1.630
		3	1.120	1.238	1.367	1.509	1.663
External	.0	1	1.462	1.617	1.787	1.972	2.173
		2	1.535	1.700	1.880	2.078	2.293
		3	1.560	1.728	1.912	2.113	2.334
External	.3	1	3.347	3.532	3.525	3.626	3.736
		2	3.487	3.578	3.678	3.787	3.905
		3	3.534	3.627	3.729	3.840	3.961

Note: $L = 5$, $N = 64$, $\alpha = .9$, $\pi = .6$

TABLE 4.6
d' for More Realistic Parameter Values

				Serial Position				
R	1	2	3	4	5	6	7	8
1	1.386	1.412	1.438	1.464	1.491	1.518	1.546	1.574
2	1.880	1.915	1.950	1.986	2.023	2.060	2.097	2.135
3	2.211	2.252	2.294	2.337	2.380	2.423	2.468	2.513
4	2.456	2.501	2.548	2.595	2.643	2.692	2.741	2.792
5	2.644	2.694	2.744	2.795	2.847	2.900	2.953	3.007

Note: $L = 8$, $N = 512$, $\alpha = .98$, $p = .05$, $\varrho = .1$

TABLE 4.7
Results of a Simulation on Similarity Reduction as a Learning
Mechanism

Trial	μ_0	μ_N	σ_0^2	σ_N^2	d'
1	1.89	1.37	10.05	8.38	.171
2	3.14	.902	27.57	18.91	.464
3	3.95	.452	43.76	27.07	.580
4	4.49	.201	56.41	37.32	.627

Note: $N = 1$, $\alpha = .9$, $\varrho = .4$, $s = .4$

encoding can handle the RRSP results quite easily, and we are not sure that similarity reduction can. For this reason, probabilistic encoding seems a slightly better bet. However, this issue can only be settled by some detailed testing of the two explanations, and that remains to be done.

SUMMARY

An augmented version of the matched-filter model that includes probabilistic encoding and interitem similarity has been presented. With a small number of assumptions we can develop explicit expressions for the means and variances of the dot-product strength distribution and we can assess the effects of list length, serial position, rate of presentation, probabilistic encoding, and similarity. Detailed testing of the model is possible, but this remains to be done.

However, it should be pointed out that there are some weaknesses and omissions. We have not yet been able to include output interference in the model, and this is very necessary in applying it, for instance, to the study-test procedure. There is no context mechanism in here. Although context effects in the usual sense are weak to nonexistent in recognition (see Bjork & Richardson-Klavehn, chap. 9 in this volume), there is still the very important question of how list items are discriminated from nonlist items. This is the real importance of context, and the model is completely mute here. Judgments of frequency pose yet a further problem (Hintzman, 1988; Hockley, 1984), so there is clearly more work to be done.

As I have suggested before (Murdock, 1982), we may help matters by adding associative information to item information. However, there is the same learning problem with associative information as there is with item information. So, we now turn to paired associates and to paired-associate learning.

THE CONVOLUTION–CORRELATION MODEL (TODAM)

Description

To model paired-associate learning, we make the same basic assumptions as previously stated. Items are represented as random vectors, the feature distribution is normal with mean zero and variance P/N, and the features of each item are encoded probabilistically. For an A–B pair, we have $p_A(t)$ and $p_B(t)$ where these are the encoding probabilities for the A and B members of the pair. Generally we will not specify the temporal dependence explicitly.

Also as stated earlier, assume that we have R presentations of a list of L paired associates in a fixed presentation order. Then the storage equation is:

$$\mathbf{M}_{r,l} = \alpha\mathbf{M}_{r,l-1} + \gamma_{1,r}p_A f_l + \gamma_{2,r}p_B g_l + \gamma_{3,r}(p_A f_l * p_B g_l) \qquad (6)$$

where $\mathbf{M}_{r,l}$ is the memory vector after the r-th presentation of the l-th pair, f and g are the item vectors corresponding to the A and B members of the pair, and the association between them is formed by convolution (*). For present purposes it is sufficient to think of convolution as simply a particular way to combine two vectors into one; for a more detailed account see, for example, Eich (1982) or Murdock (1982).

This equation says that the memory vector contains both item and associative information, the item information being represented by f and g and the associative information being represented by $f * g$. The same values of p_A and p_B that characterize the encoding probabilities for items apply to the pair, and in simulations the mutilated item vectors are used in the convolution. The weighting parameters $\gamma_{1,r}$, $\gamma_{2,r}$, and $\gamma_{3,r}$ denote the "amount of attention" paid to the A item, the B item, and the A–B pair, respectively. We generally use a limited-capacity rule so that

$$\gamma_{1,r} + \gamma_{2,r} + \gamma_{3,r} = 1.0 \qquad (7)$$

The weighting parameters are subscripted by r to indicate that they may vary over trials. As the items become more familiar, less attention may be paid to the items per se and more attention paid to the association. This change of attention can be modeled by decreasing $\gamma_{1,r}$ and $\gamma_{2,r}$ over trials then, by the limited-capacity principle (Equation 7), $\gamma_{3,r}$ would automatically increase.

The retrieval process is correlation (#). When the probe item f is presented it is correlated with the memory vector and

$$f_k \# \mathbf{M}_k = g_k' \qquad (8)$$

where g_k' is the retrieved information. Note that the retrieved information is g_k' not g_k; the retrieved information will resemble the target item g_k but it will not be identical to the target item. The retrieved information must be deblurred. That is, some process is necessary to map g_k' into g_k, and we call it "deblurring" to emphasize the fact that it is analogous to cleaning up a fuzzy image.[5]

Deblurring, then, is viewed as a separate stage of processing after the retrieval process. The "tip-of-the-tongue" effect, for instance, illustrates deblurring, and we certainly don't think of it as a search process. It is more like an image-processing operation than a search process. One possible deblurring algorithm has been suggested by Hopfield (1984) and, as noted by Golden (1986), this is isomorphic to the "Brain-state-in-a-box" of Anderson, Silver-

---

[5]Schönemann (1987) has shown that recall gets worse in a convolution–correlation model as the dimensionality of the item vectors increase, and the best recall occurs with single-element vectors. However, this applies to perfect recall, and TODAM has never claimed perfect recall. As described here, the retrieved information g' is always an approximation to g, and the deblurring process is seen as a way of implementing recall.

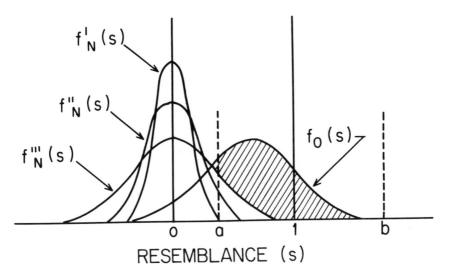

FIG. 4.2. The resemblance distributions for the probe-target pair and three "new-item" distributions. The shaded area is approximately equal to the probability of correct recall, and a and b are the tolerance limits. (Figure 18.7 from Murdock, 1987.)

stein, Ritz, and Jones (1977). We are not modeling the deblurring process, but we do want to characterize its probability of success.

The probability that g_k' will be mapped into g_k rather than g_l, $l \neq k$, is dependent on two factors, how close the match is and whether there is any better match. More specifically, for successful recall the resemblance of g_k' and g_k must be within tolerance limits (a and b) and closer to the ideal (P^2, where P is the power of the vector) than any other competitor. Probability of successful recall is then given by

$$Pr\{g_k' \to g_k\} = \int_a^b \phi_k(s) \prod_{j=1}^m [1 - \int_{P^2-s}^{P^2+s} \phi_j(x)dx]ds \qquad (9)$$

where a and b are the tolerance limits (see Fig. 4.2), $\phi_k(s)$ is the "old-item" resemblance distribution (i.e., the resemblance between g_k' and g_k), and $\phi_j(s)$ are the m "new-item" resemblance distributions (i.e., the resemblance between g_k' and g_j, $j \neq k$).[6]

As shown in Fig. 4.2, recall probability is like the m-alternative forced-choice problem of signal-detection theory. It is the probability that one observation drawn at random from the old-item distribution exceeds (here, is closer

---

[6]The resemblance between g and g' is measured by the dot product. Previously I have called this similarity, but it seems less confusing to restrict the term similarity to the inter-item similarity and use the term resemblance instead for the similarity between the retrieved information and the target information.

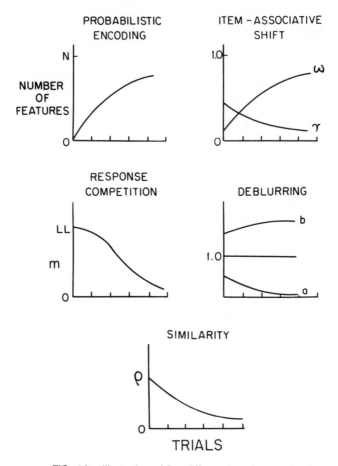

FIG. 4.3.   Illustration of five different learning mechanisms.

to P^2) than m observations each drawn at random from a separate new-item distribution. The distributions are the resemblance distributions. Roughly speaking, probability of successful recall is the cross-hatched area shown in Fig. 4.2. Although we cannot obtain a closed-form solution to Equation 9, we can compute it by numerical integration.

Learning

How does learning occur? Five different learning mechanisms are suggested: probabilistic encoding, an attentional shift, a reduction in response competition, more efficient deblurring, and a reduction in intralist similarity. These are illustrated in Fig. 4.3.

Why am I suggesting so many? Human associative learning is not simple, and it seems unrealistic to pretend that it is. Consider some of the empirical data we must account for. The basic facts of learning and forgetting, retroactive and proactive inhibition, transfer of training and generalization are fundamental. We have such empirical relationships as the length-difficulty relation, the Osgood–Martin surface, and the total-time hypothesis. We have detailed knowledge about the effects of many experimental variables (e.g., list length, presentation rate, type of material, similarity, modality of presentation, imagery and mediational instructions, rehearsal, and levels of processing), not to mention individual differences, life-span effects, and various memory pathologies. It seems rather unlikely that one or two simple mechanisms will suffice to explain all these results.

My approach, then, is to try to develop a fairly complex model that contains a number of different mechanisms, some of which may not be needed. It is probably easier in the long run to start with a fair number of processes rather than patch them in later when needed. In all fairness, I should warn the reader that I have made more progress in developing the model than in testing it. I will give a few preliminary results, and already I can say some avenues of exploration seem unpromising, but do not expect any closure. Most of the hard work of parameter estimation and model testing lies ahead.

If one accepts the necessity for a multiprocess model, why these particular processes? Let me give a brief rationale for why I selected each process. First, probabilistic encoding. If probabilistic encoding is to serve as a basic mechanism for recognition learning, then it would seem reasonable to assume that it also operates in paired-associate learning. We assume that two item vectors are convolved to form an association, and if probabilistic encoding operates on the item vectors then it must operate on the association as well.

Why the item-associative shift? As shown in Fig. 4.3, over trials the amount of attention paid to the items (or the weighting parameter γ) decreases so the amount of attention paid to the association (or the weighting parameter ω) increases. This item-associative shift is one of the main factors necessary to generate appropriate serial-position effects in our explanation of serial-order effects (Lewandowsky & Murdock, in press), so given that it works well in serial-order learning it seems reasonable to apply it here. (The parameter ω characterizes the associative component in seriation; here it would correspond to γ_3.)

In addition, some data by Bernbach (1967) and Martin (1967) are suggestive. They both found that, in a paired-associate learning task, recall probability was essentially at zero for items which were not recognized. This finding does not demand the item-associative shift we are suggesting, but it is at least supportive. Also, stage models of associative learning (e.g., Brainerd, Howe, & Desrochers, 1982; Greeno, James, DaPolito, & Polson, 1978) could be interpreted in this way. (Discrete transitions for individual pairs could be represented as a gradual change when pooled over all pairs in the list.)

Response competition has long featured prominently in interference-theory accounts of paired-associate learning (e.g., Underwood, 1983). Although generally viewed as a between-lists effect in a retroactive-inhibition design, we are considering it here as a within-lists (across trials) effect. Specifically, by response competition we mean the number of competitors m in Equation 9 or Fig. 4.2.

As shown in Fig. 4.3, m is assumed to decrease over trials. In all the fits to be reported, the value of m on Trial r is the number of incorrect recalls on Trial r-1. The assumption is that, when an item has been correctly recalled on Trial r-1, it is no longer a possible competitor in the deblurring of another item on Trial r. (The number of CN's—Correct on Trial r-1 but Not correct on Trial r—is not too large even after a single presentation; Estes, 1960; and presumably decreases with repetition.) Backward associations could mediate the editing out of committed responses.

More efficient deblurring is a nonassociative effect. It indicates that, as trials increase, more dissimilar values of g' can be mapped into g. This is modeled by setting the tolerance limits a and b further apart. As suggested by Fig. 4.3, a decreases and b increases with respect to 1.0, and the changes are symmetric.

Response integration or response learning has long been thought to be involved in paired-associate learning (e.g., Mandler, 1954; Underwood & Schulz, 1960), and responses are emitted ever more rapidly well after the stage of perfect accuracy has been reached (Waugh, 1969). This could be modeled by better deblurring. Also, because there is no retroactive inhibition in recognition (Postman & Stark, 1969), and deblurring is required only for recall, this factor is a possible explanation for the recall-recognition difference.

Finally, similarity is a classic factor in paired-associate learning, and changes in intralist generalization tendencies were an important component in the influential Gibson theory (Gibson, 1940; Underwood, 1961). Similarity reduction was discussed earlier in the section on recognition learning, and it could be involved in recall as well. Also, similarity reduction could well be involved in accounting for some of the results on A-B, A-D and A-B, C-B transfer paradigms (McGovern, 1964).

There is no lack of precedent for multifactor models of paired-associate learning. Interference theory has long been at least a two-factor theory (see, e.g., Underwood, 1983), though there has been some uncertainty as to exactly what the two factors were. McGuire (1961) developed and tested a three-factor model, and found confirmatory evidence for the three different factors (stimulus discrimination, association, and response integration). Finite-state models explicitly suggest at least two states, and there could be more.

Rather than start with too simple a model and then add on extra processes as they are needed, the approach used here is to start with possibly an overdetermined system and see what, if anything, is superfluous. We are well aware of the dangers. We could still be missing one or more essential process, but obviously we hope not. Probably the greater danger is that the implementation of one or more of these processes could be wrong. In all cases we have

TABLE 4.8
Mean and New-Item Variance for Resemblance Distributions
(For the variance we assume $\varrho = 0$)

$$\mu_0(R) = p_{AB}\Sigma b_r\gamma_{3,r}(\frac{1}{L}\Sigma a_i + \frac{L-1}{L}\varrho_{AB}\Sigma a_i)$$

$$\sigma_N^2(R) = \frac{1}{N}\Sigma a_i^2(T1 + T2 + T3) \text{ where}$$

$$T1 = \frac{3}{4}[p_A^2(\Sigma b_r\gamma_{1,r})^2 + p_A q_A\Sigma(b_r\gamma_{1,r})^2]$$

$$T2 = \frac{3}{4}[p_B^2(\Sigma b_r\gamma_{2,r})^2 + p_B q_B\Sigma(b_r\gamma_{2,r})^2]$$

$$T3 = \frac{2}{3}[p_{AB}^2(\Sigma b_r\gamma_{3,r})^2 + p_{AB} q_{AB}\Sigma(b_r\gamma_{3,r})^2]$$

where $\varrho_{AB} = \varrho_A\varrho_B$, $q_A = 1 - p_A$, $q_B = 1 - p_B$, $p_{AB} = p_A p_B$, and $q_{AB} = 1 - p_{AB}$.

chosen the simplest parameterization possible (exponential or geometric change in the parameter values over trials) and we could have the right process but the wrong parameterization.

Derivations

To obtain predicted results, we need the moments (means and variances) of the old- and new-item resemblance distributions. The derivation for the old-item mean is given in Appendix 2. This includes the similarity parameter ϱ, where ϱ is as defined earlier (i.e., the theoretical correlation coefficient of the bivariate normal distribution). The final result is shown in Table 4.8, which also gives an expression for the new-item variance (with $\varrho = 0$).

The expressions given in Table 4.8 are in terms of the model parameters (N, α, p_A, p_B, ϱ_A, and ϱ_B). For the variance they assume a new-item probe-target pair. This is equivalent to a probe-target pair $u*v$ where the list items are all $f*g$ pairs, so why is this useful? The reason is that f_k*g_k dotted with f_l*g_l is functionally $u*v$ for all $l \neq k$. It would be better to have the old-item variance than the new-item variance, but it is somewhat more complicated and we really do not need it for the present purposes. With lists of reasonable length, the additional contribution of the old-item pair is not too great.

To say a word about the new-item variance, there are three components, T_1, T_2, and T_3 where T_1 is the variance component resulting from the presence of the A items in the memory vector, T_2 is the variance component resulting from the present of the B items in the memory vector, and T_3 is the variance component associated with the A–B pairs. Each component has two parts, within repetitions (p^2) and between repetitions (pq). The $b\gamma$ products function as multipliers where, as defined in Appendix 1, b is a function of α and $\gamma_{i,r}$ captures the item-associative shift in attention over trials. A numerical example is given in Table 4.9.

TABLE 4.9
Numerical Example to Illustrate Calculation of $\sigma_N^2(R)$

r	b_r	$\gamma_{1,r}$	$\gamma_{2,r}$	$\gamma_{3,r}$	$b_r\gamma_{1,r}$	$b_r\gamma_{2,r}$	$b_r\gamma_{3,r}$
1	.440	.400	.300	.300	.176	.132	.132
2	.663	.243	.165	.592	.161	.109	.393
3	1.0	.147	.090	.762	.147	.090	.763

$$\sigma_N^2(3) = 5.742\{.05[(.632)^2(.234) + (.632)(.368)(.079)] +$$
$$.05[(.551)^2(.110) + (.551)(.449)(.037)] +$$
$$.044[(.348)^2(1.659) + (.348)(.652)(.754)]\} =$$
$$5.742\{.0056 + .0021 + .0165\} = .139$$

Note: $T = 2$ sec, $t_0 = 0$, $R = 3$, $L = 8$, $N = 15$, $\alpha = .95$, $\gamma_{1,1} = .4$, $x_1 = .5$, $\gamma_{2,1} = .3$, $x_2 = .6$, $b_1 = .5$ so $p_A = .632$, $b_2 = .4$ so $p_B = .551$.

To obtain predicted results, it is first necessary to compute the old-item mean and the new-item variance for each trial given the values of L (list length) and R (number of repetitions) in the data you are fitting. Then one must do the numerical integration implied by Equation 9 and illustrated in Fig. 4.2. This will give the predicted recall probability for each trial.

To step back from the details for a minute, we now have a way of predicting successful recall given the assumed storage and retrieval operations of convolution and correlation and the assumption of probabilisitic encoding. Given the parameters of the model one can use the equations in Table 4.8 to compute the means and variances for the resemblance distributions shown at the bottom of Fig. 4.2 for any set of experimental conditions (list length, serial position, and trials). Then, by numerically evaluating Equation 8 one can compute a recall probability value, and use this either in making predictions from the model or in fitting the model to data.

APPLICATIONS

Fitting the model to data is a two-step process. First fit the Gompertz double-exponential to the data, then fit the model to the Gompertz. The Gompertz double-exponential function is:

$$y = Lg^{h^{x-1}} \tag{10}$$

where y is the number recalled, x is the trial number, L is list length, and g and h are the two parameters of the model. Roughly, the first parameter g characterizes the curvature and the second parameter h characterizes the slope. The Gompertz is a particular type of growth curve, and it is described in Lewis (1960).

In the next section we apply the model to six different phenomena of paired-associate learning. They are mean learning curves, learning to learn, list-length effects, the length-difficulty relation, MMFR (Modified Method of Free Recall), and memory consolidation.

Mean Learning Curves

Although the Gompertz is a purely empirical description, it seems to fit paired-associate learning data quite well. An example is shown in Fig. 4.4. The data come from an unpublished study where 10 (naive) subjects each learned a single list of 30 pairs of common English words selected at random from the Vermont word pool (the predecessor to the Toronto word pool). The study-test procedure was used with a presentation time of 2 sec/pair and each subject learned to a criterion of one perfect trial. The worst, best, and average fits are shown in the figure, and there does not seem to be much differences between them.

An illustrative fit of the convolution–correlation model to the Gompertz is shown in Fig. 4.5. We fit the model to the Gompertz whose parameter values were the average of the 10 subjects of this experiment ($g = .082$, $h = .712$). We used SIMPLX (Nelder & Mead, 1965) as the parameter-estimation routine with five free parameters: α, γ (and the limited-capacity rule; see Equation 7), x (the rate constant for the decrease in attention to item information over trials), $p_A = p_B$, and "DIFF" (the difference between each tolerance and 1.0; thus, $a = .12$ and $b = 1.88$). The fit is quite good, as evidenced by a root-mean square value of .359. (By "root-mean square" value we mean the square root of the mean squared deviation between the observed and the expected values.)

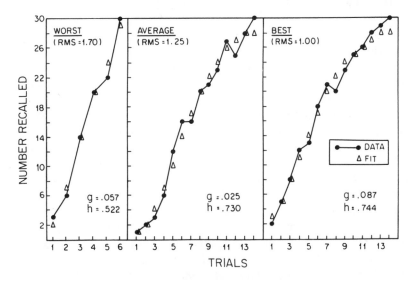

FIG. 4.4.   Worst, average, and best fit of the Gompertz double-exponential function to the learning data of 10 subjects. (Unpublished data.)

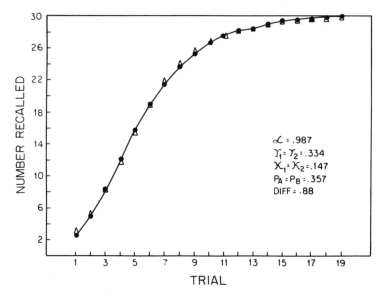

FIG. 4.5.   Fit of the convolution–correlation model to the mean learning curve (Gompertz parameters were $g = .082$, $h = .712$.)

It might be said that we are taking a small step backward by fitting a simple two-parameter function with a rather complex five-parameter function. Why not just use the Gompertz instead? The reason is that the Gompertz is "curve-fitting" of the least informative kind. It is quite unmotivated, and does not tell us anything about the processes involved in paired-associate learning. On the other hand, the convolution–correlation model is a process model with well-defined operations and links to item recognition, seriation, redintegration, and free recall. Further, as detailed earlier, it directly relates to many earlier ideas in the field.

The fact that the fit of the model to the data is so good indicates that the model can in fact fit paired-associate learning curves. As a check, the model also fits reasonably well the trial-by-trial learning curves of the individual subjects, but this is just what the Gompertz is designed to avoid. The Gompertz filters out the noise in the data so we get a clearer picture of what the model is doing. As is probably obvious, one does not have to be committed to the convolution–correlation model to use the Gompertz for this purpose. It might be useful in testing other models.

Actually, what is significant about Fig. 4.5 is what you don't see rather than what you do see. There are many other versions of the model that seem to be inadequate. If γ_3 does not increase over trials no combinations of α, p_A, or DIFF seem to work. (This statement applies for a fixed $N = 500$ to make it similar to recognition.) It is not that the chi square values become very large; they do not. Rather, the deviations of the best-fitting curve becomes suspiciously systematic, generally slightly too high for the first few trials and generally too low for the last few trials.

Learning to Learn

Using this fit as a point of departure, we then fit the model to some learning-to-learn data by Keppel, Postman, and Zavortink (1968). There were 36 lists (sessions), a study-test procedure, a presentation time of 1 sec/pair, and a 10-pair list of common words paired at random learned to a criterion of one perfect trial. The estimated Gompertz parameters (g and h, respectively) were .080 and .697 for Sessions 1-9, .039 and .614 for Sessions 10-18, and .034 and .588 for Sessions 19-27. The Gompertz program was unstable for Sessions 28-36, which is why only three of the four blocks were fitted. The fits for the first three blocks using the same Gompertz-to-TODAM procedure are shown in Fig. 4.6, and they seem quite satisfactory.

In this fit, the values of N, α, $\gamma_{1,1}$ ($= \gamma_{2,1}$) and p_A ($= p_B$) were fixed at 500, .88, .39, .43, and .92, respectively. This fit says that learning-to-learn can be accounted for by changes in a single parameter; namely, x, the rate constant for the item-associative shift. The item familiarity process proceeds more rapidly in the second block of trials than in the first, and still more rapidly in the third. In terms of Fig. 4.3, the item curve falls off more rapidly with practice so (by the limited-capacity assumption) the associative curve rises more rapidly with practice. This may be all there is to learning-to-learn.

We say "may" because we certainly are not able to reject all alternative explanations. A few of them clearly do not work, but many others have not yet been tested. However, it is gratifying to know that there is at least one version of the model that gives a simple and comprehensible interpretation

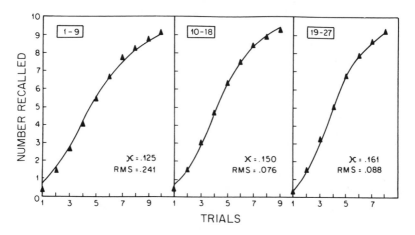

FIG. 4.6.   Fit of the convolution–correlation model to the learning-to-learn data of Keppel, Postman, and Zavortink (1968).

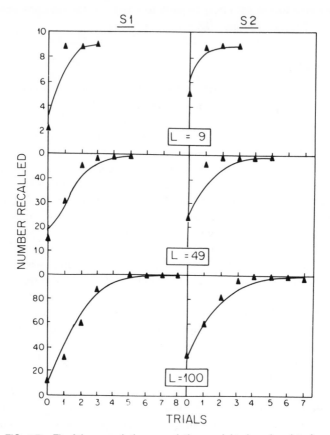

FIG. 4.7.   Fit of the convolution–correlation model to learning data from 9-,
49-, and 100-pair lists. (Data from Murdock, 1967).

of the phenomenon. Also, the simplicity and parsimony of this account may
somewhat atone for the admittedly slightly clumsy account we had to give
to fit the mean learning curve in Fig. 4.5.

List-Length Effects

Next I tried to fit some old data on list-length effects and the length-difficulty
relationship. Two valiant subjects participated in a 40-session experiment
where, on each session, each subject learned a list of either 9, 16, 25, 36, 49,
64, 81, or 100 pairs. There were eight list lengths and five replications of each.
All lists were composed of words selected at random from the Vermont word
pool (the precursor of the Toronto word pool). The study-test procedure was
used; presentation duration was 2 sec/pair for study, and testing was self-
paced. Subject 1 tested Subject 2 in the morning, and Subject 2 tested Sub-

ject 1 in the afternoon. All lists were learned to a criterion of one perfect trial. For further details, see Murdock (1967).

I tried fitting the learning curves with various versions of the model using parameter values in the general range of those reported earlier, and I was not at all satisfied with the results. I finally convinced myself that I must be in the wrong part of the parameter space, so I made a rather drastic change. Specifically, I increased the value of N, the dimensionality of the space, by an order of magnitude (from $N = 500$ to $N = 5,000$), and the results were most gratifying. Fits for three different list lengths (9, 49, and 100) are shown in Fig. 4.7, and the actual parameter values are shown in Table 4.10.

The important point is that no *free* parameters were used in fitting these data. (For the distinction between free and fixed parameters, see Hockley & Murdock, 1987.) That is, we used SIMPLX to determine the best-fitting values of α, γ, p_A ($= p_B$), and a (where a and b were symmetrical around 1), but none of the parameter values varied with list length. Having found the right part of the parameter space, we simply plugged in the eight values of L and the model generated the data shown in Fig. 4.7. The model did the work, not the parameters. As a similar example, Izawa (1985) found that her retention-interval model was able to explain the different results obtained with the study-test and the anticipation methods simply in terms of the differences in the distribution of retention intervals used by the two methods. Again, it was the model that did the work and not the parameters.

Length-Difficulty Relation

To study the length-difficulty relation, we used the fits reported in the previous section and determined the number of trials it should take each subject to learn lists of each length to criterion. This is the length-difficulty relation; the predicted and obtained results are shown in Fig. 4.8 and 4.9.

The results could not be better for Subject 1, but what about Subject 2? At first we thought there was a bug in the program, but that didn't seem to be the case. The problem may be a reliability effect. Determining trials to criteria involves reading off the value on the horizontal axis that corresponds to the intersection of the learning curve with the criterion level, and because the learning curve is generally quite flat here the dependent variable may be rather unreliable. In any case, even for Subject 2 the slope

TABLE 4.10
Parameter Estimates from SIMPLX Fits for Subjects 1 and 2

Subject	α	$\gamma_{1,1}$	x_1	p_A	DIFF
1	.996	.442	.121	.813	.912
2	.998	.406	.111	.838	.880

Note: $\gamma_{2,1} = \gamma_{1,1}$, $x_2 = x_1$, and $p_B = p_A$

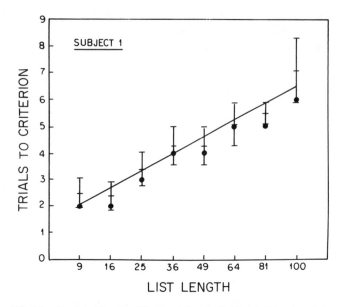

FIG. 4.8.   Predicted length-difficulty relation for Subject 1. (The closed circles are the predicted values, the vertical bars are the standard errors, and the solid line is the best fit to the data points.)

of the curve is what it should be, even if the intercept is about one trial too low.

One small problem should be mentioned. With these parameter values, with overlearning (i.e., trials beyond criterion) the old-item mean of Subject 2 got so high that recall probability decreased drastically. This problem could be remedied by allowing a change in the value of b, the upper tolerance limit, with overlearning, so it is not a major problem. However, it does indicate that the model is not quite as simple as I have implied.

The Learning Curve (again)

Fitting the data on the length-difficulty relationship necessitates a large change in the value of N, from 500 to 5,000. What effect would this change have on the previous fits? To find out, I then went back and redid the fit shown in Fig. 4.5 using the new value of N (5,000) rather than the old value of N (500). The new fit was as good if not better than the old fit; the parameter values now were $\alpha = .922$, $\gamma_{11} = \gamma_{21} = .356$, $\kappa_1 = \kappa_2 = .094$, DIFF $= .971$ and $b_1 = b_2 = .230$ that maps into $p_A = p_B = .369$. Obviously the parameter values are different, but the root-mean square value was actually slightly less (.227 vs. .389).

One might argue that if two good fits could be obtained in very different regions of the parameter space, the model is not very constrained. We would agree completely. However, we have already noted that the model is probably overdetermined, and it is designed to do far more than fit the mean learning curve. So, the fact that good fits to the mean learning curve can be obtained in different parts of the parameter space is exactly what one would expect.

Modified Method of Free Recall

Up to this point the emphasis has been exclusively on the learning of single lists. Equally important is the two-list design. One of the notable aspects of human associative memory is that people do not generally lose old associations when acquiring new associations. Or, to be more accurate, the rate of acquisition certainly exceeds the rate of loss. The associative mechanism must be designed to absorb new information without catastrophic loss of old information. In our zeal to explain the acquisition of new associations, we may sometimes lose sight of the concurrent need to retain old associations.

The appropriate experimental paradigm is the MMFR (Modified Method of Free Recall) design, where subjects are given not one but two lists to learn and then, with an A–B, A–C paradigm, asked to recall both the B and C responses to the A items as cues. The classic experiment is Barnes and Underwood (1959), where MMFR tests were given after a varying number of A–C

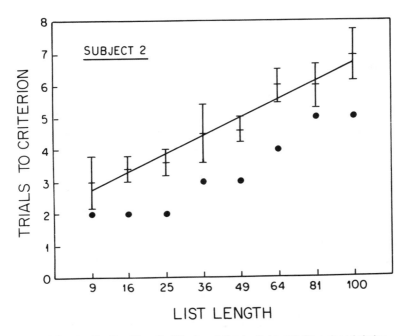

FIG. 4.9. Predicted length-difficulty relation for Subject 2. (The closed circles are the predicted values, the vertical bars are the standard errors, and the solid line is the best fit to the data points.)

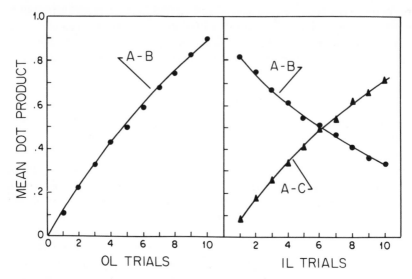

FIG. 4.10. Simulation of the convolution–correlation model for 10 trials of
A—B learning followed by 10 trials of A—C learning. The right-hand panel
shows the number of B and C recalls using the MMFR procedure.

trials. Their main finding was that the loss of the original *A–B* associations
was gradual, not sudden. As the number of trials on *A–C* learning, the acquisition of *A–C* improved gradually but the forgetting of *A–B* occurred
gradually as well.

We tried to fit the complete data (*A–B* acquisition, *A–C* acquisition, and
A–B unlearning) with several versions of the model, but we were not too successful. Although the model was certainly capable of capturing the overall
patterns in the data, it tended to overshoot or undershoot at selected points.
Probably quantitative fits are too ambitious at this stage of our knowledge;
from the point of view of model fitting, it is a rather complicated experimental paradigm. Consequently, we decided to resort to simulation to see how
the model would fare.

In the simulation we actually did the convolution and correlation, and computed the dot product of the retrieved information with all *B* responses in
the original learning (OL) and all *B* and *C* responses in the interpolated learning (IL). The dot product is a direct measure of associative strength, and is
monotonically related to recall probability. Although we would have liked
to use a value for *N* of 5,000, computing time would have been excessive so
we compromised with a value of 500. To compensate, we set $\gamma_{3,r} = 1.0$ for all
r so no item information was stored in the simulation. In a simple test of
associations, item information only functions as noise, so we chose to use

smaller-dimensional vectors with no item information rather than larger-dimensional vectors with item and associative information.[7]

In the simulation we used a value for α of .99 and $p_A = p_B = .35$; there were eight-pair lists for both original (A-B) and interpolated (A-C) learning, and there were 10 trials on each. The results of the simulation are shown in Fig. 4.10. As can be seen, unlearning as well as acquisition is gradual not sudden. So, qualitatively if not quantitatively the model can certainly generate data like that reported by Barnes and Underwood.

Consolidation

The model makes a clear prediction about consolidation. Suppose we have a retention interval filled with two different types of interpolation, one easy and one difficult. According to the model, the order in which these two interpolated tasks are presented should make no difference. If we assume one parameter (say α) for the easy interpolated task, and another parameter (say β) for the difficult interpolated task, then

$$\alpha^L(\beta^L\mathbf{M}) = (\alpha\beta)^L\mathbf{M} = (\beta\alpha)^L\mathbf{M} = \beta^L(\alpha^L\mathbf{M}) \qquad (11)$$

so the order of interpolation should be immaterial.

Unfortunately, this prediction does not seem to be correct. Landauer (1974) did exactly this experiment and found that, in line with what a consolidation notion might predict, a difficult followed by easy interpolation was more disruptive than an easy followed by a difficult interpolation. The differences were consistent across all three experiments.

However, as he noted, the difficulty manipulation was a similarity manipulation. In all the experiments the difficult interpolated pairs were more similar to the target pairs than the easy interpolated pairs were. The prediction just given is a rather global prediction, and might not hold at a more detailed level if the effects of similarity were included in the model. This has not yet been done, but it would be interesting to see if the inclusion of similarity in the model would alter the prediction to bring it more in line with the results obtained by Landauer.

Problems

In the applications previously discussed, I have not mentioned several problems that have come up. One is the fact that, as a consequence of the limited-capacity assumption, if x is greater than zero, then the strength of item infor-

---

[7]We would certainly not deny the possibility that item information could be involved in associative recall (e.g., Humphreys & Bain, 1983; Mandler, 1980), but this is simply a demonstration simulation to determine whether unlearning can be gradual.

mation decreases over trials and this is what leads to the increase in associative information over trials. As a consequence, recognition of item information could actually decrease with practice. Whether or not this happens depends on the particular parameter values. In some cases d' for recognition is still sufficiently high after many trials so good recognition performance would be expected. In other cases poor recognition performance would be expected, and this seems quite unlikely.

Another problem is that the learning curve can fit well but the actual parameter values that give rise to this curve might be somewhat unrealistic. A case in point is the revised fit to the mean learning curve with $N = 5,000$. With the particular parameter values obtained, the mean dot-product for old items was only .051 at the end of 20 trials. How could performance then be perfect? With $N = 5,000$ the variance was less than .001, so the signal-to-noise ratio was quite high. Although this is not necessarily wrong, it does strike me as being somewhat improbable.

I want to make it quite clear that the fits that I have presented in this chapter are illustrative only. I want to show that the model is in fact capable of fitting the data at a quantitative level with a few free parameters. Even if the convolution–correlation model is basically correct, it will take much more effort to work out the details. What we need now is application of the model to a wide variety of experimental phenomena with consistency of parameter values over applications. The theoretical analysis that is a necessary precursor has for the most part been done, but as I have said already the detailed application has not.

At a more general level, it should be noted that output interference is again not included in the model. Only the effects of study trials are represented, not the effects of test trials. By contrast, the work of Izawa (Chap. 8 in this volume) shows that test trials are important too. Perhaps there is some way these two apparently quite different views could be combined.

Why Probabilistic Encoding Leads to Learning

In this chapter we have suggested that probabilistic encoding might be a basic factor underlying learning. That is, learning as measured by d' will not occur in a distributed-memory model if all the elements of the item vectors are encoded on each trial; d' will stay constant at some given value that is determined by the numerical values of the parameters a and N. On the other hand, if a subset of the elements are encoded on each trial, then the value of d' will increase over trials. This holds true for both recall and recognition.

Why does probabilistic encoding enable learning to occur? Obviously, if d' increases over trials, and d' is a ratio of the old-item mean to the variance, then the mean must increase more than the variance (standard deviation). Consider the variance. The basic result is

$$p \sum_r b_r^2 + p^2 \sum_{r \neq r'} b_r b_{r'} \qquad (12)$$

The first component ($\sum b_r^2$) is the variance within repetitions and the second component ($\sum b_r b_{r'}$) is the variance across repetition. So, the variance within repetition varies with p whereas the variance across repetition varies with p^2. Because $p^2 < p$, probabilistic encoding attenuates the variance across repetition, and the smaller the value of p the greater the attenuation. This would seem to be the basic reason why probabilistic encoding leads to learning.

Throughout this chapter I have claimed that distributed memory models need some modification such as probabilistic encoding for learning to occur. This view assumes that **M**, the memory vector, is initialized to zero before list presentation starts. The situation may be different if **M** is not initialized to zero. This gets us into the issue of episodic and semantic memory; for possible views of semantic and episodic memory see Eich (1982, 1985) or McKoon, Ratcliff, and Dell (1986).

SUMMARY

We have suggested five possible factors for paired-associate learning: probabilistic encoding, an item-associative attentional shift, reduction in response competition, more efficient deblurring, and reduction in intralist similarity. Fitting the model to data is a two-step process; first, fit the Gompertz double-exponential function to the data, then fit the model to the Gompertz function. We have applied the model with some success to mean learning curves, learning to learn, list-length effects, the length-difficulty relation, MMFR, and memory consolidation.

It could be objected that, for the most part, all we have done is to fit the mean learning curve for paired-associates, and the learning curve is not too informative. Although this is true, I should point out that in principle the model is capable of making much more detailed predictions. Specifically, for any serial position in any repetition, the model can generate the mean and variance of the resemblance distributions for correct responses and all intralist intrusions, so one can predict almost any statistic from the data that one can obtain. It seems to me more reasonable to try to get the right version of the model at a higher level before getting into such fine grain detail, but eventually such detailed analyses should certainly be carried out.

Paired-associate learning is seen as more complex than recognition learning, but both are explained in a common theoretical framework. Much of the theoretical work has been done, but only enough of the detailed fitting and testing to suggest that further applications may be worthwhile. To return to the opening comment of this chapter, learning is no longer a problem for

TODAM; multiple possibilities exist. What we must do now is narrow down the possibilities.

ACKNOWLEDGMENTS

Preparation of this chapter was facilitated by Research Grant APA 146 from the Natural Sciences and Engineering Research Council of Canada and a Killam Research Fellowship from the Canada Council. I would like to thank Patrick Goebel, Bill Hockley, Steve Lewandowsky, and Roger Ratcliff for many helpful comments, and Elke Weber for much help on some of the technical aspects of the derivations.

APPENDIX 1

The derivations for the old-item mean and the old-item variance are given below.

Old-Item Mean

The old-item mean is the expected value of the dot product of the probe item with the memory vector; specifically,

$$\mu_k = E[f_k \cdot M] = E[f_k \cdot \sum_r \sum_l c_{r,l} p f_l]$$

where $c_{r,l}$ is a serial-position constant whose value depends on r ($r = 1, \ldots, R$) and l ($l = 1, \ldots, L$) and pf_l is a shorthand to denote that each element of an item is encoded with probability p and not encoded with probability $1 - p$. (This happens on each repetition of the item, so a random subset of the elements are added to the memory vector on each trial.) The upper limit of the summation over r is always R; the upper limit of the summation over l is always L.

We can switch from working with vectors to working with single random variables because

$$E[f_k \cdot \sum_r \sum_l c_{r,l} p f_l] = N \, E[Z_k \sum_r \sum_l c_{r,l} p Z_l]$$

where Z_k and Z_l are the elements that comprise f_k and f_l. There is nothing special about any particular element, so the dot product as the sum of N cross products is simply N times any given cross product. We are assuming that these vectors live in an N-dimensional Euclidean space with Cartesian coordinates. We can rewrite the expectation as

$$E[Z_k \sum_r \sum_l c_{r,l} p Z_l[= E[Z_k \sum_r \sum_l p c_{r,l} Z_l] = E[\sum_r \sum_l p c_{r,l} Z_k Z_l].$$

That is, we can think of p as acting on the serial-position constant rather than the random variable, and we can bring Z_k inside the summation. Then we can decompose the expectation into two parts; namely,

$$E[\sum_r \sum_l pc_{r,l}Z_kZ_l] = E[\sum_r pc_{r,k}Z_kZ_k + \sum_r \sum_{l\neq k} pc_{r,l}Z_kZ_l] =$$

$$E[\sum_r pc_{r,k}Z_kZ_k] + E[\sum_r \sum_{l\neq k} pc_{r,l}Z_kZ_l]$$

where the first part is the contribution of the probe item in the memory vector and the second part is the contribution of all remaining items. For the first part,

$$E[\sum_r pc_{r,k}Z_kZ_k] = E[\sum_r pc_{r,k}]E[Z^2] = p \sum_r c_{r,k}\sigma^2 = pa_k \sum_r b_r\sigma^2$$

where we can factor $c_{r,k}$ into two parts, a_k which varies with serial position and b_r which varies with repetition. This is a consequence of assuming a fixed order of presentation, and it makes the derivations easier. Both a_k and b_r are simple functions of α, the forgetting parameter, and this will be made explicit shortly. For the second part,

$$E[\sum_r \sum_{l\neq k} pc_{r,l}Z_kZ_l] = E[\sum_r \sum_{l\neq k} pc_{r,l}]E[ZZ'] = p\sum_r \sum_{l\neq k} c_{r,l}\varrho\sigma^2 =$$

$$p \sum_r b_r \sum_{l\neq k} a_l\varrho\sigma^2$$

where Z' is similar to Z by parameter ϱ and again we have decomposed $c_{r,l}$ into two parts b_r and a_l. Putting this all together we have

$$\mu_k = N(pa_k \sum_r b_r\sigma^2 + p \sum_r b_r \sum_{l\neq k} a_l\varrho\sigma^2) =$$

$$pN \sum_r b_r(a_k + \varrho \sum_{l\neq k} a_l)\sigma^2 = p \sum_r b_r(a_k + \varrho \sum_{l\neq k} a_l) = pD(A + \varrho(B-A))$$

where the definitions of A, B, and D are given in Table 4.1. (Recall that σ^2 is assumed to be P/N so if $P = 1$ then N and σ^2 cancel.) Thus, we have a simple expression for μ_k, the mean of the old-item distribution, in terms of the parameter of the model (α, the forgetting parameter; p, the encoding probability; and ϱ, the similarity parameter) and the experimental conditions (L, the list length; R, the number of presentations; and k, the serial position of the probe). Also, keep in mind that p, the encoding probability, is a function of presentation duration. This dependence does not affect the above derivation and was not explicitly specified as it was not needed.

Old-Item Variance

For the old-item variance we have

$$\sigma_k^2 = \mathrm{Var}[f \cdot M] = E[(f \cdot M)^2] - E^2[f \cdot M] = E[f \cdot M)^2] - \mu_k^2$$

and, because we already have μ_k, the mean of the old-item distribution, what is needed is the expected value of the square of the dot product. As above, let us go to the level of single random variables and we need

$$E[(Z_k \sum_r \sum_l c_{r,l} p Z_l)^2] = E[(\sum_r \sum_l p c_{r,l} Z_k Z_l)^2] = T1 + T2 + T3$$

where

$$T1 = E[\sum_r \sum_l p c_{r,l} Z_k^2 Z_l^2],$$

$$T2 = E[\sum_r \sum_{r' \neq r} \sum_l p c_{r,l} Z_k Z_l p c_{r',l} Z_k Z_l], \text{ and}$$

$$T3 = E[\sum_r \sum_{r'} \sum_l \sum_{l' \neq l} p c_{r,l} Z_k Z_l p c_{r',l'} Z_k Z_{l'}].$$

That is, we have partitioned the total summation into three components: within repetition ($T1$), between repetition ($T2$), and across serial position within each repetition ($T3$). Without presenting all the detailed steps it can be shown that

$$T1 = E[\sum_r p c_{r,k}^2 Z_k^4 + \sum_r \sum_{l \neq k} p c_{r,l}^2 Z_k^2 Z_l^2] =$$

$$p \sum_r b_r^2 (a_k^2 E[Z^4] + \sum_{l \neq k} a_l^2 E[ZZZ'Z']) =$$

$$p \sum_r b_r^2 (3a_k^2 + (1 + 2\varrho^2) \sum_{l \neq k} a_l^2) \sigma^4$$

where Z and Z' are "similar" random variables.[8] That is, they are a pair of random samples from the bivariate normal distribution with a theoretical correlation coefficient of ϱ. For $T2$ we have

$$T2 = E[\sum_r \sum_{r' \neq r} \sum_l p b_r a_l p b_{r'} a_l Z_k Z_l] =$$

$$p^2 \sum_r \sum_{r' \neq r} b_r b_{r'} E[\sum_l a_l^2 Z_k^2 Z_l^2] =$$

$$p^2 \{(\sum_r b_r)^2 - \sum_r b_r^2\} \{ \dots \} \sigma^4$$

where $\{ \dots \}$ denotes the same term as in the comparable expression for $T1$. We can conveniently combine $T1$ and $T2$ and we have

$$T1 + T2 = (p^2(\sum_r b_r)^2 + pq\sum_r b_r^2) (3a_k^2 + (1 + 2\varrho^2) \sum_{l \neq k} a_l^2) \sigma^4$$

where $q \equiv 1 - p$. For $T3$ we have:

$$T3 = E[\sum_r \sum_{r'} \sum_l \sum_{l' \neq l} p b_r a_l Z_k Z_l p b_{r'} a_{l'} Z_k Z_{l'}] =$$

$$p^2(\sum_r b_r)^2 E[\sum_l \sum_{l' \neq l} a_l Z_k Z_l a_{l'} Z_k Z_{l'}] =$$

---

[8]I would like to thank Elke Weber for showing me how to work out the expectation of products of correlated random variables.

$$\beta(a_k \sum_{1'\neq k} a_{1'} E[2ZZZZ'] = \sum_{1\neq k} \sum_{\substack{1'>1 \\ 1'\neq k}} a_l a_{1'} E[2ZZZ'Z'']) =$$

$$\beta(2a_k \sum_{1'\neq k} a_{1'} E[ZZZZ'] + \sum_{1\neq k} \sum_{1'\neq 1,k} a_l a_{1'} E[ZZZ'Z''] =$$

$$\beta(6\varrho a_k \sum_{1'\neq k} a_1 + \sum_{1\neq k} \sum_{1'\neq 1,k} a_l a_{1'} (\varrho + 2\varrho^2) \sigma^4$$

where $\beta \equiv p^2(\Sigma b_r)^2$. The final result is given in Table 4.1 in terms of the symbols A—E that are defined at the bottom of the table.

APPENDIX 2

For a list of L pairs presented R times in a fixed order, the mean resemblance μ_k of the retrieved information g_k' to the target information g_k is given by

$$\mu_k = E[g_k \cdot g_k'] = E[g_k \cdot (f_k \# M) = E[(f_k^* g_k) \cdot M]$$

(see Murdock, 1985 or Pike, 1984) where f_k is the probe item and M is the memory vector. With probabilistic encoding,

$$E[(f_k^* g_k) \cdot M] = E[(f_k^* g_k) \cdot \Sigma b_r \Sigma a_l \{\gamma_{1,r} p_A f_l + \gamma_{2,r} p_B g_l +$$

$$+ \gamma_{3,r} (p_A f_l^* p_B g_l)\}] = E[(f_k^* g_k) \cdot \Sigma b_r \gamma_{3,r} \Sigma a_l (p_A f_l^* p_B g_l)]$$

since the item components are zero $(E[f^* g] \cdot f] \sim E[ZW]E[Z] = E[Z]E[W]E[-Z] = 0)$. The terms a_l and b_r are the same as in Appendix 1. The summation ranges are $r = 1, \ldots, R$ and $1 = 1, \ldots, L$ but generally they will not be indicated explicitly. Now

$$E[(f_k^* g_k) \cdot \Sigma b_r \gamma_{3,r} \Sigma a_l (p_A f_l^* p_B g_l)] =$$

$$N^2 E[Z_k W_k \Sigma b_r \gamma_{3,r} \Sigma a_l p_A Z_l p_B W_l] = N^2 E[p_A p_B \Sigma b_r \gamma_{3,r} Z_k W_k \Sigma a_l Z_l W_l] =$$

$$N^2 E[p_A p_B \Sigma b_r \gamma_{3,r} [E[Z_k W_k \Sigma a_l Z_l W_l] =$$

$$N^2 p_A p_B \Sigma b_r \gamma_{3,r} E[Z_k W_k \Sigma a_l Z_l W_l].$$

That is, there are N^2 matching terms in the dot product of two convolutions and the coefficients are simply multipliers. Finally,

$$E[Z_k W_k \Sigma a_l Z_l W_l] = E[Z_k W_k (a_k Z_k W_k + \sum_{1\neq k} a_l Z_l W_l)] =$$

$$E[a_k Z^2 W^2 + \sum_{1\neq k} a_l ZZ'WW'] = a_k E(Z^2 W^2] + \sum_{1\neq k} a_l E \times [ZZ'WW'] =$$

$$a_k E[Z^2]E[W^2] + \sum_{1\neq k} a_l E[ZZ']E[WW'] = a_k \sigma^4 + \sum_{1\neq k} a_l \varrho_A \varrho_B \sigma^4$$

where ϱ_A is the similarity of the A items and ϱ_B is the similarity of the B items. (This assumes that the A and B items are not similar to each other.) Putting this all together we have

$$\mu_k = p_A p_B \Sigma b_r \gamma_{3,r} (a_k + \varrho_A \varrho_B \sum_{l \neq k} a_l).$$

REFERENCES

Anderson, J. A. (1973). A theory for the recognition of items for short memorized lists. *Psychological Review, 80*, 417–438.

Anderson, J. A., Silverstein, J. W., Ritz, S. A., & Jones, R. S. (1977). Distinctive features, categorical perception, and probability learning: Some applications of a neural model. *Psychological Review, 84*, 413–451.

Barnes, J.M., & Underwood, B. J. (1959). "Fate" of first-list associations in transfer theory. *Journal of Experimental Psychology, 58*, 97–105.

Bernbach, H. A. (1967). Stimulus learning and recognition in paired-associate learning. *Journal of Experimental Psychology, 75*, 512–519.

Bower, G. H. (1972). Stimulus-sampling theory of encoding variability. In A. W. Melton & E. Martin (Eds.), *Coding processes in human memory* (pp. 85–123). Washington, DC: V.H. Winston.

Brainerd, C. J., Howe, M. L., & Desrochers, A. (1982). The general theory of two-stage learning: A mathematical review with illustrations from memory development. *Psychological Bulletin, 91*, 634–665.

Eich, J. M. (1982). A composite holographic associative recall model. *Psychological Review, 89*, 627–661.

Eich, J. M. (1985). Levels of processing, encoding specificity, elaboration, and CHARM. *Psychological Review, 92*, 1–38.

Estes, W. K. (1950). Toward a statistical theory of learning. *Psychological Review, 57*, 94–107.

Estes, W. K. (1959). Component and pattern models with Markovian interpretations. In R. R. Bush & W. K. Estes (Eds.), *Studies in mathematical learning theory* (pp. 9–52). Stanford, CA: Stanford University Press.

Estes, W. K. (1960). Learning theory and the new "mental chemistry." *Psychological Review, 67*, 207–223.

Gibson, E. J. (1940). A systematic application of the concepts of generalization and differentiation to verbal learning. *Psychological Review, 47*, 196–229.

Golden, R. M. (1986). The "brain-state-in-a-box" neural model is a gradient descent algorithm. *Journal of Mathematical Psychology, 30*, 73–80.

Greeno, J. G., James, C. T., DaPolito, F., & Polson, P. G. (1978). *Associative learning: A cognitive analysis.* Englewood Cliffs, NJ: Prentice-Hall.

Hintzman, D. L. (1986). "Schema abstraction" in a multiple-trace memory model. *Psychological Review, 93*, 411–428.

Hintzman, D. L. (1988). Judgments of frequency and recognition memory in a multiple-trace model. *Psychological Review, 95*, 528–551.

Hockley, W. E. (1984). Retrieval of item frequency information in a continuous memory task. *Memory & Cognition, 12*, 229–242.

Hockley, W. E., & Murdock, B. B., Jr. (1987). A decision model for accuracy and response latency in recognition memory. *Psychological Review, 94*, 314–358.

Hopfield, J. J. (1984). Neurons with graded response have collective properties like those of two-state neurons. *Proceedings of the National Academy of Sciences, USA, 81*, 3088–3092.

Humphreys, M. S., & Bain, J. D. (1983). Recognition memory: A cue and information analysis. *Memory & Cognition, 11*, 583–600.

Izawa, C. (1985). A test of the differences between anticipation and the study-test methods of paired-associate learning. *Journal of Experimental Psychology: Learning, Memory, and Cognition, 11*, 165–184.

Johns, E. E. (1985). Effects of list organization on item recognition. *Journal of Experimental Psychology: Learning, Memory, and Cognition, 11*, 605–620.

Keppel, G., Postman, L., & Zavortink, B. (1968). Studies of learning to learn: VIII. The influence of massive amounts of training upon the learning and retention of paired-associate lists. *Journal of Verbal Learning and Verbal Behavior, 7*, 790–796.

Kohonen, T. (1977). *Associative memory: A system-theoretical approach.* Berlin: Springer-Verlag.

Landauer, T. K. (1974). Consolidation in human memory: Retrograde amnestic effects of confusable items in paired-associate learning. *Journal of Verbal Learning and Verbal Behavior, 13*, 45–53.

Lewandowsky, S., & Murdock, B. B., Jr. (in press). Memory for serial order. *Psychological Review.*

Lewis, D. (1960). *Quantitative methods in psychology.* New York: McGraw-Hill.

Loftus, G. R. (1974). Acquisition of information from rapidly presented verbal and nonverbal stimuli. *Memory & Cognition, 2*, 545–548.

Luce, R. D. (1986). *Response times.* New York: Oxford University Press.

Mandler, G. (1954). Response factors in human learning. *Psychological Review, 61*, 235–244.

Mandler, G. (1980). Recognizing: The judgment of previous occurrence. *Psychological Review, 87*, 252–271.

Martin, E. (1967). Relation between stimulus recognition and paired-associate learning. *Journal of Experimental Psychology, 74*, 500–505.

McClelland, J. L., & Rumelhart, D. E. (1985). Distributed memory and the representation of general and specific information. *Journal of Experimental Psychology: General, 114*, 159.

McGovern, J. B. (1964). Extinction of associations in four transfer paradigms. *Psychological Monographs, 16*, 78.

McGuire, W. J. (1961). A multiprocess model for paired-associate learning. *Journal of Experimental Psychology, 62*, 335–347.

McKoon, G., Ratcliff, R., & Dell, G. S. (1986). A critical evaluation of the semantic episodic distinction. *Journal of Experimental Psychology: Learning, Memory, and Cognition, 12*, 295–306.

Murdock, B. B., Jr. (1967). A fixed-point model for short-term memory. *Journal of Mathematical Psychology, 4*, 501–506.

Murdock, B. B., Jr. (1976). Item and order information in short-term serial memory. *Journal of Experimental Psychology: General, 105*, 191–216.

Murdock, B. B., Jr. (1982). A theory for the storage and retrieval of item and associative information. *Psychological Review, 89*, 609–629.

Murdock, B. B., Jr. (1985). Convolution and matrix systems: A reply to Pike. *Psychological Review, 92*, 130–132.

Murdock, B. B., Jr. (1987). Serial-order effects in a distributed memory mode. In D. S. Gorfein & R. R. Hoffman (Eds.), *Memory and learning: The Ebbinghaus centennial conference* (pp. 277–310). Hillsdale, NJ: Lawrence Erlbaum Associates.

Murdock, B. B., Jr., & Anderson, R. E. (1975). Encoding, storage, and retrieval of item information. In R. L. Solso (Ed.), *Information processing and cognition: The Loyola symposium* (pp. 145–194). Hillsdale, NJ: Lawrence Erlbaum Associates.

Murdock, B. B., Jr., & Lamon, M. (1988). The replacement effect: Repeating some items while replacing others. *Memory & Cognition, 16*, 91–101.

Nelder, J. A., & Mead, R. (1965). A simplex method for function minimization. *Computer Journal, 7*, 308–313.

Okada, R., & Burrows, D. (1973). Organizational factors in high-speed scanning. *Journal of Experimental Psychology, 101*, 77–81.

Pike, R. (1984). Comparison of convolution and matrix distributed memory systems for associative recall and recognition. *Psychological Review, 91*, 281–294.

Postman, L., & Stark, K. (1969). Role of response availability in transfer and interference. *Journal of Experimental Psychology, 79*, 168–177.

Schönemann, P. H. (1987). Some algebraic relations between involutions, convolutions, and correlations with applications to holographic memories. *Biological Cybernetiks, 56*, 367–374.

Shiffrin, R. M. (1988, August). *Models for the list-strength effect in recognition memory.* Paper presented at the Mathematical Psychology Satellite Conference, Armidale, Australia.

Underwood, B. J. (1961). An evaluation of the Gibson theory of verbal learning. In C. N. Cofer (Ed.), *Verbal learning and verbal behavior* (pp. 197–217). New York: McGraw-Hill.

Underwood, B. J. (1983). *Attributes of memory.* Glenview, IL: Scott, Foresman.

Underwood, B. J., & Schulz, R. W. (1960). *Meaningfulness and verbal learning.* Philadelphia: Lippincott.

Waugh, N. C. (1969). The effect of recency and repetition on recall latencies. *Acta Psychologica, 30*, 115–125.

Weber, E. U. (1988). Expectation and variance of item resemblance distributions in a convolution-correlation model of distributed memory. *Journal of Mathematical Psychology, 32*, 1–43.

5

Approach–Avoidance: Return to Dynamic Decision Behavior

James T. Townsend
Jerome R. Busemeyer
Purdue University

The purpose of this chapter is to resurrect an old area of research in psychology, that of the study of "approach–avoidance behavior." This research topic, more or less forgotten for some time, can perhaps serve as a linkage joining traditional motivation and learning psychology to the field of decision making. In fact, we suspect that approach–avoidance characterizes most, if not all, of a person's life decisions. "Borrowing" a cookie from Grandma's cookie jar, the dilemmas of dating and marriage proposals, college military duty, applying for jobs, and confronting the schoolyard bully are a tiny sample of such instances, which the reader can undoubtedly complement many times over.

But why disinter a research problem presumably "laid to rest?" Psychology, even in the more rigorous domains, is renowned for its faddish inclinations. Novel research problems are unearthed and mined by the innovator for the "obvious" nuggets and then as difficulties or complexities begin to appear, they tend to be abandoned for new "mother lodes." Researchers who, in the spirit of the hard sciences, continue to investigate the phenomena often meet with obstacles in publishing their results, because the research topic is "out-of-date." It is not difficult to see that sustained scientific progress is slow when pursued in this fashion. It is made worse by the inadequate treatment of classic and historic research accorded our students in many of our undergraduate and graduate programs.

In the present instance, we have on the one hand a lacuna in the formal theories of decision making and on the other, a fruitful area that formerly provided a link among motivation, learning, and decision making behavior. Formal theorization in decision making has been virtually dominated by utility theory and statistical decision theory, especially as put forth by Von Neumann and Morgenstern and advanced later by Savage and others. Much beautiful mathematical work has been accomplished in these pursuits, especially in statistical decision theory, game theory, and of course, subjective expected utility theory.

There are many advantages of these approaches, apart from their elegance and employment in telling us what our optimal behavior should be like and their possible use in artificial intelligence. One well known justification is to provide a touchstone with which to compare the not-so optimal behavior of real life creatures. This concept has proven of great value in certain areas, some related to decision making. The best known in experimental psychology is probably signal detection theory (e.g., Green & Swets, 1966). It is also fair to say that this rationale has been beneficial in decision research per se, in pointing out how human decisions depart from the more ideal assumptions or theorems of utility theory.

A missing quality, from the present viewpoint, are natural connections with biology and more fundamentally, with that heritage in psychology built on evolutionary principles. Growing out of William James and others' "functionalistic" characterizations of motivated behavior (i.e., organisms tend to do what helps them survive; close to a tautology, but of immense importance in bringing biology and psychology closer together), later "dynamic" psychologists (e.g., Angell, Woodworth, etc.,) began to forge a true psychology of motivation. Motivation went on to underpin a great deal of the theory and experiment in learning, as expressed primarily in behavioristic animal research for more than half a century (e.g., Hull, Tolman, Skinner, etc.). A valid criticism of behaviorism is that it tended to depreciate central cognition and another is that it ironically led to studying behavior in animals that was less than naturalistic with respect to their original environment. The field of ethology (e.g., Tinbergen, Lorenz, etc.) has done much to redress this latter skew. The emergence of "animal cognition" has also aided in this regard (e.g., see Roitblat, Bever, & Terrace, 1984). Nevertheless, the classical behaviorists left us a legacy of ideas that even now influence our ways of thinking about human and animal behavior.

With regard to utility theory, there often seems to be an absence of what underlying motives may drive the utility that an object or act may hold for a person. A number of other consequences tend to follow in the wake of the spirit of utility theory that carry it further from human activities. For instance utilities are usually conceived as static summaries of a fixed set of independent dimensional features or attributes. In reality these are, to the extent that they do exist, probably dynamically changing over time.

Other recent developments related to utility theory have seen a substantial increase in concern with what people actually do. This has been evident in empirical research partly stimulated by testing various tenets and consequences of utility theory (see, e.g., Tversky & Kahneman, 1981). One outcome has been the appearance of more psychologically attuned qualitative or computer simulation theories and models (e.g., Johnson & Payne, 1985). Another has been the attempt to relax certain of the assumptions of utility theory in order to better accommodate human decisional frailties. As examples, we cite Fishburn (1986), Luce and Narens (1985) and perhaps with most impact on empirical psychology, Kahneman and Tversky (1979). Kahneman and Tversky (1979) have gone far in providing intriguing evidence of humankind's straying from utility theory's predictions. In doing so, they continue a tradition starting as far back as 1738 with Bernouilli's treatment of the Petersburg paradox and later with the paradoxes of Allais (1953) and Ellsberg (1961).

Finally let us emphasize that our intent is not to denigrate the field of utility theory and the rich heritage it has brought us, but rather to help fill in the mostly unoccupied and (we feel) neglected regions where traditional psychology and biology may have something useful to say about decision making.

LEWIN'S FIELD THEORY AND RELATED NOTIONS OF APPROACH-AVOIDANCE

An "old" area of research that effectively captures the importance of dynamic conception of utilities, motivation and dynamism is so-called approach–avoidance behavior. As a twentieth–century topic, its prime and likely earliest promulgator seems to have been Lewin (1935). Lewin's theory was an example of a gestalt field theory with an emphasis on spatial relations among psychological objects, as opposed to the presumably more independent congeries of "atoms" associated with British empiricism, structuralism and to some extent behaviorism (see, e.g., Boring, 1957). The other major field "theory" (neither was formalized to any extent) was Köhler's brain field (e.g., Köhler & Held, 1949). Both flow out of gestalt tradition (e.g., Hilgard, 1956).

Lewin characterized the human as moving in a space replete with psychological and physical objects possessing attractive or repulsive qualities that would tend to draw the person toward or away from the object. Objects could also have both positive and negative qualities at the same time, resulting in ambivalence on the part of the person. The positive and negative "charges" were called "valences." In order to escape the narrow confines of geometry, which Lewin thought too confining and inapplicable, he drew on the concepts of point-set topology. Topology is that mathematical field that relinquishes such devices as angle, orthogonal dimension, linear order, and so on in order to learn what may be preserved by continuous functions of one topological space to another, without the usual assumptions of Euclidean metric and the like. Lewin apparently did not pretend to be a mathematician and was widely believed to be a genius by his followers.

On rereading some of his early works (e.g., Lewin, 1936), we expected to uncover serious misapprehensions of mathematical concepts. Surprisingly little to grouse about was found, although as noted earlier, Lewin did not himself use any actual mathematics in his theorizing. What he did was to develop metaphors based on the topological notions.

It is an open question as to how much of the actual topology will turn out to be useful in experimental arenas. From our initial perspective, it appears easier to get somewhere when we spruce up the spaces to the level of differentiable vector spaces. For then we can talk about direction, speed and related notions. We will return to Lewinian ways of depicting the psychological space, but first must fill in more of the history of approach–avoidance research.

It was not long after Lewin began to publish articles and books on dynamic psychological spaces that Clark Hull incorporated the concept of approach–avoidance in his own theory (e.g., Hull, 1938; excellent discussions of Hull's and Lewin's theories may be found in Hilgard, 1956 and in chapters in the anthology by Koch on Hull, and Estes on Lewin, *Modern Learning Theory,* 1954). It was in fact a natural extension of his ideas on drive, learning, response strength, inhibition, and extinction. Lewin began at the relatively grandiose level of complex human motivation and social movement and interaction whereas Hull started with fairly detailed (though not always entirely rigorous) assumptions at a quite microlevel of psychological processes. Nevertheless Hull intended the theoretical consequences to be applicable at least in principle to more complex human pursuits; although he never seemed overly interested in social interactions per se, in contrast to Lewin. Further, Hull used some real mathematics, although it was rather more down to earth than the topology to which Lewin verbally referred. He went so far as to define a simple differential equation for the separate approach and avoidance as functions of distance from the specified object, hereafter called the "goal object" or simply "goal." This led to exponential types of valence or gradient curves that yielded qualitative predictions for experimental situations. However, Hull never got around to linking up the approach and avoidance curves to dynamic differential equations *in time* (i.e., Hull's expressions were differential equations in space rather than time). It is interesting that during roughly the same period, Rashevsky and others were using time-differential equations (i.e., with time as an independent variable) to describe hypothetical psychological and neuropsychological systems. However, there seems to have been little or no cross-talk between these groups.

The next major figure in the short history of the subject was Neal Miller, a student of Hull. Miller (1959) and Dollard and Miller (1950), applied the ideas of approach–avoidance and other facets of a neobehavioristic theory to many aspects of psychology, with special emphasis on clinical implications. The quandary posed by a phobia such as acrophobia (fear of high places) for a person living in the age of space and flight is obvious, and qualitatively well described by approach–avoidance notions. For some reasons, after a major summary of progress to date published in Volume 2 of the influential

Psychology: A Study of a Science series (1959), Miller seems largely to have moved to other interests.

It seems strange that through all the years that concepts associated with positive and negative aspects of objects (used as is typical here, in a general sense) have been bruited about, no one has ever developed a dynamical mathematical theory to capture the essentials of Lewin's verbal and Hull's slightly more rigorous ideas. In this chapter, we begin the development of a formal theory of decisional conflict behavior, which we believe characterizes most, if not all of the major decisions in a human life. We hope also to soon begin experimentation with human subjects employing sufficiently potent positive and negative rewards that at least a modicum of realism is attained.

Our development treats positive and negatively valenced influences in a descriptively simple fashion. The exact mechanisms, psychological or biological, are mostly unspecified at this point. This is not meant to underplay the potential great importance of mental factors, such as personal feelings of efficacy, for which, for example, Bandura and his colleagues (e.g., in press) have provided ample evidence in motivated behavior. We nevertheless believe (although it is probably unprovable), that various mental facets of approach–avoidance behavior evolved over eons from reflex-like acts to more internalized cognitive behavior such as mental vicarious trial-and-error routines. Interactions or even subservience to other subprocesses such as personality and efficacy perhaps also emerged over the course of evolution.

Figure 5.1 shows the prototypical type of diagram devised by Lewin where we see, in this instance, a person (*P*) propelled by positive drive toward a goal but repelled by the negative aspects of an intermediary task, a frequent enough situation in real life. This is an example of single goal, approach–avoidance. We use the term "goal" even in cases where all valence is aversive, for simplicity of expression. Of course, just as ubiquitous are situations where there exist unpleasant consequences that arise after a pleasant goal has been reached. Notably too, the classical gambles of uncertain decision making fall readily into the framework. In particular, risk may be viewed as adding to potential aversive consequences and thereby feeding the avoidance motivation, with gain or winnings providing for approach motivation (cf. Coombs & Avrunin, 1977). Of course, the situation becomes more complex in the presence of risk-seeking people but that does not lessen the importance of the motivational distinction between the positive and negative aspects of a situation.

Figure 5.2 shows a situation in which both of two goals are aversive. In this type of situation, given an opportunity, the person may "leave the field" so to speak, as suggested by the dotted line in the Figure. However, if the dimensionality of the field is too restricted, then that may not be possible as we will see, and the individual may vacillate or come to rest at an equilibrium point.

Even in the absence of other more positive objects in the vicinity of the aversive choices, the rest of the field away from those despised objects is

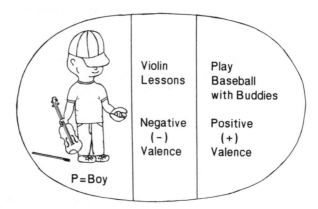

FIG. 5.1.   Example of a single-goal approach–avoidance situation when the boy (*P*) is attracted toward playing baseball(+) but repelled by a violin lesson(−) that stands between him and the attractive goal.

positive relative to the aversive negative goals. Of course, there is an infinitude of rich possibilities of such motivational fields. In this chapter, we deal with but a few of the simplest, but in a rigorous way.

Miller's verbal postulates for approach–avoidance seem a good place to start a discussion that leads to a more formal system.

1. The tendency to approach a goal is stronger the nearer the subject is to it. This is an application of Hull's principle of the goal gradient and will be called the *Gradient of Approach.*

2. The tendency to avoid a feared stimulus is stronger the nearer the subject is to it. This was an extension of the general idea of the gradient of reinforcement to avoidance learning. It will be called the *Gradient of Avoidance.*

3. The strength of avoidance increases more rapidly with nearness than does that of approach. In other words, the gradient of avoidance is steeper than that of approach. This was a new assumption necessary to account for the behavior of going part way and then stopping.

4. The strength of tendencies to approach or avoid varies directly with the strength of the drive upon which they are based. In other words, an increase in drive raises the height of the entire gradient. This assumption was necessary to explain the fact that stronger shocks stopped the animals whereas weaker shocks did not and also to explain the intuitively expected result that stronger shocks would be necessary to stop hungrier animals. This assumption was a specific application of the general notion that response strength varies with relevant drive.

5. Below the asymptote of learning, increasing the number of reinforced trials will increase the strength of the response tendency that is reinforced.

6. When two incompatible responses are in conflict, the stronger one will occur.

Miller goes on to form a set of deductions from the postulates. However the majority of the "deductions" actually seem to be more like assertions about the relations among the independent variables (deprivation, stimulus intensity, training) and what corresponds to parameters in the approach–avoidance model (e.g., slopes and intercepts of the gradients). Once the model is formalized, these turn out to be obvious consequences. Our main goal is rather to deduce relations between the dynamics of behavior (movement toward or away from goals and vacillation) and model parameters.

Hull (e.g., 1938) captured the increases of both positive and negative tendencies as the organism nears a goal conveniently set at the origin, by the spatial differential equation $dE/dD = -b/D$ where $E =$ excitatory potential (i.e., tendency toward a response), $D =$ distance from goal, and b is a constant of proportionality. This obviously leads to a solution of the form $E = a - b \log(D)$. Another suggested form for E was $E = a \exp(-hxD)$. In the former case, E evidently becomes infinitely large as one approaches the goal whereas it stays finite in the second form. The first case of E approaching infinity is not necessarily a major consideration because physics has many similar examples; for instance, the force between two bodies is said to be proportional to the squared distance between them. Thus, if the two bodies approach one another, the force ideally should approach infinity—at the time of impact, of course, a discontinuity is introduced into the dynamics. Miller (1959) pictured the gradients as linear, although explicit formulae were not given. We will later compare some different approach–avoidance curves, or "gradients" as they have traditionally been called. It is likely that

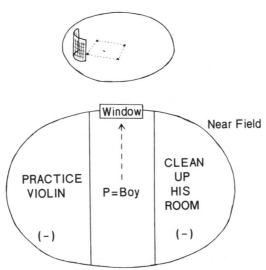

FIG. 5.2.   Example of a double-goal avoidance–avoidance situation where the person is repelled by both goals and may leave the field (dashed arrow).

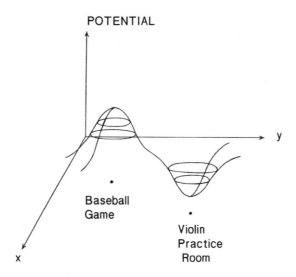

FIG. 5.3.   An example of a double-goal conflict situation where the person's approach versus avoidance *potentials* are functions of the distance from each goal (which in this case lie in two-dimensional space).

this term is borrowed from physics; let us take a moment to establish the connections.

A good starting point is to think of a goal attracting a person in analogy with a massive body attracting another body of negligible mass. In this case we might try to model the attraction in terms of a single number that applies at a given point in the space (i.e., for a given distance between them and with given coordinates). Because this number will vary over the space, it yields a so-called scalar (i.e., specified by a single number) field. For instance, if the space in which the person and goal, or two objects lie, is a plane, then the scalar field is a two-dimensional surface. An example is shown in Figure 5.3. Under certain conditions, this surface is a so-called "potential," and the partial derivatives with regard to the coordinates are the components of force of attraction, with regard to the x and y axes. Thus, from a single function, the potential, one can immediately obtain the relevant force quantities. Let $P=$ potential, then the partial derivative of P with respect to x or y respectively gives the forces along those coordinates. Further, we may gather these components into a vector, which we call the "gradient," $G = \text{grad } P = (\frac{\partial P}{\partial x}, \frac{\partial P}{\partial y})$.

It then follows from the differential calculus that a small change in the potential as we move a small distance in the space, is given us by the dot product (i.e., inner product) of this vector and the vector of change of position in the space:

$dP = G.dr$, where $dr = (dx, dy)$, the vector of changes in x and y. That is,

$$dP = \frac{\partial P}{\partial x} dx + \frac{\partial P}{\partial y} dy.$$

In a single dimension, all that was ever considered before, the gradient is just the derivative of the potential and is also therefore equivalent to the force itself. The potential and the gradient have many uses in applied mathematics, even outside physics, especially with regard to optimization and asymptotic dynamic behavior. This is largely because the direction of the gradient vector is that of maximal change of the field or surface for any point on that field.

At this point we return to Miller's postulates for more mathematical interpretation. Postulates 1 and 2 imply that the slopes or derivatives of the gradients should be positive in the direction of the goal, and 3 means that the avoidance gradient increases faster than the approach gradient near the goal so that the aversive qualities become stronger, faster as one approaches the goal. Postulate 4 asserts that the entire gradient must rise monotonically with positive (e.g., hunger, power, sex) or negative (e.g., fear, hate, disgust) drives respectively. A special case would be to multiply the gradient by a positive number (> 1) for each increase in drive. Postulate 5 simply states that the gradients are affected by learning. Postulate 6 says that we may simply subtract the gradients at any point in time or space to learn what the person will do. In a multidimensional vector space, we can still subtract vectors. However, a point that is overlooked in Postulate 6 is that under the traditional interpretation of "gradient," it is, as mentioned earlier, defined by forces that are in turn defined by a second-order differential equation (i.e., it is proportional to acceleration, rather than velocity). Thus, even though the gradients may be equal at a particular point in space giving a resultant force of zero, the velocity may not be zero so in fact the person is still acting or moving in the real or psychological space. This will be illustrated mathematically later. Nevertheless, for many purposes, and especially in spaces with dimension greater than 1, it will suffice to employ first-order systems. This will be made clear in the following.

It may be helpful to review some basics of differential equations to start things off. Such a review is located in the Appendix.

LINEAR APPROACH-AVOIDANCE IN ONE DIMENSION

There is considerable value in working out the situation for a linear gradient in one dimension. For one thing, as noted earlier, Miller (1959) used it, at least in pictorial illustration. The linear case is readily understood and solvable, even in the second order case. It is useful pedagogically, particularly because we learn through it that linearity may always be natural for the approach-avoidance problem in general.

We first inspect the single-goal approach-avoidance situation where a person is both attracted and repulsed by a single goal or choice object. Thus, her/his choice is basically whether the positive aspects of the goal outweigh the negative aspects. However, the approach–avoidance theme immediately places us in the context of a continuum of response possibilities (e.g., how far toward the object shall the person go), rather than simply an all-or-none choice. We feel that this continuum of possibilities or tendencies is really more descriptive of a person's psychology than the more traditional all-or-none depiction. After that, we observe the basic linear dynamics in a two goal-object situation.

First we outline the mathematical situation which involves only a single goal-object. The following equations show the approach and avoidance gradients respectively. Let

$P(t) =$ Position of person at time t.

$G =$ Position of Goal

$a_0 =$ Value of positive approach gradient when $P = G$ (i.e., force when goal is reached)

$a_1 =$ Slope of approach gradient

$b_0 =$ Value of avoidance gradient when $P = G$.

$b_1 =$ Slope of avoidance gradient

$k_2 =$ Slow-down or effort coefficient

In order to best capture the spirit of the theories of Lewin, Hull, and Miller, all the above parameters, including G, should be nonnegative. $P(t)$, of course, can be positive or negative. Then the germane dynamic equations are

$$F^+(t) = \frac{d^2P(t)}{dt^2} = a_0 - a_1[G - P(t)] - \frac{k_2}{2} \frac{dP(t)}{dt}$$

$$F^-(t) = \frac{d^2P(t)}{dt^2} = -[b_0 - b_1[G - P(t)] + \frac{k_2}{2} \frac{dP(t)}{dt}]$$

Where F^+ and F^- are the forces (gradients) that would determine behavior if only the positive or negative influences respectively were present. Let us first analyze $[a_0 - a_1(G - P(t))]$ for F^+, the term $-[b_0 - b_1(G - P(t))]$ for F^- is comparable. Already we come upon some awkwardness of the linear approach. Note that the intercept, when $P(t) = 0$, is $a_0 - a_1G$ so it has to be a function of the coefficient a_0 as well as the position of the goal G. This is required so that F^+ can increase as P approaches G as stipulated in the postulates. The coefficient a_1 gives the slope of ascent. So if $a_0 - a_1G > 0$ as we ordinarily assume and if $P(0) = 0$ and $\frac{dP(0)}{dt} = 0$ indicating that the starting position and velocity are both zero, then the initial force and movement are toward G (neglecting F^- for the moment) and the positive force increases as P approaches G. When $P(t) > G$ as will eventually occur, F^+ becomes even larger and goes off to infinity. This is absurd, needless to say, so we must build in a threshold terminator or a much more complex mechanism so that the person stops on reaching the goal. (Thus, a nonlinearity intrudes in spite of the initial linearity.) But, such mechanisms are very common in the application of differential equations. We shall neglect the expression for that *goal-reached* stop function in this presentation.

However, we do want to include a term for slow-down (deceleration) that might be due to mental or physical effort and the pertinent one is $\dfrac{-k_2}{2}\dfrac{dP(t)}{dt}$, the velocity. For simplicity we assume it operates the same way in F^+ and F^-. Observe further that it opposes the direction of movement whatever it is when $k_2 > 0$. (That is, $\dfrac{-k_2}{2}\dfrac{dP(t)}{dt} < 0$ if velocity is forward and vice versa if $\dfrac{dP(t)}{dt} < 0$

The typical drawings of the gradients, as in Fig. 5.4 $\dfrac{dP(t)}{dt}$ for which we would require an additional coordinate. Because we assume $\dfrac{dP(t)}{dt} = 0$ at $t = 0$ the early behavior is determined primarily by $P(t)$, so this does not do any real harm. The major effect of $\dfrac{-k_2}{2}\dfrac{dP(t)}{dt}$, from our point of view is on behavior around a point of equality, when $F^+(t) = F^-(t)$ as we shall see shortly.

Note that the equations are in the second degree so that we are effectively talking about force (without the precisely defined units to which physics is privileged). Figure 5.4 schematizes the gradients. We do not lose any generality by assuming that the person starts at the origin as noted and moves toward or away from the goal, G. There are good a priori reasons as well as experimental evidence that the avoidance gradient should ordinarily be steeper than the approach gradient as postulated, $(a_1 < b_1$, see following discussion) but there might be pathological cases where this would not be true. The point of intersection of the two gradients will also depend on the environmental and psychological circumstances. The overall resultant force is determined by the sum of the positive and negative gradients, that is,

$$F = F^+ + F^- = (a_0 - b_0) - (b_1 - a_1)P(t) - (a_1 - b_1)G = k_0 - k_1 P(t);$$

$$k_0 = a_0 - b_0 - (a_1 - b_1)G; \; k_1 = b_1 - a_1$$

Obviously postulates 1, 2, and 3 are easily captured in our model. Postulates 4 and 5 are implemented by assuming that the intercept and or slope parameters a_0, a_1, and b_0, b_1 are increasing functions of drive and learning. Miller gives no guidance as to whether the intercept or slope or both should be affected by either drive or learning. If we look to Hull, drive and learning should multiply the entire gradient equation and therefore affect both. In any event it is clear we can embed sufficient structure in our model to incorporate all the postulates.

Now, assume $k_1 > 0$ and let $k_2 = 0$. That is, the avoidance slope is sharper

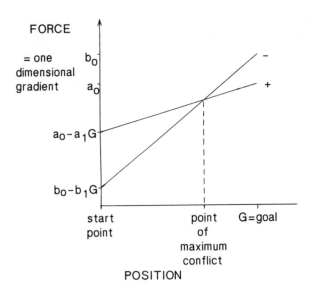

FIG. 5.4.   A typical single-goal approach–avoidance conflict situation where
the person is both attracted to and repelled by a single-goal. The (linear)
approach (+) and avoidance (−) gradients show, respectively, the forces
that would apply if only positive or negative influences were present. See
text for further discussion.

than that for approach and there is no slow-down due to effort. Using standard techniques, we find that the general solution to this case (e.g., see Luenberger, 1979) is

$$P(t) = \beta_1 \cos wt + \beta_2 \sin wt + \frac{k_0}{k_1} \text{ where } \beta_1 \text{ and } \beta_2 \text{ must be}$$

determined by the initial conditions and $w = \sqrt{k_1}$. Suppose that the initial velocity (i.e., the first derivative) is zero. Then the pertinent solution is

$$P(t) = \{\frac{k_0}{k_1}\} \; (1\text{-}\cos wt)$$

and we see that the person oscillates around the point of maximal conflict, that is, where the two gradients are equal. The frequency of oscillation is given by $\sqrt{k_1}$ and the amplitude by

$$\left| (k_0/k_1) \right| = \left| \frac{(a_0 - b_0) - (a_1 - b_1)G}{b_1 \quad - \quad a_1} \right|$$

If the amplitude exceeds the distance from the crossover point to the goal, then we would expect the person to absorb (i.e., choose, etc.) at the goal, presumably getting both the goodies as well as the baddies associated with the goal. Figure 5.5 illustrates the waveform of oscillation and below that, the point of oscillation, in the dimension of activity.

Now let $k_2 \neq 0$. The most intuitive version is with $k_2 > 0$, that is, a cost associated with "movement." We find that if $0 < k_2 < \sqrt{4k_1} = 2\sqrt{b_1 - a_1}$ then oscillation still results but the magnitude of this oscillation decreases to zero and ultimately the person goes to a point (k_0/k_1) at which $F^+ = F^-$ and stops. The solution in the latter case is given by

$$P(t) = \frac{k_0}{k_1} + c_0\, e^{\lambda_0 t} + c_1\, e^{\lambda_1 t}$$

where k_0 and k_1 are as above, and

$$\lambda_0 = \frac{-k_2 + \sqrt{k_2^2 - 4k_1}}{9}$$

$$\lambda_0 = \frac{-k_2 - \sqrt{k_2^2 - 4k_1}}{9}$$

Actually, the oscillations around (k_0/k_1) converge to zero in magnitude as t approaches infinity. Note that for $0 < (k_0/k_1) < G$, the point of equilibrium (k_0/k_1) lies between the start position and the goal.

The unusual case where the approach gradient is steeper than the avoidance gradient can be studied in the aforementioned model also. Miller (1959, p. 222) discussed this possibility. In addition to material not directly related to

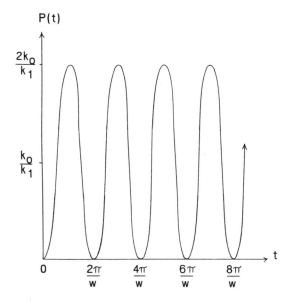

FIG. 5.5. The waveform of a person oscillating, over time, in space (psychological or physical) around the equilibrium point k_0/k_1

approach–avoidance, Miller went on to discuss matters of displacement of aggression and stimulus generalization. These are interesting and will be pursued elsewhere. Here we consider generalizations to two-goal situations and then some elementary approach–avoidance dynamics in higher dimension.

LINEAR DOUBLE APPROACH–AVOIDANCE IN ONE DIMENSION

Suppose a person faces the dilemma of two choice objects, each with its own positive and negative attributes. What does he/she do? This environment can be pictured as in Fig. 5.6 where the person starts at the origin again and on the right lies Goal 1 and on the left Goal 2. The prototypical case is shown there with the avoidance gradients being steeper than those for approach and with the approach gradient starting higher. Again ignoring the slow-down term governed by k_2 for simplicity, the two sets of resultant dynamic equations pertinent to the two goals G_1 and G_2 are

$$F_{G_1} = \frac{d^2P_1}{dt^2} = k_0 - k_1\,P(t)$$

where $k_0 = a_0 - b_0 + (b_1 - a_1)G_1$
$$k_1 = b_1 - a_1$$

and

$$F_{G_2} = \frac{d^2P_2}{dt^2} = l_0 - l_1\,P(t)$$

where $l_0 = c_0 - d_0 + (d_1 - c_1)G_2$
$$l_1 = d_1 - c_1$$

and the parameters in F_{G_2} function exactly analogously to their counterparts in F_{G_1}, but with respect to G_2, to the left of the start position. Overall then,

$$F = F_{G_1} + F_{G_2}$$
$$1 = (k_0 - l_0) - (k_1 - l_1)P(t)$$

and the several solutions are obtained in the same way as before. In particular the person will go to G_1, go to G_2 or end up at a point of positive and negative gradient equality in the event that the point of maximum conflict lies between G_1 and G_2, and if the excursion of any oscillation does not hit G_1 or G_2.

Thus, the range of qualitative behavior is like the single approach–avoidance case but the actual movements now depend on two rather than one goal and the related attractive and repulsive aspects of those two goals.

We next move to the two dimensional choice domain, that is, when the

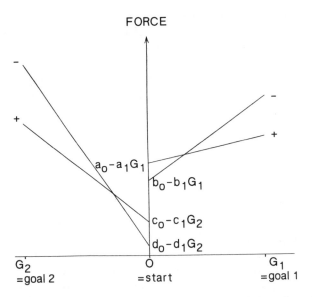

FORCE

$a_0 - a_1 G_1$

$b_0 - b_1 G_1$

$c_0 - c_1 G_2$

$d_0 - d_1 G_2$

G_2
=goal 2

O
=start

G_1
=goal 1

FIG. 5.6. An example of approach (+) and avoidance (−) gradients in a double-goal situation where each has both positive and negative attributes. As in the single-goal situation, the avoidance gradients are steeper than the approach gradients, and the approach gradients start higher.

choice space is the plane. At this point, the linear model becomes rather cumbrous so we elect to adopt a more general approach and then discuss some nonlinear special cases of interest.

MULTIDIMENSIONAL APPROACH–AVOIDANCE BEHAVIOR

We shall stay within the context of two dimensions, but the formalisms can clearly be immediately generalized to arbitrary finite dimensions. We require more structure now and therefore introduce the following new set of assumptions.

Assumptions for Multidimensional Approach–Avoidance

1. The vector representing approach toward a single goal should point directly toward that goal and a vector representing avoidance of a single goal should point directly away from that goal.

2. We define a potential that is a decreasing function of distance from a goal, $p(d)$.

3. We then extract a gradient from that potential by taking the partial derivatives of the potential with respect to the two dimensions, x and y; that is $\frac{\partial P}{\partial x}$ and $\frac{\partial P}{\partial y}$.

4. The gradient will then be a vector whose components represent the tendency toward or away from the goal on the two dimensions; that is $g(x,y) = (\frac{\partial P}{\partial x}, \frac{\partial P}{\partial y})$.

5. The length of the gradient vector gives the overall strength of approach or avoidance from the present location, P; that is if V= Valence or strength,

$$V = \sqrt{(\frac{\partial p}{\partial x})^2 + (\frac{\partial p}{\partial y})^2}$$

6.* The length (magnitude) of the gradient vector is a decreasing function of distance from the goal.

7. "Approach" in a given environment and person is defined by a family of gradients that point toward a goal and "Avoidance" is another family of functions that point away from the goal. To avoid triviality, we assume that motivational circumstances range from the case where approach always dominates, where avoidance always dominates, and where they cross. Where they cross corresponds as usual to a point of maximum conflict. The total gradient is given by the sum of the constituent gradients.

In most circumstances these assumptions will be sufficient to guarantee that there exists a point of equality of approach and avoidance for a single goal, and along a single line connecting the present location to the goal, and without consideration of other goals, that such a point be unique. This usually follows from the fact that the numerical difference of the approach and avoidance gradients will be an increasing function of distance. This function would go from a negative quantity through zero (the point of maximum conflict) on to positive quantities as distance increases from zero to large values.

Assumption 1, besides seeming psychologically reasonable, avoids messy mathematical expressions and certain complicated and mystifying behavior. For instance, cases might arise where approach equals avoidance on the two dimensions at different distances, which generally precludes a cross-over of the gradients and thus a point of maximum conflict.

The second assumption links up the present development with classical physics and says how the potential, which stands for a sort of primitive striving (akin to m/d, the attractive potential between two objects in physics, where m = product of the two masses and d = distance) toward or away from a goal. The following assumption states that we can find the components of striving on each dimension by taking the derivative of the potential with regard to each dimension. The next, number 4, simply puts the result into vector form and defines it as the gradient. The fifth assumption defines an overall valence as the magnitude (or length) of the gradient vector whereas the sixth requires that it, too, be a decreasing function of distance. The latter condition is not implied by Assumption 2, as can be seen by its expression.

Assumption 6 is starred(*) because it seems more optional. In a sense, Assumption 6 demands that the actual "movement" increase in velocity as one approaches the goal. To the extent that motor control in physical motion is ignored, this might make sense (and occurred in the one-dimensional pure approach situations discussed earlier in the linear systems examples). Otherwise, it is acceptable to permit the velocity (or force) to go to zero as one gets very close to the goal, as would happen in a smooth dynamical system acting in real time and space. Note that the more primitive notion of a gradient that increases as one approaches the goal, can be preserved even when the organism slows down in approaching it.

Interestingly, it turns out to be a little tricky to come up with a class of functions obeying all seven assumptions. Let the goal G be at the origin $G=0$. Later examples flout Assumption 6, but a two-dimensional family of functions that *will* satisfy all seven is given by the system of differential equations,

$$\frac{dx}{dt} = \frac{-axe^{b(x^2+y^2)^{-1}}}{(x^2+y^2)^2},$$

$$\frac{dy}{dt} = \frac{-aye^{b(x^2+y^2)^{-1}}}{(x^2+y^2)^2}, \text{ where } b > 0.$$

Composing this system into a velocity vector we can then write

$$g(x,y) = \frac{-a\,e^{b(x^2+y^2)^{-1}}}{(x^2+y^2)^2}\,(x,y) = F(D)\,(x,y), \text{ with } F(D) \text{ a decreasing function}$$

of distance D and (x,y) the current position vector. The vector $g(x,y)$:

1. Points directly toward ($a > 0$) or away ($a < 0$) from the goal $G=(0,0)$.

2. Comes from a potential $p(D) = \frac{a}{2b}\exp(b/D)$—where D equals x^2+y^2, that is, the euclidean distance squared, from the goal. This function $p(D)$ is a decreasing function of distance from the goal.

3. If we write a single approach–avoidance conflict situation as

$$g_{ap}(x,y) - g_{av}(x,y) = \left\{\frac{-a\,e^{b(x^2+y^2)^{-1}}}{(x^2+y^2)^2} + \frac{ce^{d(x^2+y^2)^{-1}}}{(x^2+y^2)^2}\right\}(x,y)$$

where $c > a$ and $d > b$, then there exists a unique set of points of maximum conflict where approach tendency equals avoidance tendency, approach dominates beyond that point and avoidance dominates when the organism is closer to the goal than that point. These points all satisfy $x^2+y^2 = -\{1/(d-b)\}\cdot\log(a/c)$.

4. The magnitude of the gradient as well is a decreasing function of distance from the goal.

We next use a less complex gradient that satisfies all the stipulations except number 6 and in several special cases, even that one. Consider the potential $p = a/(x^2 + y^2 + b)$. By differentiation, we then get the gradient $(dx/dt, dy/dt) = (-2ax/(x^2 + y^2 + b)^2, -2ay/(x^2 + y^2 + b)^2)$ where we can immediately absorb the "2" into the constant "a". The magnitude (length) of gradient vector is not monotonic decreasing in $\sqrt{D} = \sqrt{x^2 + y^2}$ unless $b = 0$, violating Assumption 6, but we need the b when approach–avoidance conflict is present in order to produce a cross-over of the positive and negative gradients. A separate potential is used to construct approach and avoidance gradients. The approach and avoidance gradients are added to produce the net gradient

$$\left(\frac{-ax}{(x^2 + y^2 + b)^2} + \frac{cx}{(x^2 + y^2 + d)^2} \cdot \frac{-ay}{(x^2 + y^2 + b)^2} + \frac{cy}{(x^2 + y^2 + d)^2} \right).$$

The first example is of a single goal approach–avoidance situation. As in the other two-dimensional models, we let the single goal be placed at the origin $G = (0,0)$. Figure 5.7a shows the way in which the gradient vectors point at different locations of the display. (The longer arrows will be discussed later.) It can be seen that they all point toward or away from the goal (0,0) as they should. Figure 5.7a is known as a direction field because it gives the direction of the gradients but not their magnitude. If that were also shown, in the present case, they would increase in length as the origin is approached from far away in the display but peak and then drop toward zero length close to the goal. This nonmonotonicity is because of violation of Assumption 6; if that were satisfied, then the vectors would increase in magnitude all the way to the goal.

Also shown in Fig. 5.7a are several "phase portraits" (plots) indicating the paths taken from various starting points. "Phase portrait" is simply a conventional name of a picture of the trajectory (or path) that the dynamic body (in our case, a person) takes through the space. The word "phase" has no particular relevance for us in the present context. Note that the trajectories line up with sets of direction vectors and that time is implicit and invisible. Also note that a set of equilibrium points surrounds the goal at points of maximum conflict. Close to the goal, avoidance dominates and the organism moves toward the circle of equilibrium points. On the other side of the circle, approach dominates and the organism is predicted to move toward it. Because velocity is continuous and goes to zero at the set of equilibrium points, that set is never actually met in finite time, only approached. Such an approach is depicted in Fig. 5.7b where we watch coordinate x approach the particular equilibrium point to which it is attracted, as a function of time and from two approach and two avoidance starting values.

We next go to a double goal approach–avoidance environment. Here it suffices to use the two goals $G1 = (0,0)$ and $G2 = (A,0)$. No loss of generality is entailed by letting both y goal components be 0. We may illustrate the dynamics with a model also obeying Assumption 6 by setting the b-parameter

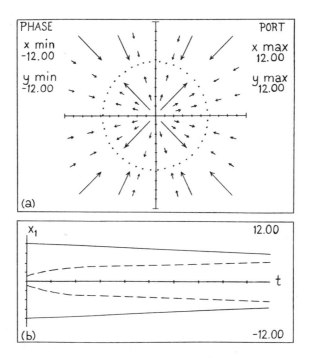

FIG. 5.7.   (a) Direction field and several phase portraits, corresponding to different starting points, of a single goal approach–avoidance situation. The dotted circle represents a set of equilibrium points. (b) A plot of the position x_1 as a function of time. The solid lines are examples of starting points greater than the equilibrium points and thus x_1 is "approaching" the goal, whereas the dashed lines are for starting points close to the goal—inside the circle— so these are "avoiding" the goal.

equal to zero. Also let $a = 1$ for simplicity. Now the gradient of approach toward $G1$ is $g_1(x,y) = (\dfrac{-x}{(x^2 + y^2)^2}, \dfrac{-y}{(x^2 + y^2)^2})$, and that of approach toward $G2$ is $g_2(x,y) = (\dfrac{-(x - A)}{((x-A)^2 + y^2)^2}, \dfrac{-y}{((x-A)^2 + y^2)^2})$. The overall gradient is found by adding the two:

$$g = g_1 + g_2 = (\dfrac{-x}{(x^2 + y^2)^2} - \dfrac{(x-A)}{((x-A)^2 + y^2)^2}, \dfrac{-y}{(x^2 + y^2)^2} + \dfrac{y}{((x-A)^2 + y^2)^2}).$$

The gradient vector field appears in Fig. 5.8 and now it can be seen that the vectors often point in directions intermediate between the two goals. However, the closer the organism is to one of the goals, or if one lies entirely to the right or left of both goals, the more directly the vector points toward the nearest one. Several phase plots are given in Fig. 5.8 and the geometric fact that the direction field vectors are tangent to a phase portrait solution becomes obvious; (Fig. 5.7a is a special case where any solution is a straight

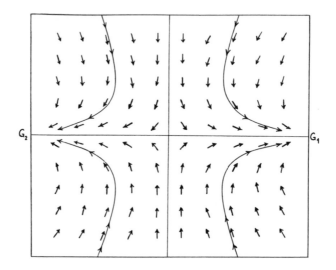

FIG. 5.8.   Gradient vector field (short arrows) and several phase plots (long arrows) approach–approach situation.

line so that all tangents lie exactly on it). Yet another feature of Fig. 5.8 is the line through the graph, separating the qualitative types of activity; it is known for this reason as a"separatrix." That line happens to coincide with the y-axis with this illustration, but in general would not. If a person were to start exactly on this line, he would never move, but rather like a pendulum balanced at the top of its swing over its pivot, any slight perturbation would cause immediate movement toward the strongest attracting goal.

The final example is a double avoidance–avoidance situation in which both goals are aversive, with no redeeming aspects. The qualitative theory of Lewin suggests that given the chance, the person will attempt to escape the area close to the aversive objects mentally or physically, as the case may be. We shall see that exactly this is predicted by our mathematical dynamics. The appropriate gradient is given by the equations for the approach–approach case but with the signs of the vector components all reversed. Figure 5.9 illustrates the direction field and some phase plots.

Observe that the vectors generally point away from the negative goals and suggest that a person will leave the field proximal to these goals. The phase portrait paths superimposed on the direction field confirm this suspicion. It is interesting that when the person is on the line joining $G1$ and $G2$, she cannot escape and must either come to rest at the best possible distance from both (as in the present case) or oscillate forever between them. This set of points is unstable, for any tiny displacement off of this line will propel the organism out of the immediate field.

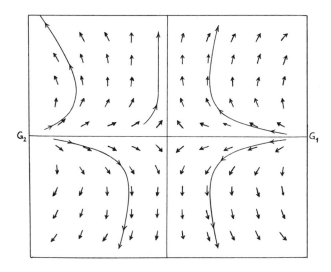

FIG. 5.9. Gradient vector field and several phase plots of a double-goal avoidance–avoidance conflict situation.

Related Theories

Two theories that use dynamic models to describe decision and choice are Atkinson and Birch's (1970) "dynamics of action" theory and Grossberg's (1978, 1980) competive systems theory. Both theories describe the dynamics of choice behavior by systems of differential equations. What is unique about the present work is the inclusion of the goal gradient hypothesis into the dynamics—the idea that intensity of motivation is a function of the distance from the goal. Although this idea could be built into the previous two models through attentional mechanisms or other means, this was not explicitly considered, and the present chapter appears to provide the first formal treatment.

Aside from the goal gradient structure the present theory does not fit readily into the competitive system framework (Grossberg, 1978, 1980). One reason is that the latter views each unit as an entity that competes through dynamic coupling with the other unit. This produces a system of differential equations in the various units. In our system, by way of contrast, the gradients sum for an arbitrary position on the part of a single "unit." This results in a single differential equation driving the dynamic behavior of the "Unit" (read person or decision mechanism). Atkinson and Birch (1970) also treat their "action tendencies" as separate entities that get integrated before comparison.

Nevertheless, one way to try to place an approach like ours into such a competitive system framework might be the following. Consider the double goal problem on a line, with a starting position at $P(0) = 0$, and the goals located at $-G$ and G. The attractiveness of each alternative at any point in time can be represented by the variables $x_1(t) = P(t)/G$ and $x_2(t) = -P(t)/G$, where $P(t)$ is the position at time t. According to Grossberg (1980, p. 382) this two alternative system is a competitive system if $\frac{\partial}{\partial x_2} \frac{dx_1}{dt} < 0$, and $\frac{\partial}{\partial x_1} \frac{dx_2}{dt} < 0$. According to our one dimensional double goal model $F = k_0 - k_1 \bullet P(t)$ and $k_1 > 0$. If it is assumed that $F = \frac{dP(t)}{dt} = \frac{G}{dt}\frac{dx_1(t)}{dt}$, then $\frac{\partial}{\partial x_2} \frac{d}{dx} x_1(t) = k > 0$, which fails to satisfy the competitive property.

More recently, Grossberg and Gutowski (1987) proposed a rather different dynamic model of risky decision making called affective balance theory. There are two major differences between our approach–avoidance theory and affective balance theory. First the latter does not incorporate the goal gradient hypothesis. Second, according to approach–avoidance theory, the competing forces produced by each alternative are processed in parallel and combined at each moment in time, but according to affective balance theory, the alternatives are processed sequentially. The forces for the first alternative are integrated over time, and the integrated value is compared to the value of the second alternative. Among other consequences this leads to different predictions concerning decision time.

WHITHER-TO NEXT?

There are many directions worth following up along the lines initiated earlier. Some of these are listed here.

1. Most experiments directly pertinent to the tenets of this theory have been done with rats. It is important to expand the studies to the human domain and specifically to be able to use negatively valenced goals that are in truth aversive to the subject, yet are harmless.

2. Among a number of particular domains of application in the social sciences, a natural and compelling one is risky decision making; that is, decision making when outcomes are uncertain and may be associated with various consequences. This has been a region of high priority in utility theory. We suggest that dynamic approach–avoidance theory can make a contribution here (cf. Townsend & Busemeyer, 1987).

3. In addition to refining and testing the theory in more numerically oriented ways with new data, it is of interest to generalize the ideas with mathematical structure not limited to euclidean vector spaces or even orthogonal coordinate spaces. Thus, investigations into manifold theory would seem appropriate (e.g., see Irwin, 1980) as would topological dynamics based on continuity and the notion of a metric but sans differentiability (e.g., see Sibirsky,

1975). Possibly less dramatic but of high importance would be the implementation of the qualitative theory of differential equations, particularly general notions of stability and limit cycles.

4. Related to (3) yet critical in its own right, is the investigation of probabilistic (read stochastic) versions of the theory. Although this must be undertaken in the near future, we believe that the deterministic theory should be developed first or at least in parallel with the stochastic theory. We suspect that something deterministic lies at the bottom of the behavior, a skeleton as it were, that is fleshed out by stochastic properties. Different versions of the stochastics can yield vastly different types of behavior, though the underlying skeleton is the same. Psychologists rarely have much to go on in deciding what stochastic structure should apply in any given milieu. Alternatively, the stochastic appearance of much human behavior could be due to deterministic, but chaotic underpinnings (see, e.g., Devaney, 1986).

5. It may be that approach–avoidance theory has something to offer practical decision making theorizing. Although utility theory and statistical decision making can represent negative vs positive gains, it may be that the emotional and motivational aspects of many, if not most, important decisions can best be captured by our type of theory. Certainly the time-dynamic character would seem valuable in accurately describing real-life decision behavior. Close in conception would be the application of these ideas in robotology and artificial intelligence, especially in situations where a mimicking of human motivational properties is desired. This in turn could help to link up goal-directed behavior in computers or robots with the burgeoning field of neural modeling and neural computation.

ACKNOWLEDGMENTS

The authors thank National Science Foundation, Memory and Cognitive Processes for support of this project under Grants #BNS 8319377 (Townsend) and BNS #8710103 (Busemeyer).

The authors also thank Helena Kadlec for her help with the figures and Kilsoon Cumings for her "creative" typing.

APPENDIX
ASPECTS OF DIFFERENTIAL EQUATIONS

Order of a Differential Equation

A differential equation describes the dynamics of a body (object, idea, etc.) by way of its derivatives. We may metaphorically think, in our case, of the first derivative as being "like" a velocity, the second as being like an acceleration and so-on. The "order" of a differential equation is the highest derivative appearing in the equation. An example of a second-order differential equation is

$$\frac{d^2x}{dt^2} = (\sin x)\, t^2 = +2 \tag{1}$$

The independent variable is time $= t$ and the dependent variable is x, usually a position in some one-dimensional space (e.g., taken with respect to a goal in our situation).

Linear versus Nonlinear Differential Equations

A "linear differential equation" is one where all of the terms are linear combinations of the dependent variable and its derivatives, possibly plus a term not involving the dependent variable. The coefficients of these dependent variable terms can in general be functions of the independent variable, as can the extra term that does not involve the dependent variable. An example of a second order linear differential equation is

$$t^3 \frac{d^2x}{dt^2} = t\, \frac{3dx}{dt} + \text{Log } t + 1 = 0. \tag{2}$$

Note that it is okay for the equation to possess nonlinear functions of the independent variable. It follows from the aforementioned that a nonlinear differential equation must have at least one nonlinear function of the dependent variable or one or more of its derivatives. Two examples are the following:

$$\{\frac{d^2x}{dt^2}\}^2 = 5\sqrt{t} \tag{3a}$$

$$6\frac{dx}{dt} - Log(x) = 0 \tag{3b}$$

In the first, the second derivative is squared, a nonlinear operation and in the second, one finds $Log(x)$, also a nonlinear operation. Equation 1 from earlier, is also nonlinear because $\sin(x)$ is nonlinear in x.

Homogeneous versus Nonhomogeneous Differential Equations

A "homogeneous differential equation" is one where terms not involving the dependent variable are absent. Equivalently, terms involving only the independent variable or constants are lacking. If it is present, then we have a "nonhomogeneous differential equation." This extra term is usually thought of as a forcing function that serves as an input to the system; that is, it "drives" the system. Thus, in contrast, a homogeneous differential equation describes a system whose entire behavior from a particular point in time is determined by where it starts and the initial values of certain of its derivatives. A nonhomogeneous system must in general include influences both from the forcing function as well as initial values. An example of a homogeneous differential equation is that of Equation 3b. Equation 1 has a forcing function given by the number "2" and Equation 3a by $5\sqrt{t}$ so both of these are nonhomogeneous. (How about Equation 2?).

The behavior of a linear system (i.e., a system defined by linear differential equations) can always be determined by adding the solution for the general homogeneous equation to a particular solution obtained with the forcing function present, but with all pertinent initial values set to zero.

Transient versus Asymptotic Behavior

We can also ask about the short term behavior of a system as well as how it acts as the duration under observation increases without limit. We may point out that while an elegant general theory of linear systems exists that perfectly describes both transient and asymptotic behavior, the only reasonably general theory that applies to large classes of nonlinear systems pertains to asymptotic behavior. Further, suitably defined "stable" linear systems have the property that the equation describing their behavior can be decomposed into a set of transient terms (i.e., terms that die out, that is go to zero) plus a set of asymptotic terms (i.e., give the position to which the system converges).

Systems of Differential Equations

When there is more than a single output of a system, or it is operating in a multidimensinoal space, as in our more general cases, a set of differential equations is needed. For instance, in the plane, we would ordinarily see a system of two differential equations, which may be generally written as

$$\frac{d^2x}{dt^2} = f(x,y,\frac{dx}{dt},\frac{dy}{dt},t), \quad \frac{d^2y}{dt^2} = g(x,y,\frac{dx}{dt},\frac{dy}{dt},t) \tag{4}$$

when we have a second order system.

A general first order two-dimensional system would be written,

$$\frac{dx}{dt} = f(x,y,t), \quad \frac{dy}{dt} = g(x,y,t) \tag{5}$$

Observe that f and g may in general be nonlinear and nonhomogeneous.

REFERENCES

Allais, M. (1953). Le comportement de l'homme rationnel devant le risque: Critique des postulats et exiomes de l'ecole americaine. *Econometrica, 21,* 503–546.

Atkinson, J. W., & Birch, D. (1970). *The dynamics of actions.* New York: Wiley.

Bandura, A. (in press). Perceived self-efficacy: Exercise of control through self-belief. In J. P. Dauwalder, V. Hobbi & M. Perez (Eds.), *Annual series of European research in behavior therapy* (Vol. 2). Lisse (NL): Swets & Zeitlinger.

Boring, E. G. (1957). *A history of experimental psychology.* New York: Appleton-Century-Crofts.

Coombs, C., & Avrunin, G. S. (1977). Single peaked functions and the theory of preference. *Psychological Review, 84,* 216–230.

Devaney, R. L. (1986). *An Introduction to Chaotic Dynamical Systems.* Menlo Park, CA: Benjamin/Cummings.

Dollard, J., & Miller, N. E. (1950). *Personality and psychotherapy: An analysis in terms of learning, thinking, and culture.* New York: McGraw-Hill.

Ellsberg, D. (1961). Risk, ambiguity, and the Savage axioms. *Quarterly Journal of Economics, 75,* 643–669.

Estes, W. K. (1954). Kurt Lewin. In Estes, Koch, MacCorquodale, Meehl, Mueller, Schoenfeld, & Verplanck (Contributors and Editors). *Modern learning theory,* (pp. 317–344). New York: Appleton-Century-Crofts.

Fishburn, P. C. (1986). *The foundations of expected utility theory.* Volume 31, Theory and Decision Library. Holland: Dordrecht.

Green, D. M., & Swets, J. A. (1966). *Signal detection theory and psychophysics.* New York: Wiley.

Grossberg, S. (1978). Competition, decision, and concensus. *Journal of Mathematical Analysis and Applications, 66,* 470–493.

Grossberg, S. (1980). Biological competition: Decision rules, pattern formation, and oscillations. *Proceedings of the National Academy of Sciences, 77,* 2338–2342.

Grossberg, S., & Gutowski, W. (1987). Neural dynamics of decision making under risk: Affective balance and cognitive-emotional interactions. *Psychological Review, 94,* 300–318.

Hilgard, E. (1956). *Theories of learning.* New York: Appleton-Century-Crofts.

Hull, C. L. (1938). The goal gradient hypothesis applied to some "field force" problems in the behavior of young children. *Psychological Review, 45,* 271–299.

Irwin, M. C. (1980). *Smooth dynamical systems.* New York: Academic Press.

Johnson, E. J., & Payne, J. W. (1985). Effort and accuracy in choice. *Management Science, 31,* 394–414.

Kahneman, D., & Tversky, A. (1979). Prospect theory: An analysis of decision under risk. *Econometrica, 47,* 263–291.

Koch, S. (1954). Clark L. Hull. In Estes, Koch, MacCorquodale, Meehl, Mueller, Schoenfeld, & Verplanck (Contributors and Editors), *Modern learning theory* (pp. 1–176). New York: Appleton-Century-Crofts.

Köhler, W., & Held, R. (1949). The cortical correlate of pattern vision. *Science, 110,* 414–419.

Lewin, K. (1935). *A dynamic theory of personality.* New York: McGraw-Hill.

Lewin, K. (1936). *Principles of topological psychology.* New York: McGraw-Hill.

Luce, R. D., & Narens, L. (1985). Classification of concatenation measurement structures according to scale type. *Journal of Mathematical Psychology, 29,* 1–72.

Luenberger, D. G. (1979). *Introduction to dynamic systems.* New York: Wiley.

Miller, N. E. (1959). Liberalization of basic S-R concepts: Extensions to conflict behavior, motivation and social learning. In S. Koch (Ed.), *Psychology: A study of a science,* Vol. II. New York: McGraw-Hill.

Roitblat, H. L., Bever, T. C., & Terrace, H. S. (Eds.). (1984). *Animal cognition.* Hillsdale, NJ: Lawrence Erlbaum Associates.

Sibirsky, K. S. (1975). *Introduction to topological dynamics.* (L. F. Boron, Trans.) Leyden: Noordhoff.

Townsend, J. T., & Busemeyer, J. R. (1987, August). *Some initial inferences from an approach–avoidance model to risky decision making.* Paper presented at the Twentieth Annual Meeting of the Mathematical Psychology Society, Berkeley, CA.

Tversky, A., & Kahneman, D. (1981). The framing of decisions and the psychology of choice. *Science, 211,* 453–458.

6

How Many Memory Systems Are There Really?: Some Evidence From the Picture Fragment Completion Task

Joan Gay Snodgrass
New York University

MULTIPLE MEMORY SYSTEMS

In 1984, Endel Tulving, in a Distinguished Scientific Contribution Award address presented at the meeting of the American Psychological Association, asked the question: "How many memory systems are there?" (Tulving, 1985). In answer to this question, he proposed a three-tiered system, arranged much like a wedding cake, in what he called a monohierarchical arrangement. The bottom layer, common to both the remaining two, he called "procedural memory"; the second layer, a specialized subsystem of the first, he called "semantic memory"; and the top layer, a specialized subsystem of the second, he called "episodic memory."

The episodic and semantic systems had been introduced more than 10 years previously (Tulving, 1972), and all three systems were outlined in his 1983 book *Elements of Episodic Memory*. What was new in his address was a clarification and modification of the relationships among the three systems, and of acceptable evidential bases for their existence, prompted in part by a series of published discussions in *Behavioral and Brain Sciences* (Baddeley, 1984; Roediger, 1984; Tulving, 1984). Figure 6.1 show these three systems, along with descriptions and examples of each level.

Procedural memory is memory for perceptual, motor, and cognitive skills. Procedural memory, according to Tulving, is not declarative in nature but rather is acquired and demonstrated by doing. For example, typing is a procedure or skill in which expertise is demonstrated by doing, not by describing. We do not care if a typist cannot describe where on the keyboard the "r" is located as long as his performance in typing demonstrates that he "knows" where it is. Semantic memory is encyclopedic knowledge about the

TULVING'S TRIPARTITE SYSTEM

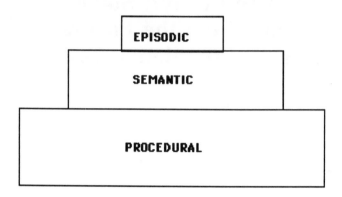

PROCEDURAL   "knowing how"

perceptual, motor, or cognitive skills

e.g., typing, reading graphs, computer programming, picture recognition

experimental: -- nonspecific practice effects on cognitive and motor tasks.

SEMANTIC "knowing that" (implicit memory)

general knowledge shared by a culture

e.g., knowledge about word meanings, and picture names

experimental -- item specific practice effects on cognitive tasks

EPISODIC "remembering that" (explicit memory)

autobiographical knowledge about self-referenced events

e.g., knowledge about occurrences of particular words and pictures

experimental -- recognition and recall memory for words and pictures

FIG. 6.1. Tulving's (1985) proposal for multiple memory systems.

world that need not be associated with autobiographical time and place of acquisition to be expressed, and is usually expressed by descriptions. Our typist's knowledge that the "r" on the keyboard is the third key from the left on the upper row is an example of semantic memory. Finally, episodic memory is knowledge about the occurrence of events that are tied to the rememberer's past and thus are autobiographical. The knowledge on the part of our typist that he typed a letter to ABC company yesterday or that he typed the word "representation" three times in the last paragraph are examples of episodic knowledge.

One test of a classification system is that people agree about the proper assignment of a task to a memory system (independent of whether people agree that the ternary classification actually represents different systems). There is general agreement among students of memory about which tasks represent episodic memory. These are all tasks in which subjects must access conscious awareness about an item's prior occurrence, and include recall, cued recall, and recognition tasks. These tasks have been described as explicit memory tasks by Graf and Schacter (1985). There is less agreement, however, about whether a particular task should be assigned to procedural or semantic memory.

Procedural memory tasks include generalized practice effects on a task as exhibited in improved performance (lower error rates or faster times) on novel or nonrepeated items. These include mirror reading of new triads of words (Cohen & Squire, 1980), which is described as "knowing how" by these investigators; reading of transformed text (Kolers, 1976); improvement in picture naming times (Mitchell & Brown, 1988); and picture fragment completion on new items after practice with a prior set (Snodgrass, Smith, Feenan, & Corwin, 1987). In addition, Cohen (1984) described improvement on the Tower of Hanoi puzzle as a procedural learning effect.

Semantic memory tasks include priming effects on perceptual tasks such as tachistoscopic identification (Jacoby & Dallas, 1981) and spelling (Jacoby & Witherspoon, 1982); word and picture fragment completion on repeated items (Warrington & Weiskrantz, 1968); mirror reading of repeated items (Cohen & Squire, 1980), described as "knowing that" by these investigators; improvement in reading transformed text with repeated sentences (Kolers, 1976); and repetition priming effects in lexical decision (Scarborough, Cortese, & Scarborough, 1977; Scarborough, Gerard, & Cortese, 1979).

Episodic memory tasks include recall or recognition tests that examine a learner's knowledge about when and where he encountered a particular stimulus. Specific examples are recognition memory for primed words that have also been presented for perceptual identification (Jacoby & Dallas, 1981; Tulving, Schacter, & Stark, 1982), or recall of when the Tower of Hanoi puzzle was last presented or whether the subject has ever encountered it before (Cohen, 1984).

Although there seems to be some disagreement in the literature about whether a particular task falls in one category or another, this classification scheme seems sufficiently comprehensive so that virtually any task calling on previous experience can be classified into one of the three categories.

We next turn to the question of how we can decide whether these systems are truly independent in the sense that a lower system can operate independently of a higher system (so the procedural system can subserve one task while both the procedural and semantic systems can subserve a second task).

Figure 6.2 presents the two patterns of empirical evidence that Tulving proposed can be used as support for these systems. The first pattern, which he

Sources of evidence for different memory systems

I. FUNCTIONAL INDEPENDENCE (Experimental)

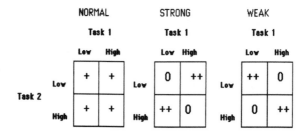

II. STOCHASTIC INDEPENDENCE (Correlational)

(by subjects, items, or subjects & items)

FIG. 6.2.   Patterns of functional and stochastic dissociation.

termed "functional independence" and which has sometimes been referred to as experimental dissociation, refers to the effects of independent variables on two tasks that are claimed to tap two different memory systems.

Single dissociation refers to the differential effect of one independent variable on each of the two tasks, and double dissociation refers to the differential effect of two independent variables on each of two tasks. There are three levels of dissociation associated with each of the single and double dissociation patterns. Normal dissociation, the most commonly proposed (and observed), is one in which one independent variable has an effect on Task 1 (indicated by a +) and no effect on Task 2 (indicated by a 0). In strong dissociation, the same independent variable has an effect in one direction on Task 1 and an effect in the opposite direction on Task 2. In weak dissociation, the same independent variable has effects on both tasks, in the same direction, but the effect is stronger in one (+ +) than in the other (+). The corresponding effects for double dissociation are also shown in Fig. 6.2. The experimental variable can be an experimenter-defined manipulation, such as depth-of-processing, modality of presentation, or number of presentations, or a subject-defined variable such as amnesic versus normal performance.

The second type of pattern is called stochastic independence. Here, we look at the relationship between performance on Task 1 and Task 2 with subjects as the unit of analysis (subject correlation), with items as the unit of analysis (item correlation), or with subject-items as the unit of analysis (subject and item correlation).

Again, these correlational patterns can occur in three levels, with normal dissociation showing no correlation, strong dissociation showing a negative correlation, and weak dissociation showing a positive correlation. For subjects, zero correlation between Task 1 and Task 2 means that subjects who do well on Task 1 do neither well nor poorly on Task 2 and vice versa. Thus, performance on the tasks by subjects is normally dissociated. When the correlation is negative, subjects who do well on Task 1 do poorly on Task 2 and vice versa, so subject performance is strongly dissociated. Finally, when the correlation is positive, subjects' performance is not dissociated between the two tasks. Similar patterns can occur for items, and for subject-items. Tulving (1985) also showed that the same set of data can produce different patterns of correlations across the three units of analysis.

Most experimental reports of dissociation have focussed on functional dissociation and/or stochastic dissociation with subject-items as the units of analysis. For example, Tulving et al. (1982) primed subjects with words, and then measured their performance on the two tasks of word fragment completion and yes/no recognition. Functional dissociation was found between delay interval and performance. Word fragment completion showed no decline in performance across a 1-week interval, whereas recognition memory declined sharply. Stochastic dissociation at the level of subject-items was also observed. Words that were successfully completed in word fragment completion were not recognized more successfully than uncompleted words, and vice versa.

Mitchell and Brown (1988) studied repetition priming effects in picture naming. They, like Tulving et al. (1982), found single normal functional dissociation for delay interval, in that facilitation in picture naming of repeated pictures showed no decrease across a 6-week interval, whereas recognition memory showed the expected decrease. They also found stochastic independence between naming latencies and recognition memory at the level of subject-items, in that correctly recognized pictures showed no more priming effects than incorrectly recognized pictures.

HISTORY OF THE PICTURE FRAGMENT
COMPLETION TASK

The picture fragment completion task is one of several tasks testing what Graf and Schacter (1985; Schacter, 1987) termed implicit memory. Implicit memory is tested by procedures that do not demand conscious recollection of the prior event whose memory is being tested. Thus, implicit memory for items previously experienced in the picture fragment completion test is exhibited by increased facility in recognizing repeated pictures. That this facilitation can occur without conscious recollection of the prior experience of identifying such pictures is testified by the many reports of patients suffering from organic amnesia who, although denying ever having seen the pictures before, nonetheless show savings on repeated items (Corkin, 1982; Schneider, 1912; Warrington & Weiskrantz, 1968). It is, of course, desirable to ensure that this type of facilitation is not attributable to some generalized practice effect on the task itself; thus, it is desirable to include among the repeated pictures some new (never-before-encountered) items to test for task practice effects.

Training on the prior items can consist of merely presenting the complete pictures and asking subjects to name them, or can consist of actual practice in identifying the items in their fragmented states. Both words and pictures have been used as stimuli in fragment completion tasks. The manner in which stimuli are rendered incomplete varies widely, particularly when words are used as stimuli. For example, words may be fragmented (Warrington & Weiskrantz, 1968), presented with only a stem (Graf, Squire, & Mandler, 1984), presented with several letters missing but with only a single completion (Tulving et al., 1982), presented tachistoscopically (Jacoby & Dallas, 1981), or masked (Marcel, 1983).

There are fewer ways of rendering pictures incomplete. Although it is always possible to present pictures tachistoscopically, presenting incomplete pictures is more problematic. Because the components of a picture are less well-defined than those of a word (which have usually been assumed to be the word's component letters), it is necessary to have a theory of picture recognition in order to systematically delete component parts (e.g., Biederman, 1985, 1987). The pictures used by Schneider (1912) to study implicit learning in Korsakoff amnesics were rendered incomplete by subpart deletion, although more recent stimulus sets (Gollin, 1960; Snodgrass et al., 1987; Vokey, Baker, Hayman, & Jacoby, 1986) have usually been constructed by random or quasi-random deletion of picture segments.

There are a number of methods that can be used to produce and test learning effects in picture fragment identification. As we shall see, the particular training procedure used has a profound effect on learning. It is also undoubtedly true that the testing procedure (or more importantly, the similarity between the testing and training procedure) also has a large effect on the magnitude of learning observed. In the next few sections I review the relatively brief literature on the picture fragment completion task, and discuss its relevance to both subject defined and experimentally manipulated variables.

Schneider's Research

According to Parkin's (1982) review of tasks showing learning in organic amnesia, the first investigation of perceptual learning in amnesics was carried out by Schneider (1912) on three Korsakoff syndrome patients. Although Schneider measured memory performance in four tasks, and on a number of other patient groups, including schizophrenics and depressives, we here consider only performance on picture fragment completion for the three Korsakoff patients and a comparison group of 25 young normals. The remaining three tasks were a figure construction task, a picture naming task, and a verbal task in which subjects learned to fill in gaps in prose passages.

The picture fragment completion task used eight objects presented at from 4 to 14 levels of completion. Pictures were rendered incomplete by subpart deletion. Because some pictures were more complex than others, the number of completion levels varied across the set of objects. Subjects were shown the pictures in ascending order of completion (i.e., with the ascending method of limits) and the level at which correct identification was accomplished was recorded, along with their correct and incorrect responses. Although Schneider did not translate these protocols into summary performance measures, I have done so here for the purpose of comparison with subsequent studies. I computed identification thresholds by averaging the levels at which subjects identified each picture.

The 25 young normal subjects (age range: 19–33) were tested only once. The three Korsakoff patients (aged 32, 48, and 51) were given varying numbers

TABLE 6.1
Comparison of Normal and Korsakoff Identification Performance
on Initial Trial (from Schneider, 1912)

Picture (max level)	Mean threshold (by levels)	
	Young normals[a]	Korsakoff patients[b]
pear (4)	1.36	2.33
mouse (8)	2.68	4.33
balance (4)	3.00	2.33
Lily of the valley (5)	3.24	5.00
coffee mill (6)	3.64	4.00
baby carriage (8)	4.36	5.00
lamp (7)	4.56	5.67
watering can (14)	8.00	9.67
Mean	3.86	4.79

Note: Level is the maximum number of levels of fragmentation available.
[a]N = 25; [b]N = 3

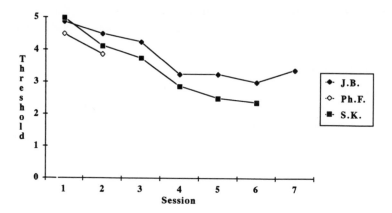

FIG. 6.3. Perceptual learning in the three Korsakoff syndrome patients studied by Schneider (1912).

of learning trials. The first (J.B.) was tested on 6 successive days, and then after 1 month; the second (Ph.F.) was tested only twice, the second time after a delay of 4 months; and the third (S.K.) was tested six times separated by anywhere from 4 days to 2 months. Table 6.1 shows performance on Trial 1 for the 25 normal subjects and three Korsakoff patients by stimulus object, and Fig. 6.3 shows the learning performance for each of the three Korsakoff patients across trials.

It is clear from Table 6.1 that the two groups of subject differed markedly in their initial identification performance (an average of one level). On the other hand, it is also clear that the same items that are difficult for the normal subjects are also difficult for the amnesics. Figure 6.3 shows that all three subjects learned across the repeated trials. Schneider also asked subjects at the end of each learning trial whether they remembered seeing the pictures before. With a few exceptions, subjects' responses were negative.

Gollin's Research

In 1960, Eugene Gollin, searching for a tool for evaluating the course of cognitive development, created a set of fragmented pictures for use in comparative–developmental research. The questions he chose to investigate were, in his words "first, how complete must the representation of a common object be in order that it be recognized; second, to what extent may the completeness of representation required for recognition be reduced as a function of training?" (Gollin, 1960, p. 289).

His stimuli were constructed by quasi-random deletion of fairly large segments of the picture. The deletions were done cumulatively, so that more complete pictures contained all of the segments of less complete pictures. He produced 23 picture series at five levels of completion, although three of the pictures were reserved for practice series. Figure 6.4 shows selected examples of his pictures at three of the five levels (1, 3, and 5). As can be seen from Fig. 6.4, even the most fragmented pictures are often identifiable, thereby producing unwanted ceiling effects, particularly for adult subjects.

Although the Gollin stimuli have been widely used in neuropsychological research (e.g., Corkin, 1982; Warrington & Weiskrantz, 1968), Gollin's empirical results concerning the effects of subject characteristics and training variables have been largely ignored. Accordingly, one purpose of this review is to present these findings and discuss them in the context of the separate memories debate.

Gollin's research, found in five papers published in the early 1960s (Gollin, 1960, 1961, 1962, 1965, 1966), was concerned with two issues: (a) the role of developmental (subject) variables, specifically age and IQ, on performance of the task; and (b) the role of training (experimental) variables on task performance; and their interaction.

In his 1960 paper, Gollin sought to determine the effect of age and IQ on task performance under a variety of different training manipulations. Identification performance was measured in two ways: by thresholds or by pro-

FIG. 6.4.   Examples of the Gollin (1960) fragmented images at Level 5 (complete), 3, and 1 (most fragmented).

portion correct. In the threshold method, subjects were shown increasingly more complete pictures by the ascending method of limits until they had correctly identified the picture. A subject's threshold was defined as the ordinal rank of the fragmentation within the series, with "1" representing the most fragmented level and "5" representing the complete picture. Thus, lower thresholds indicate better performance. In the proportion correct method, subjects were shown only the most fragmented level and scored as correct or incorrect.

Baseline threshold performance in the task improved with age, from 30 months to adult (Experiment 1). Without prior training, children identified only 5% of Level 1 pictures, whereas adults identified 38% (Experiment 3). These pretraining baseline rates were considered low enough to use identification of Level 1 pictures as a measure of training in subsequent studies.

The first training experiment (Experiment 2) consisted of giving children extensive practice in naming the complete pictures. Although the interpolated training procedure had a small effect (about 0.2 level) in reducing thresholds when the pictures were repeated, compared to the control group, simply giving the threshold test twice produced a reduction of approximately 1.1 levels for both control and experimental subjects. Thus, a single training trial with the fragmented pictures had a much larger effect than extensive training with the full pictures.

Subsequent experiments used a single level for training (either the intermediate Level 3 or the full Level 5 stimuli) and tested on Level 1, using the proportion correct measure. Experiments 4a and 4b demonstrated that training with fragmented pictures produced much greater learning than training with the full picture, and also revealed an interesting interaction of the training procedure with IQ and age. Figure 6.5 shows the effect of training level and the age–IQ variable on identification performance.

For all groups, training with Level 3 pictures produced greater learning than training with Level 5 pictures. However, the older and/or more intelligent children benefitted more from Level 5 training than the younger subjects did. The apparent interaction shown in Fig. 6.5 could, however, be attributable to ceiling effects, as all subjects were close to perfect identification performance under Level 3 training.

In subsequent experiments, Gollin (1961, 1962, 1965, 1966) examined the roles of developmental factors, delay between training and test, and the work expended during training on learning in this task. One fascinating finding is that increases in delay consistently failed to reduce identification performance as long as training was with Level 3 (fragmented) stimuli. A significant decline with delay was only observed either when training was with the full picture or when subjects were young children. Gollin (1962) manipulated the amount of effort expended during training by having subjects learn the entire series of 20 pictures by the method of serial anticipation (i.e., by turning the training procedure into an episodic memory task). Under these "high

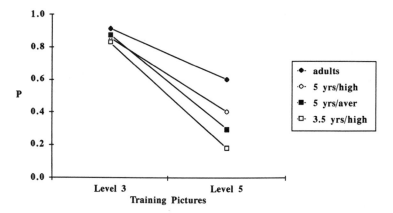

FIG. 6.5. Probability of identification (P) of Level 1 pictures as a function of the level of fragmentation (Level 3 or Level 5) of the training pictures for four groups of subjects (high = high IQ, aver = average IQ). (from Gollin, Experiment 4b, 1960).

work" conditions, identification performance actually increased with delay between 1 minute and 1 day, as is shown in Fig. 6.6.

Gollin interpreted the depressed performance immediately after training to the build-up of reactive inhibition from the intensive learning procedure. Whatever the explanation, here is an example of strong functional dissociation: Implicit memory actually improved with delay whereas explicit memory, were it to have been measured, would have undoubtedly decreased with delay.

Gollins' finding that training with moderately fragmented pictures produced greater priming than training with complete pictures was the inspiration for Experiment 3 reported here. And Gollin's exploration of the effect of delay interval in implicit memory predates many more recent reports of the immunity or relative immunity of priming facilitation to increases in retention interval.

MEASURES OF IMPLICIT LEARNING

Implicit learning can refer to either procedural learning, in which improvement occurs across presentations of novel material through some kind of generalized task practice effect, or to perceptual learning, in which improvement occurs across presentations of repeated material through item-specific effects (see Schacter (1987) for a historical review of the concept of implicit memory). In order to disambiguate abbreviations, I will hereafter refer to procedural learning as skill learning.

Not all tasks provide the opportunity of measuring both components. For example, when subjects are primed (presented with the complete stimulus)

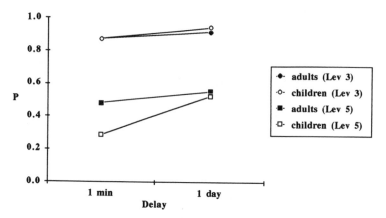

FIG. 6.6.   Probability of identification (P) of Level 1 pictures for adults and children as a function of delay and the level of fragmentation (Level 3 or Level 5) of the training pictures (from Gollin, 1962).

during training, there is no baseline from which to measure skill learning. However, in the typical priming paradigm, subjects are presented with both novel and repeated material during test, so it *is* possible to measure perceptual learning. And when subjects are repeatedly tested with the same items from session to session, there is no way to measure the skill learning component separately from the perceptual learning component, so the improvement in performance will include both types of learning.

In the following discussion, we assume that performance measures are available from the training session for training items and from the test session for both old (the repeated training) and new items. This is accomplished by exposing subjects to a subset of stimuli during a training session, and then presenting them with both repeated (old) and nonrepeated (new) items during test. Skill learning is assessed by comparing performance on new items with performance on training items, and perceptual learning is assessed by comparing performance on old items with performance on new items. Such a task was used by Snodgrass et al. (1987) and in Experiments 1 and 4 here.

Given that train, new, and old performance values are available, there are still two considerations to be made in measuring skill and perceptual learning. The first concerns the method used to measure performance during test—namely, whether the entire range of fragmentations is presented and a threshold determined for each stimulus, or whether a single level of fragmented image is presented and the subject's performance scored as a success (correct identification) or failure (incorrect identification).

Thresholds are usually measured by the ascending method of limits, in which we assume that if a stimulus is identified at a certain level, it will also be identified at all higher levels. The area under the psychometric function constructed under this assumption, weighted by the appropriate level at each point, is the mean threshold, so the threshold measure will sometimes be referred to as the area measure. This contrasts with the single level presentation method, which will sometimes be referred to as the point measure.

Strictly speaking, to compute mean thresholds it is necessary to have an underlying metric at the interval scale level for measuring fragmentation level. In practice, however, the usual metric used is the ordinal number of the fragmentation level (e.g., Gollin, 1960; Snodgrass et al., 1987; Vokey et al., 1986). This makes the mean thresholds noncomparable across experiments. However, because most experiments are concerned with changes in thresholds across an experimental manipulation, the lack of cross-experiment comparability is not usually considered a drawback. As we shall see, translation of means to probabilities of identification is dependent upon assuming that means are computed on ordinal levels; this also make probability of identification subject to the number and difficulty of levels of fragmentation.

The second measurement consideration concerns whether the improvement is measured as an absolute difference between baseline and experimental performance, or whether the improvement is measured as a relative difference. Because subject groups often differ in baseline performance, the choice between absolute and relative measures is an important one.

The factorial combination of how learning is computed from baseline (absolute vs. relative) and test type (area vs. point) produces four possible measures for both skill and perceptual learning. These are described along with their relevant learning models in the following section.

Absolute Measures

Area Measures.   Absolute area measures of skill and perceptual learning were used in Snodgrass et al. (1987). Skill learning was measured by subtracting train from new thresholds [M(new)-M(train)], and perceptual learning was measured by subtracting new from old thresholds [M(old)-M(new)]. For a more direct comparison with subsequent measures, it will be useful to translate mean threshold values into proportion correct measures.

In the method of ascending limits used to collect the threshold data used here, subjects are given eight opportunities to identify each picture (corresponding to the eight levels of fragmentation available for each picture), in which Level 1 represents the most fragmented image and Level 8, the complete picture. Virtually all subjects identify all pictures by Level 8, so the minimum possible identification score is $\frac{1}{8}$ or 0.125. The best possible performance, an identification score of 1.00, occurs when subjects identify the first (most fragmented) level. These considerations, along with the assumption that a stimulus identified at a particular level will be identified at all higher levels, leads to the following transformation for converting mean threshold (M) to proportion identified (P): $P = [k + 1] - M]/k$, where k is the number of available levels. For the present data, in which $k = 8$, $P = (9 - M)/8$.

The relationship between skill and perceptual learning measures expressed as proportions and as means are given below, where $SL(a)$ is skill learning and $PL(a)$ is perceptual learning measured as absolute differences:

$$SL(a) = P(\text{new}) - P(\text{train}) = [M(\text{train}) - M(\text{new})]/k, \text{ and}$$

$$PL(a) = P(\text{old}) - P(\text{new}) = [M(\text{new}) - M(\text{old})]/k$$

Note that when differences in proportion of identifications are used, the differences in means are divided by the number of levels (k) available for identification. Thus the proportion difference measure is useful for comparing savings across experiments using different numbers of identification levels. All measures used here have been converted to proportions. These can be converted to mean difference measures by multiplying by 8.

Point Measures.   When only a single level of fragmented image is presented, the absolute difference measure for skill learning is the difference between the proportion of correctly identified train and new items, and the absolute difference measure for perceptual learning is the difference between the proportion of correctly identified new and old items.

Compared to the area measures, which compute the average differences between the psychometric functions, the point measures are the difference between the psychometric functions at the particular level of fragmentation tested. After all measures are discussed, we present a numerical example to illustrate relationships among them.

The absolute measures assume an additive model of learning in which the effect of training is to add a constant increment of performance regardless of the absolute level of baseline performance, so that the appropriate measure is a difference score. In other words, the model assumes a linear learning function. Snodgrass and Corwin (1988) tested the additive assumption with data from Snodgrass et al. (1987), with supportive results.

Relative Measures

Despite the success of the absolute measures for the normative data, a great deal of evidence from the learning literature points to a negatively accelerated learning function, in which what is learned on a training trial is a constant proportion of what is left to be learned. This standard learning function can be expressed in terms of probability of identification as follows: $P(t+1) = P(t) + \phi[(1 - P(t)]$, where $P(t+1)$ is the probability of correct identification after training, $P(t)$ is the probability of identification before training, and ϕ is the learning parameter. Solving for ϕ leads to the following equation for learning based on the standard learning equation:

$$\phi = [P(t+1) - P(t)]/[1 - P(t)]$$

Applying this measure to skill and perceptual learning leads to the following measures.

Area Measures. Relative skill learning, $SL(r)$, is measured by:

$$SL(r) = [P(\text{new}) - P(\text{train})]/[1 - P(\text{train})]$$

Relative perceptual learning, $PL(r)$, is measured by:

$$PL(r) = [P(\text{old}) - P(\text{new})]/[1 - P(\text{new})]$$

The same measures expressed in terms of means rather than proportions are:

$$SL(r) = [M(\text{train}) - M(\text{new})]/[M(\text{train}) - 1]$$

and

$$PL(r) = [M(\text{new}) - M(\text{old})/[M(\text{new}) - 1]$$

These relative measures based on means are similar to the savings measure introduced by Ebbinghaus (1885/1913).

Point Measures. Before presenting the relative point measures, it will be useful to present a numerical example to introduce some notation. This numerical example will be used to illustrate the computation of all four sets of measures.

Table 6.2 presents some simplified data for a stimulus with four levels of fragmentation. The means for train (t), new (n), and old (o) stimuli can be computed by multiplying the proportion of identifications at each level (f) by the level of identification and summing. The mean thresholds for train, new, and old stimuli are 3.30, 3.10, and 2.50 respectively. Using the subtraction method employed in our previous research, skill and perceptual learning are 0.20 and 0.60 levels respectively. Converting means to proportions by the transformation $P = (5 - M)/4$ leads to values of P's equal to 0.425, 0.475, and 0.625 for the train, new, and old items. Both absolute and relative measures are shown in Table 6.2.

If only a single level of fragmented image is presented and we assume that prior presentations of unidentified stimuli have no effect on the ultimate level of identification, then we can compute a point measure for the set of data in Table 6.2 by using the cumulative proportions (F) of identifications. By assuming that Level 2 was presented during training and test, we obtain the point measures of skill and perceptual learning shown at the bottom of Table 6.2.

It should also be noted that the sum of the differences between the cumulative functions for train and new items, $\Sigma(F(n) - F(t))$, equals the difference in means, $M(t) - M(n)$, and the average difference equals the $SL(a)$ measure, $P(n) - P(t)$. A similar relation holds between the sum and mean dif-

TABLE 6.2
Examples of the Four Measures of Skill and Perceptual Learning

Level	f(t)	f(n)	f(o)	F(t)	F(n)	F(o)	F(n) − F(t)	F(o) − F(n)
					Measure			
1	.00	.00	.10	.00	.00	.10	.00	.10
2	.20	.25	.35	.20	.25	.45	.05	.20
3	.30	.40	.50	.50	.65	.95	.15	.30
4	.50	.35	.05	1.00	1.00	1.00	.00	.00

$M(t) = 3.30$; $M(n) = 3.10$; $M(o) = 2.50$
$P(t) = .425$; $P(n) = .475$; $P(o) = .625$
$\Sigma[F(n) - F(t)] = M(t) - M(n)$; $\Sigma[F(o) - F(n)] = M(n) - M(o)$

Area measures:
$SL(a) = P(\text{new}) - P(\text{train}) = [M(\text{train} - M(\text{new})]/4 = .05$
$PL(a) = P(\text{old}) - P(\text{new}) = [M(\text{new}) - M(\text{old})]/4 = .15$
$SL(r) = [P(\text{new}) - P(\text{train})]/[1 - P(\text{train})] = .087$
$PL(r) = [P(\text{old}) - P(\text{new})]/[1 - P(\text{new})] = .286$

Point measures (at level 2):
$SL(a) = F(\text{new}) - F(\text{train}) = .05$
$PL(a) = F(\text{old}) - F(\text{new}) = .20$
$SL(r) = [F(\text{new}) - F(\text{train})]/[1 - F(\text{train})] = .062$
$PL(r) = [F(\text{old}) - F(\text{new})]/[(1 - F(\text{new})] = .267$

Note: t = train; n = new; o = old. f is the proportion of items identified at each level. F is the cumulated proportion.

ference of the cumulative functions for new and old items and $M(n) - M(o)$ and $PL(a)$.

A test for evaluating absolute and relative models on learning in the picture fragment completion task is presented in the next section, after the general experimental procedure is described.

TESTS OF THE SEPARATE MEMORIES HYPOTHESIS

In this section, I describe some tests of the separate memories hypothesis with data collected from the fragmented pictures task. The task is structured so that in some cases all three types of memory—skill, perceptual, and episodic— can be measured.

First I describe the method for all experiments, and then I describe specific tests of both functional and stochastic independence among memory tasks.

Method of All Experiments

Apparatus and Stimuli. Stimuli were 150 pictures of objects and animals selected from Snodgrass and Vanderwart (1980), which had been prepared for presentation on the Apple Macintosh computer. The fragmented series were created on the Macintosh computer. The fragmentation algorithm is described more fully in Snodgrass et al. (1987). Briefly, the fragmentation process randomly deleted successive 16×16 pixel blocks from the picture to produce eight levels of fragmented images per stimulus. Before fragmenting, blocks containing black pixels were identified so that only these information-bearing blocks were included as candidates for deletion. The numbers of blocks retained at each level were calculated by an exponential function having the following form:

retained blocks (level) = # total blocks [aEXP(8 – level)],

where a was set to .7 and level varied from 8 (complete picture) to 1 (most fragmented). Because the pictures varied in number of total information-bearing blocks, the number of blocks displayed varied across levels. However, the percentage of blocks displayed was constant across items, from 8% at the lowest level to 100% at the complete level. At Level 6, approximately 50% of the total blocks were displayed.

Several fragmentation series were created on-line until an acceptable series was produced. An acceptable series was one in which the overall outline of the picture was preserved at the most fragmented level but critical identifying features of the picture (such as an eye or tail in the picture of an animal) were deleted at low fragmentation levels. This series was then saved for use in the subsequent picture fragment completion task. Two series were created for each picture for Experiment 4, in which a different fragmentation series was used between training and test.

The resulting fragmented pictures are similar to the Gollin (1960) stimuli in that fairly large areas of the picture are deleted. Saving the actual fragmentations permitted us to present exactly the same fragmentation series in test as in training, a procedure that parallels the Gollin procedure.

Figure 6.7 presents three examples of the fragmented images at selected levels of completion. The levels are numbered from 1 to 8, where 1 is the most fragmented image and 8 is the complete picture.

Procedure.   Two sets of experimental results will be presented. The first set is from a normative study by Snodgrass et al. (1987), referred to as Experiment 0, and the second set is from a series of four experiments (Experiments 1 through 4) that varied training conditions.

The basic task used in Experiment 0 consisted of three phases—a training phase, a brief delay filled by a distractor test, and a test phase. In the training phase, subjects were given 15 fragmented picture series to identify. Each picture series consisted of eight levels of fragmented images presented for identification by an ascending methods of limits. At the presentation of each fragmented image, subjects attempted to identify it by typing its name on the computer keyboard, or by pressing the return key if they could not iden-

FIG. 6.7.   Examples of fragmented images at Levels 8 (complete), 6, 4, and
2 (from Snodgrass, Smith, Feenan, & Corwin, 1987).

tify it. When a subject's name was correct (matched one of the possible names
for the picture stored in the computer's lexicon), subjects were informed they
were correct and the program proceeded to the next picture in the randomly
determined series.

At the end of the training phase, there was a 10-minute delay during which
subjects performed a paper-and-pencil cancellation of nine's task. Following
the delay, subjects were given the test phase of the experiment. In the test
phase, the training (now old) pictures were presented again mixed with an
equal number of new pictures. Subjects were not informed that some of the
training pictures would be repeated. However, because the number of training items was relatively small and the delay short, virtually all of the subjects
were aware that some of the training items were repeated during test.

Subjects exhibited two kinds of learning in this task: (a) skill learning, an improvement on new pictures, and (b) perceptual learning, an improvement on repeated pictures. In the original study, skill learning was measured by subtracting new thresholds from train thresholds, and perceptual learning was measured by subtracting old thresholds from new thresholds. Here we use threshold means transformed to proportions under both the absolute and relative difference methods to measure skill and perceptual learning.

A second purpose of Experiment 0 was to test the equivalence of perceptual thresholds at the three levels of training (train, new, and old) across the five sets of 30 pictures used, and to test the equivalence of the two forms of 15 pictures each of which alternately served as train/old and new pictures within each set. Across the 10 set-forms (five sets × two forms), the average skill learning was 0.20 level, and the average perceptual learning was almost 2 levels when measured as threshold differences. However, Experiment 0 also revealed a large effect of form on perceptual identification thresholds. An essential condition of the subtraction method is that the two forms within a set be matched in difficulty because both skill and perceptual learning are measured by comparing performance across forms. Even though the set-forms had been matched for picture variables thought to be important in perceptual identification, based on the Snodgrass and Vanderwart (1980) norms, only two sets (3 and 4) showed no main effect of form and no interaction between form and training. Accordingly, the tests of independence reported here are based on data from subjects receiving Sets 3 and 4 only (a total of 40 subjects from Experiment 0).

Because of the lack of equivalence between forms for Sets 1, 2, and 5, subsequent experiments used only Sets 3 and 4. The experiments were all variations on the basic task in that the same test phase was used as in the basic task, but each differed in the nature of the training phase. In Experiment 1, the training phase was identical to that used in Experiment 0 except that subjects were shown the complete picture after correct identification. Because adding complete picture priming to the basic training procedure produced no increase in perceptual learning, results from Experiment 0 and 1 will be reported together for the subject-based analyses. In Experiment 2, subjects saw no fragmented images during study. Instead, they were presented with the complete picture only and asked to name it. In Experiment 3, subjects during training were exposed to only a single level of fragmented image—the complete picture (Level 8) or one of two more fragmented picture levels (Levels 3 and 5). Upon presentation of the fragmented or complete image, subjects were required to identify it by typing in its name. If their name for the picture was incorrect, they were given feedback in the form of the picture's name. In Experiment 4, subjects were given the full ascending series to identify during training, but the fragments were changed from training to test to assess the effect of explicit fragment memory. In both Experiments 3 and 4, subjects were asked to recall the names of the pictures after the test session. Thus, for Experiments 3 and 4 (and only for these experiments), performance on an episodic memory task was available.

Comparison of Absolute and Relative Measures of Learning

Before presenting learning measures for all experiments, we first consider what the data from Experiments 0 and 1 can tell us about the plausibility of the two learning models described in the previous section on measurement. The model on which the absolute measures are based assumes that a constant increment is added to performance by the training manipulation, whereas the model on which the relative measures are based assumes that a constant proportion of what is left to be learned is added. One way of evaluating the two models is to determine the relationship between the probability of identification during training, $P(t)$, and the two measures of perceptual learning, $PL(a)$ and $PL(r)$. If the absolute model is correct, then the correlation between $P(t)$ and $PL(a)$ should be zero, and the correlation between $P(t)$ and $PL(r)$ should be positive. If the relative model is correct, then the correlation between $P(t)$ and $PL(a)$ should be negative and the correlation between $P(t)$ and $PL(r)$ should be zero. In short, the correct model of learning will show dissociation between the baseline measure, $P(t)$, and that model's measure of perceptual learning.

Two sets of correlations were computed. The first set was computed using only the 40 subjects in Experiment 0 receiving Sets 3 and 4 plus all 20 subjects in Experiment 1 ($N = 60$), and the second set was computed using all 100 subjects in Experiment 0 plus the 20 subjects in Experiment 1 ($N = 120$). All subjects in Experiment 0 were used for the second set because train and old performance is measured on the same set-form and thus their comparison is not affected by form differences.

Both sets of correlations showed the same pattern: The correlations between $P(t)$ and $PL(a)$ were $-.20$ and $-.23$ for the smaller and larger sets of subjects, $ps > .05$ and $< .025$ by one-tailed tests; and the correlations between $P(t)$ and $PL(r)$ were $+.27$ and $+.30$ for the same two sets, $ps < .05$ and $< .025$ by one-tailed tests. The correlations for the relative model are higher than those for the absolute model, thereby suggesting that the absolute model is correct (although neither model achieves that desired outcome of a zero correlation). However, because of some problems with the absolute measures, we used both sets of measures in the subsequent analyses.

Results

Table 6.3 presents the results from the five experiments based on subjects as units of analyses for those memory components available. Experiments 0 and 1 have been combined because full picture priming during training in Experiment 1 had absolutely no effect on performance. For Experiments 0 and

TABLE 6.3
Memory Measures for the Five Experiments Based on Subjects

					Measure					
Exp	N	P(t)	P(n)	P(o)	SL(a)	SL(r)	PL(a)	PL(r)	EL(o)	EL(n)
0/1	60	.54	.57	.81	.03	.07	.24	.57	N/A	N/A
2	20	N/A	.55	.66	N/A	N/A	.11	.24	N/A	N/A
3a	12	.57	.60	.78	.03	−.04	.18	.46	.69	.45
3b	12	N/A	.60	.70	N/A	N/A	.10	.25	.62	.45
4	40	.52	.55	.72	.03	.06	.18	.40	.73	.53

Note: N = number of subjects; $P(t)$ = prop train items identified; $P(n)$ = prop new items identified; $P(o)$ = prop old items identified. SL = skill learning; PL = perceptual learning; EL = episodic learning; $SL(a) = P(n) - P(t)$; $SL(r) = [P(n) - P(t)]/[1 - P(t)]$; $PL(a) = P(o) - P(n)$; $PL(r) = [P(o) - P(n)]/[1 - P(n)]$. $EL(o)$ = prop old items recalled; $EL(n)$ = prop new items recalled; N/A = not available.

1, both skill and perceptual learning are available for analysis because subjects performed picture fragment completion during training; however, no episodic learning performance was measured.

For Experiment 2, full pictures were presented during training for identification, so no training thresholds were measured nor were measures of recall collected. Thus, only the perceptual learning measures are available for Experiment 2, and so results from this experiment cannot be used to test the separate memories model. I include Experiment 2 because it provides another test of the relationship between the two measures of perceptual learning for an experimental condition that produces relatively poor performance.

For Experiment 3, one third of the training pictures were presented as complete (at Level 8), one third were presented at Level 3, and one third were presented at Level 5. Because perceptual learning was larger (and identical) for pictures presented at fragmented levels (3 and 5) than for pictures presented as complete, I have divided Experiment 3 into two subexperiments. Experiment 3a presents performance for Levels 3 and 5 priming conditions, and Experiment 3b presents performance for Level 8 priming. Identification performance on Level 8 pictures during training, as might be expected, was virtually perfect; however, performance on Levels 3 and 5 were not, so we use these point measures as estimates of training for Experiment 3a. As can be seen in Table 6.3, these point measures give comparable levels of training performance to the area measures available for the other experiments. Recall of the pictures was also measured for Experiment 3. Recall proportions are reported separately for train/old pictures (which are consistently higher) and for new pictures. Thus, Experiment 3a provides learning estimates for all three types of memory components, whereas Experiment 3b provides estimates only for the perceptual and episodic memory components.

Finally, in Experiment 4, train, new, and old thresholds as well as recall proportions are available, and thus Experiment 4 also yields estimates for all three memory components.

Functional Independence

The data shown in Table 6.3 provide tests of functional independence of the three memory components. Functional independence is supported whenever a particular manipulation has an effect on one memory component, but no (or the opposite) effect on the second. The experimental manipulations that distinguish one experimental condition from another were expected to affect perceptual learning rather than either skill or episodic learning. Accordingly we turn first to comparisons of the perceptual learning components, as measured by either the absolute measure, $PL(a)$, or the relative measure, $PL(r)$.

Perceptual Learning. The experimental conditions produced the following ordering of perceptual learning: Experiment 0/1, in which the full series of fragmented pictures were presented during training, produced the highest amount of perceptual learning; Experiments 2 and 3b, which presented only the complete picture during training, produced the lowest amounts of perceptual learning; and Experiments 3a and 4 produced intermediate amounts of perceptual learning. Experiments 3a and 4 presented fragmented pictures during training, but the training was not optimum either because only one level was shown, as in Experiment 3a, or because although the full sequence was shown, the fragmented images were different from those shown during test, as in Experiment 4. Figure 6.8 shows perceptual learning measures based on absolute differences for the five experiments.

Analyses of variance on both $PL(a)$ and $PL(r)$ showed that differences among the perceptual learning measures were significant. For $PL(a)$, $F(4, 139) = 18.08$, and for $PL(r)$, $F(4, 139) = 17.66$, both $ps < .001$. Planned comparisons among the means of both measures also revealed exactly the same patterns. Perceptual learning was higher for Experiment 0/1 than for the average of Experiments 3a and 4, which did not differ; and the average of Experiments 3a and 4 were significantly higher than the average of Experiments 3b and 2, which did not differ, $Fs(1, 139) = 16.81$ and 25.46 respectively for $PL(a)$ and 14.63 and 25.66 for $PL(r)$.

Skill Learning. Differences in skill learning were nonexistent for $SL(a)$ or extremely small for $SL(r)$, which actually was negative in Experiment 3a. The analysis of variance on $SL(a)$ across the three experiments in which it was measured showed absolutely no differences among the experiments, whereas the $SL(r)$ differences were significant, $F(2, 109) = 3.18$, $p = .046$. An unplanned comparison between the average of Experiments 0/1 and 4 with

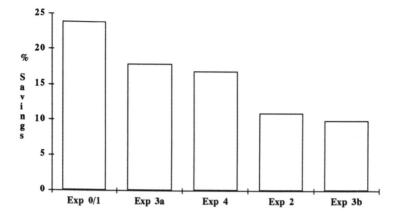

FIG. 6.8.   Savings (%) measured as the absolute difference between percentage of old and new items identified in the five experiments.

Experiment 3a showed the latter had significantly lower skill learning, $F(2, 109) = 3.14$, $p = .047$. However, the $SL(r)$ measure was somewhat more variable than the $SL(a)$ measure because dividing by a small denominator often magnified effects of outlying negative observations.

Episodic Learning.   Only three experimental conditions yielded episodic learning measures. Because Experiments 3a and 3b shared identical new picture recall scores, I only examined differences among recall of the old pictures. There was no overall difference among Experiments 3a, 3b, and 4 in old picture recall, $F(2, 61) = 2.60$, $p = .082$. However, the average of 3a and 4 was significantly different from 3b by a planned comparison, $F(1, 61) = 4.63$, $p = .035$.

In summary, then, the following patterns of learning were observed across the five experimental conditions:

for perceptual learning: Exp 0/1 > Exp 3a = Exp 4 > Exp 3b = Exp 2

for skill learning: Exp 0/1 = Exp 4 ≥ Exp 3a

for episodic learning: Exp 3a = Exp 4 > Exp 3b

Skill learning differed from perceptual learning in showing no superiority of Experiment 0/1 over Experiment 4 and in showing a somewhat questionable superiority of Experiment 4 over Experiment 3a. On the other hand, episodic learning showed exactly the ordering as perceptual learning. Accordingly, although skill and perceptual learning were functionally dissociated, episodic and perceptual learning were not: Experimental manipulations that improved perceptual learning (specifically, the presentation of fragmented pictures

	SUBJECTS	ITEMS	SUBJECT-ITEMS
SKILL/PERCEP	Exps 0/1, 3a, & 4	Exps 0, 1, & 4	✕
SKILL/EPISOD	Exps 3a & 4	Exp 4	✕
PERCEP/EPISOD	Exps 3a, 3b, & 4	Exps 3 & 4	Exps 3 & 4

FIG. 6.9.   The possible tests of stochastic independence

during training), not only improved subjects' ability to identify those pictures when subsequently presented, but they also improved subjects' ability to recall those pictures in the absence of a perceptual cue.

Stochastic Independence

Stochastic independence can be tested in each of three ways—by subjects, items, and subject-items. Similarly, stochastic independence can be tested among three memory types—skill, perceptual, and episodic. There are three possible pairings of these memory types—skill/perceptual, skill/episodic, and perceptual/episodic. All three memory pair types can be tested on subjects and on items. However, only the perceptual/episodic pair type can be tested on subject-items because the same subject must be tested on the same item in both tasks. The logic of measuring skill learning requires that it be expressed on a different set of items from the set used during training when subjects are the unit of analysis, and that it be expressed on a different set of subjects from the set used during training when items are the unit of analysis.

Figure 6.9 shows the three possible tests of stochastic independence by the three possible pairs of memory systems. Neither skill/perceptual nor skill/episodic comparisons can be made for subject-items so these two cells have been crossed out. The remaining cells show the experiments for which the remaining tests are available. When items served as the unit of analysis, Experiments 0 and 1 were analyzed separately and Experiment 3a and 3b were combined. Only data from Experiment 4 provided all three comparisons between memory systems for all three types of tests.

Tests on Subjects.   Tests of stochastic independence by subjects are based on the assumption that, to the extent that these memory systems are separate, we might expect subjects to show little or no correlation between their performance on one memory type (e.g., skill), and a second memory type (e.g., episodic). Indeed, one of the strongest pieces of evidence for the existence of separate systems has been the finding that amnesic subjects show normal or near-normal performance on skill and perceptual memory but show abnormally low performance on episodic memory tasks (e.g., Corkin, 1982; Graf & Schacter, 1985, 1987; Hirst & Volpe, 1982; Jacoby, 1982; Schacter & Graf, 1986; Warrington & Weiskrantz, 1968).

Before examining the pattern of correlations across learning measures, it is important to evaluate the measure-to-measure and task-to-task correlations. If the correlations between two measures of skill or two measures of episodic learning are low, then we would not expect a high correlation across skill and episodic memory.

Table 6.4 presents measure-to-measure and task-to-task correlations across subjects. For all experiments, identification of new and old pictures (the $P(n) - P(o)$ correlation) was positively related. For Experiments 0/1 and 4, but not for Experiment 3a, train-new and train-old correlations were also positive and significant. In Experiment 3a, training performance was measured by a point measure (i.e., by the proportion of Level 3 and 5 pictures identified when presented singly during training), rather than by an area measure.

Although the relationship between the skill and perceptual learning measures rightfully belong to the domain of memory-to-memory relation-

TABLE 6.4
Correlations Between Measures and Tasks Based on Subjects

| | Experiment | | | | |
	0/1	2	3a	3b	4
No. subs	60	20	12	12	40
Measure-to-measure					
$SL(a) - SL(r)$	.99†	N/A	.88†	N/A	.98†
$PL(a) - PL(r)$	.83†	.92†	.88†	.96†	.88†
Task-to-task					
$P(t) - P(n)$	.64†	N/A	.41	N/A	.74†
$P(n) - P(o)$	.60†	.79†	.68*	.80†	.75†
$P(t) - P(o)$	.55†	N/A	.06	N/A	.73†
$SL(a) - PL(a)$	- .36†	N/A	.26	N/A	- .42†
$SL(r) - PL(r)$	- .01	N/A	.20	N/A	- .25
$EL(o) - EL(n)$	N/A	N/A	- .22	- .27	.41†

Note: $P(t)$ = prop train items identified; $P(n)$ = prop new items identified; $P(o)$ = prop old items identified. SL = skill learning; PL = perceptual learning; EL = episodic learning; $SL(a) = P(n) - P(t)$; $SL(r) = [P(n) - P(t)]/[1 - P(t)]$; $PL(a) = P(o) - P(n)$; $PL(r) = [P(o) - P(n)]/[1 - P(n)]$. $EL(o)$ = prop old items recalled; $EL(n)$ = prop new items recalled; N/A = not available.
   $*p < .05$; $†p < .01$.

ships, they are presented in Table 6.4 to illustrate a problem with the absolute measures. The positive correlations among $P(t)$, $P(n)$, and $P(o)$ produced a negative correlation between $SL(a)$ and $PL(a)$ for Experiments 0/1 and 4. Because of the existence of these spurious correlations, and because the relation between the absolute and relative measures of skill and perceptual learning were high (see the $SL(a) - SL(r)$ and $PL(a) - PL(r)$ correlations), I use the relative measures of skill and perceptual learning in memory-to-memory comparisons.

It is worth noting that the single comparison we have between measures of episodic learning—the correlation between old and new item recall—was only significant for Experiment 4, and was actually insignificantly negative for Experiments 3a and 3b. Because of these low correlations between new and old item recall, I consider each of these measures separately in comparisons of episodic with skill and perceptual learning.

Table 6.5 shows the memory-to-memory correlations for the preferred measures of skill, perceptual, and episodic learning. There was no relationship between skill and perceptual learning, and between perceptual and episodic learning, when the basis of the comparison was by subjects. For the skill-episodic relationship, Experiment 4 showed a high and positive correlation between old item recall and skill learning, but no correlation between new item recall and skill learning. Experiment 3a showed a similar pattern of results, although the positive correlation did not reach significance. In summary, then, with a single exception, the three types of learning were dissociated

TABLE 6.5
Correlations Across Memory Tasks Based on Subjects

	Experiment			
	0/1	3a	3b	4
No. of subjects	60	12	12	40
skill/percep				
$SL(r) - PL(r)$	−.01	.20	N/A	−.25
skill/episod				
$SL(r) - EL(o)$	N/A	.45	N/A	.51*
$SL(r) - EL(n)$	N/A	−.35	N/A	.18
percep/episod				
$PL(r) - EL(o)$	N/A	−.26	−.26	.11
$PL(r) - EL(n)$	N/A	.29	−.01	.14

Note: SL = skill learning; PL = perceptual learning; EL = episodic learning; $SL(a) = P(n) - P(t)$; $SL(r) = [P(n) - P(t)]/[1 - P(t)]$; $PL(a) = P(o) - P(n)$; $PL(r) = [P(o) - P(n)]/[1 - P(n)]$. $EL(o)$ = prop old items recalled; $EL(n)$ = prop new items recalled; N/A = not available.
*$p < .05$

by subjects. The single exception makes no theoretical sense, as skill learning is an improvement between train and new performance, and the episodic learning measure with which it was correlated was based on old item performance. Accordingly, I attribute this single exception to sampling error.

Tests on Items. Tests of stochastic independence by items followed the same logic as the parallel tests by subjects. They were based on the assumption that, to the extent that these memory systems are separate, we expected an item's learning performance for skill to be unrelated to its learning performance for perceptual or episodic memory.

Item comparisons can be made across a number of different manipulations. Items can be compared across levels of training—that is, across the train, new, and old conditions within an experiment. When this is done, comparisons of train with new and new with old performance involves different subjects (because a given subject sees a different subset of new pictures from the subset used for the train/old pictures), whereas comparisons of train with old performance involve the same subjects. Nonetheless, in the normative study (Experiment 0), the correlation between train and new performance was higher ($r = +.82$) than that between train and old performance ($r = +.66$) for the 150 pictures used in the normative study.

Items can also be compared across experiments. Set 3 was common across all experiments, whereas Set 4 was not used in Experiments 2 and 3. Accordingly performance on the 30 items of Set 3 and the 60 items of Sets 3 and 4 was evaluated separately across the experiments having them in common.

Finally, items can be compared across version of fragmentation. In Experiment 4, two different versions of each fragmentation series were used. Correlations across experiments for the same version at the same level of training were higher than correlations within Experiment 4 across the two different versions. For the 60 items in Sets 3 and 4 common to Experiments 0 and 4, the average of the within-version correlations was $+.80$, whereas the average of the between-version correlations was $+.40$. When only the 30 items in Set 3 common to Experiments 0, 1, and 4 were considered, the within-version correlations averaged $+.81$, and the between-version correlations, $+.38$. Because of the large effect of fragmentation version on identification performance, it was decided to treat the two versions of fragmented pictures in Experiment 4 as separate items.

For the item analysis, Experiments 0 and 1 were separated because Experiment 1 only used the 30 items in Set 3. Experiments 3a and 3b were combined because, as only 12 subjects participated in Experiment 3, each item was seen by only two subjects at a given level of fragmentation during training; accordingly, no training measures were computed for items in Experiment 3.

Table 6.6 presents the memory measures based on items for the five experiments under this new reorganization. Note that data for Experiment 4

TABLE 6.6
Memory Measures for the Five Experiments (based on items)

Exp	N	P(t)	P(n)	P(o)	SL(a)	SL(r)	PL(a)	PL(r)	EL(o)	EL(n)
0	60	.54	.57	.80	.03	.06	.24	.55	N/A	N/A
1	30	.54	.58	.84	.04	.09	.25	.60	N/A	N/A
2	30	N/A	.55	.66	N/A	N/A	.11	.22	N/A	N/A
3	30	N/A	.60	.75	N/A	N/A	.15	.38	.67	.45
4[a]	60/120	.52	.55	.72	.03	.06	.17	.38	.73	.53

Note: $P(t)$ = prop train items identified; $P(n)$ = prop new items identified; $P(o)$ = prop old items identified. SL = skill learning; PL = perceptual learning; EL = episodic learning; $SL(a) = P(n) - P(t)$; $SL(r) = [P(n) - P(t)]/[1 - P(t)]$; $PL(a) = P(o) - P(n)$; $PL(r) = [P(o) - P(n)]/[1 - P(n)]$. $EL(o)$ = prop old items recalled; $EL(n)$ = prop new items recalled; N/A = not available.
[a]The two fragmented series for each pictures are treated as separate items for the skill and perceptual learning measures, but they are combined for the episodic measures.

were based on 120 items when the perceptual identification measures are determined, because of the separation of the two versions of fragmented images, but they were based on only 60 items when the episodic learning measures were computed. This is because subjects saw one version of fragmented image during training and the second during testing, so it was impossible to disentangle the effect of version on episodic learning of old items. Although version could have been separately analyzed for new items, it was not considered worthwhile.

Means based on items were virtually identical to those based on subjects except for the relative learning measures. Nonetheless, it was of interest to determine whether the statistical comparisons obtained previously among means based on subjects were replicated when items served as the units of analysis. The item-based perceptual learning measures followed the same ordering of experimental conditions as for subjects: namely, that Experiments 0 and 1 were the best, followed by Experiments 3 and 4, followed by Experiment 2. Analyses of variance on both perceptual learning measures were consistent with this ordering. For both $PL(a)$ and $PL(r)$, the overall differences among experiments were significant, $Fs(4, 264) = 11.60$ and 21.08 respectively, both $ps < .001$. Planned comparisons on both perceptual learning measures showed the following ordering of means.

Exp $0 =$ Exp $1 >$ Exp $3 =$ Exp $4 >$ Exp 2 (all comparisons at $p < .001$).

There were no differences among the experiments in skill learning when measured by $SL(a)$ or $SL(r)$. The significant differences in $SL(r)$ in the subject-based analysis was due to Experiment 3a, which is not represented here.

Episodic learning differences were analyzed in two ways. First, because Experiment 4 used both Sets 3 and 4 whereas Experiment 3 used only Set 3), we analyzed the difference between episodic learning for old and new training levels of the items by a mixed design, with experiment as a between-subject variable. With this less sensitive analysis, there was no significant difference between Experiments 3 and 4, $F(1, 88) = 3.06$, $p = .08$; a large difference between old and new recall performance, $F(1, 88) = 66.79$, $p < .001$, and no interaction ($F < 1$). When only Set 3 from Experiment 4 was analyzed in a completely within-subjects analysis of variance, Experiment 4 produced better recall performance than Experiment 3, $F(1, 29) = 12.57$, $p < .01$, there was the same large difference between old and new recall performance, and no interaction. The significant effect of experiment in the second analysis arises in part because in Experiment 4, Set 3 pictures produced better recall performance than Set 4 pictures (.67 vs. .64 overall), so eliminating Set 4 pictures from the analysis enhanced the difference between experiments.

In summary, then, the following patterns of learning were observed across the five experiments, when items were used as units of analysis:

for perceptual learning: Exp 0 = Exp 1 > Exp 3 = Exp 4 > Exp 2

for skill learning: Exp 0 = Exp 1 = Exp 4

for episodic learning: Exp 4 ≥ Exp 3

Again, skill learning was functionally dissociated from perceptual and episodic learning. However, because Experiment 3 was not subdivided into its fragmented and complete picture priming conditions, the similarity of patterns observed for both perceptual and episodic learning by subjects were

TABLE 6.7
Correlations Between Measures and Tasks Based on Items

	Experiment				
	0	*1*	*2*	*3*	*4*[a]
No. items	60	30	30	30	60/120
Measure-to-measure					
SL(a) – SL(r)	.98†	.98†	N/A	N/A	.96†
PL(a) – PL(r)	.67†	.68†	.92†	.88†	.89†
Task-to-task					
P(t) – P(n)	.78†	.89†	N/A	N/A	.75†
P(n) – P(o)	.60†	.52†	.80†	.49†	.55†
P(t) – P(o)	.62†	.56†	N/A	N/A	.51†
SL(a) – PL(a)	– .51†	– .45†	N/A	N/A	– .32†
SL(r) – PL(r)	– .12	– .45†	N/A	N/A	– .26*
EL(o) – EL(n)	N/A	N/A	N/A	.22	.60†

$*p < .05$; †$p < .01$

[a]The two fragmented series for each pictures are treated as separate items for the skill and perceptual learning measures, but are combined for the episodic measures.

TABLE 6.8
Correlations Across Memory Tasks Based on Items

	Experiment			
	0	1	3	4[a]
No. of items	60	30	30	60/120
skill/percep				
$SL(r) - PL(r)$	−.12	−.45†	N/A	−.26*
skill/episod				
$SL(r) - EL(o)$	N/A	N/A	N/A	−.09*
$SL(r) - EL(n)$	N/A	N/A	N/A	−.04
percep/episod				
$PL(r) - EL(o)$	N/A	N/A	−.10	.18
$PL(r) - EL(n)$	N/A	N/A	.16	.09

*$p < .05$; †$p < .01$
[a]The two fragmented series for each picture are treated as separate items for the skill and perceptual learning measures, but are combined for the episodic measures.

obscured—episodic and perceptual learning were no longer parallel, and thus could be said to be partially dissociated.

Table 6.7 presents the correlations between measures and tasks based on items. As for the subject analysis, it was remarkable that the correlations between train and new performance were so high, based as they are on different subjects. Again, it points to the powerful effect of items in determining performance.

There were some differences between the patterns of correlations for the item-based and subject-based analyses. First, the correlations between $SL(r)$ and $PL(r)$ were significantly negative for two of the three experiments, whereas they were not in the subject-based analysis. Second, the correlation between the episodic components for Experiment 4 was stronger for items than for subjects.

Table 6.8 presents correlations across memory tasks. As noted previously, there was a significant negative correlation between the skill and perceptual learning measures for two of the three experiments for which they were available. I take this particular pattern of evidence with some reservations, however, because it is probably an artifact of the measurement procedure. None of the other memory-to-memory correlations was significant, so I conclude that virtually all of the item-based analyses support the separate memories position.

Tests on Subject-Items. Subject-item tests can only be carried out for Experiments 3 and 4, which measured both perceptual and episodic learning, because the same subject's performance must be obtained on the same item for at least two different tasks. Support for the separate memories position is obtained when a difference in a set of subject-items is obtained for one task, but no or the opposite difference is obtained for the second.

The most straightforward comparison is to determine whether identification performance during the course of training is different for recalled than for nonrecalled items, as measured by either of the perceptual learning measures. A relationship between episodic and perceptual learning is demonstrated whenever it can be shown that perceptual learning for recalled items is greater than for nonrecalled items.

In order to facilitate comparisons across Experiments 3 and 4, I combined data from priming Levels 3 and 5 in Experiment 3 (eliminating Level 8), and used only data for Set 3 from Experiment 4. This has the effect of equating perceptual learning measures across the two experiments. The results of a 2 (experiment) by 2 (recall status) by 2 (training level) mixed analysis of variance showed that both the main effect of recall and the recall by training interaction was significant, $F(1, 29) = 4.41$, $p = .04$ and $F(1, 29) = 4.10$, $p = .05$. There was no main effect of experiment nor did experiment interact with anything else. Planned comparisons showed that the difference between new picture identification for recalled and nonrecalled items was highly significant, $F(1, 29) = 10.64$, $p = .003$, whereas the difference between old item identification for recalled and nonrecalled items was not, $F < 1$.

Table 6.9 and Fig. 6.10 show new and old item performance for recalled and nonrecalled pictures combined across experiments, and Table 6.9 also shows the perceptual learning measures, based on differences between old and new recalled and nonrecalled pictures by subjects. It is apparent that recalled pictures only differed from nonrecalled pictures for new items, not for old items.

The analysis of the perceptual learning measures showed that perceptual learning was significantly greater for recalled than nonrecalled pictures for $PL(a)$ but not for $PL(r)$, $Fs(1, 30) = 4.75$ and 2.83, $ps = .04$ and .10 respectively. It is clear that this difference in perceptual learning occurred because new item identification was worse for recalled pictures, not because old item identification was better. This is an important result, because it shows the importance of measuring both new and old picture identification performance.

TABLE 6.9
Perceptual Identification and Perceptual Learning for Recalled and
Nonrecalled Pictures Combined Across Experiments 3 and 4 (Set 3 Only)

	recalled	nonrecalled
$P(n)$	.55	.63
$P(o)$	.76	.76
$PL(a)$	.21	.13
$PL(r)$	.47	.33

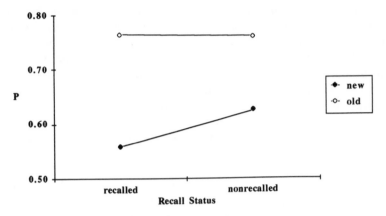

FIG. 6.10. Probability of identification (P) for new and old recalled and nonrecalled pictures in Experiments 3 and 4.

If only old picture identification had been considered, we would have concluded, along with several other investigators using the method of stochastic independence for subject-items, that perceptual and episodic learning were dissociated. In fact, in Experiment 4, recalled pictures had lower train performance (.54) than nonrecalled pictures (.59), although this difference did not reach significance.

The nature of the relationship between identification performance and recall suggests that when a picture is difficult to identify the first time it is presented (i.e., when it is a training or new item), it is easier to recall. Under this interpretation, the fact that perceptual learning is greater for recalled than for nonrecalled pictures is an artifact of the way in which perceptual learning is measured, and says nothing about the relationship between these two types of memory.

Discussion

Although most of the tests of stochastic independence showed normal dissociation between pairs of memory components, two showed strong dissociation (a negative correlation) and two showed association (a positive correlation).

Subject-based tests revealed a single positive memory-to-memory correlation, that between skill learning and old item recall for Experiment 4. Subjects who showed most learning between training and new items also showed highest recall for old (but not for new) items. Because that relationship seemed inexplicable, I attribute it to sampling error.

Item-based tests revealed that two of three correlations between skill and perceptual learning were negative, thereby supporting strong dissociation and the separate memories position. There is, however, a measurement problem in comparing skill and perceptual learning. Both learning measures have in common new item identification performance, $P(n)$, which is added to the skill learning measure and subtracted from the perceptual learning measure. When a correlation is computed between a gain score measured from baseline and the baseline measure, the correlation tends to be spuriously negative because it contains the error of measurement of the baseline measurement common to both (Lord & Novick, 1968, p. 73). Although the negative correlations between skill and perceptual learning disappeared for the relative measures $SL(r)$ and $PL(r)$ in the subject-based analyses, they reappeared in the item analysis. Thus these negative correlations between skill and perceptual learning would appear to be due to measurement artifact rather than to strong dissociation between skill and perceptual learning.

Finally, subject-item based tests showed a positive correlation between perceptual and episodic learning. However, this positive association was attributable to a difference in new identification scores, not to a difference in old identification scores. This positive correlation would appear to be spurious as it reflects the influence of effortfulness on recall performance for both old and new items.

Having disposed of all of the evidence *against* Tulving's proposal that there are separate memory modules, are we now prepared to conclude that these experiments support the separate memories position? The answer to that is, alas, "no." The exercise of showing how all the nonzero correlations should be zero could also be turned around to show how all the zero correlations should really be positive. There are issues of measurement that must be solved before any definitive interpretation of patterns of positive, negative, or zero associations can be interpreted.

Certainly, we have shown that real data can evidence the same sort of variable patterns when evaluated across the three units of analyses that Tulving (1985) demonstrated with artificial data. Patterns of dissociations or associations from subjects to items to subject-items are not predictable. Accordingly, I argue that dissociation or association effects based on the various units of analysis on which they are computed must be interpreted with caution.

GENERAL DISCUSSION

In this discussion, I consider various interpretations of dissociations between implicit and explicit memory tasks, and then I present a synthesis. Schacter (1987) reviewed three theoretical views that attempt to account for dissociation between implicit and explicit memory. Here I consider each of these in turn in the light of results from the present set of experiments. The three views are activation, processing differences or similarities between encoding and test, and the separate memories position with which this paper began.

First, however, I would like to clarify my usage of certain terms. I use the terms "procedural," "semantic," and "episodic" to describe different memory tasks, even though by such usage I do not mean to commit myself to the separate memories model. Similarly, I use the terms "priming," "perceptual learning," and "item-specific learning effects" interchangeably to refer to the facilitation observed on repeated items, even though some of these terms are not neutral with respect to the locus of the facilitation effect.

Earlier, I identified priming effects in word and picture fragment completion with the semantic system. Most memory theorists agree that priming is an implicit memory phenomenon, although they disagree about whether it should be attributed to the procedural or semantic systems. Tulving (1985) suggested that priming effects in word fragment completion might occur in the procedural system, the semantic system, or in yet a fourth system that he whimsically called QM for Question Mark. But because we can clearly distinguish between performance improvements expressed on novel items and performance improvements expressed on repeated items, this distinction should be reflected in our terms for these two types of learning. Therefore, I identify the first kind of learning with the procedural system and the second kind of learning with the semantic system. Thus procedural or skill learning refers to task practice effects and priming or perceptual learning refers to item practice effects.

Let me examine the basic picture fragment completion task in more detail to clarify my usage of terms and to illustrate the theoretical debate. During the initial study phase, subjects are confronted with a task that is, in my view, relentlessly semantic. They are asked to identify a picture from a few fragments. Such a task clearly relies on semantic memory for its execution. Subjects need to access information about the way objects (or their line drawing representations) look and to find information about the names of these objects. This information has accumulated over the years into the subject's semantic system and, at this point in the subject's life, is presumably not associated with a single episode of learning. Thus, this phase of the task is decidedly not an episodic memory task. In addition to accessing information about the appearance and names of specific items, however, subjects must also use some general skills in recognizing objects. Such object recognition skills fall within the procedural memory system.

In the test phase of the experiment, subjects are shown both old and new pictures. When they are confronted with new pictures, their performance shows a small improvement over the training pictures. Somehow, their experience with the training pictures has increased their facility in the task. Although the act of identifying new pictures relies on semantic memory in the same way that the act of identifying training pictures did, the *increase* in facility between training and testing reflects some improvement in the general procedure of object recognition. That is, the *improvement* is procedural in nature, even though the task on which such improvement is exhibited—identification of new pictures—is semantic. This improvement may consist of learning to see connections among fragments representing lines and curves of the picture's outline, because subjects appear to need to see some minimal number of fragmented images during training to exhibit such skill learning.

When subjects are confronted with old pictures in the test session, they show a much larger improvement compared to the training pictures, the priming or perceptual learning effect. It is the site and nature of this improvement—the priming or perceptual learning effect—that is in question.

The activation model of priming (Graf & Mandler, 1984; Mandler, 1980; Morton, 1979) holds that the act of identifying a repeated picture is, like the act of identifying a training or new picture, based upon retrieval of information from semantic memory. However, because this information in semantic memory has recently been accessed, it exhibits increased availability or priming that leads to facilitation in picture identification.

Under the activation model, the priming effect reflects a change in the state of a subject such that an impoverished stimulus that, without prior exposure, would remain a meaningless jumble of lines and curves, comes to more easily *evoke* its stored semantic memory image. Such evocation occurs without conscious effort on the part of the observer, and indeed may be impeded by effortful recollection. Such a process could be viewed as the lowering of a threshold for the stored visual image, represented either as a set of features or as a prototypical visual image (Snodgrass, 1980, 1984). The fragmented image acts like a key in a lock, producing a perceptible image where otherwise there would be only a meaningless jumble. The "key-in-the-lock" metaphor accords well with phenomenological experience in this task.

The activation explanation places the locus of priming effects squarely in the domain of the semantic system, and thus is consistent with the separate memories view. Schacter (1987) pointed out two problems with the activation view in accounting for priming effects in normal subjects. The first is the sometimes long-lasting effects of a single priming experience, and the second is the apparent priming effects observed for new associations. The long lasting effects of priming are problematic because, according to Tulving's (1983) characterization, retrieval from semantic memory leaves it unchanged. New associations are presumably formed in episodic memory, and thus priming effects for new associations must occur there if the distinctions between semantic and episodic memory systems are to be maintained.

The processing explanation of priming holds that the similarity of processing operations between study and test determines the amount of learning (Craik, 1983; Jacoby, 1983; Kolers & Roediger, 1984; Roediger & Blaxton, 1987; Roediger & Weldon, 1987). Priming effects are optimal when the test representation most closely matches the study representation. Because priming by its definition relies on presentation of some version of the stimulus for learning to be exhibited, performance in priming tasks has also been described as data-driven, in contrast to episodic tasks such as recall that are conceptually-driven (Roediger & Blaxton, 1987).

The processing similarity explanation strongly resembles the principle of encoding specificity proposed by Tulving (1972, 1983; Tulving & Thomson, 1971) to account for context effects in episodic learning. It differs from encoding specificity in emphasizing processing similarities rather than stimulus context similarities; however, because priming tasks depend upon presenting the same stimulus again, it is hard to distinguish the two positions operationally. The processing similarity explanation differs from both the activation model and the separate memories model in assuming that priming effects reflect the establishment of new episodic representations.

The processing similarity/encoding specificity approach gives a good account of the present data. Perceptual learning was best when the study and test conditions were identical, and was worst when the study and test conditions differed (as in Experiment 2 and 3b when complete pictures were used as primes). Furthermore, it gives a good account of the particular pattern of associations between recall and identification: Recall was best when identification was worst—that is, when subjects on the first presentation of an item needed to do a good deal of work.

To recapitulate, the activation and separate memories position are similar in asserting that priming effects occur in the semantic system (although Tulving has admitted the possibility of yet a fourth system). Their problems are similar in the difficulty of reconciling the extreme longevity of priming with short-lived activation of the semantic system (Corkin (1982) showed that the amnesic H. M. showed priming for the Gollin picture task after 14 years!); and with the fact that priming effects seem to be subject to the same principle of encoding specificity seen in episodic memory. Yet to assert that because priming and episodic memory tasks rely on the same processes and principles, they must occur in the same system means giving up the useful distinction between semantic and episodic memory.

In order to preserve Tulving's distinction between semantic and episodic memory systems, we need to change some of the properties of semantic memory. Specifically, we need to propose that the principle of encoding specificity applies to both semantic and episodic memory. Retrieval from semantic memory under perceptually distinct conditions can leave a context-dependent tag that is easily accessed by reintegrating the initial study contexts. For reasons that are unclear (see Schacter, 1987), such a tag does not seem to contain the self-referential information about time and place of occurrence that would identify it easily as having occurred in the learner's autobiographical past. Thus, retrieval of previously stored information during a priming task seems often to be unaccompanied by conscious recollection of the episode of learning (and seems never to be accompanied by such recollection in amnesic subjects).

The relative longevity of priming may depend not only on the degree of similarity between the encoding and retrieval episodes, but also the similarity of each of these to other episodes in the subject's day-to-day life. Thus, in the Tulving et al. (1982) experiment, recognition as to whether or not a word is old may suffer over a 1-week interval because subjects have experienced similar or identical words during the intervening period. Word fragment completion may not, because subjects have not experienced similar word fragments during the intervening period (a crossword puzzle addict, on the other hand, might show a decrement). Similarly, H. M. could show savings in the Gollin pictures because the encoding to retrieval similarity was unique compared to his other experiences during the 14-year interval.

In summary, then, it seems to me that a synthesis of theories might deal with not only the present set of results, but the overwhelming mass of data in the literature on functional and stochastic associations and dissociations. By accepting the important role of encoding-test similarity, by permitting greater context-dependent effects in semantic memory, and by considering not only the encoding-to-test similarity but the encoding/test to other environments similarity, we might be able to reconcile conflicting results and interpretations.

ACKNOWLEDGMENTS

The author would like to thank Kelly Feenan and Youmin Kim for their help in running subjects and analyzing data. June Corwin and Kelly Feenan provided supportive and illuminating discussions about the interpretations of the results presented here. This research was supported in part by a Research Challenge Fund grant from New York University and a University Research Initiative Program grant from the Air Force Office of Scientific Research.

REFERENCES

Baddeley, A. (1984). Neuropsychological evidence and the semantic/episodic distinction. *Behavioral and Brain Sciences, 7,* 238–239.

Biederman, I. (1985). Human image understanding: Recent experiments and theory. *Computer Vision, Graphics, and Image Processing, 32,* 29–73.

Biederman, I. (1987). Recognition-by-components: A theory of human image understanding. *Psychological Review, 94,* 115–147.

Cohen, N. J. (1984). Preserved learning capacity in amnesia: Evidence for multiple memory systems. In L. R. Squire & N. Butters (Eds.), *Neuropsychology of Memory* (pp. 83–103). New York: Guilford Press.

Cohen, N. J. & Squire, L. R. (1980). Preserved learning and retention of pattern-analyzing skill in amnesia: Dissociation of knowing how and knowing that. *Science, 210,* 207–210.

Corkin, S. (1982). Some relationships between global amnesias and the memory impairments in Alzheimer's disease. In S. Corkin, K. L. Davis, J. H. Growdon, E. Usdin, & R. J. Wurtman (Eds.), *Alzheimer's Disease: A report of progress* (pp. 149–164). New York: Raven Press.

Craik, F. I. M. (1983). On the transfer of information from temporary to permanent memory. *Philosophical Transactions of the Royal Society of London, 302,* 341–359.

Ebbinghaus, H. (1913). Memory: A contribution to experimental psychology (H. A. Ruger &

C. E. Bussenius, Trans.). New York: Teachers College, Columbia University. (Original work published 1885)

Gollin, E. S. (1960). Developmental studies of visual recognition of incomplete objects. *Perceptual and Motor Skills, 11*, 289–298.

Gollin, E. S. (1961). Further studies of visual recognition of incomplete objects. *Perceptual and Motor Skills, 13*, 307–314.

Gollin, E. S. (1962). Factors affecting the visual recognition of incomplete objects: A comparative investigation of children and adults. *Perceptual and Motor Skills, 15*, 583–590.

Gollin, E. S. (1965). Perceptual learning of incomplete pictures. *Perceptual and Motor Skills, 21*, 439–445.

Gollin, E. S. (1966). Serial learning and perceptual recognition in children: Training, delay, and order effects. *Perceptual and Motor Skills, 23*, 751–758.

Graf, P., & Mandler, G. (1984). Activation makes words more accessible, but not necessarily more retrievable. *Journal of Verbal Learning and Verbal Behavior, 23*, 553–568.

Graf, P., & Schacter, D. L. (1985). Implicit and explicit memory for new associations in normal and amnesic patients. *Journal of Experimental Psychology: Learning, Memory, and Cognition, 11*, 501–518.

Graf, P., & Schacter, D. L. (1987). Selective effects of interference on implicit and explicit memory for new associations. *Journal of Experimental Psychology: Learning, Memory, and Cognition, 13*, 45–53.

Graf, P., Squire, L. R., & Mandler, G. (1984). The information that amnesic patients do not forget. *Journal of Experimental Psychology: Learning, Memory, and Cognition, 10*, 164–178.

Hirst, W., & Volpe, B. T. (1982). Automatic and effortful encoding in amnesia. In L. S. Cermak (Ed.), *Human memory and amnesia* (pp. 369–386). Hillsdale, NJ: Lawrence Erlbaum Associates.

Jacoby, L. L. (1982). Knowing and remembering: Some parallels in the behavior of Korsakoff patients and normals. In L. S. Cermak (Ed.), *Human memory and amnesia* (pp. 97–122). Hillsdale, NJ: Lawrence Erlbaum Associates.

Jacoby, L. L. (1983). Perceptual enhancement: Persistent effects of an experience. *Journal of Experimental Psychology: Learning, Memory, and Cognition, 9*, 21–38.

Jacoby, L. L., & Dallas, M. (1981). On the relationship between autobiographical memory and perceptual learning. *Journal of Experimental Psychology: General, 110*, 306–340.

Jacoby, L. L., & Witherspoon, D. (1982). Remembering without awareness. *Canadian Journal of Psychology, 36*, 300–324.

Kolers, P. A. (1976). Reading a year later. *Journal of Experimental Psychology: Human Learning and Memory, 2*, 554–565.

Kolers, P. A., & Roediger, H. L., III (1984). Procedures of mind. *Journal of Verbal Learning and Verbal Behavior, 23*, 425–449.

Lord, F. M., & Novick, M. R. (1968). *Statistical theories of mental test scores*. Reading, MA: Addison-Wesley.

Mandler, G. (1980). Recognizing: The judgment of previous occurrence. *Psychological Review, 87*, 252–271.

Marcel, A. J. (1983). Conscious and unconscious perception: Experiments on visual masking and word recognition. *Cognitive Psychology, 15*, 197–237.

Mitchell, D. B., & Brown, A. S. (1988). Persistent repetition priming in picture naming and its dissociation from recognition memory. *Journal of Experimental Psychology: Learning, Memory, & Cognition, 14*, 213–222.

Morton, J. (1979). Facilitation in word recognition: Experiments causing change in the logogen models. In P. A. Kolers, M. E. Wrolstead, & H. Bouma (Eds.), *Processing of visible language 1* (pp. 259–268). New York: Plenum.

Parkin, A. J. (1982). Residual learning capability in organic amnesia. *Cortex, 18*, 417–440.

Roediger, H. L. (1984). Does current evidence from dissociation experiments favor the episodic/semantic distinction? *Behavioral and Brain Sciences, 7*, 252–254.

Roediger, H. L., & Blaxton, T. A. (1987). Retrieval modes produce dissociations in memory for surface information. In D. S. Gorfein & R. R. Hoffman (Eds.), *Memory and cognitive processes: The Ebbinghaus centennial conference* (pp. 349–379). Hillsdale, NJ: Lawrence Erlbaum Associates.

Roediger, H. L., & Weldon, M. S. (1987). Reversing the picture superiority effect. In M. A. McDaniel & M. Pressley (Eds.), *Imagery and related mnemonic processes: Theories, individual differences, and applications* (pp. 151–174). New York: Springer-Verlag.

Scarborough, D. L., Cortese, C., & Scarborough, H. (1977). Frequency and repetition effects in lexical memory. *Journal of Experimental Psychology: Human Perception and Performance, 3*, 1–17.

Scarborough, D. L., Gerard, L., & Cortese, C. (1979). Accessing lexical memory: The transfer of word repetition effects across task and modality. *Memory & Cognition, 7*, 3–12.

Schacter, D. L. (1987). Implicit memory: History and current status. *Journal of Experimental Psychology: Learning, Memory, and Cognition, 13*, 501–518.

Schacter, D. L., & Graf, P. (1986). Preserved learning in amnesic patients: Perspectives from research on direct priming. *Journal of Clinical and Experimental Neuropsychology, 8*, 727–743.

Schneider, K. (1912). Über einige klinisch-pathologische Untersuchungsmethoden und ihre Ergebnisse: Zugleich ein Beitrag zur Psychopathologie der Korsakowschen Psychose [On certain clinical-pathological methods of research and their results. Together with a contribution to the psychopathology of Korsakoff's psychosis]. *Zeitschrift fur Neurologie und Psychiatrie, 8*, 553–616.

Snodgrass, J. G. (1980). Toward a model for picture and word processing. In P. A. Kolers, M. E. Wrolstad, & H. Bouma (Eds.), *Processing of visible language 2* (pp. 565–584). New York: Plenum.

Snodgrass, J. G. (1984). Concepts and their surface representations. *Journal of Verbal Learning and Verbal Behavior, 23*, 3–22.

Snodgrass, J. G., & Corwin, J. (1988). Perceptual identification thresholds for 150 fragmented pictures from the Snodgrass and Vanderwart picture set. *Perceptual and Motor Skills, 67*, 3–36. (Monograph Supplement 1-V67)

Snodgrass, J. G., Smith, B., Feenan, K., & Corwin, J. (1987). Fragmenting pictures on the Apple Macintosh computer for experimental and clinical applications. *Behavior Research Methods, Instruments, & Computers, 19*, 270–274.

Snodgrass, J. G., & Vanderwart, M. (1980). A standardized set of 260 pictures: Norms for naming agreement, familiarity, and visual complexity. *Journal of Experimental Psychology: Human Learning and Memory, 6*, 174–215.

Tulving, E. (1972). Episodic and semantic memory. In E. Tulving & W. Donaldson (Eds.), *Organization of memory* (pp. 381–403). New York: Academic Press.

Tulving, E. (1983). *Elements of episodic memory*. New York: Oxford University press.

Tulving, E. (1984). Precis of elements of episodic memory. *Behavioral and Brain Sciences, 7*, 223–268.

Tulving, E. (1985). How many memory systems are there? *American Psychologist, 4*, 385–398.

Tulving, E., Schacter, D. L., & Stark, H. A. (1982). Priming effects in word-fragment completion are independent of recognition memory. *Journal of Experimental Psychology: Learning, Memory, and Cognition, 8*, 336–342.

Tulving, E., & Thomson, D. M. (1971). Retrieval processes in recognition memory: Effects of associative context. *Journal of Experimental Psychology, 87*, 116–124.

Vokey, J. R., Baker, J. G., Hayman, G., & Jacoby, L. L. (1986). Perceptual identification of visually degraded stimuli. *Behavior Research Methods, Instruments, & Computers, 18*, 1–9.

Warrington, E. K., & Weiskrantz, L. (1968). New method of testing long-term retention with special reference to amnesic patients. *Nature, 217*, 972–974.

7

Hypermnesia: Improvements in Recall With Repeated Testing

Henry L. Roediger, III
Rice University

Bradford H. Challis
Purdue University

Memory is never so perplexing a capacity as when it fails. Everyone has had the experience of trying repeatedly to recall something well known, but failing utterly. Just as curious is the experience of the forgotten fact or name suddenly reappearing at some later point, even without a conscious intention to remember it. In his monumental experimental monograph, *Über Das Gedächtnis*, Ebbinghaus (1885/1964) noted that "Names, faces, bits of knowledge and experience that had seemed lost for years suddenly appear before the mind, especially in dreams, with every detail present and in great vividness; and it is hard to see whence they came and how they managed to keep hidden so well in the meantime" (p. 62).

The phenomenon of spontaneous remembering after retrieval failures is difficult to study empirically. One method sometimes used to investigate such memory failures and recoveries involves having people keep diaries of such experiences (Reason & Lucas, 1984). This method provides descriptive information and may be useful in the first stages of investigating the phenomenon. However, most researchers have preferred experimental methods, dating back to the turn of the century. The typical strategy has been to provide subjects with material to remember and then to test them repeatedly with no intervening study. The usual finding is that people remember material on later tests that they failed to produce on earlier tests. Because the nature of the external retrieval conditions typically does not change between tests, these represent cases of spontaneous remembering. Ballard (1913) provided the first well known series of experiments demonstrating these phenomena. Following presentation of different types of material to school children, he gave them repeated tests at various intervals of time since learning (but with no intervening study opportunities). He discovered that the children almost always recalled material on later tests that they could not recall on earlier tests, and that frequently the total amount recalled improved on the later tests. (That is, recovery of material between tests outweighed forgetting.)

REMINISCENCE AND HYPERMNESIA

We describe later experiments by W. Brown (1923) to illustrate the basic phenomena from this sort of experiment and to introduce some terminology. Brown asked the basic question that formed the title of his paper, "To what extent is memory measured by a single recall?" Brown performed two experiments. In the first, he asked college students to recall as many of the 48 states as possible during a 5-minute period. A half hour later, without any warning, he gave them the same task again. The interest was in determining differences in performance between the two tests. The second experiment was similar, except that in this case students were given 48 words to memorize, with each word presented four times. Once again, an initial 5-minute recall occurred immediately after learning, and second test followed after 30 minutes.

The results from Brown's experiments are presented in Table 7.1. The first two rows represent the total number of items recalled on the first (T_1) and second (T_2) tests, respectively, with the difference ($T_2 - T_1$) in the third row. The fact that subjects performed better on the second test than on the first test was the finding that provided so much interest to Ballard and others. After all, the second test occurs a considerable amount of time after the first test and thus one would normally expect forgetting to occur between the two tests, at least in retention of the list. However, performance on the second test was actually better than that on the first test. (No inferential statistics were applied to Brown's data, but results like his have been frequently replicated, as the remainder of this chapter attests.)

Brown also broke down performance into two components of interest, intertest forgetting and intertest recovery. Despite the fact that more items were recalled on the second test than on the first test, some items were actually forgotten between the two tests. That is, states or words recalled on the first test were forgotten on the second test. These data are presented in the fourth row of Table 7.1, and indicate that more words than states were forgotten be-

TABLE 7.1
Results From Brown's (1923) Experiments

	States	Word List	
Test 1	36.31	25.48	
Test 2	39.66	26.77	
Difference ($T_2 - T_1$)	3.35	1.29	Hypermnesia
Intertest Forgetting	1.94	3.04	
Intertest Recovery	5.29	4.33	Reminiscence

tween tests. In the fifth row is the number of items recovered between the two tests, or items not recalled on the first test that were recalled on the second. Obviously, the overall improvement between tests for states (and to a lesser extent for words) reflects the fact that intertest recovery exceeded intertest forgetting in Brown's experiments.

Ballard (1913) defined reminiscence as "the remembering again of the forgotten without re-learning" (p. v). The proper index of reminiscence then is intertest recovery—the number of items recalled on a second test that could not be recalled on a first test (with no intervening study between tests). However, Ballard (1913) occasionally examined reminiscence by reporting the overall gain between two tests, even though he clearly made the distinction between improvement between two tests and intertest recovery (pp. 17-18). Unfortunately, as Erdelyi (1984) and Payne (1987) have documented, this inconsistency in applying the term reminiscence led other researchers to the conclusion that reminiscence was not a reliable phenomenon. These investigators defined reminiscence as overall improvement between tests and noted that many experiments failed to reveal this outcome. For example, Buxton (1943) reviewed the literature and concluded that reminiscence was an unreliable phenomenon. However, the careful examination of the literature provided by Payne (1987) reveals that, when properly defined as intertest recovery, reminiscence almost always occurs in experiments involving repeated memory tests. That is, information is recalled on later tests that could not be recalled on earlier ones, even though overall improvement in the amount of information recalled between tests might not occur. Buxton's (1943) pessimistic review was probably partly responsible for the decline in theoretical and empirical interest in reminiscence until the issue was reopened by important new work by Matthew Erdelyi in the 1970s.[1]

Because of the historical confusion in using the term *reminiscence*, the current chapter will follow the relatively recent practice of defining reminiscence (as did Ballard) as intertest recovery, or recall of items on a second (or later) test that could not be recalled on a first. The overall improvement between tests will be referred to as *hypermnesia*, following the reintroduction of this term by Erdelyi and Becker (1974). Hypermnesia reflects the fact that performance increases between tests over time, in contrast to more typical forgetting or amnesia over time.

HYPERMNESIA

The resurgence of interest in hypermnesia can be traced to important studies of Erdelyi and his colleagues (e.g., Erdelyi & Becker, 1974; Erdelyi & Klein-

---

[1]At least three other lines of research have employed repeated testing paradigms: (a) Estes' (1960) "RTT" paradigm with paired associate learning (see, for example, Izawa, 1971, 1981); (b) Tulving's (1967) repeated free recall paradigm with very limited recall time; and (c) the issue of improvements over time in motor learning (Eysenck & Frith, 1977). These literatures are only partially relevant to issues of the present chapter and will be cited when appropriate.

bard, 1978). We present the results of an experiment by Erdelyi, Finkelstein, Herrell, Miller, and Thomas (1976) because it serves to make both the relevant empirical and theoretical points most strongly. Three groups of subjects were shown different types of material with instructions to study the items carefully in preparation for a recall test. One group received 60 pictures, simple sketches of objects such as *flag* or *trumpet*. Another group received 60 words, the names of the pictures. A third group of subjects was also shown the 60 words, but in addition, were instructed to form vivid images of each named object as it was presented.

Following study, subjects were given three successive 7-minute tests at retention intervals of 1 minute, 15 minutes, and 29 minutes and told to provide as many list items as possible. (Subjects who studied pictures were told to write down names of the pictures.) A forced recall procedure was used on each test; subjects were given sheets with 40 spaces and told to write down 40 items, even if they had to guess. The forced recall procedure insured that response criteria did not change across test. (Prior work had shown that 40 responses would be well above the average number recalled.) Between tests, subjects were instructed to sit back and think about the stimulus set in preparation for the next test.

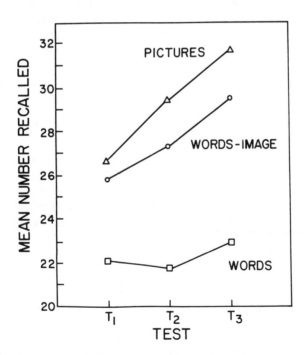

FIG. 7.1. Results of Erdelyi et al. (1976). Recall of pictures and imaged words increased across tests, but recall of words studied without imagery instructions did not.

TABLE 7.2
Forgetting and Reminiscence in Erdelyi et al. (1976)

	Forgetting		Reminiscence	
	Number[1]	As a Proportion of Test 1 Recall	Number[2]	As a Proportion of Remaining Targets
Pictures	5.0	.19	9.1	.27
Words-Image	4.4	.17	7.4	.22
Words	3.3	.15	3.6	.09

[1]Number of items recalled on Test 1 that were not recalled on either Test 2 or Test 3 (or both).
[2]Number of items not recalled on Test 1 but later recalled on either Test 2 or Test 3 (or both).

The results are shown in Fig. 7.1. As can be seen, recall of pictures increased substantially across the three tests. When words had been studied without imagery instructions, the total number recalled was relatively constant. However, when words had been presented with instructions to form images, recall resembled the pattern for pictures. Thus, both pictures and imaged words showed hypermnesia, whereas presentation of words with no special instructions did not. The picture/word difference replicated prior experiments by Erdelyi and Becker (1974). In response to this consistent pattern of results, Erdelyi et al. (1976) proposed that hypermnesia only occurred for information coded in memory in an imaginal format: Pictures and imaged words showed the effect, whereas recall of verbal materials did not in their experiment or in many others (but see Brown, 1923 and Table 7.1).

Further evidence for the idea that pictures and words whose referents were imagined are especially susceptible to "spontaneous recovery" after being forgotten can be found in Table 7.2, which presents intertest forgetting and reminiscence in Erdelyi et al.'s (1976) experiment. The left hand side of the table shows the number of items that were recalled on the first test, but were forgotten on Test 2, on Test 3, or on both. The number of pictures forgotten was actually somewhat greater than the number of words forgotten, with the Words-Image condition falling in between. However, because more pictures than words were recalled on Test 1, more opportunities existed for forgetting in this condition. When the forgetting figures are expressed as a proportion of the number of items forgotten after Test 1 relative to the number of items recalled during Test 1 (the second column), the differences in forgetting among types of material are less apparent. Thus, forgetting of pictures or words—given that they were recalled on Test 1—was roughly constant in the Erdelyi et al. (1976) data.[2]

---

[2]The forgetting data in Table 7.2 ignore one type of forgetting across three tests: items forgotten on Test 1, recalled on Test 2, but forgotten again on Test 3. The mean number of items exhibiting this pattern of forgetting in each condition was .9 for Pictures, .6 for Imagined Words, and .6 for Words studied without imagery instructions.

On the other hand, the reminiscence results at the right side of Table 7.2 exhibit a very different pattern. The third column shows the number of new items recalled after Test 1 for the three conditions. The Picture groups exhibited more spontaneous recovery than did the Words-Image group, which in turn outperformed the group that studied only Words without special instructions. These differences become even larger when taken as a proportion of the number of potential items that could be recalled after Test 1, because the pool of remaining target pictures was smaller than that for target words due to differential recall in Test 1. (That is, because 26.65 Pictures were recalled and 22.10 Words were recalled on Test 1, the pool of remaining targets was 33.35 for Pictures and 37.90 for Words. The proportions in the rightmost column reflect observed reminiscence relative to the total possible amount.) Thus, much greater reminiscence occurred for pictures and imagined words than for words, although even with words subjects recalled 9% of the targets on Tests 2 and 3 that were not produced on Test 1. In line with the findings of many others (e.g., Tulving, 1967), reminiscence occurs for words but often tends to be balanced by intertest forgetting. Pictures and imaged words show hypermnesia because the reminiscence outweighs the intertest forgetting.

The remainder of this chapter is devoted to reviewing research, largely from our laboratory, seeking to answer basic questions about reminiscence and hypermnesia. The questions include: What causes hypermnesia? Is repeated testing necessary for its occurrence? Is the forced recall procedure a necessary condition? Why is hypermnesia greater for pictures (and for imaged words) than for words? Do other variables also affect hypermnesia? What theoretical constructs are necessary for understanding it? The following sections are devoted to answering these questions, as well as to raising a few other issues.

THE ROLE OF REPEATED TESTING

One fundamental question about hypermnesia is the extent to which repeated testing is responsible for the phenomenon. This issue arose in the early work on reminiscence in which investigators sought to determine whether improvements across time could occur without repeated testing. Indeed, when repeated testing was eliminated by using between-subjects designs, the typical finding was either forgetting or no change of material over time (see McGeoch & Irion, 1952, chap. 5).

Shapiro and Erdelyi (1974) examined this issue again using Erdelyi's newly developed paradigm involving recall of pictures and words. They presented subjects with either 60 pictures or 60 words and then tested them once, either after a delay of 30 seconds or of 5 minutes. Both variables were manipulated between subjects. During the retention interval, subjects were instructed to review the material covertly. Shapiro and Erdelyi reported that people who studied pictures performed better after 5 minutes than after 30 seconds (33.1 vs. 29.6, respectively), but there was no reliable difference in performance between the two tests for people who studied words (22.8 vs. 24.3). If taken at face value, these results would indicate that recall increased over the retention interval for pictures without practice due to testing. However, the procedure of providing subjects with a 5-minute interval to think about the material may have effectively extended the subjects' recall time, or permitted them practice at repeatedly retrieving the items. Of course, one would then need to explain why the improvement occurred for pictures but not words, but a possible solution to this issue is described in the following section.

Roediger and Payne (1982) also addressed the issue of whether improvements in net recall across repeated tests were attributable to some change in the memory trace correlated with time (e.g., consolidation of imaginal representations) or was due to practice effects arising from repeated tests. To separate these explanations, they presented subjects with a set of 60 pictures and then gave them three successive free recall tests. Three different groups of subjects were tested, with the primary variable being the delay of the first test. The retention interval prior to the first test was filled by reading a passage from the *Scientific American* to prevent rehearsal or retrieval practice on the pictures. Reading was deemed unlikely to provide much retroactive interference for the pictures. Thus, for the three different groups, the first test occurred after either a Short, Intermediate, or Long delay. For subjects in the Intermediate and Long delay conditions, their first test began at the same time that the Short delay subjects began their second and third tests, respectively (see Table 7.3). The design outlined in Table 7.3 disentangles the natural confounding in repeated testing studies between retention interval and the number of prior tests.

Three facts emerge from the data presented in Table 7.3. First, by looking at the rows, note that hypermnesia occurred in each condition, as recall improved across the three tests. (The magnitude was the same as in the Picture condition in Erdelyi et al., 1976.) Second, an examination of the downward diagonals in Table 7.3 shows that improvements in recall did not occur across

TABLE 7.3
Results from Roediger and Payne (1982)

Condition	Study	Retention Interval $t \longrightarrow$			
Short	60 Pictures	T_1 25.6	T_2 27.9	T_3 30.1	
Intermediate	60 Pictures		T_1 25.1	T_2 27.5	T_3 29.8
Long	60 Pictures			T_1 25.6	T_2 28.9	T_3 31.3

retention intervals in the absence of repeated testing. For example, subjects in the Immediate, Short, and Long delay conditions recalled 25.6, 25.1, and 25.6 items, respectively, on their initial tests. On the other hand, when the retention interval was held constant, recall increased directly with the number of prior tests. For example, in the middle column of Table 7.3, data are shown for the three groups with the retention interval held constant but the number of previous tests varied. Looking from the bottom to the top of the column (T_1, T_2, and T_3), it is obvious that recall improved directly as a function of prior tests and that the increase is the same as in the "normal" repeated testing conditions represented by data in the rows. The conclusion from Table 7.3 is that hypermnesia for pictures depends directly on the number of prior tests and does not occur over time in absence of retrieval practice.

CUMULATIVE RECALL AND
THE RECALL LEVEL HYPOTHESIS

At about the time Erdelyi and Becker (1974) were publishing their seminal work on hypermnesia, the senior author was engaged in two other lines of work in which cumulative recall data were being collected (Roediger, Stellon, & Tulving, 1977; Roediger & Tulving, 1979). Cumulative recall curves portray how recall changes over time during testing and can be collected by the simple expedient of asking subjects to draw lines at regular intervals during the testing period. Because such data illuminate dynamic aspects of recall, they have been studied, sporadically, for over 40 years. For example, the data in Fig. 7.2 come from Bousfield and Sedgewick (1944), who asked subjects to write down as many items as they could from common categories during a 16-minute period. As can be seen, group cumulative recall curves are quite orderly and are well fit by an exponential equation of the following form: $n(t) = n(\infty)(1 - e^{-\lambda t})$, where $n(t)$ represents the number of items that have been recalled by time t, $n(\infty)$ is the asymptote of the function (the lower bound estimate of the number of items accessible), e is the base of the natural algorithm, and λ is the rate of approaching the asymptote.

Surprisingly little work has been directed at understanding the dynamics of cumulative recall (although see Indow & Togano, 1970 and Vorberg & Ulrich, 1987). Our current interest lies in the use of such an analysis in understanding reminiscence and hypermnesia. One more fact about the curves shown in Fig. 7.2 is necessary for our analysis: The parameter reflecting the rate of approaching the asymptote, λ, is negatively correlated with the asymptotic level of recall, $n(\infty)$. The more items one knows in a category, the slower is one's rate of approaching the asymptotic level. This can be seen in Fig. 7.2 by comparing the cumulative recall curves from different sized categories. When recalling smaller categories, such as *unpleasant objects* or *European cities*, subjects approached the asymptote more quickly than when recalling

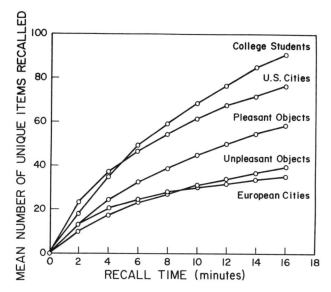

FIG. 7.2. Cumulative recall curves obtained by Bousfield and Sedgewick (1944).

larger categories, such as *pleasant objects*, or *U.S. cities*. For example, if we use recall at 16 minutes as an estimate of asymptotic recall, at 10 minutes subjects recalling European cities produced 85% of the responses whereas subjects recalling fellow college students recalled 76% of their responses (and note that the latter subjects had obviously not reached asymptote). The importance of the negative correlation between λ and $n(\infty)$ in our interpretation of hypermnesia will become apparent.

The question that initiated our work on hypermnesia was whether subjects given three successive tests in the standard Erdelyi and Becker (1974) paradigm would recall more information than would subjects given a single test of equivalent duration. Because cumulative recall curves often show gains even after long periods of time, as in Fig. 7.2, it seemed possible that the procedure of giving successive tests showed increases in recall simply because subjects were given additional time on later tests. Roediger and Thorpe (1978, Experiment 1) asked this question by presenting subjects either with 60 pictures or 60 words (the names of the pictures) and then testing them either with three successive 7-minute tests or one extended (21-minute) test. Free recall instructions were given in all tests and subjects were asked to draw a line after each minute of the test.

Three interesting facts emerged from this experiment. Two of these can be gleaned from results shown in Fig. 7.3, which portrays cumulative recall of the two groups of subjects given three successive tests after studying either pictures or words. First, note that hypermnesia occurred for both pictures

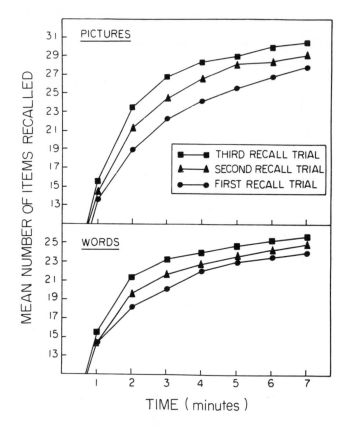

FIG. 7.3. Cumulative recall curves over three successive free recall tests
of either pictures or words (Roediger & Thorpe, 1978, Experiment 1).

and for words, although it seems somewhat greater for pictures. The usual
method of portraying hypermnesia results, such as in Fig. 7.1 of this chapter,
is simply to present the number of items recalled at the end of each test—the
far right hand points in Fig. 7.3. However, a second interesting fact to emerge
from this analysis is that the magnitude of hypermnesia might be greater if
somewhat shorter tests were given (e.g., 3 to 4 minutes, rather than 7).[3] Also,
note from Fig. 7.3 that if only 1 minute had been given for recall, no evidence
of hypermnesia would have been obtained. Erdelyi and Becker (1974) noted
that early findings of hypermnesia might not have been well replicated because
people typically employed verbal materials in their experiments. The data in

_____

[3]This claim rests on the assumption that three 3-minute tests would reveal the same pattern
of improvement as would three 7-minute tests at the end of the third minute, an untested assumption (but see Payne, 1986, Experiment 3). We would like to thank J. H. Neely for calling this
to our attention.

Fig. 7.3 suggest that another consideration in obtaining the effect is the amount of recall time provided, because in many experiments this was quite brief. For example, Tulving (1967, Experiment 2) gave subjects test periods of 36 seconds to report orally 36 studied words. Although he obtained reminiscence, no hypermnesia was observed due to great intertest forgetting. Presumably, subjects need ample time to recall prior items and new ones, as is evident in Fig. 7.3.

The third finding of Roediger and Thorpe (1978) is displayed in Fig. 7.4, where recall of pictures and words is shown for the entire 21-minute test period. For subjects given three tests, recall of an item was scored the first time it was recalled, with subsequent repeated recalls ignored. Thus, all four groups were scored by the same criterion. Although pictures were obviously recalled better than words, no difference existed in the number of unique items recalled between subjects given three successive tests and those given one long test of equivalent duration. In some sense, then, hypermnesia occurs because subjects are simply not given "long enough" on the first test to recall all the information they know.

But why should hypermnesia be greater for pictures than for words? Erdelyi suggested that the critical variable was whether or not information was coded in an imaginal format, but another possibility exists. Pictures are better recalled than are words studied with no special instructions, as seen in Fig.

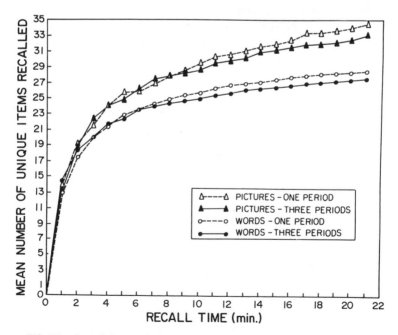

FIG. 7.4.   Cumulative recall of pictures and words over 21 minutes (Roediger & Thorpe, 1978, Experiment 1).

7.1 and 7.3 and in numerous other experiments. Perhaps level of recall, rather than imaginal coding, is the relevant variable. Indeed, examination of cumulative recall curves such as those shown in Fig. 7.2 and 7.4, has suggested to us a straightforward rationale for supposing that this is so.

THE CUMULATIVE RECALL LEVEL HYPOTHESIS

The logic underlying the recall level hypothesis of hypermnesia depends on several assumptions and will be illustrated with reference to the idealized cumulative recall curves in Fig. 7.5. The following assumptions are needed to explain hypermnesia (Roediger, Payne, Gillespie, & Lean, 1982; Roediger, 1982):

1. Hypermnesia, or increased recall across repeated tests, produces equivalent total recall as compared to performance of subjects given a single test of the same duration. The results of Roediger and Thorpe (1978, Experiment 1) support this assumption and it has been repeatedly verified (see Payne, 1986, 1987).

2. Because the total number of items recalled in repeated tests is equivalent to cumulative recall, properties of cumulative recall curves may be critical for understanding the phenomenon.

3. Cumulative recall curves typically exhibit a negative correlation between the asymptotic level of recall, $n(\infty)$, and the rate of approaching that asymptote, λ (Bousfield & Sedgewick, 1944).

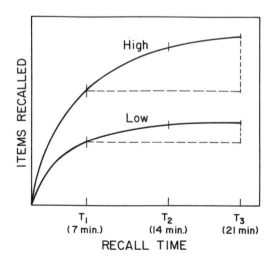

FIG. 7.5.   Hypothetical cumulative recall curves to illustrate the logic of the cumulative recall level hypothesis.

4. Because the rate of approaching the asymptote is greater with lower levels of asymptotic recall, if recall is stopped prior to the asymptote, performance will be nearer the asymptotic level in cases of lower than of higher recall. This is illustrated in Fig. 7.5. Performance at the first test (T_1) is closer to the asymptotic level of recall in the case of the Low curve than of the High curve. To take an actual example, recall at the end of the first test in the three conditions of Erdelyi et al.'s (1976) experiment was 75% of eventual recall for subjects recalling pictures, 78% for those recalling imagined words, and 86% those recalling words without instructions (see Fig. 7.1). Thus, the higher the overall level of asymptotic recall, the greater the potential for further gains in recall after Test 1.

5. Therefore, hypermnesia (growth in recall over repeated tests) will be correlated with cumulative recall level, $n(\infty)$, or, more precisely, with the difference between cumulative recall and recall on a first test (cumulative recall $- T_1$ recall). If the logic is correct, then the reason for greater recall in one condition than another should not matter. That is, the picture/word contrast is not special in producing hypermnesia and similar results should be found by varying cumulative recall level in other ways.

6. Another assumption was noted only in passing in the original Roediger et al. (1982) formulation but it has turned out to be critical. This is the assumption that intertest forgetting does not vary with recall level. Roediger and his colleagues noted that "Differential intertest forgetting between conditions is not taken into consideration in this account" (p. 639). Of course, evidence available at the time was consistent with the assumption that intertest forgetting did not differ over conditions (Erdelyi et al., 1976, as shown in Table 7.2 here, and Roediger & Thorpe, 1978, their Table 1). However, as will be documented later, this assumption is the weakest link in the recall level hypothesis (Payne, 1986).

The cumulative recall level hypothesis of hypermnesia provided a reasonable account of most, but not all, of the extant evidence in 1982 (see Erdelyi, 1982 and Roediger, 1982 for differing opinions on this issue, however). For example, Erdelyi et al.'s (1976) finding that hypermnesia was greater for pictures than for words accords well with the formulation. In addition, when words were studied under conditions encouraging their recoding into an imaginal format, asymptotic recall increased and so did hypermnesia. Of course, the Erdelyi et al. results are similarly in accord with the hypothesis that imagery is the critical factor.

Given this situation, the obvious need was for experiments that would manipulate cumulative recall level over a wide range (but by manipulations that would not involve imagery) to see if hypermnesia still correlated with cumulative recall level. Roediger et al. (1982) reported three experiments that conformed to this general prescription and found positive results. Only Experiment 3 will be reported here, because it manipulated level of recall over the widest range. In this experiment we asked subjects to free recall natural

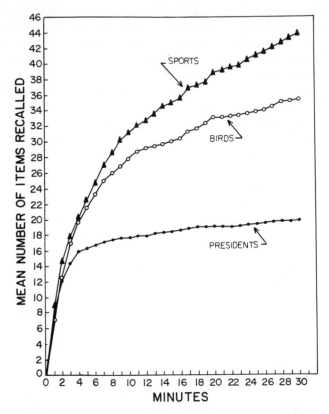

FIG. 7.6.   Cumulative recall of Presidents, Birds, and Sports over 30 minutes (Roediger et al., 1982, Experiment 3).

categories from semantic memory. We picked three categories (Presidents, Birds, and Sports) that varied considerably in size in order to induce differences in asymptotic levels of recall. Subjects were given three successive 10-minute tests, with short breaks between tests simply to collect recall sheets and pass out new ones. The instructions were to recall as many members of one category as possible each time.

The cumulative recall curves for the 30 minutes of testing are shown in Fig. 7.6 and indicate that we did succeed in manipulating asymptotic level of recall. (Indeed, recall of sports, and to a lesser extent of birds, were not at asymptote even after 30 minutes.) Also apparent from Fig. 7.6 is the fact that at the end of the first test, subjects in the various conditions had attained different proportions of their eventual level of recall. Little room for further improvement after 10 minutes existed in the condition in which subjects recalled Presidents, but subjects who recalled sports were far from asymptote after 10 minutes and therefore had considerable room for improvement. The prediction of the recall level hypothesis is simply that hypermnesia should be a direct correlate of the difference between initial and asymptotic levels of recall, as shown in Fig. 7.5. Hypermnesia is plotted in the customary way in Fig. 7.7, and this expectation is indeed borne out. Hypermnesia was greater for sports than for birds, and greater for subjects recalling both these categories than for those recalling Presidents. The interaction between number of tests and the conditions was statistically significant. However, even in the case of recall of Presidents, reliable hypermnesia was obtained, because almost all subjects showed the effect.

The experiment just reported accords well with the cumulative recall level hypothesis: Manipulation of cumulative recall level predicted hypermnesia, and in a situation where imagery probably played little differential role in recall of the three categories (but see Erdelyi, 1982). Roediger et al. (1982) reported two other experiments in which recall was manipulated either through a levels of processing manipulation with words (Experiment 1) or by one or three repetitions of nonsense syllables (Experiment 2). The expected result was obtained in both cases, with hypermnesia greater for those cases in which there was greater cumulative recall. Payne and Roediger (1987) obtained similar results.

PROBLEMS FOR THE RECALL LEVEL HYPOTHESIS

The cumulative recall level hypothesis of hypermnesia is built on the five assumptions previously described. Erdelyi (1987) has pointed out that the recall

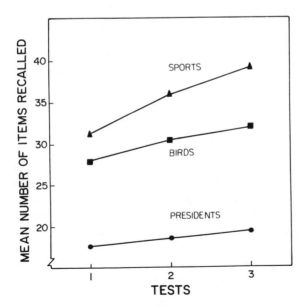

FIG. 7.7. Recall of Presidents, Birds, and Sports across three successive tests (Roediger et al., 1982, Experiment 3).

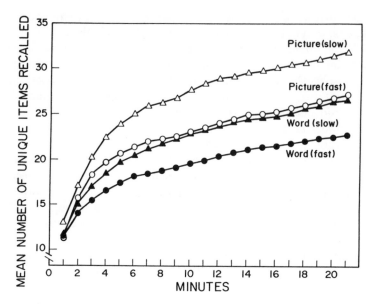

FIG. 7.8. Cumulative recall of pictures and words presented at different rates of presentation (Payne, 1986).

level hypothesis is really a statement about reminiscence, with the assumption that hypermnesia can be directly predicted from the amount of reminiscence. He further points out that this is true only if one ignores the possibility of forgetting between tests. Indeed, the original formulation proposed by Roediger et al. (1982) did assume, almost in passing, that the amount of intertest forgetting would not differ across conditions of interest. However, this assumption turns out to be wrong in some cases, as demonstrated in experiments by Payne (1986).

Payne's (1986) experiments were designed as a test of several aspects of the cumulative recall level hypothesis. For present purposes, the first two reported experiments (Experiments 1 and 1A) are the most relevant. He presented subjects with pictures or words and manipulated the level of their recall by varying the number of presentations of the material or the amount of study time. The idea guiding Payne's work was to break the natural correlation between type of material and level of recall. When presentation conditions are held constant, pictures are better recalled than words. By manipulating the number of presentations and the amount of time, Payne sought to achieve conditions in which words would be recalled as well as or better than pictures. Assuming this condition was met, he could then determine if, under these conditions, hypermnesia would be greater for words than for pictures.

Two examples from Payne's results illustrate his major findings. In Experiment 1A, the cumulative recall curve for words presented at a slow rate was

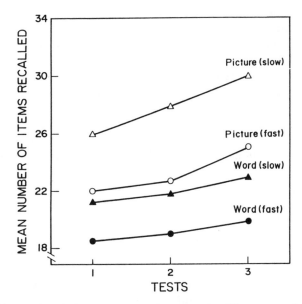

FIG. 7.9.   Recall of pictures and words presented at different rates of presentation across three successive tests (Payne, 1986).

roughly equivalent to that of pictures presented at a fast rate, as shown in the middle curves of Fig. 7.8. Thus, by the logic of the cumulative recall level hypothesis, one would expect equivalent hypermnesia in these conditions. However, the results showed greater hypermnesia for pictures than for words (Fig. 7.9, middle lines). The reason for this occurrence was that greater intertest forgetting occurred for words than for pictures, thus offsetting the equivalent amounts of reminiscence. The same pattern was obtained in another experiment in which cumulative recall was equated by presenting words more often than pictures. Thus, the assumption that intertest forgetting is equivalent for different types of materials (or other conditions) was not met and consequently predictions from the cumulative recall level hypothesis were not borne out. When recall of pictures and words was equated at asymptote, pictures were more likely to be recalled across tests than were words. Waring and Payne (1987) provided other data that also challenge the cumulative recall level hypothesis on similar grounds.

It is unclear why Payne (1986) found that variation in materials led to differential intertest forgetting, but Erdelyi et al. (1976) and Roediger and Thorpe (1978) did not. However, to the extent that intertest forgetting differs across other independent variables that affect recall level, the cumulative recall level hypothesis may be compromised. Payne (1986) modified the cumulative recall level hypothesis so as to take into account intertest forgetting. Quite obviously, the cumulative recall level hypothesis sets an upper bound on the amount of hypermnesia that can be attained and points to factors critical in determining the phenomenon, but the problem of interest forgetting must be taken into account (Erdelyi, 1987).

Payne (1986, Table 3) reported a correlational analysis that can be interpreted as good support for the cumulative recall level hypothesis. Across subjects, he correlated (a) the amount of hypermnesia $(T_3 - T_1)$ and (b) the difference between cumulative recall and performance on the first test (Cumulative recall $- T_1$). This latter entity is, according to the hypothesis, responsible for hypermnesia (see Assumption 5 in the previous section). Payne (1986) found correlations of .82 and .91 for two groups of subjects recalling pictures, and correlations of .74 and .76 for two groups recalling words. All four correlation were impressive, and were higher than when hypermnesia was correlated with other values (recall on Test 1, or cumulative recall) across subjects. The higher correlations for subjects recalling pictures than those recalling words probably owes to the fact that, in Payne's (1986) experiments, less intertest forgetting occurred for pictures than for words.

Our conclusion is that the cumulative recall level hypothesis captures primary factors for predicting hypermnesia. However, it obviously founders when intertest forgetting is great, when it varies across conditions, and/or when it is negatively correlated with reminiscence. The conditions leading to such occurrences are poorly understood.

THEORETICAL MECHANISMS EXPLAINING HYPERMNESIA

The cumulative recall level hypothesis of hypermnesia provides a functional account of the phenomenon by identifying conditions thought to be necessary for its occurrence. However, as formulated, no molecular theoretical mechanisms are implicated. What theoretical mechanisms might cause hypermnesia? Interestingly, the two primary mechanisms usually introduced to explain hypermnesia date back to the time of Ballard (1913) and Brown (1923) and are still the most prominently mentioned today. One is the assumption that the act of retrieving and recalling information serves to make this information more likely to be accessible in the future (Erdelyi & Becker, 1974; Roediger & Thorpe, 1978). Much evidence supports this idea (e.g., Darley & Murdock, 1971), although apparently provision must be made for differential effects of prior recall on later recall for different types of material in some cases (pictures and words; Payne, 1986).

A second assumption is required to account for increased recall over time— for reminiscence or spontaneous recovery. One natural theoretical suggestion to account for reminiscence is Estes' (1955, 1959) stimulus sampling theory, which was originally applied to the similar problem of spontaneous recovery following extinction of a conditioned response. Reminiscence may be due to repeated sampling of elements from memory, with the particular elements sampled changing within increased delays due to inherent variability in the population of elements being sampled. Stated somewhat differently, the increased recall with extended time and effort may be related to other cases where recall improves due to presentation of explicit retrieval cues (Roediger & Thorpe, 1978, p. 304). Just as provision of external retrieval cues can sometimes greatly increase recall (Tulving & Pearlstone, 1966), perhaps increased recall across time is due to changes in internal retrieval cues used by subjects (Tulving, 1974).

Direct evidence on this second assumption is less prevalent, but an experiment by Payne (1986, Experiment 4) is at least suggestive. Prior work by Tulving and Psotka (1971) and by Paris (1978) had shown that hypermnesia occurred for free recall of categorized lists. The primary question in Payne's experiment was whether or not the increased recall across repeated tests was due to (a) more different categories being added to recall, (b) more items being recalled from the same categories that had already appeared in recall, or (c) both factors. If the improved recall across repeated tests is due to the addition of novel categories during the later tests, then this would provide support for the idea that subjects are cuing themselves by thinking of category names in later recall attempts. Indeed, Payne's data showed that additional recall on repeated tests was due to increases in the number of categories recalled across tests, rather than an increase in the number of items per category recalled.

The most explicit account of hypermnesia occurs in the SAM (Search of Associative Memory) model of Raaijmakers and Shiffrin (1980, 1981). Two parameters in their model correspond to the two factors described above. "Incrementing" is the process whereby a recalled item is strengthened and made more likely to be recalled in the future; a second parameter is responsible for repeated sampling with replacement over long periods of time, at least until the same information is repeatedly retrieved and the recall process stops. Simulations have shown that both these parameters are needed within the model for hypermnesia to occur. Although the SAM model provides the best theoretical account of hypermnesia, the two critical ideas are really quite old ones and have been repeatedly mentioned as the leading candidates. Also, both ideas are embarrassingly close to redescriptions of the relevant data, and thus we may hope for future theoretical developments that might permit clearer insight into these phenomena.

Recall Criteria and Hypermnesia

The concluding section of this chapter concerns the problem of recall criteria, which has often been neglected in the analyzing recall processes in remembering. In studies of recognition memory, researchers have worried for years over the problem of guessing and of various corrections for guessing. The application of signal detection theory to recognition memory (e.g., Bernbach, 1967) and the use of other correction procedures have had great impact. However, the issue of differences in recall criteria across conditions has rarely been raised. Of course, the problem of recall criteria and whether or not reported memories are accurate or fabrications occurs in many situations, such as eyewitness testimony (Wells & Loftus, 1984) and hypnotic memory enhancement (Smith, 1983). Klatzky and Erdelyi (1985) provided an excellent discussion of the criterion problem in recall, considering especially recall under hypnosis.

We became interested in the problem of recall criteria through our investigations of hypermnesia, and in particular in attempting to determine why some researchers find little evidence for hypermnesia for words, whereas our studies have routinely shown this effect (cf. Erdelyi et al., 1976; Roediger & Thorpe, 1978). One possible reason for the difference is that we have typically employed free recall with instructions warning subjects against guessing, whereas Erdelyi and others have employed a forced recall procedure in which subjects are instructed to produce a fixed number of responses, guessing when necessary. Presumably subjects are much more conservative in responding when engaged in free recall than in forced recall, as the low intrusion rates in free recall attest. The forced recall procedure insures that response criteria cannot change across successive tests, but this possibility remains open when free recall is employed. Perhaps hypermnesia occurs for words in free recall, but not forced recall, because subjects loosen their recall criteria across the tests in the former case and are more willing to guess on later tests.

In order to test this possibility, Roediger and Payne (1985) had subjects study 70 words and then take three successive tests. However, different groups of subjects received tests under one of three instructional conditions. The free recall group received typical free recall instructions with a warning against guessing; the forced recall group was told to write down at least 40 responses on each test; a third group, referred to as the uninhibited free recall condition (after Bousfield & Rosner, 1970) was told to try to remember the words as well as possible, but to report any items that came to mind during the test phase, whether or not they deemed the retrieved responses correct.

This instructional manipulation had a huge effect on the intrusion rate across the 24 minutes of testing (three 8-minute tests), as can be seen in Table 7.4. Free recall subjects intruded 7.5 items, uninhibited recall subjects intruded 28.8, and forced recall subjects intruded 71.4 across 24 minutes. (The rates in Table 7.4 are means of the three tests.) However, despite this huge difference in recall criteria as reflected by the intrusion rates, hypermnesia was the same in all three conditions, as can be seen in Table 7.4. Thus, the differences in testing procedure do not explain the variable outcomes in obtaining hypermnesia for words. However, of more interest in the present context is the fact that overall recall levels did not differ despite wide variations in recall criteria. That is, even though subjects in the forced recall condition produced many more intrusions than did free recall subjects, the total number of words correctly recalled did not differ. Across the 24-minute testing period, free recall subjects produced 31.2 target

TABLE 7.4
Results From Roediger and Payne (1985)

Test	Tests				Mean
Instructions	1	2	3	Mean	Intrusions
Free Recall	25.1	26.6	28.2	26.6	2.5
Uninhibited Recall	24.3	26.4	28.4	26.4	9.6
Forced Recall	25.1	26.0	27.4	26.2	23.8
Mean	24.8	26.3	28.0		

items whereas the figures for the uninhibited recall and forced recall conditions were 31.0 and 30.9, respectively. Surprisingly, varying recall criteria had no effect on the total number of words correctly recalled.

Roediger and Challis (in preparation) performed several other experiments exploring this unexpected effect. These experiments have led to a further puzzle, which we do not yet understand. However, we will present selected data from one experiment to illustrate the problem. Four groups of subjects in this experiment studied 60 pictures and then received either free recall or forced recall tests. Two groups of subjects received two tests, one relatively soon after presentation of the material (Immediate) and then the same type of test again after a 1 week delay (Delayed). Subjects were given 10 minutes to recall the material, with forced recall subjects being required to write down 60 items (and encouraged to write more if they so desired). Free recall subjects were cautioned against guessing, but asked to continue trying during the entire testing period. Two other groups of subjects received the same set of pictures, but were only tested after a one week delay. Following each test, subjects were asked to give confidence ratings as to how likely each recalled item was to have actually occurred in the study list. Subjects rated each item on a 6-point scale, where 1 indicated that subjects were highly confident that the items had not appeared on the study list and 6 indicated high confidence that the item had appeared on the study list.

Results are shown in Table 7.5. The top two rows contain performance of the two groups tested twice. Notice that on the immediate test, the forced recall subjects produced more correct responses than did the free recall subjects (a significant difference). However, when performance was conditionalized only on those items subjects believed to have actually appeared on the study list (4, 5, and 6 responses on the confidence scale), the number of items recalled did not differ between free and forced recall conditions. This occurred despite the fact that the intrusion rates differed substantially, as shown in the third column. This pattern of results was replicated when these subjects were tested a week later, although overall performance was of course lower; again forced recall subjects produced significantly more correct responses during the test, but this difference disappeared when guesses were eliminated.

A different pattern of results was obtained in the two groups that were

TABLE 7.5
Results From Roediger and Challis (in preparation)

	Test 1 (Immediate)			Test 2 (One Week Delay)		
	Correct	High Conf.*	Errors**	Correct	High Conf.*	Errors**
Free	29.2	28.2	1.8	23.2	20.9	3.1
Forced	32.8	28.8	35.6	29.2	21.0	48.2
			Delayed Test Only			
Free				16.7	11.5	5.3
Forced				25.9	15.1	42.5

*The number of correctly recalled items that subjects later judged to have been from the study list.
**The number of intrusions.

only given a delayed test (see the bottom of Table 7.5). Forced recall subjects again produced more correct responses than did free recall subjects, but this difference survived (in attenuated form) even when guesses were eliminated and credit was given only for responses that subjects judged to be correct. We generally replicated this pattern under other conditions of presentation: Variation in recall criteria appears to have an effect on recall on delayed, but not on immediate, tests.

The theoretical interpretation of these results is unclear, to say the least. However, two points can be made. First, unlike the Roediger and Payne (1985) experiments, we did find an effect of recall criteria in recall of pictures (see also Erdelyi, Finks, & Feigen-Pfau, in press). Forced recall subjects produced more correct responses than did free recall subjects, although the differences in "hit rates" seems relatively slight when compared to the huge difference in intrusions (or the "false alarm" rates). Perhaps the concrete and higher frequency nature of the materials used in this experiment—because we had to use items that could be converted into recognizable sketches—permitted better guessing. The second point is that, when subjects provided confidence ratings, the effect of varying recall criteria either disappeared (top of Table 7.5) or shriveled (bottom of Table 7.5). Thus, even when subjects produced more correct items under forced recall conditions, they were largely unaware of this benefit. This may represent a type of free association priming as studied in implicit memory tests (see Schacter, 1987). The unravelling of these puzzles must await further research.

CONCLUDING COMMENTS

This chapter has delineated one approach to the problems of reminiscence and hypermnesia. The cumulative recall level hypothesis has the advantage of (a) providing an explicit (if functional) formulation of these phenomena, (b) stating and bolstering its six primary assumptions, (c) providing a testable account, and (d) drawing attention to the dynamics of recall over time. Although the cumulative recall hypothesis can account for a number of findings in the hypermnesia literature, it founders on the assumption of equivalent intertest forgetting across conditions. Whenever conditions differ in intertest forgetting, the recall level hypothesis may not accurately predict hypermnesia (Payne, 1986). However, if differences in intertest forgetting are slight, and if levels of recall are varied over a large range (as in Roediger et al. (1982), Experiment 3; see Fig. 7.5 and 7.6), then the recall level hypothesis may survive despite the invalidity of the intertest forgetting assumption. Future work will likely center on development of theoretical mechanisms to explain hypermnesia, although the SAM model (Raaijmakers & Shiffrin, 1980) provides a reasonable account. In addition, another profitable direction for future research will be the exploration of how differences in recall criteria affect remembering.

ACKNOWLEDGMENT

Research reported in this chapter was supported by Grant R01 HD15054 from the National Institute of Child Health and Human Development.

REFERENCES

Ballard, P. B. (1913). Oblivescence and reminiscence. *British Journal of Psychology Monograph Supplements, 1*, 1–82.

Bernbach, H. A. (1967). Decision processes in memory. *Psychological Review, 74*, 462–480.

Bousfield, W. A., & Rosner, S. R. (1970). Free versus uninhibited recall. *Psychonomic Science, 20*, 75–76.

Bousfield, W. A., & Sedgewick, C. H. W. (1944). An analysis of sequences in restricted associative responses. *Journal of General Psychology, 30*, 149–165.

Brown, W. (1923). To what extent is memory measured by a single recall trial? *Journal of Experimental Psychology, 6*, 377–382.

Buxton, C. E. (1943). The status of research in reminiscence. *Psychological Bulletin, 40*, 313–340.

Darley, C. F., & Murdock, B. B. (1971). Effects of prior free recall testing on final recall and recognition. *Journal of Experimental Psychology, 91*, 66–73.

Ebbinghaus, H. (1964). *Memory: A contribution to experimental psychology.* (H. A. Ruger & C. E. Bussenius, Trans.) New York: Dover. (Original work published 1885)

Erdelyi, M. (1982). A note on the level of recall, level of processing, and imagery hypotheses of hypermnesia. *Journal of Verbal Learning and Verbal Behavior, 21*, 656–661.

Erdelyi, M. (1984). The recovery of unconscious (inaccessible) memories: Laboratory studies of hypermnesia. In G. H. Bower (Ed.), *The psychology of learning and motivation: Advances in research and theory* (Vol. 18, pp. 95–127). New York: Academic Press.

Erdelyi, M. (1987). *On the distinction between reminiscence and hypermnesia (and that between cumulative recall and recall) with some theoretical consequences.* Unpublished manuscript.

Erdelyi, M. H., & Becker, J. (1974). Hypermnesia for pictures: Incremental memory for pictures but not for words in multiple recall trials. *Cognitive Psychology, 6,* 159–171.

Erdelyi, M. H., Finkelstein, S., Herrell, N., Miller, B., & Thomas, J. (1976). Coding modality vs. input modality in hypermnesia: Is a rose a rose a rose? *Cognition, 4,* 311–319.

Erdelyi, M. H., Finks, J., & Feigin-Pfau, M. B. (in press). The effect of response bias on recall performance, with some observations on processing bias. *Journal of Experimental Psychology: General.*

Erdelyi, M. H., & Kleinbard, J. (1978). Has Ebbinghaus decayed with time?: The growth of recall (hypermnesia) over days. *Journal of Experimental Psychology: Human Learning and Memory, 4,* 275–289.

Estes, W. K. (1955). Statistical theory of spontaneous recovery and regression. *Psychological Review, 62,* 145–154.

Estes, W. K. (1959). The statistical approach to learning theory. In S. Koch (Ed.), *Psychology: A study of science* (Vol II, pp. 380–490). New York: McGraw-Hill.

Estes, W. K. (1960). Learning theory and the new "mental chemistry." *Psychological Review, 67,* 207–223.

Eysenck, H. J., & Frith, C. D. (1977). *Reminiscence, motivation, and personality.* New York: Plenum.

Indow, T., & Togano, K. (1970). On retrieving sequence from long term memory. *Psychological Review, 77,* 317–331.

Izawa, C. (1971). The test potentiating model. *Journal of Mathematical Psychology, 8,* 200–224.

Izawa, C. (1981). Toward a quantitative theory of performance differences between anticipation and study-test procedures: The retention interval model. *Scandinavian Journal of Psychology, 22,* 79–91.

Klatzky, R. L., & Erdelyi, M. (1985). The response criterion problem in tests of hypnosis and memory. *International Journal of Clinical and Experimental Hypnosis, 33,* 246–257.

McGeoch, J. A., & Irion, A. L. (1952). *The psychology of human learning.* New York: Longmans, Green.

Paris, S. G. (1978). Memory organization during children's repeated recall. *Developmental Psychology, 14,* 99–106.

Payne, D. G. (1986). Hypermnesia for pictures and words: Testing the recall level hypothesis. *Journal of Experimental Psychology: Learning, Memory, and Cognition, 12,* 16–29.

Payne, D. G. (1987). Hypermnesia and reminiscence in recall: A historical and empirical review. *Psychological Bulletin, 101,* 5–27.

Payne, D. G. & Roediger, H. L. (1987). Hypermnesia occurs in recall but not recognition. *American Journal of Psychology, 100,* 145–166.

Raaijmakers, J. G. W., & Shiffrin, R. M. (1980). SAM: A theory of probabilistic search of associative memory. In G. H. Bower (Ed.), *The psychology of learning and motivation: Advances in research and theory* (Vol. 14, pp. 207–262). New York: Academic Press.

Raaijmakers, J. G. W., & Shiffrin, R. M. (1981). Search of associative memory. *Psychological Review, 88,* 93–134.

Reason, J., & Lucas, D. (1984). Using cognitive diaries to investigate naturally occurring memory blocks. In J. E. Harris & P. E. Morris (Eds.), *Everyday memory: Actions and absentmindness* (pp. 53–70). London: Academic Press.

Roediger, H. L. (1982). Hypermnesia: The importance of recall time and asymptotic level of recall. *Journal of Verbal Learning and Verbal Behavior, 21,* 662–665.

Roediger, H. L, & Challis, B. H. (in preparation). *Varying recall criteria has differential effects on immediate and delayed recall.*

Roediger, H. L., & Payne, D. G. (1982). Hypermnesia: The effects of repeated testing. *Journal of Experimental Psychology: Learning, Memory, and Cognition, 8,* 66–72.

Roediger, H. L., & Payne, D. G. (1985). Response criteria do not affect recall level or hypermnesia: A puzzle for generate/recognize theories. *Memory & Cognition, 13,* 1–7.

Roediger, H. L., Payne, D., Gillespie, G. L., & Lean, D. S. (1982). Hypermnesia as determined by level of recall. *Journal of Verbal Learning and Verbal Behavior, 21*, 635-665.

Roediger, H. L., Stellon, C., & Tulving, E. (1977). Inhibition from part-list cues and rate of recall. *Journal of Experimental Psychology: Human Learning and Memory, 3*, 174-188.

Roediger, H. L., & Thorpe, L. A. (1978). The role of recall time in producing hypermnesia. *Memory & Cognition, 6*, 296-305.

Roediger, H. L., & Tulving, E. (1979). Exclusion of learned material from recall as a postretrieval operation. *Journal of Verbal Learning and Verbal Behavior, 18*, 601-615.

Schacter, D. L. (1987). Implicit memory: History and current status. *Journal of Experimental Psychology: Learning, Memory, and Cognition, 13*, 501-518.

Shapiro, S. R., & Erdelyi, M. H. (1974). Hypermnesia for pictures but not for words. *Journal of Experimental Psychology, 103*, 1218-1219.

Smith, M. C. (1983). Hypnotic memory enhancement of witnesses: Does it work? *Psychological Bulletin, 94*, 387-407.

Tulving, E. (1967). The effects of presentation and recall in free recall learning. *Journal of Verbal Learning and Verbal Behavior, 6*, 175-184.

Tulving, E. (1974). Cue-dependent forgetting. *American Scientist, 62*, 74-82.

Tulving, E., & Pearlstone, Z. (1966). Availability versus accessibility of information in memory for words. *Journal of Verbal Learning and Verbal Behavior, 5*, 381-391.

Tulving, E., & Psotka, J. (1971). Retroactive inhibition in free recall: Inaccessibility of information available in the memory store. *Journal of Experimental Psychology, 87*, 1-8.

Vorberg, D., & Ulrich, R. (1987). Random search with unequal search rates: Serial and parallel generalizations of McGill's model. *Journal of Mathematical Psychology, 31*, 1-23.

Waring, S. M., & Payne, D. G. (1987, April). *Imagery, level of recall, and organization of recall in hypermnesia.* Paper presented at the meetings of the Eastern Psychological Association, Washington, D.C..

Wells, G. L., & Loftus, E. F. (Eds.). (1984). *Eyewitness testimony: Psychological perspectives.* Cambridge, England: Cambridge University Press.

8

Introduction. Similarities and Differences Between Anticipation and Study-Test Item Information Presentation Methods

Chizuko Izawa
Tulane University

One of my long-term research interests since undergraduate days in Tokyo has been the optimization of learning and retention, much of that concern stems from daily life. It would not be surprising even if we would find reasons for: (a) the recent recognition of "cultural illiteracy" among American high school students, (b) their limited knowledge of overseas cultures (Asia in particular) and (c) recent suboptimal performance in foreign policy making, the underemphasis on foreign language skills and the generally poor quality of education in the United States. A great many conditions seem to cry for improvement.

By contrast, in nearly all other industrialized nations (e.g., Japan) foreign language learning is a "must" for students in middle school or above. Their willingness may in part stem from their awareness that international relations and therefore languages are of great importance, as is the ability to digest new developments anywhere in the world. All this has great survival value for nations and persons striving to compete successfully as producers of high technology and in other domains of today's world economy.

For intellectuals in Japan, foreign language learning is among the foremost prerequisites and its importance rises sharply as their aspirations grow. Thus, the undergraduate degree at the University of Tokyo requires two foreign languages, 2 years each, in addition to the major subject. I, for example, took three western languages—English, French, and German—as well as Chinese literature. If you want to be in an elite class in Tokyo, you have to be able to do business in Japanese, discuss international affairs in English, do some science in German, read Confucius and poetry in Chinese, and fall in love in French.

A few hours of effort per week per language, however, does not carry you very far. It was only an intellectual hobby. The real challenge, however, came when I arrived at Stanford and first faced William K. Estes, now author of our lead chapter (the scientific portion), along with a classroom of the brightest graduate students in psychology, including several contributors to this volume. All of my classmates had for a quarter century lived the English language 24 hours a day. By contrast, my experience with English was still in its infancy, altogether the equivalent of about 20 months. Optimal learning was an absolute necessity for my daily survival, academically and otherwise.

Of the scores of experimental variables already investigated or to be investigated in our laboratory on issues relevant to optimization of learning and retention phenomena, we will, in the present chapter, focus mostly on item presentation or learning method issues. The paired-associate or cued-recall learning situation is particularly relevant in this context, as it closely resembles the learning of new or foreign words, if we view the first term, the cue (stimulus) or a-term of the pair as a new or foreign word, and the second, the target (response) or b-term as its translation. Such a paired-associate learning situation can be schematically demonstrated, as in Equation 1 under the *traditional anticipation method* (considered the standard for over a century; cf. Ebbinghaus, 1885) where each test (T, question) event is followed by its study (S, answer) event for an n-item list, when items are presented in random order from cycle to cycle:

$$a_1 - ? , a_1 - b_1, a_2 - ? , a_2 - b_2, \ldots, a_j - ? , \boxed{a_j - b_j}, \ldots, a_n - ? , a_n - b_n ;$$
$$[\text{intercycle interval}]; \tag{1}$$
$$a_5 - ? , a_5 - b_5, a_8 - ? , a_8 - b_8, \ldots, \overline{\underline{a_j - ?}}, a_j - b_j , \ldots, a_2 - ? , a_2 - b_2 ;$$

in which the a-term stands for the cue (stimulus) term, the b-term stands for the target (response) term of the pair, and Subscript j identifies Pair j respectively within the n-pair list, where $j = 1, 2, 3, \ldots, n$, and $n \geq 1$.

When the same list is presented under the *study-test method* (reinforcement-test or RT method, a relative newcomer that came to be used frequently in the 1960s and thereafter) where S and T events are administered on separate cycles. They may be shown schematically as in Equation 2:

$$a_1 - b_1, a_2 - b_2, \ldots, \boxed{a_j - b_j}, \ldots, a_n - b_n ; [\text{intercycle interval}];$$
$$a_5 - ? , a_8 - ? , \ldots, \overline{\underline{a_j - ?}}, \ldots, a_2 - ? ; [\text{intercycle interval}];$$
$$a_4 - b_4, a_j - b_j , \ldots, a_n - b_n , \ldots, a_3 - b_3 ; [\text{intercycle interval}]; \tag{2}$$
$$a_n - ? , a_6 - ? , \ldots, a_7 - ? , \ldots, a_j - ? .$$

Three types of theories are proposed to account for performance differences between study-test and anticipation methods. The operant conditioning feedback model expects the anticipation method that enjoys the benefit of immediate feedback to be advantageous, whereas the task alternation (e.g., Battig & Brackett, 1961), or differential acquisition or encoding (e.g., Kanak, Cole,

& Eckert, 1972; Kanak & Neuner, 1970) theories predict the study-test method to be superior, because of its favorable task arrangement, or its greater encoding or acquisition power compared to the anticipation method. However, the empirical evidence has not given consistent support to any of these theories or models.

The fact is, over the last 3 decades, more than 120 experiments have been conducted to examine the relative efficacy of the two methods. Yet, outcomes were inconsistent: Although about 55% indicate superior performance for the study-test method, about 45% demonstrate little differences between them (Izawa, Hayden, & Isham, 1980; Kanak, Cole, & Eckert, 1972). This inconsistency was a source of difficulty and frustration in devising our theoretical accounts (cf. Cofer, Diamond, Olsen, Stein, & Walker, 1967).

In order to resolve this difficulty, Izawa (1972, 1977, 1981e) suggested that the retention or S-T interval (between boxes in broken and solid lines in Equations 1 and 2) controls performance differences between anticipation and study-test methods to a major degree, and specified that individual retention intervals distribute triangularly (a probability density function) for the methods as shown in Fig. 8.1 in terms of intervening events (adapted from Izawa, 1972) for an n-pair (item) list where n, the list length, is any positive whole number equal to or greater than 2. When $n = 1$, the two methods become identical and can no longer be distinguished (cf. Izawa, 1979c).

The overlap area of the two distribution curves (40%) of Fig. 8.1 cor-

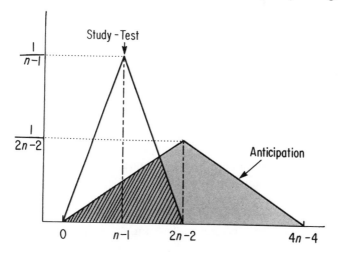

Number of intervening events between an S and its subsequent T

FIG. 8.1.   Triangular distributions of intervening events (items) in the retention (S-T, from an S event to its T event) interval for the anticipation (shaded) and the study-test methods under the whole list design commonly used in the learning of linguistic materials (adapted from Izawa, 1972).

responds to the probability that the retention interval of an item (pair) may be the same for the two methods, whereas the nonoverlap area specifies the probability that the retention interval is shorter for the study-test method than the anticipation method.

If a given pair is critical (defined as being in the short-term memory system, STM), it is likely to remain critical after short retention (S-T) intervals, but not after long ones. Because the critical pairs are likely to be retrievable at test (T), performance levels of the two techniques will be determined primarily by the relative frequencies of critical items falling into overlap and nonoverlap areas of the distributions (Fig. 8.1).

The identity model (Izawa, 1985a) evolved from and is a special case of the retention interval model (Izawa, 1981e). It sought to account for performance differences between study-test and anticipation method based on the above rationales. By viewing events as being constituted of four states: CA (conditioned and active), $C\bar{A}$ (conditioned, but not active), UA (unconditioned, but active) and $U\bar{A}$ (unconditioned and not active), the identity model postulates identical processes for *both* methods per event. That is, encoding or acquisition processes are postulated as occurring as in Matrix S in Equation 3 for each S event, whereas retrieval of a target item occurs on each T event, as in Matrix T in Equation 4:

$$S = \begin{array}{c} \\ CA_v \\ C\bar{A}_v \\ UA_v \\ U\bar{A}_v \end{array} \begin{array}{cccc} CA_{v+1} & C\bar{A}_{v+1} & UA_{v+1} & U\bar{A}_{v+1} \\ \left[\begin{array}{cccc} 1 & 0 & 0 & 0 \\ 0 & 1 & 0 & 0 \\ c & 0 & 1-c & 0 \\ 0 & 0 & 0 & 1 \end{array}\right] \end{array} \qquad (3)$$

$$T = \begin{array}{c} \\ CA_v \\ C\bar{A}_v \\ UA_v \\ U\bar{A}_v \end{array} \begin{array}{cccc} CA_{v+1} & C\bar{A}_{v+1} & UA_{v+1} & U\bar{A}_{v+1} \\ \left[\begin{array}{cccc} 1 & 0 & 0 & 0 \\ k' & 1-k' & 0 & 0 \\ 0 & 0 & 1-k & k \\ 0 & 0 & k' & 1-k' \end{array}\right] \end{array} \qquad (4)$$

Probability c specifies the encoding probability of study (S) event of a target, whereas k and k' determine probability that an element moves from the active (A) to inactive state $(\bar{A})$, during the retrieval or test (T) event of a target. Each matrix presents the transition taking place from Cycle v to Cycle $v+1$.

The retention-storage processes undergoing during the intercycle rest interval is summarized in Matrix r_I in Equation 5:

$$r_I = \begin{array}{c} \\ CA_v \\ C\bar{A}_v \\ UA_v \\ U\bar{A}_v \end{array} \begin{array}{cccc} CA_{v+1} & C\bar{A}_{v+1} & UA_{v+1} & U\bar{A}_{v+1} \\ \left[\begin{array}{cccc} 1-g & g & 0 & 0 \\ g' & 1-g' & 0 & 0 \\ 0 & 0 & 1-g & g \\ 0 & 0 & g' & 1-g' \end{array}\right] \end{array} \qquad (5)$$

The retention storage processes in intervening work intervals are entered in Matrices r_S and r_T, specifying processes of $(n-1)/2$, S and T events respectively, on the average, of other items within an n-pair list, as in Equations 6 and 7:

$$
r_S = \begin{array}{c} \\ CA_\nu \\ C\bar{A}_\nu \\ UA_\nu \\ U\bar{A}_\nu \end{array}
\begin{array}{c} CA_{\nu+1} \\ \left[\begin{array}{cccc} & & & \\ 1-e \\ e' \\ 0 \\ 0 \end{array}\right. \end{array}
\begin{array}{c} C\bar{A}_{\nu+1} \\ e \\ 1-e' \\ 0 \\ 0 \end{array}
\begin{array}{c} UA_{\nu+1} \\ 0 \\ 0 \\ 1-e \\ e' \end{array}
\begin{array}{c} U\bar{A}_{\nu+1} \\ \left.\begin{array}{c} 0 \\ 0 \\ e \\ 1-e' \end{array}\right] \end{array}
\tag{6}
$$

$$
r_T = \begin{array}{c} \\ CA_\nu \\ C\bar{A}_\nu \\ UA_\nu \\ U\bar{A}_\nu \end{array}
\begin{array}{c} CA_{\nu+1} \\ \left[\begin{array}{cccc} & & & \\ 1-f \\ f' \\ 0 \\ 0 \end{array}\right. \end{array}
\begin{array}{c} C\bar{A}_{\nu+1} \\ f \\ 1-f' \\ 0 \\ 0 \end{array}
\begin{array}{c} UA_{\nu+1} \\ 0 \\ 0 \\ 1-f \\ f' \end{array}
\begin{array}{c} U\bar{A}_{\nu+1} \\ \left.\begin{array}{c} 0 \\ 0 \\ f \\ 1-f' \end{array}\right] \end{array}
\tag{7}
$$

Components g, e, and f show probabilities of an element escaping from the active set to the inactive one during the intercycle interval, over intervening S and T events of other items, respectively, whereas components g', e', and f' are probabilities of an element's move to the opposite direction in three respective retention interval events (Matrices r_I, r_S, and r_T). For further details, see Izawa (1985a).

Although the aforementioned theoretical formulations were advanced for forward associations in paired-associate learning in Equations 1 and 2, the bulk of studies address backward associations (cf. Asch & Ebenholtz, 1962; Izawa, 1965, 1967c; Rubin, 1983). Backward association learning may be schematized as in Equations 8 and 9, respectively, for anticipation and study-test methods:

$$a_1 - ?, a_1 - b_1, a_2 - ?, a_2 - b_2, \ldots, a_j - ?, \boxed{a_j - b_j}, \ldots, a_n - ?, a_n - b_n;$$
$$\text{[intercycle interval];} \tag{8}$$
$$b_5 - ?, b_5 - a_5, b_8 - ?, b_8 - a_8, \ldots, \overline{\underline{b_j - ?}}, b_j - a_j, \ldots, b_2 - ?, b_2 - a_2;$$

$$a_1 - b_1, a_2 - b_2, \ldots, \boxed{a_j - b_j}, \ldots, a_n - b_n; \text{ [intercycle interval];}$$
$$b_5 - ?, b_8 - ?, \ldots, \overline{\underline{b_j - ?}}, \ldots, b_2 - ?; \text{ [intercycle interval];} \tag{9}$$
$$a_4 - b_4, a_j - b_j, \ldots, a_n - b_n, \ldots, a_3 - b_3; \text{ [intercycle interval];}$$
$$b_n - ?, b_6 - ?, \ldots, b_7 - ?, \ldots, b_j - ?.$$

Differences in directionality in associations notwithstanding, the key factor for the identity model, that is, the S-S, T-T, S-T, and T-S intervals for backward association learning in Equations 8 and 9 are identical to those in Equations 1 and 2 for forward association learning. Thus, the current approach should hold in backward association learning situations, as well. This was affirmed by a series of experiments (e.g., Izawa, 1981c).

The identical temporal factors were also found in recognition memory for verbal discrimination learning situations. The latter learning situations can be summarized in Equations 10 and 11, respectively, for anticipation and study-test methods where learning was measured by recognition:

$$a_1\ b_1,\ a_1,\ b_2\ a_2, a_2, \ldots,\ a_j\ _{b_j},\ \boxed{a_j},\ \ldots, b_n\ a_n, a_n\ ;$$
$$\text{[intercycle interval]};\tag{10}$$
$$b_5\ a_5,\ a_5,\ a_8\ b_8, a_8, \ldots, \overline{\underline{b_j\ a_{j_{\rfloor}}}},\ a_j\ , \ldots, b_2\ a_2, a_2\ ;$$

$$
\begin{array}{llll}
a_1 & , a_2 & , \ldots, \boxed{a_j} & , \ldots, a_n & ; \text{[intercycle interval]};\\
b_5 a_5 & , a_8\ b_8 & , \ldots, \overline{\underline{b_j\ a_{j_{\rfloor}}}}, & \ldots, b_2\ a_2 & ; \text{[intercycle interval]};\\
a_4 & , a_j & , \ldots, a_n & , \ldots, a_3 & ; \text{[intercycle interval]};\\
b_n\ a_n & , a_1\ b_1 & , \ldots, a_7\ b_7 & , \ldots, b_j\ a_j & .
\end{array}
\tag{11}
$$

Although similarities and differences between recall and recognition have been debated throughout the history of learning linguistic materials, we have found previously that both types of memory measures seem to obtain similar results with respect to the effects of test trials (cf. Part 3 of this chapter; Izawa, 1966, 1967a, 1967b, 1968, 1969, 1970a, 1970b, 1971, 1976, 1989 *in press*; Tulving & Arbuckle, 1966). We subsequently found that data for the retention interval were similar; as confirmed by Izawa and Morrison (1979) via a series of verbal discrimination (recognition) learning experiments that favored the current approach.

In all of the aforementioned cued recall (paired-associate) and recognition (verbal discrimination) learning situations (Equations 1-2, 8-9, 10-11), we discussed the effects of a random item presentation order because it is commonly utilized to avoid the contaminating effects of serial order cues in recall and recognition learning situations.

Theoretically, however, randomness in item presentation orders is neither necessary nor sufficient for the identity model. When the random item presentation order is completely absent, say for example, when items are presented under a constant order on all cycles, there are no variations in retention interval distributions under either the anticipation or study-test method. However, their respective means are the same as those under random presentation order. Consequently there is no theoretical reason why the identity model cannot be tested utilizing a constant item presentation order. That the model is, indeed, able to withstand such a test is evident from detailed empirical examinations of the identity model that excluded the random item presentation order effect; see Izawa (1979a, 1979b).

Consequently, the identity model appears to have considerable generality for both recall and recognition memory, with a variety of learning materials. For further background information including the model's theoretical evolution, please refer to Izawa (1972, 1974, 1977, 1978, 1979a, 1979b, 1980, 1981a, 1981b, 1981c, 1981d, 1981e, 1983, 1985a, 1985b), Izawa, Bell, and Hayden (1984),

Izawa and Hayden (1978), and Izawa, Hayden, and Isham (1980). Both the general retention interval model and its special case, the identity model, have enjoyed substantial support from a number of quantitative investigations (e.g., Izawa, 1981b, 1981d, 1981e, 1982a, 1982b, 1985a).

Questions that remain to be answered include the generalizability and the tenability of the model in various learning situations other than those utilizing visual presentations of the linguistic materials to be learned. We proceeded, therefore, to use three different sensory departments in a qualitative and quantitative examination of the identity model, including novel sublist manipulations. A total of *nine new* experiments were especially planned and executed for investigating the identity model in this chapter. Since all experiments had common features, for simplicity of exposition, we numbered all experiments presented in the chapter, sequentially without regard to the chapter's subdivisions. Similarly, all equations, tables, and figures are so numbered.

However, the three sensory modalities here considered were emphasized to different degrees, in accordance with varied purposes and different collaborators. Therefore, the remainder of this chapter is composed of three parts, each with a distinct title and different authors.

The identity model is tested both qualitatively and quantitatively via four experiments conducted with visual information processing in Part 1. Three experiments in Part 2 address the efficacy of auditory information processing as compared with visual information processing. In Part 3, two experiments explore the validity of the model and its generality for learning Euclidean distance and location by means of kinesthetic movements, an uncultivated domain for assessing the item information procedures under consideration.

REFERENCES

Asch, S. E., & Ebenholtz, S. M. (1962). The principle of associative symmetry. *Proceedings of the American Philosophical Society, 106*, 135–163.

Battig, W. F., & Brackett, H. R. (1961). Comparison of anticipation and recall methods in paired-associate learning. *Psychological Reports, 9*, 59–65.

Cofer, C. N., Diamond, F., Olsen, R. A., Stein, J. S., & Walker, H. (1967). Comparison of anticipation and recall methods in paired-associate learning. *Journal of Experimental Psychology, 75*, 545–558.

Ebbinghaus, H. (1885). Über das Gedächtnis: Untersuchungen zur experimentellen Psychologie [On Memory: Investigations in experimental psychology]. Leipzig, Germany: Duncker & Humbolt.

Izawa, C. (1965). Backward association in paired-associate learning. *Japanese Psychological Research, 7*, 47–60.

Izawa, C. (1966). Reinforcement-test sequences in paired-associate learning. *Psychological Reports, 18*, 879–919.

Izawa, C. (1967a). Function of test trials in paired-associate learning. *Journal of Experimental Psychology, 75*, 194–209.

Izawa, C. (1967b). Mixed- versus unmixed-list designs in paired-associate learning. *Psychological Reports, 20*, 1191–1200.

Izawa, C. (1967c). Effects of meaningfulness and familiarization upon backward associations in paired-associate learning. *Japanese Psychological Research, 9*, 95–110.

Izawa, C. (1968). Effects of reinforcement, neutral and test trials upon paired-associate acquisition and retention. *Psychological Reports, 23*, 947–959.

Izawa, C. (1969). Comparison of reinforcement and test trials in paired-associate learning. *Journal of Experimental Psychology, 81*, 600–603.

Izawa, C. (1970a). Optimal potentiating effects and forgetting-prevention effects of tests in paired-associate learning. *Journal of Experimental Psychology, 83*, 340–344.

Izawa, C. (1970b). Reinforcement-test-blank acquisition programming under the unmixed-list design in paired-associate learning. *Psychonomic Science, 19*, 75–77.

Izawa, C. (1971). The test trial potentiating model. *Journal of Mathematical Psychology, 8*, 200–224.

Izawa, C. (1972). Retention interval hypothesis and evidence for its basic assumptions. *Journal of Experimental Psychology, 96*, 17–24.

Izawa, C. (1974). Retention interval hypothesis and list lengths: Comparison of anticipation and reinforcement (study)-test procedures. *Canadian Journal of Psychology, 28*, 214–224.

Izawa, C. (1976). Vocalized and silent tests in paired-associate learning. *American Journal of Psychology, 89*, 681–693.

Izawa, C. (1977). Theoretical and empirical performance differences between anticipation and study-test methods: Retention interval hypothesis vs. spaced practice effects. *Japanese Psychological Research, 19*, 31–38.

Izawa, C. (1978). Effects of two retention interval components on performance differences between study-test and anticipation methods in paired-associate learning. *Scandinavian Journal of Psychology, 19*, 151–158.

Izawa, C. (1979a). A test of the retention interval hypothesis with a constant item presentation order. *Japanese Psychological Research, 21*, 200–206.

Izawa, C. (1979b). Comparisons of learning procedures: Effects of constant and random presentations. *Acta Psychologica, 42*, 133–143.

Izawa, C. (1979c). Toward a comprehensive theory of variable performance differences and differential spaced practice effects between anticipation and study-test methods. *Journal of General Psychology, 100*, 63–83.

Izawa, C. (1980). Empirical examinations of the retention interval hypothesis: Comparisons of learning methods when learning is difficult. *Journal of General Psychology, 103*, 117–129.

Izawa, C. (1981a). Order learning and item presentation methods. *Journal of General Psychology, 105*, 45–83.

Izawa, C. (1981b). Quantitative tests of the retention interval model. *Journal of General Psychology, 105*, 273–292.

Izawa, C. (1981c). The retention interval hypothesis and backward associations *Australian Journal of Psychology, 33*, 229–241.

Izawa, C. (1981d). The retention interval model: Qualitative and quantitative examinations. *Japanese Psychological Research, 23*, 101–112.

Izawa, C. (1981e). Toward a quantitative theory for performance differences between anticipation and study-test procedures: The retention interval model. *Scandinavian Journal of Psychology, 22*, 79–91.

Izawa, C. (1982a). Fundamental similarities and differences between study-test and anticipation item presentation procedures in the learning of linguistic items: Quantitative test of the retention interval model via varied parameter estimation modes. *Psychologia, 25*, 1–17.

Izawa, C. (1982b). The retention interval model examined by delayed test performances. *Journal of General Psychology, 106*, 219–231.

Izawa, C. (1983). The generality of the retention interval model. *Journal of General Psychology, 108*, 113–134.

Izawa, C. (1985a). A test of the differences between anticipation and study-test methods of paired-associate learning. *Journal of Experimental Psychology: Learning, Memory, and Cognition, 11*, 165–184.

Izawa, C. (1985b). The identity model and factors controlling the superiority of study-test method over the anticipation method. *Journal of General Psychology, 112*, 65–78.

Izawa, C. (1989 *in press*). A search for the control factors in the repetition effect. *Japanese Psychological Review, 31*(3).

Izawa, C., Bell, D., & Hayden, R. G. (1984). Auditory information processing and its method of presentation. *Japanese Psychological Research, 26*, 12–23.

Izawa, C., & Hayden, R. G. (1978). Effects of method of presentation with spaced practice. *Psychologia, 21*, 16–26.

Izawa, C., Hayden, R. G., & Isham, K. L. (1980). Sensory modality and method of item information presentation in memory. *Acta Psychologica, 44*, 131–145.

Izawa, C., & Morrison, J. E. (1979). Verbal discrimination learning: Effects of method of presentation, practice distribution, and learning material. *Journal of General Psychology, 101*, 75–101.

Kanak, N. J., Cole, L. E., & Eckert, E. (1972). Implicit associative responses in verbal discrimination acquisition. *Journal of Experimental Psychology, 93*, 309–319.

Kanak, N. J., & Neuner, S. D. (1970). Associative symmetry and item availability as a function of five methods of paired-associate acquisition. *Journal of Experimental Psychology, 86*, 288–295.

Rubin, D. C. (1983). Associative asymmetry, availability, and retrieval. *Memory & Cognition, 11*, 83–92.

Tulving, E., & Arbuckle, T. Y. (1966). Input and output interference in short-term associative memory. *Journal of Experimental Psychology, 72*, 145–150.

8

Part 1. A Test of the Identity Model: Encoding Processes Differ Little Between Anticipation and Study-Test Methods

Chizuko Izawa
Tulane University

In the previous section of this chapter, we established the substantial generality of the identity model which states that the standard anticipation method and the newer study-test method of the information presentation differ little, except for inherent differential mean lengths of the retention (S-T) interval (between a study and test events) and different distributions of the retention intervals. We did, indeed, isolate the key factor differentiating the two information presentation methods: the retention interval effect based on short-term memory (STM) processes (cf. Izawa, 1972, 1974, 1977, 1978, 1979a, 1979b, 1979c, 1980, 1981a, 1981b, 1981c, 1981d, 1982a, 1982b, 1983, 1985a, 1985b; Izawa, Bell, & Hayden, 1984; Izawa & Hayden, 1978; Izawa, Hayden, & Isham, 1980).

A great majority of support for the retention interval effect, however, is indirect by nature, because (a) the S-T interval effect was demonstrated within method and (b) it was impossible to manipulate the same mean S-T interval for both anticipation and study-test method concurrently without destroying the inherent characteristics of the respective methods. In order to overcome these unsatisfactory aspects of *interprocedural* comparisons, Izawa (1985a) introduced a novel procedure: the sublist manipulation technique. In an effort to deal with the direct evidence, we expanded the sublist manipulation technique as to be described subsequently in the current part of this chapter.

The identity model assumes all processes postulated in Equations 3-7 are identical for both methods. The only differences between the two methods boil down to the differential work retention (S-T) interval. Namely, there are inherently two Matrices r_S and r_T respectively for the anticipation method, whereas only one each for the study-test method, with the whole list design that are usually utilized in this field for practically all cases.

If the above is correct, the identity model makes a strong prediction that the two methods should produce approximately the same level of performance, when the mean retention intervals were created equal for both study-test and anticipation methods. Such a prediction is testable. We, therefore, created the *identical or nearly identical mean S-T retention intervals interprocedurally between anticipation and study-test methods.* If the major difference between the methods is indeed the inherently different mean S-T intervals (cf. Fig. 8.1), the identity model expects small performance differences, when the mean S-T intervals were made equal or nearly so interprocedurally. Thus, we generated such S-T intervals, with the respective inherent characteristics of the methods intact. We present a few such random samples, out of massive data at hand, to show a state of affairs sufficiently in this chapter. Our current conclusion and the extent of their support for the identity model remain the same for the rest of our data as well.

EXPERIMENTS 1 AND 2

In each of Experiments 1 and 2, a 2×2 factorial design was utilized with two methods, study-test versus anticipation method; and two intercycle intervals, 0 seconds (massed practice) versus 30 seconds (spaced practice). A 20-pair list was constructed for each experiment with materials allowing manipulations of learning difficulty, that is, Consonant-Vowel-Consonant (CVC)-double-digit pairs. A harder list was used in Experiment 1 with low meaningfulness (m', Noble, 1961) ranging 1.50-1.69, and with low association values of digits (a', Battig & Spera, 1962) ranging from 0.72-2.25, whereas the values for a relatively easier list in Experiment 2 were 2.43-2.81 for an m' and 0.79-3.09 for a'. Two different learning difficulty levels were used because differences between anticipation and study-test methods may vary substantially, depending on learning difficulty of a given list (e.g., Izawa, 1980, 1985b).

Each list was subdivided into three sublists in such a way that the mean learning difficulty was the same for all, based on actual pre-experimental (pilot) data, as well as a priori m' and a' values. The three sublists thus constructed consisted of 5 items each in Sublists A (Item Identification Numbers 1-5) and Sublists C (Items 16-20) respectively, and 10 items in Sublist B (Items 6-15), in each experiment. The items assigned to each sublist remain the same between the two methods within each experiment.

Anticipation Sublists A, B, and C are entered in Italics, large, or bold type respectively; see Fig. 8.2 (adopted from Izawa, 1985a) in Experiments 1 and 2. Under the anticipation method, long and short S-T intervals are manipulable only on alternate cycles. The sublist presentation order was ABC on every odd-numbered anticipation cycle (even-numbered S trials experienced by the subject, because the data from the first anticipation cycle reflects no S trial

			Study (S) Opportunities with the Anticipation Method (Anticipation Cycle)				
Sublist		Item Position	S_0 (1)	S_1 (2)	S_2 (3)	S_3 (4)	. . . .
S Cycle Even	Odd		ABC	CBA	ABC	CBA	
A	C	1	a_1 -	▲ a_{17} -	a_4 -	▲ a_{18} -	
		2	a_1 - b_1	a_{17} - b_{17}	a_4 - b_4	a_{18} - b_{18}	
		3	a_2 -	▲ a_{16} -	a_2 -	▲ a_{20} -	
		4	a_2 - b_2	a_{16} - b_{16}	a_2 - b_2	a_{20} - b_{20}	
		5	a_3 -	▲ a_{18} -	a_1 -	▲ a_{17} -	
		6	a_3 - b_3	a_{18} - b_{18}	a_1 - b_1	a_{17} - b_{17}	
		7	a_4 -	▲ a_{20} -	a_5 -	▲ a_{16} -	
		8	a_4 - b_4	a_{20} - b_{20}	a_5 - b_5	a_{16} - b_{16}	
		9	a_5 -	▲ a_{19} -	a_3 -	▲ a_{19} -	
		10	a_5 - b_5	a_{19} - b_{19}	a_3 - b_3	a_{19} - b_{19}	
B	B	11	a_6 -	a_{13} -	a_{14} -	a_{11} -	
		12	a_6 - b_6	a_{13} - b_{13}	a_{14} - b_{14}	a_{11} - b_{11}	
		.	.	.	.	.	
		.	.	.	.	.	
		29	a_{15} -	a_9 -	a_8 -	a_{12} -	
		30	a_{15} - b_{15}	a_9 - b_9	a_8 - b_8	a_{12} - b_{12}	
C	A	31	a_{16} -	a_3 -	a_{19} -	a_2 -	
		32	▲ a_{16} - b_{16}	a_3 - b_3	▲ a_{19} - b_{19}	a_2 - b_2	
		33	a_{17} -	a_1 -	a_{18} -	a_4 -	
		34	▲ a_{17} - b_{17}	a_1 - b_1	▲ a_{18} - b_{18}	a_4 - b_4	
		35	a_{18} -	a_2 -	a_{17} -	a_3 -	
		36	▲ a_{18} - b_{18}	a_2 - b_2	▲ a_{17} - b_{17}	a_3 - b_3	
		37	a_{19} -	a_5 -	a_{20} -	a_5 -	
		38	▲ a_{19} - b_{19}	a_5 - b_5	▲ a_{20} - b_{20}	a_5 - b_5	
		39	a_{20} -	a_4 -	a_{16} -	a_1 -	
		40	▲ a_{20} - b_{20}	a_4 - b_4	▲ a_{16} - b_{16}	a_1 - b_1	

FIG. 8.2.   Sublist item presentation arrangements under the anticipation method in Experiments 1 and 2 (after Izawa, 1985a; a- and b-terms are stimulus (cue) and response (target) terms of a pair, which is identified by its subscript. Sublist A (in Italics) appeared first on all even S (odd anticipation) cycles and last on all odd S (even anticipation) cycles, whereas the opposite held for Sublist C (in bold type). Sublist B items (in large type) were always in the middle item-positions).

effects; thus labeled S_0) and CBA on every even anticipation (odd numbered S) cycle. For convenience and simplicity of exposition in appropriate comparisons with the study-test method, we henceforth refer to anticipation cycles in terms of S trials experienced. The presentation order of the items within sublist was randomized from cycle to cycle at the designated sublist positions, respectively.

The aforementioned arrangement produced short retention intervals that varied from 0 to 16 intervening events, with a mean of 8 events for Anticipa-

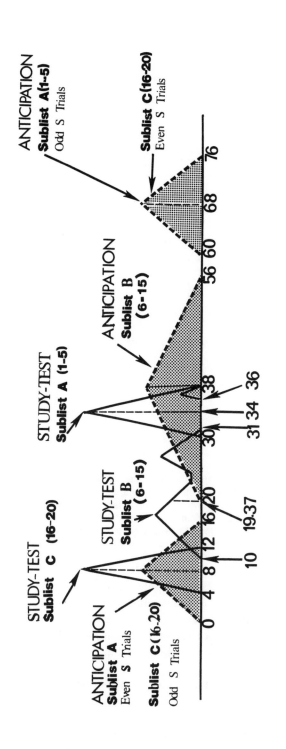

Number of Intervening Events between S and its Subsequent T

FIG. 8.3. Distributions of intervening events in the retention (S-T) intervals for each sublist under anticipation (shaded) and study-test methods in Experiments 1 and 2.

213

Sublist Cycle S T	Item Position	S_1 ABCB	T_1 BCBA	S_2 ABCB	T_2 BCBA	. . . .
		Study (S) and Test (T) Cycles with the Study-Test Method				
B	1	$a_1 - b_1$	$a_{13}-$	$a_4 - b_4$	$a_{11}-$	
	2	$a_2 - b_2$	$a_7 -$	$a_2 - b_2$	$a_8 -$	
A	3	$a_3 - b_3$	$a_{17}-$	$a_1 - b_1$	$a_{18}-$	
	4	$a_4 - b_4$	$a_{16}-$	$a_5 - b_5$	$a_{20}-$	
C	5	$a_5 - b_5$	$a_{18}-$	$a_3 - b_3$	$a_{17}-$	
	6	$a_6 - b_6$	$a_{20}-$	$a_{14}-b_{14}$	$a_{16}-$	
	7	$a_7 - b_7$	$a_{19}-$	$a_{12}-b_{12}$	$a_{19}-$	
B	8	$a_8 - b_8$	$a_{10}-$	$a_6 - b_6$	$a_{13}-$	
	9	$a_9 - b_9$	$a_8 -$	$a_9 - b_9$	$a_6 -$	
	10	$a_{10}-b_{10}$	$a_{15}-$	$a_{11}-b_{11}$	$a_9 -$	
	11	$a_{11}-b_{11}$	$a_6 -$	$a_7 - b_7$	$a_{10}-$	
B	12	$a_{12}-b_{12}$	$a_{11}-$	$a_{10}-b_{10}$	$a_{14}-$	
	13	$a_{13}-b_{13}$	$a_{12}-$	$a_{15}-b_{15}$	$a_7 -$	
	14	$a_{16} - b_{16}$	$a_{14}-$	$a_{19} - b_{19}$	$a_{15}-$	
	15	$a_{17} - b_{17}$	$a_9 -$	$a_{18} - b_{18}$	$a_{12}-$	
C	16	$a_{18} - b_{18}$	$a_3 -$	$a_{17} - b_{17}$	$a_2 -$	
	17	$a_{19} - b_{19}$	$a_1 -$	$a_{20} - b_{20}$	$a_4 -$	
A	18	$a_{20} - b_{20}$	$a_2 -$	$a_{16} - b_{16}$	$a_3 -$	
B	19	$a_{14}-b_{14}$	$a_5 -$	$a_{13}-b_{13}$	$a_5 -$	
	20	$a_{15}-b_{15}$	$a_4 -$	$a_8 - b_8$	$a_1 -$	

FIG. 8.4. Sublist item presentation arrangements under the study-test method in Experiments 1 and 2 (Sublist A items (in Italics) are restricted to Item Positions 1-5 on all study (S) cycles, and 16-20 on all test (T) cycles, whereas those in Sublist C (in bold type) occupied Item Positions 14-18 on S cycles and 3-7 on T cycles. Sublist B items (in large type) took all the remaining positions).

tion Sublist A on every even S trial as well as for Anticipation Sublist C on every odd S trial. On all other cycles, these two sublists had the long retention intervals distributed between 60 to 76 intervening events with a mean of 68, see Fig. 8.3. Anticipation Sublist B was placed in the middle positions, generating a medium retention interval for the anticipation method with a mean of 38 intervening events, with the lower and upper limits of 20 and 56 events, respectively.

In order to create the same *mean* S-T intervals for both methods, on every S cycle Study-Test Sublist C items were placed in the last 7 item positions except the two final ones (Item Positions 14-18), and the initial 7 positions save the first two (Item Positions 3-7) on every T cycle, as summarized in Fig. 8.4. This arrangement resulted in a mean retention interval for the study-test method, identical to that of the short retention interval in the anticipation method (Fig. 8.3), although the range or the base for the triangular distribution of the study-test method was one-half that of the anticipation method, that is, ranging from 4 to 12 intervening events.

Study-Test Sublist A items were always placed in the first five item positions on every S cycle and the last five positions on the T cycles, producing the long retention interval for the study-test method. This longest mean retention interval approximated the mean medium retention interval for the anticipation method (34 vs. 38 intervening intervals, Fig. 8.3). The nearly equal mean retention intervals between Study-Test Sublist A and Anticipation Sublist B are very important, because the crucial retention intervals appear consistently on every cycle without any alterations, albeit the distribution variance was much larger for the anticipation method, the base of the triangle being 4.5 times wider than that for the study-test method counterpart.

All other item positions utilized Sublist B items under the study-test method, and their retention intervals in terms of the intervening events are unorthodox; a result of several combinations of triangular distributions as entered in Fig. 8.3; they ranged from 10 to 38, with a mean of 19.37 intervening events.

Whereas the mean S-T (retention) intervals are identical for both study-test (Sublist C) and anticipation (Sublists A and C) methods, there are concerns regarding short and long alternations with the anticipation method along with its compensating S-S and T-T interval effects (cf. Izawa, 1985a for detailed discussion). Yet, these comparisons of the two methods, although weak, would constitute useful tests. These tests may reveal the potent influence of S-T intervals powerful enough to be detected. There seems little contamination of this nature in comparisons between Study-Test Sublist A and Anticipation Sublist B, which seem to provide a strong test of S-T interval effects, if conducted interprocedurally. These latter tests are especially significant, as the mean S-S and T-T are the same for both methods and constant from cycle to cycle.

A practical aspect in optimizing acquisition of any new word or language, includes spaced practice effects. In order to acquire a set of words, is it better to rest between trials? We added this dimension of inquiry to the item presentation method in this part of the present chapter. The variations of this factor consisted of massed practice with no intercycle intervals (cf. Equations 1 and 2), and spaced practice with 30 second intercycle intervals. Thus, all sublist variations were tried with both massed and spaced practice.

The presentation rate was 3 seconds per each S and T event. Intercycle intervals were 0 seconds each for Conditions 1 (study-test) and 2 (anticipation), and 30 seconds for Conditions 3 (study-test) and 4 (anticipation). Subjects were volunteers from Introductory Psychology classes at Tulane, 15 per condition in each experiment, for a total of 120 students in this set of two experiments.

A practice task, consisting of two lists of three pairs each was learned by all subjects, one list under the study-test method and the other under the anticipation method. The practice task served to (a) acquaint all subjects with both procedures so as not to bias them toward one method or the other, and (b) provide data to assess the influence of the subject variable.

The Two Item Information Presentation Methods Differ Little

The extant models, except for the identity model (and its sire, the retention interval model), take no retention interval into consideration, in accounting for performance differences between anticipation and study-test methods. Regardless of the length of the retention interval or acquisition situation, the feedback model predicts superiority for the anticipation method, whereas the study-test method is expected to be advantageous with the task alternation (e.g., Battig & Brackett, 1961) and differential acquisition (e.g., Kanak & Neuner, 1970) models. The differential "encoding model" (Barch & Levine, 1967; Part 2 of this chapter) expects the superiority of the anticipation method when encoding is difficult, but the advantage for the study-test method when encoding is easy.

Contrary to the latter four models that assume explicitly or implicitly that it is greater acquisition (conditioning) power or encoding capability which makes one method superior to the other, it is axiomatic to the identity model that encoding processes occurring on study (S) events differ little between study-test and anticipation methods. According to the identity model, performance differences between the two item information presentation methods are primarily attributable to their inherently different mean retention (S-T) intervals and the number of critical items in short-term memory system.

Therefore, when the retention interval is equated for both anticipation and study-test methods by novel sublist manipulation techniques (Fig. 8.2 and 8.4), the identity model predicts nearly similar performance levels, *ceteris paribus*, from both item presentation procedures. But, predictions from the other models remain the same, *vide supra*; for them, the retention interval is irrelevant, therefore it cannot influence their predictions.

Data from the practice task, administered to all those participated, indicated no significant differences on the subject variable among the four conditions within each of the first two experiments (although the subjects in the anticipation condition had trends to be inferior in Experiment 2), ensuring overall comparibility of the four groups. Such comparibility within experiment, held throughout all other experiments in the present chapter as well.

We repeatedly replicated the retention (S-T) interval effects *within* method and found throughout the present study (within subject comparisons), that the shorter the interval, the better the performance, just as in Izawa (1972, 1985a) and Izawa and Morrison (1979). However, in the present study, our emphasis is on making interprocedural comparisons *between* anticipation and study-test methods. Because there were three sublists per condition, there are nine possible interprocedural (between subject) comparisons between the two methods, with massed or spaced practice. Here and for all experiments, there is the trend that longer retention interval differentials enhance performance differences between the methods. However, considering the main goal for this part of our chapter, that is interprocedural comparisons with equal retention (S-T) intervals, we settle for just one set of random samples of unequal (S-T) interval cases for our four experiments in this part of the chapter.

Comparison of the anticipation method with the study-test method under the novel sublist manipulation technique indicates that shorter retention intervals enhanced performance, regardless of method. That, however, usually does not produce a significance, unless the differences between S-T intervals

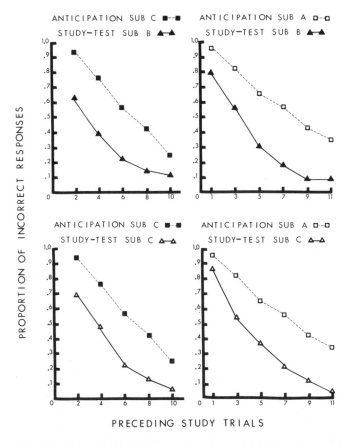

FIG. 8.5. Performance differences between anticipation and study-test sublists when the mean S-T intervals differentials are very large with massed practice in Experiment 2.

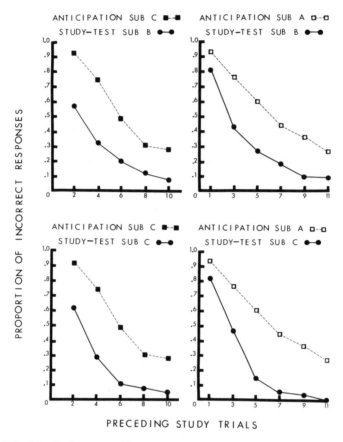

FIG. 8.6. Performance differences between anticipation and study-test sublists when the mean S-T intervals differentials are very large with spaced practice in Experiment 2.

are sufficiently large. In the current learning situation, such cases were generally observed only among the large S-T differentials, that is, 30 intervening events or more. See, for example, Study-Test Sublist C compared either with Anticipation Sublist B (8 vs. 38) or with Anticipation Sublists A and C, on odd and even S trials (8 vs. 68), respectively. These comparisons in Experiment 2, for example, produced the kinds of results shown in Fig. 8.5 and 8.6 for massed and spaced practice, respectively. The differences were all highly significant: $F(1, 28)$'s were 24.84 and 31.39 when Anticipation Sublists A and C on odd and even S trials, respectively, were compared to Study-Test Sublist B, and 14.63 and 18.92 when contrasted to Study-Test Sublist C (Fig. 8.5), $p < 0.001$ each. The same interprocedural comparisons with spaced practice produced $F(1, 28)$'s of 16.37, 11.40, 21.90, and 17.78, respectively, with p's < 0.01 (Fig. 8.6).

We now return to our main focus, interprocedural comparisons of anticipation and study-test methods with identical or nearly identical retention (S-T) intervals. The creation of the retention intervals of the similar lengths was crucial for differentiating alternative models, and to account for performance differences between the two methods and the methods' differential efficacy, if any.

A strong test was performed in the comparisons of Study-Test Sublist A and Anticipation Sublist B. On the average, all other temporal intervals (S-S, T-T and T-S) were held constant, or nearly so. Most importantly, the crucial S-T intervals in question were approximately the same in both methods (Fig. 8.3). See the lower panels of Fig. 8.7 and 8.8. There were scarcely any differences between anticipation and study-test methods in Experiment 1 with either massed practice (Fig. 8.7) or spaced practice (Fig. 8.8). The differences between the two methods with massed practice were especially small. The identity of the two methods held up very well, although the study-test method

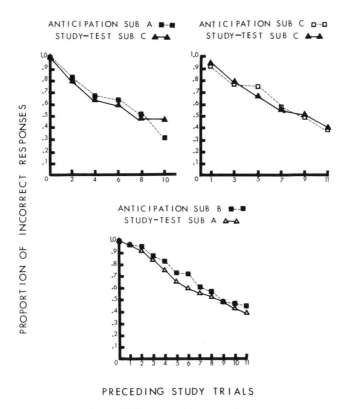

FIG. 8.7.   Performance comparisons of sublists between study-test and anticipation methods when the mean S-T intervals were either identical or nearly identical with massed practice (0 second intercycle intervals) in Experiment 1.

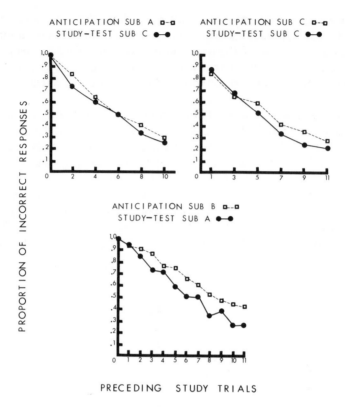

FIG. 8.8.   Performance comparisons of sublists between study-test and anticipation methods when the mean S-T intervals were either identical or nearly identical with spaced practice (30 second intercycle intervals) in Experiment 1.

had a slightly shorter S-T interval (by 4 intervening events) than the anticipation method, and therefore, was thought to have a slight advantage.

The current identity of the two item presentation methods does deny the possibility of differential acquisition and task alternation models; both models expect superior performances for the study-test method. But this was not the case. However, the absence of significance between Anticipation Sublist B and Study-Test Sublist A can also be derived from the feedback model. That is, the mean feedback (T-S) intervals for these sublists are also nearly identical; there are 0 intervening events for the former, but 4 for the latter. This difference in the mean feedback (T-S) intervals is the same as that of the mean retention (S-T) intervals.

In order to differentiate between the identity and feedback models, they must provide different predictions of outcomes from identical situations. Such situations are indeed provided. For instance, in the comparisons between Study-Test Sublist C and Anticipation Sublists C (on odd S trials) and A (on even S trials) where the mean feedback (T-S) interval always contained 0 intervening events under the anticipation method, there were as many as 30 intervening events under the study-test method. Yet, this latter comparison had the identical mean retention (S-T) interval for both methods in 8 intervening events.

Consequently, the feedback model predicts the superiority for the anticipation method, whereas the identity model expects no differences between the two methods in the Study-Test Sublist C versus Anticipation Sublists C (odd Ss) and A (even Ss) comparisons. To procure a verdict based on data, turn to the two top panels of Fig. 8.7 and 8.8, respectively. The anticipation method was not superior; that is, the data did not support the feedback model. Instead, performance differentials between the two item information presentation methods were infinitesimal, both with massed practice (Fig. 8.7) and with spaced practice (Fig. 8.8). The evidence clearly favors the identity model.

Opposed effects likely to cancel each other are probably attributable to alternating S-S and T-T intervals in addition to the critical S-T (retention) interval. Nonetheless, the positive evidence obtained for the identity model seems particularly impressive, because the four cases in this particular combination of the two methods should be regarded as conservative (weak) tests, at best. A total of six study-test versus anticipation methods comparisons using similar retention intervals, at both short and medium retention intervals, would indeed constitute important additional evidence on behalf of the identity model.

Figures 8.9 and 8.10 present these six cases of the study-test versus anticipation sublist comparisons with the identical or nearly identical retention intervals manipulated, respectively, with massed and spaced practice in Experiment 2, where relatively easier materials were learned (cf. Fig. 8.2, 8.3, and 8.4). Relative interprocedural differences in Experiment 2 were not generally as small as those in Experiment 1. However, no significant differences were found between Study-Test Sublist A and Anticipation Sublist B for either massed or spaced practice (bottom panels in Fig. 8.9 and 8.10, respectively). These are strong tests of the identity model.

How about weaker tests with mutually cancelling effects? All comparisons between Study-Test Sublist C and Anticipation Sublists A and C, respectively, on even and odd S trials were similarly small to the point of nonsignificance, except one: Anticipation Sublist A on even S trials was compared with Study-Test Sublist C, with massed practice, $F(1, 28) = 7.53$, with $p < 0.05$.

Of the 12 cases comparing the two methods with equal retention intervals, we encountered one aberration (8%). This may be thought of as a direct challenge to the identity model, or simply as reflecting some artifactual contamination, perhaps attributable to the subject variable, which strongly suggested that subjects in the anticipation conditions were inferior to those in the study-test conditions. This may have contributed to an overestimation of the differences between the two methods, as the anticipation curves stayed artificially high in proportions of incorrect responses. Notice also that this

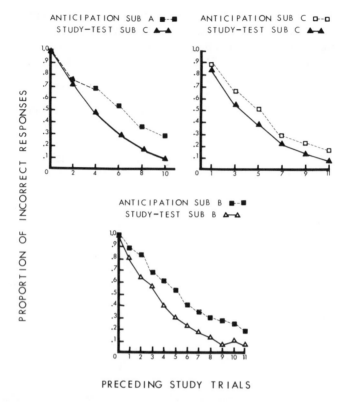

FIG. 8.9.   Performance comparisons of sublists between study-test and anticipation methods when the mean S-T intervals were either identical or nearly identical with massed practice in Experiment 2.

deviation was in one of the four weak tests, where all S-T, S-S and T-T intervals alternated between one anticipation cycle and the next, that is, mutually opposing unmeasureable forces that may have masked the crucial effect. Quite interestingly, the direction of this deviation is opposite to the expectation from the feedback model.

If the deviation were genuine, not attributed to artifacts, it should be easily reproduced. We will do just that by rerunning Experiment 2 next, instead of further speculation. There is no substitute for direct evidence.

QUANTITATIVE EXAMINATIONS OF THE IDENTITY MODEL

In order to express the identity model in a mathematical form, to facilitate comparisons with empirical data, we followed the procedure created by Izawa (1985a). For computational convenience, Parameter c in Equation 3 was set to be 1, which was assumed to be the same for both study-test and anticipation methods. The mathematical equations thus derived for each sublist are each a function of e, e', f, f', g, g', k, and k'.

Therefore, once a set of the eight parameters are estimated, we are able to make numerical predictions from the identity model. If it were our aim to produce the closest possible fit between theory and data, a powerful computer could determine the best parameter values by utilizing all data points. Instead, we adopted a much more restricted parameter estimation technique to test the model under more stringent criteria.

Only a single sublist in one method out of six with spaced practice was used for estimating the eight parameters (let us call this the primary parameter estimation; spaced practice gives a more stable and unique set of Parameter g and g': see Izawa, 1981b, 1985a for details), and predictions for all other sublist performances were made using that set of parameter values for both anticipation and study-test methods. Of the eight parameters, the identity model predicts Parameters k and k' to differ for massed and spaced prac-

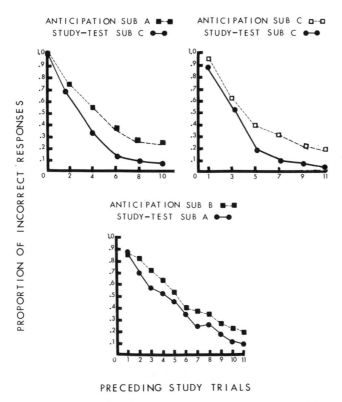

FIG. 8.10. Performance comparisons of sublists between study-test and anticipation methods when the mean S-T intervals were either identical or nearly identical with spaced practice in Experiment 2.

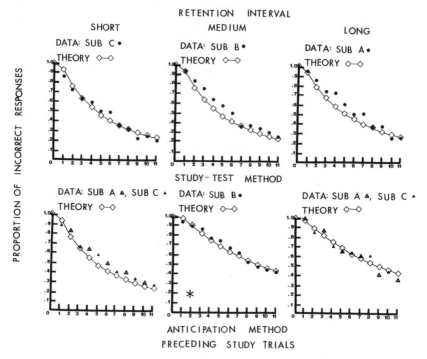

FIG. 8.11.   The identity model (open dots) as contrasted to the sublist data (solid dots) with spaced practice in Experiment 1, with all eight parameter values estimated solely from Anticipation Sublist B (indicated by the * sign; the primary parameter estimation).

tice, respectively. For that reason, a set of k and k' values alone were estimated from a single sublist in one method with massed practice (let us call this the secondary parameter estimation) to be utilized in all massed practice sublists with both methods. The secondary parameter estimation was achieved by holding the other six primary parameters (from a spaced practice sublist) invariant. The same procedure was adopted in all four experiments in Part 1 of this chapter.

This means that only a single set of Parameters e, e', f, f', g, g' (the invariant primary parameters) was used for all of the 12 sublists within each experiment in both massed and spaced practice as well as under study-test and anticipation methods, independent of whichever method's sublist was selected randomly for estimating the six invariant primary parameters.

Under the present parameter estimation technique, then, only a fraction of data points impacted parameter estimations: Out of a total of as many as 144 data points within each in Experiments 1 and 2, only 12 points (one sublist) were utilized for the primary parameter estimation (e, e', f, f', g, g', k, and k') for spaced practice data; for massed practice data, another

12 data points (one massed practice sublist) were involved in the estimation of the secondary parameters (k and k'). That is, as few as 16.7% of all data points influenced parameter estimations, whereas a great majority that is, 120 data points or 83.3% did not.

Because we eliminated such a large percentage of the data points from parameter estimations, our curve-fitting is not expected to be at its most impressive. If, however, satisfactory outcomes were realized with this highly restrictive parameter estimation technique, any success here would underscore the soundness of the basic assumptions of the identity model more powerfully than if the alternative estimation techniques had been tried.

For Experiment 1, a spaced practice sublist thus selected was Anticipation Sublist B (identified by an asterisk (*) in Fig. 8.11). The obtained set of Parameters e, e', f, f', g, g', k, and k' values were: .999, .051, .959, .201, .724, .011, .934, and .051, respectively. The general trends found earlier (Izawa, 1981b, 1985a) were again apparent in this and all other experiments here, that is, within each matrix, the parameters without prime ($'$) were larger than those with it, $e > e'$, $f > f'$, $g > g'$, and $k > k'$.

Using these parameter values, theoretical predictions were made on the basis of the identity model and entered in the lower center panel of Fig. 8.11. Agreement between the observed data and the model was almost ideal: Tested by chi square, the results were highly satisfactory: $\chi^2(3, N = 180) = .173, p > .95$. There were no significant differences between data and the model. (This extreme closeness between theory and data was made possible by using all data points for parameter estimations with this particular sublist. Closeness of this order would have been possible for *all* other sublists if we used all of the 144 data points in each of the experiments.)

Via the same set of eight primary parameters as above, the performances of the remaining five sublists were predicted for spaced practice from the identity model not only for the anticipation method sublists (one of them was used for the primary parameter estimation), but also for the study-test method sublists that were totally independent of any spaced practice parameter estimation in Experiment 1. As seen in every panel in Fig. 8.11, the identity model predicted data very satisfactorily under both study-test method (upper panels) and anticipation method (lower panels) for all lengths of retention intervals: short, medium, and long ones (left, center, and right panels, respectively). The overall agreement between the model and data is very close. Deviations were nonsignificant: $\chi^2(64, N = 1080) = 2.645, p > .99$.

The difference between massed and spaced practice in the identity model can be translated into differential values of Parameters k and k' between the two types of practice in the current situation, whereas invariance is expected between them for Parameters e, e', f, f', g, and g', respectively. Therefore, Parameters k and k' alone were estimated from Study-Test Sublist C for massed practice in Experimental 1 (indicated by an * in Fig. 8.12). The values thus estimated were .729 and .041, respectfully. Relative relationships between

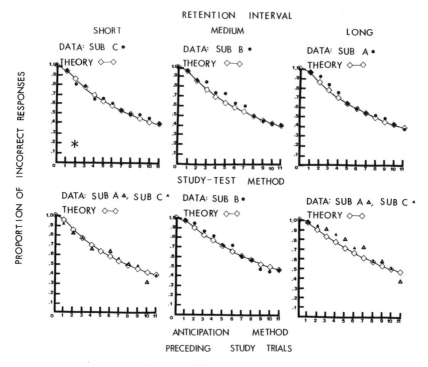

FIG. 8.12. The identity model (open dots) as compared with the sublist data (solid dots) with massed practice in Experiment 1, with Parameters k and k' alone estimated from Study-Test Sublist C only (shown by the * sign; the secondary parameter estimation).

k and k' and between massed and spaced practice are both in the directions anticipated by the identity model; said relationships were also noted elsewhere (Izawa, 1985a). Using this secondary parameter estimation (k and k' for massed practice), along with the primary one (invariant e, e', f, f', and g, and g' for all sublists), the predictions for all sublists with massed practice are entered in Fig. 8.12 for both study-test (upper panels) and anticipation (lower panels) methods to compare with actual data.

The identity model also has an excellent fit with massed practice. An overall chi square, $\chi^2(70, N = 1080)$ was merely in the order of 1.308, $p > .99$, indicating that deviations of data from the predictions are minor and thus do not challenge the model. It seems remarkable that only two of eight parameters were estimated from one sublist (12 data points). Even then such close agreements were obtained between theory and data not only for that sublist (within subjects), but also for all remaining five sublists (60 data points) across both item presentation methods that were totally independent of parameter estimations (between subjects). This, in turn, seems to validate the basic processes occurring in each event (Equations 3-7) that are postulated to be identical between the two methods in the identity model.

For Experiment 2, a primary set of eight parameters was estimated from Study-Test Sublist B with spaced practice (Fig. 8.13, upper center panel). The obtained values were .994, .140, .425, .415, .945, .031, .745, and .070, respectively, for Parameters e, e', f, f', g, g', k, and k'. The predictions from the identity model are contrasted with actual spaced practice data from Experiment 2 in Fig. 8.13. Although the deviations from the model were moderate on a few trials in the middle learning stage, with Study-Test Sublist A (long retention interval, upper right panel in Fig. 8.13), deviations on the other sublists were generally small. An overall chi square test demonstrated that the deviations were far too small to be significant: $\chi^2(64, N = 1080) = 6.216$, $p > .99$.

While holding the invariant six primary parameters (from a spaced practice sublist) constant, Parameters k and k' for massed practice were estimated from Anticipation Sublist B (Fig. 8.14, lower center panel) alone: $k = .877$

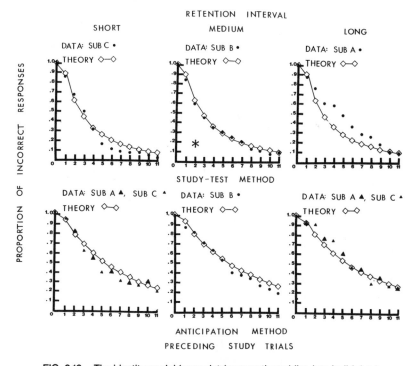

FIG. 8.13.   The identity model (open dots) versus the sublist data (solid dots) with spaced practice in Experiment 2 with all parameter values estimated solely from Study-Test Sublist B (indicated by the * sign; the primary parameter estimation).

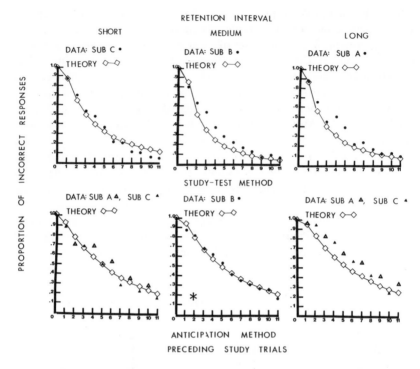

FIG. 8.14.   The identity model (open dots) versus the sublist data (solid dots) with massed practice in Experiment 2 with Parameters *k* and *k'* alone estimated from Anticipation Sublist B only (shown by the * sign; the secondary parameter estimation).

and $k' = .099$. The theoretical and the observed values for each massed practice sublist in Experiment 2 are compared in Fig. 8.14. Here, apparently, subjects using massed practice with the anticipation method experienced differential learning difficulty between Sublists A and C; see the zig-zag courses of improvement attributed to alternating sublists with both short and long retention intervals (lower left and right panels). Such learning curves make fit with any theory problematic. Yet, the identity model, overall, produced nonsignificant deviations from massed practice data from Experiment 2: $\chi^2(70, N = 1080) = 10.459$, $p > .99$.

EXPERIMENT 3

In Experiment 2, one significant deviation occurred among 12 comparisons of anticipation and study-test methods, with equal retention intervals, in our qualitative data analyses. At that point the rate of deviation was 8%. In our previous study (Izawa, 1985a) one case out of 16 defied the identity model;

the failure rate was 6%. Deviations of this magnitude (6%-8%) however do not constitute a serious challenge to the validity of any theory. Indeed, the more empirical tests there are, the more such deviations are likely to occur due to the random intrusions by unknown artifacts.

On the other hand, one could also misconstrue the rate of deviation as a bit too high. There were two concerns about the results of Experiment 2. The major one stemmed from nonsignificant but sizable differences in the subject variable: The subjects in the anticipation method were poorer than those in the study-test method. This particular fact may have contributed, in part, to larger overall performance differences in general. In Experiment 2, one of the six comparisons of study-test and anticipation methods with equal retention intervals reached a significance level at $p = 0.05$.

Another, if minor, concern was the way the study-test method items were arranged in its sublist in order to generate the same mean retention interval as for the anticipation method. (See Fig. 8.1.) The variance of the retention interval distribution is always greater for the anticipation method than the study-test method when using the usual whole list design. In Experiments 1 and 2, sublists were manipulated intentionally to mimic that state of affairs, to create in such a way as to make the retention interval distribution variation range for the anticipation method exactly twice as large as for the study-test method (Fig. 8.3, Study-Test Sublist C vs. Anticipation Sublists C and A on odd and even S trials, respectively). In a sense, however, one of the advantages of the study-test method may be its greater homogeneity in retention interval length compared to the anticipation method. This would be true for either the whole list situation or the sublist situation as in Experiments 1 and 2.

In order to mitigate both concerns, Experiment 2 was rerun as Experiment 3 using the same learning materials, but with a slightly different sublist item manipulation to create *identical* retention interval distributions (means, ranges, and variances included) in both methods: We placed Study-Test Sublist C items in the exact same item locations as those with the corresponding anticipation sublists. Note that S and T events occur alternately with the anticipation method. The study (S) events of Anticipation Sublist C on the first anticipation cycle (S_0 in Fig. 8.2), for example, occurred on the last five S-items positions (cross Item Positions 32, 34, 36, 38, and 40) marked by open triangle dots (adopted from Izawa, 1985a).

The same Sublist C items were placed in identical locations from the ends of the S cycle under the study-test method, that is, Item Positions 12, 14, 16, 18, and 20 in Fig. 8.15. The same identical item presentation arrangements were made for test (T) events of Sublists C for both anticipation and study-test methods to generate the shortest identical S-T intervals: Identified by solid triangle dots, the T events appeared on Item Positions 1, 3, 5, 7, and 9 under both Study-Test T cycles and even-numbered anticipation cycles (odd-numbered Ss), cf. Fig. 8.2 vs. 8.15.

Sublist Cycle S	T	Item Position	S_1 AB BC	T_1 CB BA	S_2 AB BC	T_2 CB BA	....
A		1	$a_1 - b_1$	▲ a_{17} -	$a_4 - b_4$	▲ a_{18} -	
		2	$a_2 - b_2$	a_{13}-	$a_2 - b_2$	a_{11}-	
		3	$a_3 - b_3$	▲ a_{16} -	$a_1 - b_1$	▲ a_{20} -	
		4	$a_4 - b_4$	a_7 -	$a_5 - b_5$	a_8 -	
		5	$a_5 - b_5$	▲ a_{18} -	$a_3 - b_3$	▲ a_{17} -	
	C+B	---	---	---	---	---	
B		6	$a_6 - b_6$	a_{10}-	$a_{14}-b_{14}$	a_{13}-	
		7	$a_7 - b_7$	▲ a_{20} -	$a_{12}-b_{12}$	▲ a_{16} -	
		8	$a_8 - b_8$	a_8 -	$a_6 - b_6$	a_6 -	
		9	$a_9 - b_9$	▲ a_{19} -	$a_9 - b_9$	▲ a_{19} -	
		10	$a_{10}-b_{10}$	a_{15}-	$a_{11}-b_{11}$	a_9 -	
B		11	$a_{11}-b_{11}$	a_6 -	$a_7 - b_7$	a_{10}-	
		12	△ $a_{16} - b_{16}$	a_{11}-	△ $a_{19} - b_{19}$	a_{14}-	
		13	$a_{12}-b_{12}$	a_{12}-	$a_{10}-b_{10}$	a_7 -	
		14	△ $a_{17} - b_{17}$	a_{14}-	△ $a_{18} - b_{18}$	a_{15}-	
		15	$a_{13}-b_{13}$	a_9 -	$a_{15}-b_{15}$	a_{12}-	
	B+C	---	---	---	---	---	
A		16	△ $a_{18} - b_{18}$	a_3 -	△ $a_{17} - b_{17}$	a_2 -	
		17	$a_{14}-b_{14}$	a_1 -	$a_{13}-b_{13}$	a_4 -	
		18	△ $a_{19} - b_{19}$	a_2 -	△ $a_{20} - b_{20}$	a_3 -	
		19	$a_{15}-b_{15}$	a_5 -	$a_8 - b_8$	a_5 -	
		20	△ $a_{20} - b_{20}$	a_4 -	△ $a_{16} - b_{16}$	a_1 -	

FIG. 8.15. Sublist item presentation arrangements with the study-test method in Experiment 3 (after Izawa, 1985a: In order to create the identical S-T interval distributions including the mean and the variance to those with the anticipation method, Sublist C items were presented on every other item position at the end of S cycles as indicated by open triangle dots, and at the beginning of T cycles as indicated by solid triangle dots).

The sublist item arrangement under the anticipation method in Experiment 3 was identical to those in Experiments 1 and 2 (Fig. 8.2). The item positions not occupied by either Sublists A or C under the study-test method were filled by the Study-Test Sublist B items. The resultant Study-Test Sublists C and B distributions are identical to those of Study-Test Sublists C and B ', respectively, in Experiment 4 shown in Fig. 8.21. The retention interval distributions of Study-Test Sublist A and all of those sublists under the anticipation method in Experiment 3 were the same as shown in Fig. 8.3.

Both study-test and anticipation conditions were run with massed practice with 0 seconds intercycle intervals in Experiment 3. A new set of 20 volunteers from another Introductory Psychology class participated in Experiment 3, with 10 volunteers each in study-test and anticipation conditions. All other experimental procedures in Experiment 3 were the same as in Experiment 2.

Figure 8.16 presents data for both the study-test and anticipation method sublists, with identical (upper panels) and nearly identical (bottom panel) retention intervals in Experiment 3. The two methods differed little in all of the three comparisons, including a strong test, that is, Study-Test Sublist A versus Anticipation Sublist B, and two weak tests: Study-Test Sublist C compared with Anticipation Sublists A and C, respectively, on odd and even S trials, all ps being greater than 0.15.

The significant performance differences between Anticipation Sublist A and Study-Test Sublist C on even S trials in Experiment 2 were not replicated in Experiment 3 (upper left, Fig. 8.9 vs. 8.16), although the same material was learned and the identical mean retention intervals were employed (with a minor modification in variance for the Study-Test Sublist C). Apparently, the deviation noted in Experiment 2 was indeed a random artifact that could not be reproduced.

It is interesting to note that the differences between the two methods, with identical mean retention intervals tended to be somewhat larger (but not

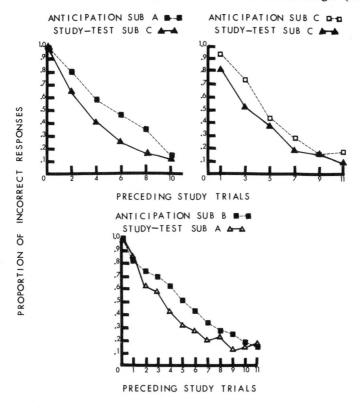

FIG. 8.16. Performance differences between study-test and anticipation sublists when their mean retention (S-T) intervals were the same or practically the same in Experiment 3.

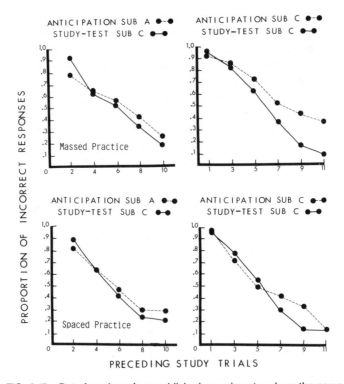

FIG. 8.17. Data from Izawa's unpublished experiments, where the same linguistic materials as those in our Experiment 3 were learned with the identical item presentation arrangements for Study-Test Sublist C and Anticipation Sublists C and A, respectively, on odd and even S cycles, to generate the short identical S-T interval distributions under both methods including both means and variances (cf. Fig. 8.15), under both massed practice with 0 second intercycle interval (upper panels), and spaced practice with 30 second intercycle intervals (lower panels).

significantly so) when different sublists were involved in the comparison: For both Fig. 8.9 and 8.16, the left upper panels (Sublists A vs. C) produced slightly larger differences than the right upper panels (the same Sublist C) suggesting possible involvements of sublist differences in learning difficulties. This manifested also in quantitative analyses in some of the current experiments.

It is most likely that the deviation observed in Experiment 2 stemmed from the fact that strong subject variable trends were manifest and that therefore performance level (excessive errors) was underestimated for the anticipation method, inflating performance differences. This view is supported by the overall performance differences between the two methods, for all combinations of Experiment 2. They were larger, albeit nonsignificantly, than in Experiment 3 (Fig. 8.9 vs. 8.16).

Although our random sampling procedure did not apply here, we have two unpublished sets of experiments in which the *same* materials as in Experiments 2 and 3 were learned, and the same Study-Test Sublist C was compared with the Anticipation Sublists A and C on even and odd S trials, respectively. Because replicability is the issue here, it may be advisable to include a sneak preview of the four additional comparisons of the same sublists. None of these four comparisons resulted in differences of any appreciable magnitude, see Fig. 8.17. The top panels in Fig. 8.17 demonstrate the state of affairs for massed practice, whereas the bottom ones deal with spaced practice. Thus, an important replication failed again in four additional comparisons (unpublished study by Izawa) as well.

In summary, a total of 13 comparisons employing identical learning materials in Experiments 2 (6 comparisons), 3 (3 comparisons) and Izawa's unpublished experiments (4 comparisons) produced only one deviation (7.7%). It seems eminently logical, then, to conclude that the aberration of Experiment 2 was in all likelihood an artifact of the subject variable; one that we could not replicate.

In the quantitative examination of the identity model via data from Experiment 3, the eight-primary-parameter estimation was made from Study-

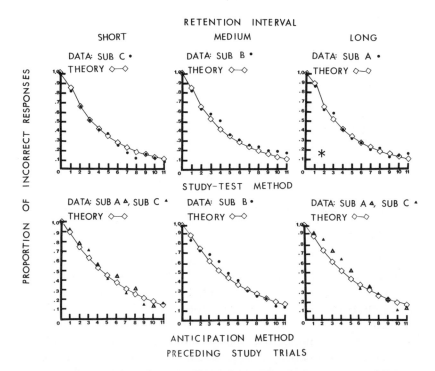

FIG. 8.18.   The identity model (open dots) as contrasted to the sublist data (solid dots) in Experiment 3 with all the parameter values estimated solely from Study-Test Sublist A (indicated by the * sign).

Sublist S Cycle Even / Odd	Item Position	Study (S) Opportunities with the Anticipation Method (Anticipation Cycle)				
		S_0 (1) ABB'C	S_1 (2) CB'BA	S_2 (3) ABB'C	S_3 (4) CB'BA	....
A C	1	a_1 -	▲ a_{27} -	a_4 -	▲ a_{28} -	
	2	$a_1 - b_1$	$a_{27} - b_{27}$	$a_4 - b_4$	$a_{28} - b_{28}$	
	3	a_2 -	▲ a_{26} -	a_2 -	▲ a_{30} -	
	4	$a_2 - b_2$	$a_{26} - b_{26}$	$a_2 - b_2$	$a_{30} - b_{30}$	
	5	a_3 -	▲ a_{28} -	a_1 -	▲ a_{27} -	
	6	$a_3 - b_3$	$a_{28} - b_{28}$	$a_1 - b_1$	$a_{27} - b_{27}$	
	7	a_4 -	▲ a_{30} -	a_5 -	▲ a_{26} -	
	8	$a_4 - b_4$	$a_{30} - b_{30}$	$a_5 - b_5$	$a_{26} - b_{26}$	
	9	a_5 -	▲ a_{29} -	a_3 -	▲ a_{29} -	
	10	$a_5 - b_5$	$a_{29} - b_{29}$	$a_3 - b_3$	$a_{29} - b_{29}$	
B B'	11	a_6 -	a_{24} -	a_{14} -	a_{20} -	
	12	$a_6 - b_6$	$a_{24} - b_{24}$	$a_{14} - b_{14}$	$a_{20} - b_{20}$	
	:	:	:	:	:	
	29	a_{15} -	a_{17} -	a_8 -	a_{18} -	
	30	$a_{15} - b_{15}$	$a_{17} - b_{17}$	$a_8 - b_8$	$a_{18} - b_{18}$	
B' B	31	a_{16} -	a_{13} -	a_{19} -	a_{11} -	
	32	$a_{16} - b_{16}$	$a_{13} - b_{13}$	$a_{19} - b_{19}$	$a_{11} - b_{11}$	
	:	:	:	:	:	
	49	a_{25} -	a_9 -	a_{22} -	a_{12} -	
	50	$a_{25} - b_{25}$	$a_9 - b_9$	$a_{22} - b_{22}$	$a_{12} - b_{12}$	
C A	51	a_{26} -	a_3 -	a_{29} -	a_2 -	
	52	▲ $a_{26} - b_{26}$	$a_3 - b_3$	▲ $a_{29} - b_{29}$	$a_2 - b_2$	
	53	a_{27} -	a_1 -	a_{28} -	a_4 -	
	54	▲ $a_{27} - b_{27}$	$a_1 - b_1$	▲ $a_{28} - b_{28}$	$a_4 - b_4$	
	55	a_{28} -	a_2 -	a_{27} -	a_3 -	
	56	▲ $a_{28} - b_{28}$	$a_2 - b_2$	▲ $a_{27} - b_{27}$	$a_3 - b_3$	
	57	a_{29} -	a_5 -	a_{30} -	a_5 -	
	58	▲ $a_{29} - b_{29}$	$a_5 - b_5$	▲ $a_{30} - b_{30}$	$a_5 - b_5$	
	59	a_{30} -	a_4 -	a_{26} -	a_1 -	
	60	▲ $a_{30} - b_{30}$	$a_4 - b_4$	▲ $a_{26} - b_{26}$	$a_1 - b_1$	

FIG. 8.19.   Sublists arrangements under the anticipation method in Experiment 4 (Items 1-5, 6-15, 16-25, and 26-30 inclusive, respectively, belonged to Sublists A, B, B', and C).

Test Sublist A (Fig. 8.18, upper right panel, the long retention interval) alone. The estimated e, e', f, f', g, g', k, and k' values were, respectively, .100, .051, .800, .126, .600, .051, .251, and .001. Figure 8.18 compares data with predicted values from the identity model for all the sublists, both study-test and anticipation methods. In Experiment 3 also, the effect of alternating Anticipation Sublists A and C, stemming from differential learning difficulty in the sublists, seems particularly prominent in the short retention interval (lower left panel of Fig. 8.18). Yet, considering all sublists, the overall chi square value was far too small to seriously challenge the identity model: $\chi^2(64, N = 720) = 5.719$, $p > .99$.

Sublist Cycle S T	Item Position	Study (S) and Test (T) Cycles with the Study-Test Method				
		S_1 ABB'C	T_1 CB'BA	S_2 ABB'C	T_2 CB'BA	. . . .
A	1	$a_1 - b_1$	▲ a_{27}^-	$a_4 - b_4$	▲ a_{28}^-	
	2	$a_2 - b_2$	a_{22}^-	$a_2 - b_2$	a_{20}^-	
	3	$a_3 - b_3$	▲ a_{26}^-	$a_1 - b_1$	▲ a_{30}^-	
	4	$a_4 - b_4$	a_{18}^-	$a_5 - b_5$	a_{17}^-	
	5	$a_5 - b_5$	▲ a_{28}^-	$a_3 - b_3$	▲ a_{27}^-	
B'+C						
	6	$a_6 - b_6$	a_{21}^-	$a_{14}-b_{14}$	a_{25}^-	
	7	$a_7 - b_7$	▲ a_{30}^-	$a_{13}-b_{13}$	▲ a_{26}^-	
	8	$a_8 - b_8$	a_{17}^-	$a_9 - b_9$	a_{22}^-	
	9	$a_9 - b_9$	▲ a_{29}^-	$a_{11}-b_{11}$	▲ a_{29}^-	
B	10	$a_{10}-b_{10}$	a_{16}^-	$a_{15}-b_{15}$	a_{16}^-	
	11	$a_{11}-b_{11}$	a_{19}^-	$a_{12}-b_{12}$	a_{23}^-	
B'	.	.	.	.	.	
	.	.	.	.	.	
	15	$a_{15}-b_{15}$	a_{24}^-	$a_8 - b_8$	a_{18}^-	
	16	$a_{16}-b_{16}$	a_{13}^-	$a_{18}-b_{18}$	a_{11}^-	
B'	.	.	.	.	.	
	.	.	.	.	.	
B	20	$a_{20}-b_{20}$	a_7^-	$a_{21}-b_{21}$	a_{14}^-	
	21	$a_{21}-b_{21}$	a_{15}^-	$a_{24}-b_{24}$	a_9^-	
	22	▲ $a_{26} - b_{26}$	a_{10}^-	▲ $a_{29} - b_{29}$	a_{10}^-	
	23	$a_{22}-b_{22}$	a_{12}^-	$a_{23}-b_{23}$	a_{13}^-	
	24	▲ $a_{27} - b_{27}$	a_6^-	▲ $a_{28} - b_{28}$	a_7^-	
	25	$a_{23}-b_{23}$	a_9^-	$a_{25}-b_{25}$	a_{12}^-	
B'+C						
	26	▲ $a_{28} - b_{28}$	a_3^-	▲ $a_{27} - b_{27}$	a_2^-	
	27	$a_{24}-b_{24}$	a_1^-	$a_{16}-b_{16}$	a_4^-	
A	28	▲ $a_{29} - b_{29}$	a_2^-	▲ $a_{30} - b_{30}$	a_3^-	
	29	$a_{25}-b_{25}$	a_5^-	$a_{22}-b_{22}$	a_5^-	
	30	▲ $a_{30} - b_{30}$	a_4^-	▲ $a_{26} - b_{26}$	a_1^-	

FIG. 8.20. Sublist arrangements under the study-test method in Experiment 4 (Items 1-5, 6-15, 16-25, and 26-30 inclusive, respectively, belonged to Sublists A, B, B', and C).

EXPERIMENT 4

The similarity of the anticipation and study-test methods with equal retention (S-T) interval was further pursued in Experiment 4. A much longer list was employed, $n = 30$, that is, 50% longer than the previous three experiments in the present study. The sublist manipulations for Sublists A and C utilized in Experiment 3 were also used in Experiment 4. Here, however, an additional 10 items were included, they were of the same measured learning difficulty as the other three sublists. This addition is labeled as Sublist B ' and placed next to, or between Sublists B and C, as shown in Fig. 8.19 and 8.20, respectively, for the anticipation and study-test methods. The

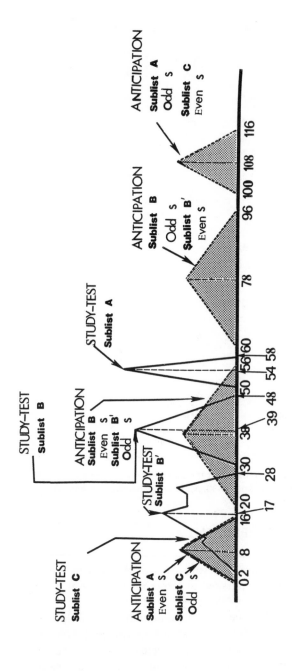

FIG. 8.21. Distributions of intervening events in the retention (S-T) intervals for each sublist under anticipation (shaded) and study-test methods in Experiment 4.

Number of Intervening Events between S and its Subsequent T

list used for Sublists A, B, and C in Experiment 4, was the same as those in Experiment 1.

This means that the S-T interval distributions for Study-Test Sublist C and Anticipation Sublists C (odd Ss) and A (even Ss) are identical for Experiment 4, each becoming a replication of Experiments 2 and 3, as all sublists had the same mean retention intervals. Thus, we provided still more opportunities to examine the replicability of earlier findings with 8 intervening events in the mean short S-T interval.

In total, including the same S-T interval of much greater length, newly created interprocedural comparisons in Experiment 4 generated eight additional opportunities to test the identity of the two methods. The S-T interval for Study-Test Sublist B had almost the same number of intervening events as those for Anticipation Sublist B (even Ss) or B ' (odd Ss), 39 versus 38 intervening events. Figure 8.21 gives the S-T interval distributions for all sublists with both anticipation and study-test methods in Experiment 4.

Another set of 40 volunteers from Introductory Psychology classes at Tulane participated, 20 each for massed and spaced practice, and 10 in each condition. Tested by the practice task, common to all subjects, there were no significant performance differences among the conditions in the subject variable.

The Identity of the Study-Test and Anticipation Methods Holds for Long Lists Also

Unlike earlier experiments in the present part, none of the interprocedural comparisons contained constant intervals for the anticipation method except for feedback (T-S) intervals that were found to generate minimal effects. Thus, all comparisons in Experiment 4 involved alternating long and short S-T, S-S, and T-S intervals in each anticipation sublist, although all four intervals were constant in any given study-test sublist. Consequently, these are weak (conservative) tests. However, should the retention interval effect be strong enough to overpower the contaminating effects of the alternations for three out of four temporal intervals in the anticipation method, we would still be able to observe the identity of the two methods.

Figure 8.22 and 8.23 present, respectively, data with massed and spaced practice in Experiment 4, which compared anticipation and study-test methods with equal S-T (retention) intervals. Study-Test Sublist C is compared with Anticipation Sublists A and C on even and odd S cycles, respectively, as shown in the top panels of Fig. 8.22 and 8.23 (the short identical retention interval). Similarly, Study-Test Sublist B is contrasted with Anticipation Sublists B and B ' on even and odd S cycles, respectively, as shown in the bottom panels (the long identical retention interval).

Throughout all eight interprocedural comparisons, the two methods did not differ significantly. Apparently, the retention interval effect was so power-

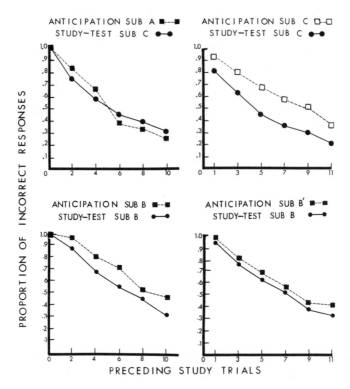

FIG. 8.22. Interprocedural comparisons of sublists when their mean S-T (retention) intervals were either identical or virtually identical in length, with massed practice (0 second intercycle intervals) in Experiment 4.

ful that it overrode all opposing effects (due to three alternating intervals under the anticipation method).

The findings clearly support the identity model. Even the largest differences observed in Anticipation Sublist C versus Study-Test Sublist C (Fig. 8.22, upper right) did not reach any accepted significance level, $F(1, 18) = 2.45, p > 0.15$. The other seven comparisons seen in Fig. 8.22 and 8.23 were much smaller and nonsignificant. Thus, the identity of the two item presentation methods did hold firm for a much longer list, provided that the same mean S-T intervals were used with both methods.

The results here obtained repeatedly affirm that encoding and retrieval processes differ little between the anticipation and study-test methods. They indicate also that the differences noted are attributable to the storage-retention processes occurring in the retention (S-T) intervals, which are inherently different for the methods when the commonly utilized whole list design is employed (Fig. 8.1).

In obtaining theoretical expressions for the sublists under both item presentation methods in Experiment 4 ($n = 30$) from the identity model, notice that:

The mean retention intervals for Sublists C, B ', B, and A under the study-test method had 8, 17, 39, and 54 intervening events, respectively, for short, medium-short, medium-long, and long retention intervals. The short, medium-short, medium-long, and long retention intervals under the anticipation method had 8, 38, 78, and 108 intervening events, respectively, occurring for Sublists A-even S and C-odd S, Sublists B-even S and B '-odd S, Sublists B-odd S, B '-even S, and Sublists A-odd S and C-even S trials. When the shortest retention interval was regarded as Unit 1 length, the other three can be regarded as the multiples of 2, 5, and 7 (taking the nearest whole number) with the study-test method, and Units 1, 5, 10, and 14 with the anticipation method, respectively. The latter units were used for calculating theoretical values from the identity model.

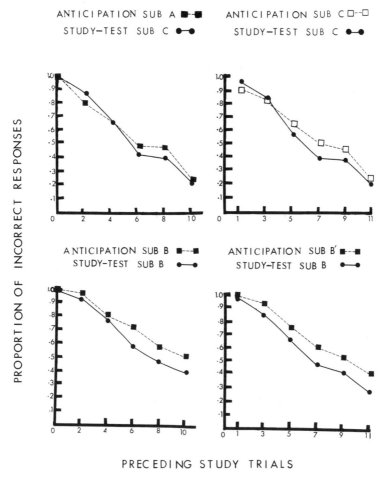

FIG. 8.23.   Interprocedural comparisons of sublists when their mean S-T (retention) intervals were either identical or virtually identical in length, with spaced practice (30 second intercycle intervals) in Experiment 4.

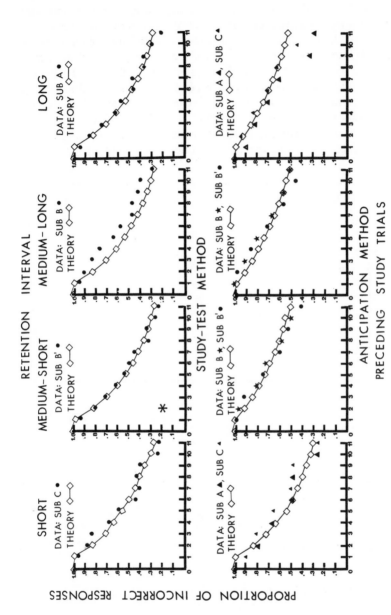

FIG. 8.24. The identity model (open dots) as compared with the sublist data (solid dots) with spaced practice in Experiment 4, with all the parameter values estimated solely from Study-Test Sublist B' (shown by the * sign; the primary parameter estimation).

240

Although there were two sublists each, with both massed and spaced practice more in Experiment 4 than any of the previous ones, we again used only one spaced practice sublist for estimating the primary eight parameters, and one massed practice sublist for estimating the secondary parameters for k and k'. That is, in Experiment 4 only 24 data points (2 sublists, 1 each with spaced and massed practice) out of 192 points (16 sublists, 8 under the study-test method and the remaining 8 under the anticipation method) were utilized, that is, only 12.5% of all points. Can the identity model also withstand that rigorous test here?

Study-Test Sublist B' with the medium-short retention interval alone was used in estimating the primary eight parameters for spaced practice (Fig. 8.24, upper panel, the second from the left). The values thus obtained were: $e = .854$, $e' = .051$, $f = .969$, $f' = .236$, $g = .999$, $g' = .001$, $k = .720$, and $k' = .007$. Via these parameter values alone, performances on a total of eight sublists were predicted from the identity model under both anticipation and study-test methods with spaced practice; see Fig. 8.24. Although two data points in Anticipation Sublist A (even S trials, the long retention interval) did not fit the model very well, all of the remaining 94 points were reasonably well approximated by the model. With an overall $\chi^2(88, N = 960) = 5.91$, $p > .99$, the overall deviations from the model were far removed from significance.

The secondary parameter estimation for Parameters k and k' for massed practice were made solely via the Study-Test Sublist B with the medium-long retention interval (Fig. 8.25, upper panel, the second from the right); $k = .659$ and $k' = .021$. Figure 8.25 presents the numerical predictions made from the identity contrasted with massed practice data from Experiment 4.

As often happens, when a sublist is randomly chosen for primary parameter estimation (6 invariant parameters plus 2 parameters exclusively for spaced practice) or estimation of the secondary parameters (2 exclusively for massed practice), one may involve a relatively long retention interval under one method, however, the larger deviations are likely to occur with relatively shorter intervals under the other method, or vice versa. For example, see Study-Test Sublist B (the medium-long retention interval, parameter estimation) versus Anticipation Sublists C and A on odd and even S trials respectively (the short retention interval, relatively larger deviations), as illustrated in Fig. 8.25 by the third upper panel (from the left) versus the first lower panel (between subjects).

Even in the latter case (short retention interval), Sublist A data agreed closely with the identity model, although Sublist C involved larger deviations, demonstrating differences in learning difficulty for subjects in the massed practice anticipation condition. A few deviations notwithstanding, from a global perspective, predictions from the identity model closely agreed with massed practice data as well: $\chi^2(94, N = 960) = 4.344$ is far too small to be significant, $p > .99$. These seem to be remarkable outcomes since only two of the eight parameters were estimated from 12.5% of massed practice data (Fig. 8.25); the remaining 87.5% of data did not influence the estimates.

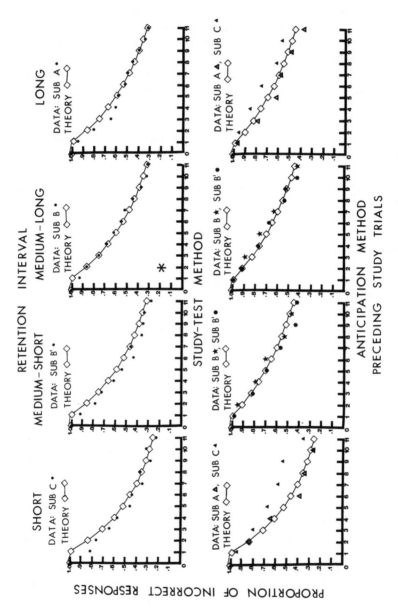

FIG. 8.25. The identity model (open dots) as contrasted to the sublist data (solid dots) with massed practice in Experiment 4, with Parameters k and k' alone estimated from Study-Test Sublist B only (indicated by the * sign; the secondary parameter estimation).

In summary, utilizing random samples of experiments, we compared anticipation and study-test methods qualitatively by applying equal retention (S-T) intervals 23 times in four experiments; these were reported in detail, in this portion of our chapter. Of them, one sublist comparison deviated from qualitative expectation of the identity model, a failure rate of 4%. If we include four additional comparisons employing identical learning materials and sublist arrangements as in Experiment 3 (Fig. 8.17, unpublished data from Izawa), the aberration was one out of 27, that is, 3.7%. Even when we include our previous study (Izawa, 1985a) where one significant departure from the identity model occurred in 16 comparisons, one could argue for 2 failures out of 43, or 4.7%. (This failure rate is about the same as for all unpublished experiments considered, either separately or jointly with the current data.) Deviations of this magnitude do not seem to warrant concern about the soundness of the identity model.

The identity model was thus supported by the outcomes (qualitative, quantitative, theoretical, empirical) obtained from the present and previous experiments (including Izawa, 1985a) as well as by Experiment 4, which was performed with 50% longer lists.

A possibility might still exist, however, that these two methods maintain unique properties that stem from their inherent characteristics. For instance, trends were observed pointing to the greater superiority of methods incorporating shorter S-T intervals. The study-test method, however, tended to benefit more than the anticipation method. Yet, such trends were just too small to merit further discussion at this juncture.

At the quantitative level also, the soundness of the basic assumptions underlying the identity model were verified by a total of seven sets of quantitative analyses (Fig. 8.11-8.14, 8.18, 8.24-8.25) with both massed and spaced practices in Experiments 1, 2, and 4, and with massed practice alone in Experiment 3. Only four sets of the invariant six parameters (e, e', f, f', g, and g'), one set per experiment (plus seven sets of Parameter k and k', one set per practice, massed or spaced) made it possible to accurately predict as many as 552 data points for a total of four experiments. Of these data points, only a fraction, 84 points (15%) provided input for parameter estimations, whereas the remaining 468 data points (85%) were not involved.

Thus, the identity model did, indeed, withstand very stringent quantitative examination in all of our experiments that employed different learning materials (learning difficulty levels) for different subjects and with different designs. Unquestionably, the model was solidly supported by the outcomes of these studies.

The time seems ripe, now, to move on to examine the generality of the identity model in different types of experimental situations with different sensory modalities. We next apply the identity model to auditory and tactual information processing in Parts 2 and 3, respectively.

PART 1 REFERENCES

Barch, A. M., & Levine, J. R. (1967). Presentation method in auditory identification learning. *Journal of Verbal Learning and Verbal Behavior, 6,* 282–288.

Battig, W. F., & Brackett, H. R. (1961). Comparison of anticipation and recall methods in paired-associate learning. *Psychological Reports, 9,* 59–65.

Battig, W. F., & Spera, A. J. (1962). Rated association values of numbers from 0-100. *Journal of Verbal Learning and Verbal Behavior, 1,* 200–202.

Izawa, C. (1972). Retention interval hypothesis and evidence for its basic assumptions. *Journal of Experimental Psychology, 96,* 17–24.

Izawa, C. (1974). Retention interval hypothesis and list lengths: Comparison of anticipation and reinforcement (study)-test procedures. *Canadian Journal of Psychology, 28,* 214–224.

Izawa, C. (1977). Theoretical and empirical performance differences between anticipation and study-test methods: Retention interval hypothesis vs. spaced practice effects. *Japanese Psychological Research, 19,* 31–38.

Izawa, C. (1978). Effects of two retention interval components on performance differences between study-test and anticipation methods in paired-associate learning. *Scandinavian Journal of Psychology, 19,* 151–158.

Izawa, C. (1979a). A test of the retention interval hypothesis with a constant item presentation order. *Japanese Psychological Research, 21,* 200–206.

Izawa, C. (1979b). Comparisons of learning procedures: Effects of constant and random presentations. *Acta Psychologica, 42,* 133–143.

Izawa, C. (1979c). Toward a comprehensive theory of variable performance differences and differential spaced practice effects between anticipation and study-test methods. *Journal of General Psychology, 100,* 63–83.

Izawa, C. (1980). Empirical examinations of the retention interval hypothesis: Comparisons of learning methods when learning is difficult. *Journal of General Psychology, 103,* 117–129.

Izawa, C. (1981a). Quantitative tests of the retention interval model. *Journal of General Psychology, 105,* 273–292.

Izawa, C. (1981b). The retention interval hypothesis and backward associations *Australian Journal of Psychology, 33,* 229–241.

Izawa, C. (1981c). The retention interval model: Qualitative and quantitative examinations. *Japanese Psychological Research, 23,* 101–112.

Izawa, C. (1981d). Toward a quantitative theory for performance differences between anticipation and study-test procedures: The retention interval model. *Scandinavian Journal of Psychology, 22,* 79–91.

Izawa, C. (1982a). Fundamental similarities and differences between study-test and anticipation item presentation procedures in the learning of linguistic items: Quantitative tests of the retention interval model via varied parameter estimation modes. *Psychologia, 25,* 1–17.

Izawa, C. (1982b). The retention interval model examined by delayed test performances. *Journal of General Psychology, 106,* 219–231.

Izawa, C. (1983). The generality of the retention interval model. *Journal of General Psychology, 108,* 113–134.

Izawa, C. (1985a). A test of the differences between anticipation and study-test methods of paired-associate learning. *Journal of Experimental Psychology: Learning, Memory, and Cognition, 11,* 165–184.

Izawa, C. (1985b). The identity model and factors controlling the superiority of study-test method over the anticipation method. *Journal of General Psychology, 112,* 65–78.

Izawa, C., Bell, D., & Hayden, R. G. (1984). Auditory information processing and its method of presentation. *Japanese Psychological Research, 26,* 12–23.

Izawa, C., & Hayden, R. G. (1978). Effects of method of presentation with spaced practice. *Psychologia, 21,* 16–26.

Izawa, C., Hayden, R. G., & Isham, K. L. (1980). Sensory modality and method of item information presentation in memory. *Acta Psychologica, 44*, 131–145.

Izawa, C., & Morrison, J. E. (1979). Verbal discrimination learning: Effects of method of presentation, practice distribution, and learning material. *Journal of General Psychology, 101*, 75–101.

Kanak, N. J., & Neuner, S. D. (1970). Associative symmetry and item availability as a function of five methods of paired-associate acquisition. *Journal of Experimental Psychology, 86*, 288–295.

Noble, C. E. (1961). Measurements of association value (a), rated associations (a '), and scaled meaningfulness (m ') for the 2100 CVC combinations of the English alphabet. *Psychological Reports, 8*, 487–521.

8

Part 2. Comparisons of Visual and Auditory Information Processing Under Two Item Information Presentation Methods

Chizuko Izawa
Robert G. Hayden
Tulane University

For 103 years now since Ebbinghaus (1885), a great majority of human learning and memory phenomena have been investigated in the sensory context of vision. It was considered the primary input channel for stimulus-item information. The identity model was no exception; its theoretical formulation and evolution are based on the visual processing of data. However, the identity model is not sensory modality specific. Irrespective of sensory modality, temporal relationships between study (S) and test (T) events remain the same under the anticipation and study-test methods in Equations 1 and 2 given earlier in this chapter, as do the retention (S-T) interval distributions (Fig. 8.1). Consequently, there seems no reason why the identity model, if valid, should not withstand empirical scrutiny when auditory stimuli are involved.

There were keen interests among volunteers who assisted with the present research in relative efficacy of visually processing (reading the text) versus auditory processing (listening to the same text), an issue highly relevant for determining how to optimize encoding (acquisition) and retention.

Comparisons between vision and hearing have been made virtually throughout the entire history of experimental psychology. Yet, the results are very mixed. A few examples from any period of the history will convey this state of affairs; relatively recent ones of the last 3 decades or so, will suffice. The question of relative efficacy of the two sensory modalities, may be pursued empirically, independent of one's theoretical position that human memory is organized by mode of presentation. This suggests separate representations in memory for auditory and visual information processing (cf. Margrain, 1967; Murdock, 1974; Wallach & Averbach, 1955; Warrington & Shallice, 1972). Murdock (1968), for example, maintained that auditory storage is temporally mediated, whereas visual storage is spacially mediated. Even if the types of information processing are not separate, however, it still seems reasonable to ask which is more efficient in the learning situation under consideration here. Morton (1970), Sperling and Speelman (1970), and Treisman, Sykes, and Gelade (1977) all have something to offer in this context.

Highly varied outcomes in the field of our interest may be illustrated by the recency effect. It produces better performance under auditory rather than visual presentation given immediate recall, that is, the modality effect (e.g., Craik, 1969; Crowder & Morton, 1969; Murdock, 1967, 1968; Watkins & Watkins, 1977). No such modality effects were observed with longer retention intervals (e.g., Tulving & Madigan, 1970). Here, long retention intervals (delayed tests), were associated with visual information processing being superior to auditory processing (e.g., Kroll, Parks, Parkinson, Bieber, & Johnson, 1970; Parkinson, 1972), whereas Engle and Mobley (1976) found no differences except for immediate tests. With the Peterson-Brown technique, visual presentation conditions generally outperform auditory ones (e.g., Johansson, Lindberg, & Svensson, 1974; Scarborough, 1972). In investigating effects of different recall intervals, Kool and Tripathi (1978) also found the visual mode superior. Kraft and Jenkins (1981) demonstrated the lag effect with passages auditorily presented. For further relevant discussions of modality effects and visual versus auditory sensory modalities, we refer you to Whitten and Bjork (1977), DeBoth and Dominowski (1979), Glenberg and Swanson (1986), and Horton and Mills (1984), among others.

The complexity of issues in this area is further illustrated by Metcalfe, Glavanov, and Murdock (1981), who found significant interaction between the input modality and type of recall: Visual presentation resulted in superior recall over the auditory one in the spatial condition, but the opposite was true in the temporal conditions (contradicting Murdock's earlier study).

Auditory versus visual comparisons in other (nonimmediate recall) learning situations with linguistic materials are even more variable, as seen in Berry, Detterman, and Mulhern (1973), Janssen (1976), Mueller (1977), Schulz and Kasschau (1966), and Williams and Derks (1963). In related but more remote areas such as educational, developmental, or clinical psychology, similar levels of diversity seem to prevail in comparative studies of the two sensory departments.

Relative strengths of one sensory department over the other may be evaluated, as recently became popular, by exposing the subject to both simultaneously (e.g., Walk & Pick, 1981). In this line of research also, inconsistency is the rule, rather than the exception: As the complete, or extremely strong dominance of vision over auditory perception was reported (e.g., Howard & Templeton, 1966), some others countered with findings that it is audition that strongly dominated vision in temporal tasks (e.g., Easton & Basala, 1982; Myers, Cotton, & Hilp, 1981; Walker & Scott, 1981).

If the modality information is processed automatically as suggested by Lehman (1982), then encoding such automatically processed information should not require extensive effort on the part of the subject (cf. Hasher & Zacks, 1979). The fact that positive evidence is obtainable in incidental learning situations (e.g., Lehman, 1982) seems to support such a contention. If indeed, modality information is encoded and retained effortlessly, the effect of the modality itself may be so trivial that it may generate no lasting effect of any magnitude, despite Murdock's modality specific memory position, which is supported by Hasher and Zacks (1979), but contradicted by Bray and Batchelder (1972) and Lehman and Hanzel (1981, data on children).

There is another item of interest. Rehearsals that emerged as a prominent feature in short-term memory models may enter as a relevant issue here. This follows from the fact that aloud versus silent rehearsals may be analogous to auditory versus visual presentation (cf. Atkinson & Shiffrin, 1968). Murdock (1966) found visual presentation with vocalization to be inferior to auditory presentation in the penultimate item and superior on the first few items. Murdock (1967) also found that if visually presented material was rehearsed silently performance was worse compared to auditory presentation over the whole list. However, according to Norman (1966), there were no differences between modalities in the rates of information decay. In an attempt to reconcile apparent inconsistent outcomes in the study (acquisition), retention, and test phases of learning, as well as rehearsals, Izawa (1976) distinguished the short-term effects of vocalization from its longer-term effects. In light of recent investigations (e.g., Turner, LaPointe, Cantor, Reeves, Griffeth, & Engle, 1987), that kind of approach appears particularly worthwhile.

Let us limit our discussion in this part of the chapter primarily to cognitive processes involving sensory modalities in the basic learning situations with paired-associates (cued recall) under the list design. The target issue, the relative efficiency of the anticipation method versus the study-test method, was seldom considered in the context of cross sensory modal input channels. We reviewed 120 experiments covering the past 5 decades that compared the two item presentation methods. Only one study considered cross sensory modalities (Izawa, Hayden, & Isham, 1980).

Indeed, the paucity of studies comparing the two item presentation methods under the auditory modality is staggering: Only about 4% of the extant anticipation versus study-test method comparisons focused on audition. To make the matter worse, the inconsistency of data is far greater for studies with the auditory modality than those employing vision. But even this lesser contradiction remained unresolved, despite efforts by distinguished colleagues (e.g., Cofer, Diamond, Olsen, Stein, & Walker, 1967).

Quite strikingly, Barch and Levine (1967) obtained substantially better performance under the anticipation method than under the study-test method, when paired-associates were presented aurally, as with Morse code signals (as stimulus or a-terms in Equations 1 and 2), and two-digits (as response or b-terms). The findings are not only highly unusual (only 1 out of more than 120 experiments examined were conducted during the past half century), but also directly challenge the very core of the identity model. Thus, Barch and Levine (1967) seemed to merit our full scrutiny.

Intriguingly enough, when Barch and Levine substituted words for Morse code signals, they obtained completely opposite results: The study-test method was now reliably superior. The latter results were consistent with those by Battig and Wu (1965) in paired-associated learning and Kanak, Cole, and Eckert (1972) in verbal discrimination learning, each utilized the auditory item presentation mode.

However, in other paired-associated learning situations such as those by Izawa, Hayden, and Isham (1980) or those by Izawa, Bell, and Hayden (1984), no tangible differences were observed between the two methods. Thus, the varied results from the handful of extant auditory studies, if selected properly, could support virtually any theoretical approach in comparing anticipation with study-test methods. The much greater variability as well as the absence of definitive studies for the auditory modality seems to beg for further in-depth investigation. Our study in Part 2 was planned, in part, to rectify this chaotic state of affairs, characterizing auditory data.

In order to account for divergent results within their study, Barch and Levine (1967) advanced a position that the anticipation method should excel over the study-test method when the stimuli are difficult to encode, and that such a prediction should not be limited to auditory Morse Code signals (p. 267). However, when stimuli are easy to encode, they claimed that the study-test method should be distinctly advantaged. Henceforth, we refer to their model as the encoding model.

Note that the encoding model embodies learning difficulty as the critical controlling factor determining the relative efficacy of the two item presentation methods under investigation in this chapter. Coincidentally, the level of learning difficulty happened to be very salient to the identity model as well (e.g., Izawa, 1980, 1983, 1985). Now that the same factor, learning difficulty, enters distinctly to control relative performance standing of the two methods, we seem to have arrived on common ground for assessing the relative merits of these two alternative models.

In contrast to the encoding model, expectations of the identity model are as follows: When learning is extremely difficult, only a very few items are learned. Consequently, the total number of critical items in the short-term memory (STM) system is also likely to be small. With an insufficient amount of critical items in STM, regardless of where they fall in the retention interval distribution curves (Fig. 8.1), their differential lengths of retention (S-T) intervals are unlikely to generate large enough effects to lead to substantial performance differences between the methods. If correct, the resultant outcome will show the study-test method to have little, if any, advantage over the anticipation method.

In the same vein, when items are extremely easy and readily overlearned and go to the long-term memory (LTM) system effortlessly, few items remain in STM as critical items. This situation is also likely to lead to an insufficient differentiation in the retention (S-T) interval distributions of the critical items, and therefore, relatively small performance differences between the two item presentation methods.

When learning is moderately difficult, however, a substantial number of items are learned and become critical in STM. In this situation, two outcomes are possible. One possibility is: If a sufficient number of critical items fall into the nonoverlap areas in the distribution (Fig. 8.1), these retention (S-T) intervals under the study-test method are likely to be shorter than those under the anticipation method. Therefore, a distinctly superior performance is more likely under the former method. Another possibility is, however, if sufficient critical items concentrate in the overlap area instead, retention (S-T) interval lengths of these critical items are likely to be the same for both study-test and anticipation methods. Then, resultant performance differences between the two methods are expected to be minimal.

Consequently, the two alternative theoretical positions, represented by the encoding and identity models, make for highly contrasting predictions concerning the relative efficiency of the two item presentation methods, as a function of the learning or encoding difficulty level. For example, when learning is extremely difficult, the encoding model predicts superior results for the anticipation method, whereas the identity model anticipates little performance differences between the two methods under investigation. Also, when learning is very easy, the former model expects the study-test method to be advantageous, whereas the latter assumes similar performance level for both methods. And when learning is intermediate, the encoding model does not seem to have any explicit predictions. It may not be unreasonable to infer, however, that small performance differences are likely between the methods. This follows from the fact that performance with intermediately difficult cases falls midway between the two extremes of difficulty, from which the encoding model predicted diametrically opposite outcomes. The identity model, on the other hand, is explicit about predictions for situations of middling difficulty: with some reservations for the possible absence of performance differences (this possibility being the same for both models), these situations are likely to lead to a considerable advantage for the study-test method over the anticipation method.

Consequently, the learning or encoding difficulty dimension provides an ideal variable for testing empirically, the relative merit of the two rival theories. Experiment 5 was designed to conduct such a test, by manipulating the encoding difficulty levels by word frequency (Thorndike & Lorge, 1944; cf. Underwood, 1982).

EXPERIMENT 5

A $2 \times 2 \times 3$ factorial was utilized involving two sensory departments: visual versus auditory, two information processing methods: anticipation versus study-test method, and three levels of learning difficulty: easy, medium, and difficult. Three learning lists were each composed of 20 paired associates (list length, $n = 20$), derived from 40 two to three syllable words. The words in the easy list occurred 100 times or more per million in Thorndike and Lorge (1944), in the intermediate list they occurred five times per 4 million, and those in the difficult list, demonstrated four occurrences per 18 million.

Auditory presentations involved a male voice, a Realistic Tape Recorder Model CTR-42, and visual presentations were via a Stowe Memory Drum B-549. With a 2 sec presentation rate per item for both study (S, paired-presentation of both terms) and test (T, presentation of cue or the first term alone) events. During S event, the subject voiced presented pairs. During each T event, subjects responded orally, after voicing the stimulus term of the pair. As is commonly done, item presentation order was randomized from one cycle to the next under both methods. In order to equate the test trial experiences that were shown to be significant (Izawa, 1971a, 1971b) for both methods, the study-test conditions commenced with a test cycle.

There were 132 Introductory Psychology students at Tulane who volunteered for the experiment. The experiments were run individually, 11 subjects in each of the 12 conditions. Prior to the main task, there was a practice task consisting of both anticipation and study-test methods under both visual and auditory modalities for all subjects so as not to bias any condition differentially. Judging from practice task data, there were no group differences in the subject variable in Experiment 5.

Comparisons of Visual and
Auditory Information Processing

Figure 8.26 summarizes performances under the 12 conditions in terms of incorrect responses (overt errors plus omissions). Large differences resulted as a function of learning difficulties: $F(2, 120) = 80.48$, $p < 0.0001$. The performance levels lined up neatly in accordance with those of learning difficulty for both auditory (upper panels) and visual (lower ones) presentations. Difficulty levels based on the word frequency count did, in fact, produce the expected effect, in this empirical examination of the two alternative models.

Of major interest in Experiment 5 was the relative performance levels between the auditory and visual presentations. As can be easily inferred from Fig. 8.26, there were highly significant differences between the two sensory modalities: $F(1, 120) = 21.80$, $p < 0.0001$ in favor of visual information processing. The overall superiority of the visual presentation held for both study-test and anticipation methods, with no significant interactions in the between-subject factors of the $2 \times 2 \times 3$ analyses of variance (ANOVA). However, the trial (within subject) factor interacted highly significantly with all the other between-subject factors (mode, difficulty level, and method): in all double,

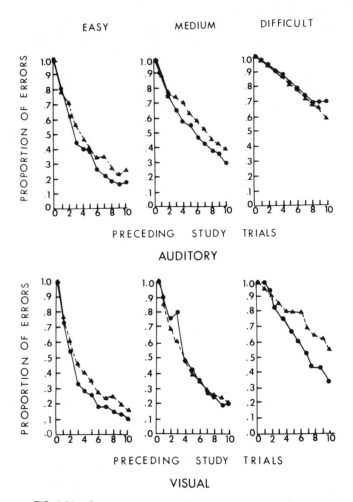

FIG. 8.26.   Group data under both anticipation (triangular dots connected with broken lines) and study-test (circle dots connected with solid lines) methods for three levels of learning difficulty under the auditory (upper panels) and the visual (lower panels) modes in Experiment 5.

triple, and quadruple interactions $ps < 0.001$, except for the triple interactions of the trial $\times$ level $\times$ method that resulted in $p = 0.19$.

Throughout all data analyses in Experiment 5, as well as in all other experiments in this part of the chapter, both main factors of the trial and the sensory modality were *always* highly significant. Independent of scope of analyses, global or minute, performances under the visual item presentation excelled the auditory one consistently. (We will not repeat this information in subsequent analyses.)

The superior performances under the visual modality over the auditory modality reinforces the work of Izawa, Hayden, and Isham (1980), which compared these modalities under both methods of information presentation using nonsense syllables. This work is in line with Schulz and Hopkins (1968) and Schulz and Kasschau (1966) (both with low m') as well as Williams and Derks (1963) (with intermediate m'); each of these studies employed the list design as in the present study.

The mean S-T intervals for the study-test and anticipation methods were 38 and 76 sec respectively, derived from $(n-1)d$ and $2(n-1)d$, where n and d are the list length and presentation rate in seconds, respectively (for details, see Izawa, 1972). The delayed tests in short-term memory studies are comparable to the S-T intervals in this order. In fact, studies by Johansson et al. (1974), Kroll and Kellicutt (1972), Parkinson (1972), Scarborough (1972), and Salzberg, Parks, Kroll, and Parkinson (1971) exemplify this. On the other hand, small differences were found between the two sensory modalities by Engle and Mobley (1976, no immediate tests), McGeoch (1942) and Mueller (1977).

In short-term memory studies, it often seems to be assumed that vocalizing the visually presented items has the same effects as an auditory presentation, because auditory stimulation is involved (e.g., Penney, 1975). If the assumption was correct, the following two possibilities existed: (a) On the one hand, both visual and auditory presentation modes should have generated approximately the same results, because the visual mode accompanied by vocalization is assumed to be equivalent to the auditory mode. This, however, was not supported, and (b) on the other hand, it is more plausible to expect that the auditory mode should have advantages over the visual one, because the former may be regarded as having two auditory presentations per event, once by the experimenter, followed by another (repeated) by the subject, whereas vocalizing visually given items is assumed to be equivalent to only one auditory presentation. This second expectation also remained unsupported. Indeed, our data demonstrated that the reverse was true.

It should be noted that, in a strict sense, it may be impossible to achieve equivalence of item presentations for visual and auditory modalities. That is, both terms of a pair appear simultaneously under visual presentation, but in the auditory mode they appear sequentially, the stimulus (cue, a-) term, followed by the response (target, b-) term. Furthermore, although the presentation rate is the same for both modalities, under visual conditions, both terms of the pair on each S event and the first term alone on each T event are visible for the full 2 sec. By contrast, auditory presentations vanish almost immediately after the presentation. Should a momentary inattentiveness or distraction cause the subject to miss, or misunderstand the first term of the pair, any effective utilization of S or T events is unlikely during the remaining time of the 2 sec presentation; the first term has already disappeared by the time the second (response) term is presented in an S event.

In addition, both simultaneity of presentation and the persistence of both terms of the pair is possible only under the visual conditions: This alone may facilitate performance compared to the auditory conditions, because the visual mode is advantaged in supplying missing information, correcting misunderstood information (misinformation), and facilitating consolidation, rehearsal, or other processes that may be required by certain theoretical approaches.

From another perspective, disparate encoding processes may be involved with each sensory department during the acquisition phase, or the S events. Quite possibly, only a low or shallow level of encoding prevails when repeating the auditorily presented words, but a higher, or more elaborate level of encoding may be involved or necessary for vocalizing visually presented information. This follows from the fact that at minimum, it is crucial for the subject to select the correct phoneme. Viewed differently, greater discriminability may be inherent to visual information processing, compared to auditory processing. Exaggerated differences of this sort may be found in dyslexia; if correct, it would support this view. Whatever the theoretical approaches taken in accounting for modality differences under the list design, Experiment 5 provides support for the advantage of the visual over auditory presentations for both study-test and anticipation item information processing methods.

Comparisons of Study-Test and Anticipation Item Presentation Method

We now direct our primary attention to the central issue of this chapter. Performance differences between anticipation and study-test methods in a $2 \times 2 \times 3$ ANOVA did not quite reach significance, rather it approximated significance: $F(1, 120) = 3.87$, $p = 0.0515$. However, the method factor interacted significantly with the trial: $F(10, 600) = 6.12$, $p < 0.0001$ and trial and level factors: $F(20, 600) = 2.43$, $p = 0.0005$, respectively, indicating that performance between the two item presentation methods differs depending on the stage of learning, and the degree of learning difficulty.

An overall analysis of procedural differences, however, may be of little value, unless more fine-grained analyses are performed for evaluating both the encoding and the identity models, the two rival theories under examination. Both difficulty level and modality were quite significant, ps < 0.0001. Because substantial differences prevailed between sensory modalities, we conducted separate analyses for each modality. Under the visual item presentation mode, the difficulty level was still highly significant: $F(2, 60) = 32.46$, $p < 0.0001$. It is very interesting that under the visual mode, the two methods became clearly significant: $F(1, 60) = 5.62$, $p < 0.03$, and interacted reliably with both the trial and trial-by-level: $F(10, 600) = 6.12$, $p < 0.0001$, and $F(20, 600) = 2.43$,

$p < 0.0005$, respectively. Thus, performance differences varied depending on the learning stage, considered singly or jointly with the learning difficulty.

It is of interest here that under the auditory presentation, there were no performance differences at all between anticipation and study-test methods. Nonsignificance prevailed even when each list was analyzed separately. The only factors that produced significance were the level of difficulty, trials, and the trial by level interactions. No significance was obtained for auditory presentations where encoding is quite difficult. The encoding model predicts that the anticipation method should be superior, whereas the identity model expects little differences between the two methods. Thus, current data support the identity model. Nonsignificance failed to support either the Skinnerian feedback model or differential acquisition (Kanak & Neuner, 1970) or task alternation (Battig & Brackett, 1961) models, which predict the superiority for the anticipation method and the study-test methods, respectively (see the introductory section of this chapter for details).

According to the identity model, significance requires that sufficient encoding take place. Under the visual presentation where more learning took place, such a situation was apparently approached. Although the advantage for the study-test method when encoding is *relatively* greater, it can be predicted from a host of models including the encoding, task alternation, differential acquisition models, as well as the identity model. The identity model seems to be the only one that can handle both more difficult auditory data and relatively less difficult visual data.

The encoding model (Barch & Levine, 1967) expects the anticipation method to be significantly superior when learning is very difficult, but predicts a large advantage for the study-test method when learning is very easy. Although there are no explicit expectations for the medium list, a compromise between the two opposite effects, that is, little performance differences between the two methods may be inferred to take place. That is, strong interactions between the difficulty level and performance differences between the methods are suggested.

Indeed, we see in Fig. 8.26 that in accord with the encoding model no reliable differences occurred between the two item presentation methods for the medium list either for audition (upper panel) or vision (lower panel) in the middle column. However, *both* of this model's expectations, that is, (a) sizable superiority of the anticipation method with the difficult list (right panels) and (b) that of the study-test method with the easy list (left panels), failed to materialize. Even large trends in the opposite direction are observed with the difficult list under the visual mode. The large interactions between the method the list predicted from the encoding model were also absent: $F(1, 120) = 0.24$, $p > 0.50$. It is unsettling that the cases (medium in difficulty) bypassed in the encoding model without any explicit statements were the only ones (i.e., our inferences) supported by data, whereas the model's explicit prediction did not receive any empirical backup.

In contrast, the identity model predicts negligible differences between anticipation and study-test methods when learning difficulty levels are extreme, due to insufficient numbers of critical items in STM (not enough have entered STM when too hard, whereas the most critical items have left STM when too easy). See both left and right panels of Fig. 8.26, the superiority of the study-test method is quite unimpressive, and overall insignificant.

When learning is of intermediate difficulty, the identity model assumes a sufficient number of critical items are generated in STM. However, depending on how they distribute among their retention interval lengths, the model anticipates two possible outcomes: (a) a large advantage for the study-test method when a sufficient number of the critical items fall in the nonoverlap areas (Fig. 8.1), but (b) little between-method differences when enough of them concentrate in the overlap area, where items with both methods have S-T intervals of the same length. The latter, that is (b), appears to have occurred in Experiment 5. As shown in the middle panels of Fig. 8.26, there was no significance between the two methods.

The current data seem in accord with the identity model, but diverge considerably from the encoding model. It is just possible, however, that so far the data analyses may not have done justice to the latter model, if in our analysis some elements crucial to that model were overlooked. In order to minimize the likelihood of such an oversight and to explore the possibility of new support for the encoding model, elaborate analyses from additional perspectives were initiated.

First, we estimate conditioning (encoding) probability or learning rate per study (S) trial, derived from proportions correct for the first time given incorrect on all previous trials; see Table 8.1. In general, there was a trend for the conditioning probability to increase from the first S to subsequent ones, and after reaching certain plateaus, it declined, but toward the end of the experiment when the number of relevant cases became too small, the probabilities became quite variable. The weighted mean, the best estimate of the learning rate for each condition, lined up neatly with the difficulty dimension. Within list, although the statistics are mixed, the learning rate was usually greater for the study-test method than for the anticipation method; on the average the study-test method had the edge.

Other statistics entered in Table 8.1 are: the mean test (T) trials to the first correct response, those to the last incorrect responses, and the number of items never learned at the end of the experiment; these seem to convey wholly consistent messages: (a) performance was controlled significantly by the difficulty dimension (the larger in these values, the harder the learning); (b) in general, more frequently than not the study-test method showed some advantage, however, interprocedural differences were quite small under the auditory information processing; and (c) the statistics uniformly favored the visual over the auditory modality. Overall, statistics in Table 8.1 were consistent internally and with the ANOVA results reported earlier.

TABLE 8.1

Proportion Correct for the First Time Given Incorrect on All Previous Trials (Conditioning Probability), Mean Test Trials to the First Correct Response and Last Incorrect Response, and Number of Items Never Learned in Each Condition under Auditory and Visual Modalities in Experiment 5

Modality	Difficulty level	Method	Proportion correct for the first time given incorrect on all previous trials											Mean T trials to the first correct (SD)	Mean T trials to the last error (SD)	No. of items never learned
			Preceding study trials										Weighted Mean			
			1	2	3	4	5	6	7	8	9	10				
Auditory	Easy	Anticipation	.200	.165	.204	.231	.200	.236	.164	.174	.289	.148	.199	4.848 (2.527)	6.177 (3.842)	23
		N	220	176	147	117	90	72	55	46	38	27				
		Study-Test	.191	.253	.293	.255	.143	.233	.239	.257	.192	.143	.229	4.480 (2.323)	5.627 (3.723)	18
		N	220	178	133	94	70	60	46	35	26	21				
	Medium	Anticipation	.100	.136	.129	.081	.131	.118	.105	.138	.111	.181	.120	5.696 (2.877)	7.727 (3.508)	59
		N	220	198	171	149	137	119	105	94	81	72				
		Study-Test	.077	.148	.156	.185	.101	.131	.086	.200	.132	.153	.134	5.547 (2.676)	7.550 (3.472)	50
		N	220	203	173	146	119	107	93	85	68	59				
	Difficult	Anticipation	.023	.042	.049	.056	.059	.052	.091	.087	.037	.091	.056	6.800 (2.686)	9.459 (2.538)	120
		N	220	215	206	196	185	174	165	150	137	132				
		Study-Test	.005	.018	.060	.040	.041	.054	.046	.077	.039	.027	.040	6.787 (2.384)	10.091 (1.933)	145
		N	220	219	215	202	194	186	176	168	155	149				
Visual	Easy	Anticipation	.236	.250	.270	.207	.233	.286	.275	.241	.227	.118	.243	4.381 (2.301)	5.514 (3.675)	15
		N	220	168	126	92	73	56	40	29	22	17				
		Study-Test	.273	.313	.391	.359	.256	.344	.238	.125	.143	.167	.303	3.833 (1.896)	4.777 (3.435)	10
		N	220	180	110	67	43	32	21	16	14	12				
	Medium	Anticipation	.150	.230	.183	.243	.259	.217	.319	.219	.240	.158	.211	4.870 (2.367)	6.240 (3.604)	16
		N	220	170	131	107	81	60	47	32	25	19				
		Study-Test	.100	.162	.217	.262	.188	.269	.246	.256	.250	.208	.193	5.249 (2.381)	6.355 (3.439)	19
		N	220	198	166	130	96	78	57	43	32	24				
	Difficult	Anticipation	.036	.052	.090	.077	.053	.038	.117	.066	.094	.113	.066	6.568 (2.851)	9.173 (2.796)	102
		N	220	212	201	183	169	160	154	136	127	115				
		Study-Test	.005	.050	.135	.189	.171	.165	.139	.264	.094	.241	.125	6.477 (2.330)	7.718 (2.972)	44
		N	220	219	208	180	146	121	101	87	64	58				

N = the number of cases.

257

TABLE 8.2
Overt Errors, Total Errors and Proportions of Overt Errors in Each
Condition in Auditory and Visual Modalities in Experiment 5

Modality	Difficulty Level	Method	Overt Errors			All Errors			Overt Error Proportion
			Mean	SD	Total	Mean	SD	Total	
Auditory	Easy	Anticipation	1.000	1.602	220	5.418	3.459	1192	.185
		Study-Test	.577	1.118	127	4.795	3.243	1055	.120
	Medium	Anticipation	1.064	1.735	234	7.045	3.512	1550	.151
		Study-Test	.995	1.598	219	6.727	3.415	1480	.148
	Difficult	Anticipation	.641	1.383	141	9.050	2.796	1991	.071
		Study-Test	.664	1.184	146	9.636	2.306	2120	.069
Visual	Easy	Anticipation	.818	1.393	180	4.686	3.226	1031	.175
		Study-Test	.950	1.441	209	3.868	2.807	851	.246
	Medium	Anticipation	.759	1.228	167	5.305	3.166	1061	.157
		Study-Test	.582	1.354	128	5.436	2.996	1196	.107
	Difficult	Anticipation	.668	1.140	147	8.664	2.989	1906	.077
		Study-Test	.482	1.013	106	7.132	2.898	1569	.068

In search of yet another hidden factor, we note that the data analyses conducted so far were based on the total incorrect responses, the combination of (a) overt errors (wrong responses) and (b) omissions (failure to respond). To uncover effects conceivably overlooked in the earlier analyses, overt errors were separated and the proportion of overt errors per condition was obtained and entered in Table 8.2 (last column). The overt error proportions turned out to be fairly small, indicating that a great majority of incorrect responses consisted of failures to respond (omissions).

Small, undecisive trends were detected: The subject seemed to have ventured more unsuccessful guesses and committed more overt errors, when the list was easy. Such overt guesses appeared more frequently with the anticipation method than with the study-test method under auditory presentation, but the opposite seemed to hold when the visual modality was involved.

In order to examine the larger performance advantage of the study-test method over the anticipation method under the visual mode, we further scrutinized the two methods under *each* list. No tangible differences were obtained for either easy or medium lists. However, the two methods differed reliably with the hard list; $F(1, 20) = 5.26$, $p < 0.04$. The trial also interacted significantly with the method: $F(10, 200) = 8.13$, $p > 0.0001$.

Significant differences in favor of the study-test method over the anticipation method may be difficult to reconcile with the encoding model, as that model expects opposite results, i.e., a large advantage for the anticipation method. It would also create a problem for the identity model, if we were to take the difficult list to be hard no matter how it is given to the subjects, whereas the latter model expects no difference when learning is difficult. The last qualifier is important. As the lower right panel of Fig. 8.26 shows, the learning of the list labeled difficult was *not really* difficult when presented visually. This follows from the fact that the subjects did learn nearly half, 40%–60% of the list at the end of the experiment, which may belong to an intermediately difficult learning situation. If so, a large advantage for the study-test method is in agreement with the identity model. The difficulty level under discussion should be defined by the subject, not the experimenter, because the number of critical items in STM is controlled by the subject's performance and not a priori by the experimenter.

If the difficult list presented under the visual presentation modality belongs de facto to learning situation of intermediate difficulty, then in theory the encoding model should be given equal opportunity to reinterpret outcomes. Few performance differences should be expected from the encoding model for an intermediately difficult list. Again, the outcome was contrary to encoding model predictions.

As suggested by the foregoing, there is considerable ambiguity concerning what we mean by "learning difficulty." One operational definition was made by the experimenter: The greater the Thorndike and Lorge Frequency Count, the easier is learning, and vice versa.

An a priori criterion of learning difficulty may not necessarily apply across modalities. The auditory presentation was significantly more difficult to acquire than the visual one, given an identical list. Consider the data in Fig. 8.26 at a global level. The easy list condition under the auditory presentation mode (top left) is equivalent, at performance level, to the medium list condition under the visual mode. Similarly, the medium list under auditory modality was equivalent to the difficult list under the visual modality. Hence, it was no surprise that the relatively large difference between the two methods occurred in the difficult condition under visual presentation because it was about the same as the medium learning difficulty list under the other mode.

Let us, therefore, view data from the learner's perspective of difficulty as inferred from performance. This is quite important, as the learning difficulty plays a key role in differentiating the current alternative models. Note that any given list, however designated by the experimenter, may be regarded as very easy by some subjects, and as very difficult by others. It is therefore, imperative that we examine individual differences closely by examining data in terms of subject determined levels of difficulty.

To this end, data from the two best performers (lowest in incorrect responses) and the two poorest performers (highest in incorrect responses) were selected from each condition and entered, respectively, in Fig. 8.27 and 8.28. As seen in Fig. 8.27, for the best performers, no list was really very difficult. Conversely, Fig. 8.28 indicates that none of the lists were very easy for the poorest learners.

As evident by comparing Fig. 8.27 and 8.28, by far the greatest differences occurred between the best and worst subjects: $F(1, 24) = 481.52$, $p < 0.00001$.

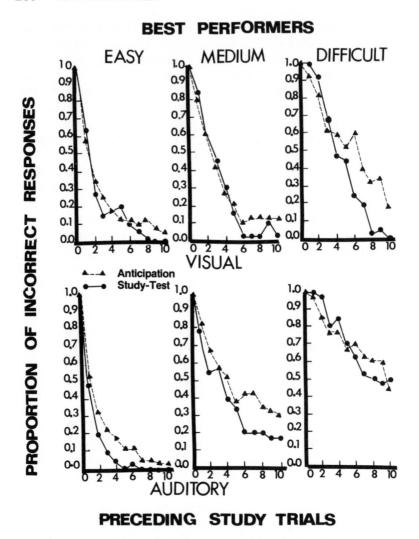

FIG 8.27. Performance of the two best learners from each condition under both visual (upper panels) and auditory (lower panels) information presentation modes, respectively, in Experiment 5.

Here also, modalities and difficulty levels (lists) differed significantly, with respective $F(1, 24) = 25.21$, and $F(2, 24) = 161.63$, each $p < 0.0001$. For these extreme performers, overall differences between anticipation and study-test methods were large, and highly reliable: $F(1, 24) = 22.62$, $p < 0.0001$. Suggestive trends hinted that method interacted with modality, but there were no signs that method interacted with list, see both Fig. 8.27 and 8.28. The triple interactions: group × mode × list were highly significant: $F(2, 24) = 11.20$, $p < 0.001$, and the group × method × mode approached significance: $F(1, 24) = 4.11$, $p \doteq 0.05$.

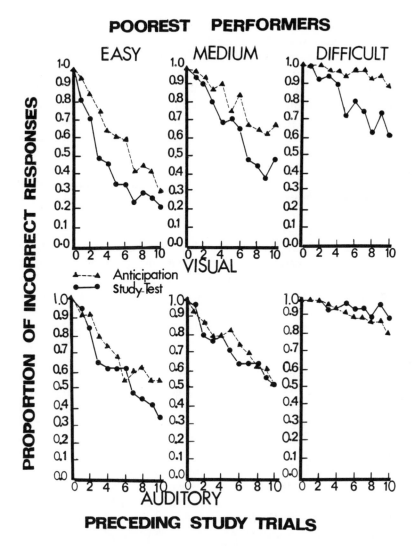

FIG. 8.28. Performance of the two poorest learners from each condition under both visual (upper panels) and auditory (lower panels) information presentation modes, respectively, in Experiment 5.

For the within-subject factor, the trial, interacted significantly with all primary between-subject factors. The presentation method, most relevant to this section, was no exception; it interacted with trials at a highly reliable level: $F(10, 240) = 6.13$, $p < 0.00001$. So it was true for group by trial interactions: $F(10, 240) = 48.92$, $p < 0.00001$. There were also pervasive trends of methods triply interacting with the mode by trial as well as with list by the trial, p being approximately 0.06.

Given the significant differences between the two groups of subjects, Fig. 8.27 versus Fig. 8.28, we conducted separate analyses. For the best performers, aside from usual confirmation of reliable modality and list difference effects, our main interest, performance differences between anticipation and study-test methods were significant: $F(1, 12) = 7.03$, $p < 0.05$. Very interestingly, the method factor did not interact reliably with the list or with the modality; it interacted significantly only with the trial, confirming that for the best performers, the task was easy regardless of the list or the modality! The only way the list had an effect in reference to the method was in triple interactions with the trial: $F(20, 120) = 1.66$, $p = 0.05$.

The six panels in Fig. 8.27 present data for the best performers. As defined by performance, we seem to have obtained roughly two types of results: (a) extremely easy learning (top left and center panels and bottom left panel) and (b) learning of intermediate difficulty (top right panel, bottom center and right panels). There were no significant differences between the two methods in three extremely easy situations. This is in agreement with the identity model, but in disagreement with the encoding model, which predicts a large advantage for the study-test method. In the situations of intermediate difficulty, the encoding model predicts small differences between the two methods, empirically supported by the difficult list under the auditory presentation (bottom right), but the model was not supported in the other two panels that show a substantial advantage for the study-test method (visual difficulty list and auditory medium list). The two types of outcomes in intermediate situations correspond to the two types of predictions by the identity model.

In a sense, the auditorily difficult list can be classified as a relatively difficult situation. If one grants that classification, nonsignificant differences between the two methods do not support the encoding model any longer, because it explicitly predicts a large advantage for the anticipation method. Lack of significance in a difficult learning situation is quite in line with the identity model. Overall, then, whichever way one may classify a given panel, the encoding model encounters difficulties in a great majority of cases in Fig. 8.27 with the best learners. However, the identity model seems to be supported at each level of learning difficulty.

What of the poorest learners? As seen in Fig. 8.28, no situation was really easy for them. Their ANOVA demonstrated that all major between- and within-subject factors generated significant effects of primary interest here. For the item presentation method: $F(1, 12) = 17.20$, $p < 0.002$, in favor of the study-test method. Method interacted with modality: $F(1, 12) = 8.59$, $p < 0.02$, and the trial: $F(10, 120) = 2.88$, $p = 0.003$, but did not interact reliably with level of difficulty, suggesting this group of subjects performed poorly regardless of the list. The only other significant result pertaining to method involved the four-way interactions (trial $\times$ mode $\times$ method $\times$ list): $F(20, 120) = 1.88$, $p < 0.02$.

Because the sensory modality factor was significant: $F(1, 12) = 7.98$,

$p < 0.02$, for the poorest learners, we conducted separate analyses on each modality to obtain finer-grained information. It is intriguing to see that the sources of significant performance differences between the two methods derived entirely from the visual modality: $F(1, 6) = 15.28$, $p < 0.01$, here considerable acquisition was achieved. Under the auditory mode learning was overall considerably more difficult and interprocedural differences were too small to be reliable. Similarly, the method interacted significantly with the trial but only for vision: $F(20, 60) = 4.29$, $p < 0.001$. As always the list generated large effects, but did not interact with the method for either sensory mode.

The aforementioned analyses verified that even the *experimenter designated* easy list was, in fact, not easy for the poorest learners: At the performance level, the easy list for the poorest performers was subjectly equivalent to or harder than the difficult list for the best performers. This state of affairs is clearly illustrated by comparing the right panels of Fig. 8.27 (best) and the left ones of Fig. 8.28 (poorest). For the worst learners the remaining lists were even harder. In fact, within Fig. 8.28, the easiest cases (left panels under both modes) belonged to intermediate situations, together with the center panels (medium list under both modes), in terms of their performances. Thus, for the poorest subjects, there were de facto only two types of difficulty levels: (a) intermediate (the above four panels), and (b) difficult learning situations (two right panels).

The encoding model expects little differences between the anticipation and the study-test method when learning is intermediate: This is supported by two cases under the auditory mode (left and center lower panels), but not by the other two cases under the visual mode (the same lists). Indeed, all four cases solidly sustained the alternative, the identity model that predicts either large or small advantage for the study-test method vis-à-vis the anticipation method depending on the distributions of critical items in STM, which are assumed to be sufficient in number in intermediate situations.

In extremely difficult situations, the right panels under both modes, one expects the anticipation method to be significantly superior via the encoding model. This, however, was not borne out in either of the two cases. The identity model, on the other hand, expects small differences between procedures. The performance differences were large and reliable for the difficult list under the visual mode; this was the only case of departure from the model, however, when the same list was presented under the auditory mode, an even harder learning situation, no differences between the two item presentation methods were observed; this fits precisely with the identity model.

Performance under the most difficult condition for the best performers was objectively equivalent to or for them even easier than the learning by the poorest performers under the least demanding conditions. This applied to both visual and auditory presentations. It would therefore be interesting for purposes of comparison to view Fig. 8.27 and 8.28 side by side. Displayed from left to right are degrees of learning difficulty, from easiest to most difficult. The upper panels display data from the visual modality whereas the lower ones deal with auditory presentations. The greater variety of learning situations, from extremely easy to extremely difficult, allows us to test the two alternative theoretical positions fairly. This is compellingly illustrated in Fig. 8.27 and 8.28.

Examine the six panels per row (learning situations, Fig. 8.27 and 8.28). For the visual mode (top row), the first two on the left (Fig. 8.27) can be regarded as easy, the next three (both figures) as medium, and the far right (Fig. 8.28) as difficult. For auditory presentations the far left (Fig. 8.27) should be seen as very easy, the next four panels (both figures) are intermediate, and the far right (Fig. 8.28) is seen as very difficult.

For each sensory modality, the encoding model predicts a pronounced superiority for the study-test method when learning is very easy, and a large advantage for the anticipation method in extremely difficult learning situations, whereas in intermediate situations the differences between methods will be small (i.e., each method interacts with the level of difficulty). Nonsignificance was indeed borne out in three of four situations of medium difficulty under the auditory mode, but neither the easy nor the difficult situations supported the encoding model (lower panels). It was far worse under the visual modality (upper panels). None of the encoding model predictions coincided with data.

By contrast, the identity model does not predict significant superiority for the study-test method at all levels of learning difficulty; however, it is expected that superiority can become significant in some situations of intermediate learning difficulty. See the 12 panels of Fig. 8.27 and 8.28. All of the predictions from the identity model were well sustained for both modalities except in the difficult situation under the visual mode: nonsignificance in extreme situations as well as the possibility of either large or small advantage for the study-test method in intermediate situations.

In summary, data from extreme performers support the encoding model in 3 out of 12 cases (25%), while upholding the identity model in 11 out of 12 cases (92%). Because the encoding model asserts that the anticipation method is superior when encoding is difficult, we attempted in every way to examine very difficult learning situations that were indeed created by the poorest learners in Fig. 8.28. But we failed to discover any sign of an advantage for the anticipation method anywhere. Similarly, the pronounced advantage the encoding model predicts for the study-test method, when encoding is very easy, is completely absent from the data shown in the panels for best learners on the extreme left of Fig. 8.27.

EXPERIMENTS 6 AND 7

In a sense, all words no matter how difficult or rare they may be, can be conceived of being easier to learn than nonwords. If so, there was a slight possibility that our materials in Experiment 5 do not make for a fair test of the encoding model. One class of nonwords scrutinized for learning difficulty was nonsense syllables as defined by several norms. That type of learning material was fortunately utilized by Izawa, Hayden, and Isham (1980) in a 2×2 factorial design employing two item presentation methods (study-test vs. anticipation) and two sensory modalities (auditory vs. visual). The findings paralleled ours: that is, significantly better learning was found under the visual rather than the auditory mode.

Performance differences between study-test and anticipation methods were reliably large and favored the former method under visual presentation, but only negligibly under auditory presentation, and displayed significant mode by method interactions. Their results, just as those of Experiment 5, were clearly in line with the identity model, but in disagreement with the encoding model. Although their learning situations were quite difficult with the error rate being greater than 60% under the auditory modality, the expected superiority for the anticipation method from the encoding model is nowhere to be found.

It is granted that the anticipation method's superiority was not limited to Morse code (in concurrence with Barch and Levine, 1967). However, should there be any fundamental differences on the one hand between verbal (linguistic) materials used in Experiment 5 or CVCs' (nonwords, but still linguistic materials) employed by Izawa et al. (1980) and on the other hand nonverbal materials (e.g., the Morse code signals utilized by Barch and Levine), it would be inappropriate to generalize our findings to their Morse code data. If all inputs are always coded and verbally rehearsed (cf. Conrad, 1964; Morton, 1970), experiments with nonverbal materials, which may be difficult to encode verbally, may involve the processes quite different from those of verbal materials. Thus, it would not be surprising to find it more difficult to remember nonverbal items such as faces in long retention intervals. Consequently, two experiments (6 and 7) were conducted on Morse code.

It is of added interest that Nazzaro and Nazzaro (1970) found that audible Morse code patterns were learned more easily than visual ones. The present two experiments seek to test the generalizability of their findings.

We conducted not one, but two experiments using procedures identical to Barch and Levine, including the identical learning list that consisted of 8 Morse code signals paired with two-digit numbers. However, unlike their group testing situations where the responses were written in by the subjects, the subjects' data in Experiments 6 and 7 were obtained subject by subject; responses were recorded by the experimenter. Auditory presentations of the Morse code signals was via tape recorder, it reproduced signals generated via telegraph keys during the actual transmission of the Morse code signals. The other experimental procedures were the same as Experiment 5. An additional 80 subjects, 40 subjects in each of the two experiments, came from the same subject pool; that is, volunteers from Introductory Psychology courses at Tulane.

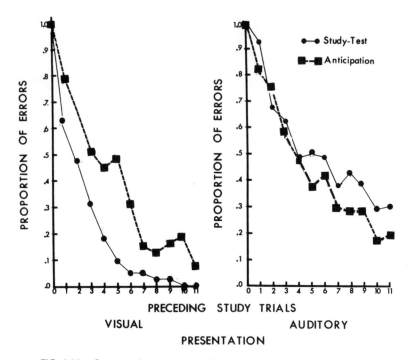

FIG. 8.29. Group performance of study-test and anticipation methods under visual (left) and auditory (right) information processing methods in Experiment 6.

Comparisons of Visual and Auditory Sensory Modalities

Figures 8.29 and 8.30 present group data for Experiments 6 and 7, respectively. First, we performed an overall ANOVA incorporating both experiments. Consistent with the earlier practice task analyses, no detectable differences occurred between the two experiments. The sensory modality was the only significant between-subject main factor: $F(1, 72) = 22.20$, $p < 0.0001$, which interacted reliably with the trial: $F(11, 792) = 3.50$, $p < 0.001$, and with both the method and the experiment (triple interaction). Both Fig. 8.29 and 8.30 demonstrate these significant effects: substantially better performances for the visual rather than the auditory mode, which differed greatly depending on the trial, as well as clear modality differences for the two item presentation methods between the two experiments, respectively.

In each of Experiments 6 and 7 also, a highly significant modality effect attested to the superiority of visual information processing, as did the trial effect in all analyses, joint or separate. A case in point: The superiority of the visual over the auditory modality holds firmly in the ANOVA for each experiment. $F(1, 36)$'s were 13.10 and 9.32, respectively, in Experiments 6 and 7, each with $p < 0.005$. The new findings that emerged in separate analyses

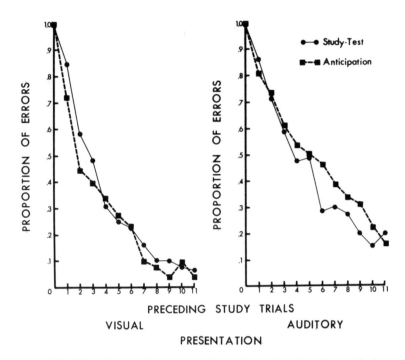

FIG. 8.30. Group performances of study-test and anticipation methods under visual (left) and auditory (right) information processing methods in Experiment 7.

per experiment as contrasted with a joint analyses was that the mode by method interactions were significant in Experiment 6: $F(1, 36) = 5.52, p < 0.03$ (as clearly detectable in Fig. 8.29, but far from significant in Experiment 7 [Fig. 8.30]). However, the trial × mode × method triple interactions that remained large in Experiment 6: $F(11, 396) = 1.78, p = 0.055$, all but disappeared in Experiment 7.

Visual presentation turned out to be decisively and consistently superior to auditory presentation throughout the present three experiments plus that by Izawa et al. (1980). In it, both natural and artificial words along with nonverbal Morse code signals were learned in paired-associate cued recall learning under the list design.

Comparisons of Anticipation and Study-Test Item Presentation Methods

All of the above ANOVAs run both jointly and separately per experiment resulted in significant differences between modalities, but nonsignificant differences between the presentation methods. To detect effects masked in larger ANOVAs where modality differences dominated the entire outcomes, we

TABLE 8.3

Proportion Correct for the First Time Given Incorrect on All Previous Trials (Conditioning Probability), Mean Test Trials to the First Correct Response, and Number of Items Never Learned in Each Condition under Auditory and Visual Modalities in Experiments 6 and 7

| Experiment | Modality | Method | Proportion correct for the first time given incorrect on all previous trials — Preceding study trials | | | | | | | | | | | Mean trials to the first correct (SD) | Mean trials to the last error (SD) | No. of items never learned |
			1	2	3	4	5	6	7	8	9	10	Weighted Mean[a]			
Exp. 6	Auditory	Anticipation	.175	.136	.263	.286	.267	.273	.375				.229	5.000 (2.385)	7.450 (3.765)	2
		N[b]	80	66	57	42	30	22	16							
		Study-test	.075	.297	.173	.372	.259	.050	.158	.063	.200	.417	.204	4.945 (2.527)	7.875 (3.960)	7
		N	80	74	52	43	27	20	19	16	15	12				
	Visual	Anticipation	.263	.271	.442	.208	.105	.353	.545				.296	4.141 (2.208)	6.313 (3.592)	2
		N	80	59	43	24	19	17	11							
		Study-test	.367	.280	.361	.522	.364	.571					.369	3.650 (1.843)	3.152 (2.214)	0
		N	79	50	36	23	11	7								
Exp. 7	Auditory	Anticipation	.163	.194	.259	.200	.219	.320	.176	.214	.091	.400	.212	5.105 (2.740)	7.986 (3.228)	4
		N	80	67	54	40	32	25	17	14	11	10				
		Study-test	.125	.243	.226	.293	.207	.348	.333	.400			.231	5.013 (2.452)	6.863 (3.758)	2
		N	80	70	53	41	29	23	15	10						
	Visual	Anticipation	.275	.397	.314	.292	.353	.364					.324	3.975 (2.123)	4.538 (3.253)	0
		N	80	58	35	24	17	11								
		Study-test	.150	.309	.362	.400	.167	.267	.364				.272	4.492 (2.331)	4.675 (3.209)	1
		N	80	68	47	30	18	15	11							

[a] Based on the cases with $N \geqslant 10$.

[b] N = the number of cases.

TABLE 8.4

Overt Errors and Proportions of Overt Errors in Each Condition in
Auditory and Visual Modalities in Experiments 6 and 7

			Overt Errors			All Errors			Overt Error Proportion
Experiment	Modality	Method	Mean	SD	Total	Mean	SD	Total	
Exp. 6	Auditory	Anticipation	3.263	2.509	261	5.600	2.984	448	.583
		Study-Test	3.538	2.873	283	6.413	3.510	513	.552
	Visual	Anticipation	2.438	2.074	195	4.863	2.801	389	.501
		Study-Test	0.850	1.032	68	2.825	1.881	226	.301
Exp. 7	Auditory	Anticipation	3.575	2.796	286	6.225	2.994	498	.574
		Study-Test	2.563	2.594	205	5.513	3.102	441	.465
	Visual	Anticipation	1.838	2.213	147	3.750	2.602	300	.490
		Study-Test	1.900	2.197	152	4.213	2.768	337	.451

achieved needed separations for the modality. In Experiment 6, as is clear from Fig. 8.29, the study-test method differed little from the anticipation method under the auditory modality, but excelled the anticipation method significantly under the visual modality: $F(1, 18) = 10.62$, $p < 0.005$. Although method did not interact with trial for auditory data, it did so significantly for visual data: $F(11, 198) = 2.51$, $p < 0.01$. The differential outcomes derive from interprocedural differences between the two sensory departments in Experiment 6. Here Morse code signals and Izawa et al.'s (1980) nonsense syllables produced identical results.

However, in Experiment 7, performance differences between anticipation and study-test methods were too small to be reliable for either visual or auditory information processing. Method did not interact with trial under either mode in Experiment 7.

The present auditory conditions in Experiments 6 and 7 utilized Barch and Levine's (1967) learning materials, the only difference being that their subjects were run in groups, and ours individually. Yet, we were unable to replicate the superiority of the anticipation method in any of these two experiments (see right panels of Fig. 8.29 and 8.30). Contrary to the encoding model the results for these two methods differed little in each experiment with auditory presentations.

In spite of these varied results (nonsignificance for the auditory mode in the present experiments as well as either significant or nonsignificant differences favoring the study-test method under the visual mode), the identity model can unequivocally account for all such findings.

Table 8.3 provides the conditioning probability or acquisition (learning) rate per study (S) trial for each condition in Experiments 6 and 7. The weighted means and other statistics in Table 8.3 uniformly indicate superior performances for the visual over the auditory mode. Within each modality, relative standings between anticipation and study-test methods seem inconsistent but

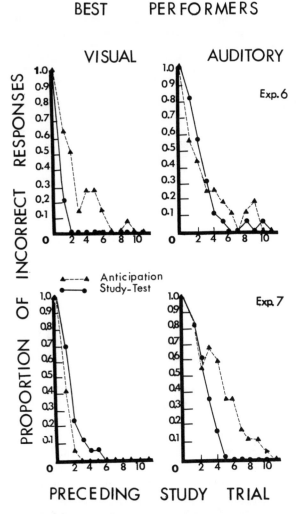

FIG. 8.31. Performance of the two best learners from each condition under both visual (left) and auditory (right) information presentation modes in Experiments 6 (upper panels) and 7 (lower panels).

did not differ greatly from each other, in general. These facts correspond well to the ANOVA reported earlier.

Table 8.4 shows the overt and total errors separately, and the last column gives the proportion of overt errors relative to the total errors for Experiments 6 and 7. In contrast to the same statistics in Experiment 5 that used words, when Morse code signals were paired with digits, the subjects ventured many more guesses in Experiments 6 and 7. There were trends showing that subjects guess more under the anticipation than the study-test method.

POOREST PERFORMERS

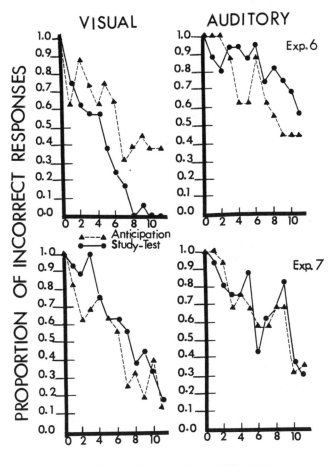

FIG. 8.32. Performance of the two poorest learners from each condition under both visual (left) and auditory (right) information presentation modes in Experiment 6 (top) and 7 (bottom).

Although Barch and Levine seemed to assume that a Morse-code-signal paired with a number would be difficult to encode, the four panels of Fig. 8.29 and 8.30 demonstrate considerable acquisition in each case, even under the more difficult auditory conditions (as compared with visual ones). In a certain sense, all four situations in these two figures may be regarded as being of more or less intermediate difficulty in terms of actual performance. Here all four cases can be accounted for by the identity model, but nonsignificance in three out of four cases may also be in accord with the encoding model. Indeed, the encoding model might perform even better. To examine this further we procured more clearly defined learning difficulty situations of greater variety and analyzed data for both the two best and the two poorest subjects per condition in Experiments 6 and 7. Figures 8.31 and 8.32 give data from these extreme performers, for Experiments 6 (top panels) and 7 (bottom panels).

A global analysis of the variance indicated that the greatest differences occurred between the best and worst subjects: $F(1, 16) = 556.74$, $p < 0.0001$. For these divergent subjects also, the visual modality was significantly better than the auditory one: $F(1, 16) = 95.53$, with $p < 0.0001$. Comparing Experiments 6 and 7 there were no significant differences between these extreme subjects, reconfirming the compatibility of the two experiments.

Most importantly, there was no overall significance between study-test and anticipation methods. Of the six double between-subject interactions, the only one that reached significance was between the method and the performer: $F(1, 16) = 4.57$, $p < 0.05$. The method by experiment and modality by performer interactions approached significance: respective $F(1, 16)$s were both 4.250, $ps = 0.056$. Whereas the within-subject factor, the trial interacted with the mode as usual, as well as with the performer: $F(11, 176) = 13.78$, $p < 0.0001$, it did not interact with method. Among the triple or higher level interactions that involve method, significance was limited to the following four interactions, each accompanied by the modality factor: the mode $\times$ method $\times$ experiment and the mode $\times$ method $\times$ performer, $F(1, 16)$s being 34.57 and 5.25, $ps < 0.04$, plus the trial $\times$ mode $\times$ method $\times$ performer and the trial $\times$ mode $\times$ method $\times$ experiment $\times$ performer, $F(11, 176)$s being 3.32 and 2.05, $ps < 0.03$, respectively.

In order to achieve fine grained analyses and to relate graphical data presentation more closely to ANOVA results, we conducted an ANOVA for each experiment. A new fact emerged: the study-test method was significantly better than the anticipation method in Experiment 6: $F(1, 8) = 5.46$, $p < 0.05$, but not so in Experiment 7. View Fig. 8.31 and 8.32 side by side, with the former on the left, and examine the differences between upper and lower panels.

The mode $\times$ method interactions did occur for both: $F(1, 8)$s were 18.48 and 16.86 with $p < 0.05$, respectively, in Experiments 6 and 7. Whereas significance of the mode $\times$ performer interactions were limited to Experiment 6 with $F(1, 8) = 13.97$, $p < 0.006$ (upper panels), the large method $\times$ performer interactions were confined to Experiment 7 only with $F(1, 8) = 8.49$, $p < .02$ (lower panels). The within subject trial factor interacted with the between-subject factors in similar fashion for both experiments excepting trial $\times$ mode $\times$ method $\times$ performer quadruplicate interactions that were significant only in Experiment 6, $F(11, 88) = 4.87$, $p < 0.0001$.

Next, we separated the performer factor within each experiment; it had generated the strongest effects above. In Experiment 6, interestingly, there were no differences between sensory modalities among "best performers," for whom all situations were easy. Furthermore, there were no meaningful performance differences between the two methods. These findings favor the identity model over the encoding model, which anticipates the study-test method to be superior. From a practical point of view, then, learning was so easy for the best performers that neither the method with which item information is presented nor the sensory modality produced any difference at all.

A still finer grained analysis of the best performers in Experiment 6 indicated that there was no significance between anticipation and study-test methods under audition, and a lack of interaction between trial and method (Fig. 8.31, top right). Under the visual modality, however, the two methods did generate reliable differences: $F(1, 2) = 841.00$, $p < 0.002$, and interacted significantly with the trial: $F(11, 22) = 5.69$, $p. = 0.0003$ (Fig. 8.31, top left).

In sharp contrast, for the poorest performers there were large modality effects favoring vision: $F(1, 4) = 131.64$, $p = 0.0003$ (upper panels, Fig. 8.32), as well as significant method by mode interactions: $F(1, 4) = 43$, $p < 0.003$. For the poorest learners, then, the sensory modality and method did matter. In Experiment 6, superior performance was attained with the study-test method under the visual mode: $F(1, 2) = 33.92$, $p < 0.03$. Performance under audition was worst where both item presentation methods produced similarly, poor scores. No trial method interactions occurred in either mode.

In Experiment 7, the modality produced reliable effects for both the best and the poorest learners: $F(1, 4)$s were 66.06 and 11.11, respectively with $p < 0.03$. For the poorest learners there were no differences between anticipation and study-test methods, however, the procedural differences did approach significance for the best learners: $F(1, 4) = 5.71$, $p = 0.075$. The method by mode interactions, not significant for the poorest, were significant for the best: $F(1, 4) = 25.20$, $p < 0.008$. In both groups, however, trial interacted with mode: $F(11, 44)$s being 4.35 and 2.86, ps < 0.01, respectively.

Further analyses indicated that the study-test method excelled significantly under the auditory mode where learning progressed relatively slowly for the best performers: $F(1, 4) = 38.44$, $p = 0.025$, but not under the visual mode, here acquisition was extremely easy and progressed very rapidly (Fig. 8.31, lower panels). For the poorest learners no procedural difference was detected under either mode (Fig. 8.32, lower panels).

Let us now view Fig. 8.31 and 8.32 side by side, with the former (best performers) on the left. The four panels in each experiment lined up nicely: Learning difficulty increased from left to right for this set of learning materials. With learning very easy, the encoding model expects superiority from the study-test method and when learning is very difficult, the encoding model expects superiority from the anticipation method. Neither model forecasts differences for intermediate situations. In Experiment 6, the first two panels (Fig. 8.31, top panels) support the encoding model, but the last two (Fig. 8.32, top panels) do not. Here an intermediate state made for significant superiority of the study-test method, but for the very difficult situation there were no differences between the two methods. In Experiment 7, only one of the four situations supported the encoding model: no significance in an intermediate situation (Fig. 8.32, bottom left). Thus, in Experiments 6 and 7 the encoding model is in line with the data in only three out of eight cases.

The identity model avers that nonsignificance can occur in learning situations at any level of difficulty except for the possibility of notable superiority for the study-test method in intermediate situations. However, one deviation from identity model predictions occurred in the easy situations of Experiment 6 (Fig. 8.31, top left, visual) where the study-test method was distinctly superior. But, all other situations in Experiments 6 and 7 supported the identity model. That is, seven out of eight situations clearly upheld the identity model.

In summary, we had a total of 30 panels in this part of our chapter that illustrated performance under the anticipation and study-test methods (Fig. 8.26–8.32). Of the 30, 18 cases deviated from the expectations of the encoding model, a failure rate of 60%. Furthermore, the 12 situations in conformity with the encoding model were all, save one, nonsignificant for levels of intermediate difficulty situations for which the model makes no explicit theoretical statements. If one relies on explicit predictions from the encoding model to test it, we must note that only in one case did the data support it.

In contrast, the identity model was overwhelmingly supported by the data in our three current experiments: 28 out of 30 cases were correctly predicted from the identity model. One deviation each occurred in very easy and very difficult learning situations. The failure rate was 6.7% (2/30; it becomes 4.7% when Izawa et al. [1980, 1984] data were considered jointly). It does not seem to pose a serious challenge to this model.

Moreover, interestingly enough, the two deviations above were limited to the visual mode. When the auditory one alone was considered separately, no case deviated from the identity model in any of the 15 comparisons in Part 2, or any of 11 comparisons in Izawa et al. (1980; 1984).

Auditory information is transmitted sequentially in time; no two words can be processed simultaneously. It seems intuitively appealing to assume that the anticipation method which utilizes immediate feedback (see Equation 1) must benefit from this. The powerful Skinnerian feedback model and the current encoding model by Barch and Levine notwithstanding, nowhere in our data were there such expected advantage for the anticipation method.

Consequently, it is disturbing that the predictive accuracy of the anticipation method did not fare well under the visual mode. It also did badly in each situation in which learning materials were presented auditorily, as was the case in all three current experiments, one with words, and the other two with learning materials identical with those of Barch and Levine. Even in the situations where encoding is very difficult, which was assumed to be an ideal situation for the anticipation method, encoding model expectations did not materialize. Comparisons between anticipation and study-test methods using the auditory mode were for the most part not significant. Indeed, when performance differences were large on infrequent occasions, their direction was opposite to prediction (i.e., the study-test method was superior to the anticipation method). The findings by Izawa et al. (1980) concur with these results.

The apparent discrepancy between Barch and Levine and our present studies remains mystifying. We are so concerned about their results because they came from an extraordinarily large sample of subjects (a total of 652), 520 students in large group testing situations (Experiment 1), and 132 in small group and some single subject testing situations (Experiment 2). It was our assumption that this large sample made for accuracy. But a partial reason for the discrepancy between their data and ours might be found in the fact that: (a) they used group testing situations, and (b) the subjects recorded their own responses. Such experimental procedures enable subject to respond *after* the target or response term was presented under the anticipation method: This was impossible in our experiments; here each subject was run, one at a time, and all responses were recorded by the experimenter.

It seems entirely reasonable to conclude that the identity model survived best throughout all the micro- and macro-analyses designed to examine results from nearly every angle conceivable for the three experiments, including two replications from Barch and Levine's study. These findings, aside from underlining the basic soundness of the identity model also substantiated its generalizability to another modality, namely, the auditory dimension.

PART 2 REFERENCES

Atkinson, R. C., & Shiffrin, R. M. (1968). A proposed system and its control processes. In K. W. Spence & J. T. Spence (Eds.), *The psychology of learning and motivation: Advances in research and theory, Vol. 2.* New York: Academic Press.

Barch, A. M., & Levine, J. R. (1967). Presentation method in auditory identification learning. *Journal of Verbal Learning and Verbal Behavior, 6,* 282–288.

Battig, W. F., & Brackett, H. R. (1961). Comparison of anticipation and recall methods in paired-associate learning. *Psychological Reports, 9,* 59–65.

Battig, W. F., & Wu, R. D. (1965). Comparison of recall and anticipation paired-associate procedures within mixed aurally-presented lists. *Psychonomic Science, 3,* 233–234.

Berry, F. M., Detterman, D. K., & Mulhern, T. (1973). Stimulus encoding as a function of modality: Aural versus visual paired-associate learning. *Journal of Experimental Psychology, 99,* 140–142.

Bray, N. W., & Batchelder, W. H. (1972). Effects of instructions and retention interval on memory of presentation mode. *Journal of Verbal Learning and Verbal Behavior, 11,* 367–374.

Cofer, C. N., Diamond, F., Olsen, R. A., Stein, J. S., & Walker, H. (1967). Comparison of anticipation and recall methods in paired-associate learning. *Journal of Experimental Psychology, 75,* 545–558.

Conrad, R. (1964). Acoustic confusions in immediate memory. *British Journal of Psychology, 55,* 75–84.

Craik, F. I. M. (1969). Modality effects in short-term storage. *Journal of Verbal Learning and Verbal Behavior, 8,* 658–664.

Crowder, R. G., & Morton, J. (1969). Precategorical acoustic storage (PAS). *Perception & Psychophysics, 5,* 365–373.

DeBoth, J., & Dominowski, R. L. (1979). Individual differences in learning: Visual vs. auditory presentation. *Journal of Educational Psychology, 70,* 498–505.

Easton, R. D., & Basala, M. (1982). Perceptual dominance during lipreading. *Perception & Psychophysics, 32,* 562–570.

Ebbinghaus, H. (1885). *Über das Gedächtnis: Untersuchungen zur experimentellen Psychologie* [On memory: Investigations in experimental psychology]. Leipzig, Germany: Duncker & Humbolt.

Engle, R. W., & Mobley, L. A. (1976). The modality effect: What happens in long-term memory? *Journal of Verbal Learning and Verbal Behavior, 15,* 519–527.

Glenberg, A. M., & Swanson, N. G. (1986). A temporal distinctiveness theory of recency and modality effects. *Journal of Experimental Psychology: Learning, Memory, and Cognition, 12,* 3–15.

Hasher, L., & Zacks, R. T. (1979). Automatic and effortful processes in memory. *Journal of Experimental Psychology: General, 108,* 356–388.

Horton, D. L., & Mills, C. B. (1984). Human learning and memory. *Annual Review of Psychology, 35,* 361–394.

Howard, I. P., & Templeton, W. B. (1966). *Human Spatial Orientation.* New York: Wiley.

Izawa, C. (1971a). Massed and spaced practice in paired-associate learning: List versus item distributions. *Journal of Experimental Psychology, 89,* 10–21.

Izawa, C. (1971b). The test trial potentiating model. *Journal of Mathematical Psychology, 8,* 200–224.

Izawa, C. (1972). Retention interval hypothesis and evidence for its basic assumptions. *Journal of Experimental Psychology, 96,* 17–24.

Izawa, C. (1976). Vocalized and silent tests in paired-associated learning. *American Journal of Psychology, 89,* 681–693.

Izawa, C. (1980). Empirical examinations of the retention interval hypothesis: Comparisons of learning methods when learning is difficult. *Journal of General Psychology, 103,* 117–129.

Izawa, C. (1983). The generality of the retention interval model. *Journal of General Psychology, 108,* 113–134.

Izawa, C. (1985). The identity model and factors controlling the superiority of study-test method over the anticipation method. *Journal of General Psychology, 112,* 65–78.

Izawa, C., Bell, D., & Hayden, R. G. (1984). Auditory information processing and its method of presentation. *Japanese Psychological Research, 26,* 12–23.

Izawa, C., Hayden, R. G., & Isham, K. L. (1980). Sensory modality and method of item information presentation in memory, *Acta Psychologia, 44,* 131–145.

Janssen, W. H. (1976). Selective interference in paired-associate and free recall learning: Messing up the image. *Acta Psychologica 40,* 35–48.

Johansson, B. S., Lindberg, L. G., & Svensson, M. L. (1974). Effects of encoding strategy, presentation modality, and scoring method on STM performance with the Peterson and Peterson technique. *Memory & Cognition, 2,* 656–662.

Kanak, N. J., Cole, L. E., & Eckert, E. (1972). Implicit associative responses in verbal discrimination acquisition. *Journal of Experimental Psychology, 93,* 309–319.

Kanak, N. J., & Neuner, S. D. (1970). Associative symmetry and item availability as a function of five methods of paired-associate acquisition. *Journal of Experimental Psychology, 86,* 288–295.

Kool, V. K., & Tripathi, K. (1978). Short-term recall as a function of presentation of material of varying load to identical and different modality. *Psychologia, 21,* 204–209.

Kraft, R. N., & Jenkins, J. J. (1981). The lag effect with aurally presented passages. *Bulletin of the Psychonomic society, 17,* 132–134.

Kroll, N. E. A., & Kellicut, M. H. (1972). Short-term recall as a function of covert rehearsal and of intervening task. *Journal of Verbal Learning and Verbal Behavior, 11,* 196–204.

Kroll, N. E. A., Parks, T., Parkinson, S. R., Bieber, S. L., & Johnson A. L. (1970). Short-term memory while shadowing: Recall of visually and of aurally presented letters. *Journal of Experimental Psychology, 85,* 220–224.

Lehman, E. B. (1982). Memory for modality: Evidence for an automatic process. *Memory & Cognition, 10,* 554–564.

Lehman, E. B., & Hanzel, S. H. (1981). A developmental study of memory for presentation modality. *Journal of General Psychology, 105,* 155–164.

Margrain, S. A. (1967). Short-term memory as a function of input modality. *Quarterly Journal of Experimental Psychology, 19,* 109–114.

McGeoch, J. A. (1942). *The psychology of human learning.* New York: Longmans, Green.

Metcalfe, J., Glavanov, D., & Murdock, M. (1981). Spatial and temporal processing in the auditory and visual modalities. *Memory & Cognition, 9,* 351–359.

Morton, J. (1970). A functional model for memory. In D. A. Norman (Ed.), *Models of human memory* (pp. 203–254). New York: Academic Press.

Mueller, J. H. (1977). Test anxiety, input modality, and levels of organization in free recall. *Bulletin of Psychonomic Society, 9,* 67–69.

Murdock, B. B., Jr. (1966). The criterion problem in short-term memory. *Journal of Experimental Psychology, 72,* 317–324.

Murdock, B. B., Jr. (1967). Auditory and visual stores in short-term memory. *Acta Psychologica, 27,* 316–324.

Murdock, B. B., Jr. (1968). Modality effects in short-term memory. *Journal of Experimental Psychology, 77,* 79–86.

Murdock, B. B., Jr. (1974). *Human memory: Theory and data.* Hillsdale, NJ: Lawrence Erlbaum Associates.

Myers, A. K., Cotton, B., & Hilp, H. A. (1981). Matching of the rate of concurrent tone bursts and light flashes as a function of flash surround luminance. *Perception & Psychophysics, 30,* 33–38.

Nazzaro, J. R., & Nazzaro, J. N. (1970). Auditory versus visual learning of temporal patterns. *Journal of Experimental Psychology, 84,* 477–478.

Norman, D. A. (1966). Acquisition and retention in short-term memory. *Journal of Experimental Psychology, 72,* 369–381.

Parkinson, S. R. (1972). Short-term memory while shadowing multiple-item recall of visually and of aurally presented letters. *Journal of Experimental Psychology, 92,* 256–265.

Penney, C. G. (1975). Modality effects in short-term memory. *Psychological Bulletin, 82,* 68–84.

Salzberg, P. M., Parks, T. E., Kroll, N. E. A., & Parkinson, S. R. (1971). Retroactive effects of phonemic similarity on short-term recall of visual and auditory stimuli. *Journal of Experimental Psychology, 91,* 43–46.

Scarborough, D. L. (1972). Stimulus modality effects on forgetting in short-term memory. *Journal of Experimental Psychology, 95,* 285–289.

Schulz, R. W., & Hopkins, R. H. (1968). Presentation mode and meaningfulness as variables in several verbal-learning tasks. *Journal of Verbal Learning and Verbal Behavior, 7,* 1–13.

Schulz, R. W., & Kasschau, R. A. (1966). Serial learning as a function of meaningfulness and mode of presentation with audio and visual stimuli of equivalent duration. *Journal of Experimental Psychology, 71,* 350–354.

Sperling, G., & Speelman, R. G. (1970). Acoustic similarity and auditory short-term memory: Experiments and a model. In D. A. Norman (Ed.), *Models of human memory.* New York: Academic Press.

Thorndike, E. L., & Lorge, I. (1944). *The teacher's word book of 30,000 words.* New York: Bureau of Publications, Teachers College, Columbia University.

Treisman, A. M., Sykes, M., & Gelade, G. (1977). Attention and stimulus integration. In S. Dornic (Ed.), *Attention and performance VI.* Hillsdale, NJ: Lawrence Erlbaum Associates.

Tulving, E., & Madigan, S. A. (1970). Memory and verbal learning. *Annual Review of Psychology, 21,* 437–484.

Turner, M. L., LaPointe, L. B., Cantor, J., Reeves, C. H., Griffeth, R. H., & Engle, R. W. (1987). Recency and suffix effects found with auditory presentation and with mouthed visual presentation: They're not the same thing. *Journal of Memory and Language, 26,* 138–164.

Underwood, B. J. (1982). Paired associate learning: Data on pair difficulty and variables that influence difficulty. *Memory & Cognition, 10,* 610–617.

Walk, R. D., & Pick, H. L., Jr. (1981). *Intersensory perception and sensory integration.* New York: Plenum.

Walker, J. T., & Scott, K. (1981). Auditory-visual conflicts in the perceived duration of lights, tones and gaps. *Journal of Experimental Psychology: Human Perception and Performance, 7,* 1327–1339.

Wallach, H., & Averbach, E. (1955). On memory modalities. *American Journal of Psychology, 68,* 249–257.

Warrington, E. K., & Shallice, T. (1972). Neuropsychological evidence of visual storage in short-term memory tasks. *Quarterly Journal of Experimental Psychology, 24,* 30–40.

Watkins, O. C., & Watkins, M. J. (1977). Serial recall and the modality effect: Effects of word frequency. *Journal of Experimental Psychology: Human Learning and Memory, 3,* 712–718.

Whitten, W. B., & Bjork, R. A. (1977). Learning from tests: Effects of spacing. *Journal of Verbal Learning and Verbal Behavior, 16,* 465–478.

Williams, J. M., & Derks, P. L. (1963). Mode of presentation and the acquisition of paired associates that differ in pronounceability and association value. *Journal of Verbal Learning and Verbal Behavior, 2,* 453–456.

8

Part 3. Effects of the Item Presentation Methods and Test Trials on Euclidean Distances and Location Learning via the Tactile Sense

Chizuko Izawa
Dean L. Patterson
Tulane University

Although a tremendous backlog of research on sensory processes has accumulated since Aristotle's doctrine of the five senses, the focus of said research has favored vision over all other senses (cf. Rock & Victor, 1964). Audition is a far removed second. Following this typical pattern, both the formulation and tests of the identity model primarily involved the sense of vision (Part 1 of this chapter) and to a much smaller degree, auditory presentations (Part 2 of this chapter).

Not being modality specific, there is no reason why the identity model cannot utilize data from any of the three remaining senses, even if generalizing to a third modality may seem a bit too ambitious. Of the three less pursued sensory departments, the tactile sense seems most frequently relevant to the issue of maximizing learning and retention, inclusive of encoding, storage, and retrieval processes, with which we are most concerned here. This concern derives from the fact that motor skill learning heavily involves haptic and kinesthetic information processing. (For a provocative discussion of motor schemata of kinesthetic experiences, see Solso's chapter in this volume.)

Motor skill learning under the tactile mode, involves a great deal of physical activity training, as seen not only in aesthetically skilled performances by, for example, dancers, musicians, artists, athletes, craftsmen, and a variety of professionals and workmen, but also in the daily activities of ordinary people. Some of these skills are job related, whereas other skills are essential for daily living.

In this final part of our chapter, we explore the kinesthetic cognitive motor system, involved in the learning of radically different types of nonverbal materials in order to examine the generality of both the identity model and its antecedent, the test trial potentiating model (Izawa, 1971b), on a new dimension. Until now, comparing anticipation with study-test stimulus information presentation methods seems to have been rarely pursued in examining the learning of Euclidean distances and locations. Given that alarming paucity of research on tactual memory and its processes, the two experiments in Part 3 were intended also to fill this hiatus.

Can a model formulated on the basis of linguistic learning data based on vision, our most dominant and sophisticated sensory modality, also be applicable to the kinds of learning data derived from studies utilizing nonverbal (often difficult to encode verbally) materials, involving the tactile system, a lower order, less sophisticated modality?

The answer to this question depends, in part, on how much overlap or similarity there is between visual and tactile sensations. In view of the fact that the identity model does hold for the auditory mode as well (Part 2), it seems necessary to include also that modality in our discussions.

On the one hand, there are reports favoring modality specific encoding processes such as Millar (1972a, 1972b) and Tversky (1969), or suggesting differences between visual and haptic modalities, such as Goodnow (1971), Jones and Connolly (1970), O'Connor and Hermelin (1978) and Posner (1967). For example, the view expressed by Kirman and Kirman (1985) that the tactile modality is too different or too primitive; that is, "the tactile system acts as though it contains a low-pass filter for processing" (p. 258) may imply that some processes are uniquely tactile, and not found in either visual or auditory modalities. If so, haptic information processing demands its own theory, distinctly different from those dealing with visual and/or auditory information processing.

On the other hand, there is extant the assumption that sensory stimulus inputs are always coded verbally (e.g., Conrad, 1964; Morton, 1970) and some reports show no qualitative differences between verbal and motor learning (e.g., Ammons, 1960; Ammons, Farr, Block, Neumann, Dey, Marion, & Ammons, 1958; Fleishman & Parker, 1962) when utilizing forgetting or retention curves. Verbal short-term memory processes, unveiled by Peterson and Peterson (1959) and affirmed by Hellyer (1962), could be demonstrated by a simple motor response task (e.g., Adams & Dijkstra, 1966) also. According to Zakay and Shilo (1985), the tactile modality was similar to the visual modality. The typical repetition effect that occurred within and between modalities (Turpin & Stelmach, 1984), as well as similar intra- and intermodality effects also suggest comparability of kinesthetic and visual sensory modalities. Indeed, similarity between verbal and motor learning may be greater than commonly assumed (cf. Adams, 1983). If correct, it appears possible that both the identity model and the test trial potentiating model can be profitably utilized in the domain of motor skill learning.

There is another line of research that evaluates the relative strengths of sensory modalities, to which a subject is exposed simultaneously (cross-modal comparisons). Recent trends suggest a growth of interest in cross-modal studies that compare the processes of sensory interaction and intersensory organization (e.g., Walk & Pick, 1981). Interestingly enough, neither the cross-modal approach, nor the other lines of research delineated earlier, have reported consistent results. The complete or very strong dominance of vision over touch (e.g., Easton & Moran, 1978; Gibson, 1933; Hay, Pick, & Ikeda, 1965; Kinney & Luria, 1970; Miller, 1972; Rock & Victor, 1964; Singer & Day, 1969; Teghtsoonian & Teghtsoonian, 1970), or over auditory perception (e.g., Howard & Templeton, 1966) was frequently reported.

Many others question the dominance of vision on the ground that a strong auditory bias or tactual information may intermingle with visual information (e.g., Fishkin, Pishkin, & Stahl, 1975; Lederman & Abbott, 1981; Walker & Scott, 1981). In macrospatial tasks, vision strongly dominates touch, proprioception and audition, whereas in temporal tasks, audition strongly dominates vision (e.g., Myers, Cotton, & Hilp, 1981; Walker & Scott, 1981). Lederman, Thorne, and Jones (1986) found that vision dominated touch in assessing spatial density, however, touch dominated when judging the roughness of the same stimulus surfaces. They were led to favor the modality appropriateness hypothesis, subscribed to by O'Connor and Hermelin (1972) and by Freides (1974).

Results seem also mixed for cross-modal comparisons of the visual and haptic senses employing factorial designs. Although Millar (1972a) found that visual-haptic matches were neither more accurate nor faster than haptic-haptic matches, Hall and Newman (1987) found that for the training-test combination, the haptic–haptic condition was significantly inferior to the visual–haptic condition.

Hatta, Yamamoto, and Mito (1984), using both the aged and young subjects, observed that processes in listening parallel those of tactile recognition processes. Similarly, Keele, Pokorny, Corcos, and Ivry (1985) contended that auditory perception and motor production may share some common mechanisms, suggesting the possibility that our models may be investigated under both auditory and kinesthetic modalities in a similar fashion.

Although many favor common explanations for motor and verbal learning, inconsistencies still seem to be the rule, rather than the exception, for investigations comparing cognitive motor and kinesthetic sensory modes. To clarify the issue, we approached kinesthetic-motor information processing in reference to the item information presentation methods; study-test versus anticipation method, examinations via the identity model plus its predecessor model. The most relevant phenomena to our approach include retention interval effect and retroactive inhibition, as well as effects of test trials.

Examination of these phenomena with motor learning studies has also produced mixed results. Wrisberg (1975) obtained large retention losses for the 50 seconds retention interval in only one of two conditions. Inconsistency also seems to prevail for retroactive inhibition with motor learning (e.g., Craft & Hinriches, 1971; Herman & Baily, 1970; Pepper & Herman, 1970; Stelmach,

1970; Williams, Beaver, Spence, & Rundell, 1969). Stelmach and Walsh (1972) obtained positive findings, but Posner and Konick (1966) and Stelmach and Barber (1970) generated negative ones.

When contemplating anticipation versus study-test comparisons in motor learning studies, we were unable to locate such work. One of the major reasons for this may be the training procedures used in kinesthetic motor-skill learning; it varies from study to study. No standard procedures appear to exist. For example, some of the past motor learning experiments have alternated study and test trials, which are basically the same as the study-test method (Equation 2) as seen in Wrisberg and Schmidt (1975). However, many other experimenters have administered either repeated study trials or repeated test trials (e.g., Adams & Dijkstra, 1966; Duffy, Montague, Laabs, & Hillix, 1975).

Researchers have shown little interest in determining the relative merits of these procedures common to motor learning studies. One notable exception was Hagman (1983) who compared three training sequences: ST (study-test method), STTTTT (one study trial followed by five test trials) and SSSSST (five S trials followed by one T trial), precisely in tune with a design developed and extensively applied for over 2 decades by Izawa (1966, 1967a, 1967b, 1968, 1969, 1970a, 1970b, 1971b, 1976, 1989) in verbal learning experiments.

Hagman and Izawa's design succeeded in unraveling the effects of repeated study and repeated tests. In view of the paucity of similar investigations in motor learning, our experiments in Part 3 were designed to pursue effects of test (T) and training (S) sequences. We sought to examine the replicability of their findings with both verbal and motor learning, to see if the test trial potentiating model (Izawa, 1971b) would be supported. What is most impressive are the clear demonstrations of positive effects from unreinforced test trials. These are manifested in two demonstrable empirical functions: (a) the test trial potentiating effect, unique to the test trials (Izawa, 1966, 1967a, 1967b, 1969), and (b) the forgetting prevention effect. The test trial potentiating model was formulated to account for both of these empirical effects.

Impressive positive performance increments over successive tests without intervening study trials, that is, hypermnesia, have been repeatedly demonstrated by Erdlyi and his colleagues since 1974 and subsequently by Roediger and his associates. We direct you to Roediger and Challis' chapter in this volume for their review of literature and discussion, including fascinating differences between pictorial materials and words; findings both enlightening and challenging for theory in this domain.

The positive effects of unreinforced test trials do not seem to be limited to explicit learning of verbal and motor skill materials aforementioned. Gollin (1960, Experiment 2) produced large improvements in performance by simply giving another threshold test using the picture fragment completion task for implicit memory. For a comprehensive discussion of implicit memory, please consult the chapter by Snodgrass in this volume.

In an attempt to procure the type of data previously unavailable, we introduced the anticipation method in motor learning situations, to compare with the study-test method. Along with other S-T sequences, S, T, or both are repeated to form a pattern throughout the acquisition or training period.

In order to create a situation as close as possible to the list design in verbal paired-associate learning situations (Equations 1 and 2), care was taken to generate either a few Euclidean distances (Experiment 8), or a few Euclidean locations (Experiment 9), respectively (rather than one each, as is often done in motor-skill learning experiments), which were presented under the haptic mode with neither visual nor auditory cues (i.e., the single sensory modality presentation). Distance, here, refers to extent of movement (the length of a straight line between the start and end points, specific location is not relevant). Location, however, refers to a movement stopping position in Euclidean space. Operationally, these two are separated by changing the starting point within and between cycles (on both study (S) and test (T) trials). Thus, location becomes an irrelevant and unreliable cue for recalling distance, and vice versa.

EXPERIMENT 8

The task of Experiment 8 was to learn to produce four Euclidean distances of straight lines via dynamic tracing responses using a slide without visual and auditory cues, that is, a movement-based distance learning under the kinesthetic sense, requiring the movement of the right arm. The four distances were 5, 11, 25, and 40 cm in length, and labeled respectively as Distances I, U, N, and S, thereby avoiding numerical references in order to minimize artifacts attributable to preconceived lengths.

Forty Introductory Psychology students at Tulane, 10 per condition, learned the four distances according to S and T trial sequences specified for each of the four conditions in Experiment 8 as shown in Fig. 8.33. An acquisition cycle consists of the presentation of all the four items (distances in Experiment 8, locations in Experiment 9), presented in random order from cycle to cycle. One anticipation method trial required two (T-S) cycles by definition, since each item was first presented as a T event, immediately followed by its S event. That is, each item was presented twice per anticipation cycle, whereas in all other (i.e., S-T) conditions, each item was presented only once per cycle, whether it was an S or a T cycle. In the standard study-test condition (Condition ST), S and T cycles came alternately, whereas in Conditions SSST and STTT, three S cycles preceded a T and three T cycles followed an S cycle, respectively.

For each condition in Experiment 8, there was a distinct repetitive pattern: TS, ST, SSST, and STTT for Conditions Anticipation, Study-Test, SSST,

Condition	Acquisition Cycles																
	1	2	3	4	5	6	7	8	9	10	11	12	13 . . . 22	23	24	25	26
Anticipation (TS)	T –	S_1	T –	S_2	T –	S_3	T –	S_4	T –	S_5	T –	S_6	T . . . S_{11}	T –	S_{12}	T –	S_{13}
Study-Test (ST)	T	S_1	T	S_2	T	S_3	T	S_4	T	S_5	T	S_6	T . . . S_{11}	T	S_{12}	T	S_{13}
SSST	T	S_1	S_2	S_3	T	S_4	S_5	S_6	T	S_7	S_8	S_9	T . . . S_{16}	S_{17}	S_{18}	T	S_{19}
STTT	T	S_1	T	T	T	S_2	T	T	T	S_3	T	T	T . . . S_6	T	T	T	S_7

FIG. 8.33. Experimental design: Study (S) and test (T) event sequences during the acquisition period, Experiments 8 (Euclidean distance learning) and 9 (Euclidean location learning).

and STTT. In order to be comparable to the anticipation method that inherently starts with a T trial, all other conditions were given an initial T trial, prior to each respective repetitive pattern commenced. Each repetitive sequence was continued until the 26th cycle (Fig. 8.33) where all conditions had S trials, marking the end of the acquisition phase. Because the anticipation cycle is analogous to two cycles of T-S trials, the method inherently ends with an S event. Thus, we selected a convenient cycle that fell in an S event for all conditions, right after completing the sixth 4-cycle repetitive patterns for all. In addition, the time interval prior to the first delayed test could be manipulated in the same manner for all four conditions, if the end point was an S cycle.

Two delayed tests followed the acquisition period: the first test (DT₁), 3 minutes after the end of the acquisition phase and the other (DT₂), 24 hours later. The delayed tests are very important, from theoretical, empirical, and applied standpoints. Theory: the identity model assumes that performance differences between anticipation and study-test methods are attributable to short-term memory components in differential retention interval distributions between the two methods. If we remove these short-term components in delayed test situations, the model anticipates no basic differences between the two methods of presenting item information, and therefore, expects the same performance levels for both. Can this theoretical expectation hold in motor learning situations also?

The delayed test to evaluate long-term memory (LTM) has another special significance in examining the effect of tests (Ts) in motor learning for comparing three S-T conditions. Hagman (1983) produced distinctly superior long-term retention for conditions which had repetitive Ts as compared with those that did not in both distance and location learning situations. Can the superiority of Condition STTT over Condition SSST be reproduced in our situation, in which the repetitive patterns were two cycles shorter than Hagman's?

The right-handed subjects, assigned to each condition randomly, were run individually and blindfolded to eliminate visual cues. White-noise masked auditory cues emanating from the moving parts of the equipment on the lab table. The equipment consisted of a free-moving slide, mounted on a ruled aluminum bar to measure the distance moved by subjects. Pegs marked starting and stopping points. The slide was always moved from left to right.

During an S event (the experimenter defined event), the subject moved the slide until stopped by the peg which indicated the end point of a specified distance. During a T event (the subject defined event), the subject attempted to reproduce a learned distance of a specified length, unaided, with the end point peg absent.

The subjects in each condition were further divided into subgroups of five, in order to alternate starting positions within and between cycles. The two starting positions were 5 cm on each side of the center point of the subject, whose body position was fixed. Care was taken to insure that each distance occurred approximately one quarter of the time in each starting position throughout the experiment. Time allowed per item on each trial was 10 sec, with 10 sec intercycle intervals.

Comparisons of Anticipation and Study-Test Item Presentation Methods in Euclidean Distance Learning

Item differences within the list are commonly found in linguistic material or verbal learning studies. Similarly in our motor skill learning studies, there were large differences among the four distances, when measured by either signed errors or absolute errors made when reproducing the four horizontal distances. A trend emerged, namely, that the greater the length, the greater the errors, (cf. Lederman, Klatzky, and Barber, 1985). However, our main goal here is to examine the general predictive power of the identity model in the tactile dimension within the motor learning domain, testing it in the same manner we used for verbal learning under the list design.

Thus, we analyze the data in terms of the list, considering four distances together, rather than dealing with the idiosyncrasies of each distance. Analyses of our outcomes were of absolute (unsigned) errors, as in Hagman (1983), in order to prevent giving false impression of accuracy that might result from canceling out overshot and undershot scores.

Figure 8.34 presents learning curves in terms of absolute errors for the anticipation and study-test conditions. Although the study-test method showed a nonsignificant superiority early in learning, the curves crossed after S_5 and several more times thereafter; differences between the two methods became much smaller. Overall differences between anticipation and study-test methods were far too small to be considered reliable: $F(1, 18) = .33$, $p > 0.20$.

Small differences between anticipation and study-test methods during the acquisition phase are contrary to the feedback model that calls for superiority of the anticipation method. It is also at variance with the task alternation model (Battig & Brackett, 1961) and the acquisition differential model (Kanak & Neuner, 1970). However, the current results are in line with one of the two predictions of the identity model that accommodates two types of outcomes: (a) large or (b) small differences between the methods in favor of the study-test method, contingent on the number of critical items that falls into the nonoverlap areas of the retention interval distributions (see Fig. 8.1).

Let us, next, consider long-term retention processes of anticipation and study-test methods. Large memory loss ($p < 0.01$) did occur during the 3 minute retention interval following the last cycle of the acquisition period with both methods, in spite of the fact that another S cycle (i.e., S_{13}) intervened between the last T (Acquisition Cycle 25) and the 3 minute delayed test (see Fig. 8.33). This was no surprise. Nevertheless, it was striking that no further retention loss ensued during the next 24 hours ($p > 0.50$), that is, on the delayed Test 2.

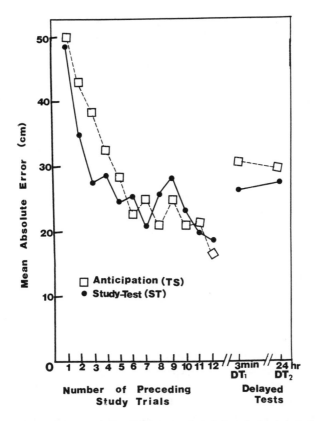

FIG. 8.34.   Comparison of anticipation and study-test methods in both acquisition phase and long-term retention (delayed tests) in the learning of
Euclidean distances, Experiment 8.

The most important finding from a theoretical perspective is that the two
methods do not differ significantly either on the first delayed (short delay)
test, the second delayed (long delay) test, or on both: $F(1, 18) = 1.56$, $p > 0.20$.
Just as the absence of differences in acquisition could not be accounted for
by the aforementioned alternative models, the lack of significance in long-
term retention in the delayed tests were also out of tune with these models.
They expected superiority for either the study-test method or the anticipation method; but none of these models appear to have the theoretical capability
to make differential predictions on the basis of acquisition performance.

By contrast, the lack of differences between study-test and anticipation
methods on delayed tests support the identity model. This follows from the
fact that the differences between the two methods are, according to the model,
due to the number of critical items in short-term memory, falling into the
nonoverlap areas under the distribution curves of the retention intervals (from
the S event of an item to its subsequent T event). For details see Izawa (1985a,

1985b; Fig. 8.1 of this chapter). The crucial issue here is that the basic differences between the two methods stem from the fact that (a) new encoding occurring on S events is identical for both methods as well as for each T event, the intercycle interval, intervening S and T events of other items within the list (Equations 3-7), and that (b) the performance differences stem primarily from the different numbers of intervening S and T events of the other items (t_s and t_T), twice as many under the anticipation method as under the study-test method on the average. In summary, two methods differ only for short-term memory processes in the retention interval during the acquisition period.

Therefore, if such short-term memory components are either minimized or eliminated in the delayed tests where long-term memory components tend to control performances, the identity model would expect nearly the same levels of performances for both anticipation and study-test methods. This was confirmed during Experiment 8 on the kinesthetic learning of Euclidean distance.

Effects of Test Trials on Motor Learning of Euclidean Distances

In order to examine test trial potentiating effects or the effectiveness of each S event, performance under each condition of Experiment 8 is shown in terms of the equal number of S opportunities for each condition experienced in Fig. 8.35. All four conditions of Experiment 8 involved tests following S_3 and S_6. These two tests provide appropriate data to examine the relative efficiency of the study and test sequences in Euclidean distance learning.

Analyses of variance yielded reliable, large differences for the main effects of conditions, two tests jointly, or separately: $F(3, 36) = 3.13$, $p < .05$ after S_3; and $F(3, 36) = 4.30$, $p < .01$ after S_6. In each case, the STTT group showed the least error, followed by either the anticipation (TS) or the study-test (ST) conditions (these two did not differ from each other; see the preceding section, Fig. 8.34), both of which were superior to Condition SSST in all cases. In every repetitive pattern of four cycles, the SSST group received only one T trial, and both anticipation and study-test groups, each experienced two Ts, while the STTT group benefited from three Ts. The curves lined up neatly in accordance with the density of the T trials; the more tests, the better the performance.

Apparently, the intensity of the test effects in making the subsequent S event more effective by increasing encoding power, that is, the test trial potentiating effect, was far greater than foreseen. This is dramatically illustrated in SSST versus STST versus STTT comparison: Conditions differ only by one T from condition to condition, maximum being only two Ts per four-cycle repetitive pattern. However, the absolute performance differences among these three S-T conditions were phenomenal (Fig. 8.35).

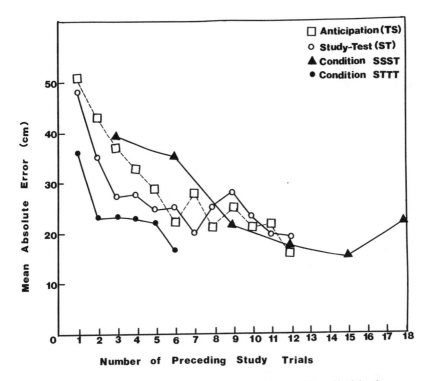

FIG. 8.35. Performance comparisons of all four conditions (Anticipation or TS, standard study-test or ST, SSST and STTT) as a function of preceding study (S) trials in Euclidean distance learning, Experiment 8.

Present findings are precisely in the direction predicted by the test trial potentiating model (Izawa, 1971b), and closely parallel the already accumulated supporting data in verbal learning. Thus, there seems now to be solid support for that model from our motor learning data and also those of Hagman (1983). The test trial potentiating effects in motor learning, illustrated in Condition SSST versus STTT (Fig. 8.35), seem potent indeed!

Lack of significance between performance differences under anticipation (TS) and study-test (ST) methods in both the haptic learning and retention of Euclidean distances (Fig. 8.34) did support the identity as discussed in the previous section. Also, please note that the same prediction holds for the test trial potentiating model. In Fig. 8.33 and 8.35, both anticipation and study-test methods receive the identical number of unreinforced tests. Therefore, both conditions benefitted equally from the test experiences. Given the same levels of encoding (acquisition), attributable to the equal number of S trials, both study-test and anticipation conditions were influenced to exactly the same degree by test trial potentiating effects, thus, performance levels were alike.

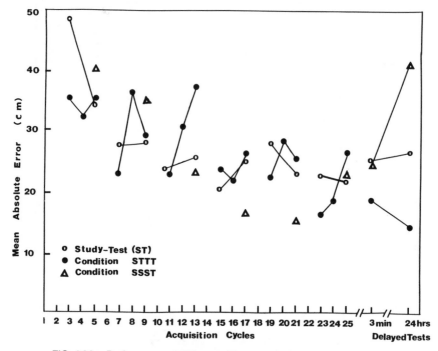

FIG. 8.36. Performances within repetitive pattern (4-cycle unit) and long-term retention (delayed tests) of the three study(S)-and-test(T) sequence conditions in Euclidean distance learning, Experiment 8.

These outcomes derived from the test trial potentiating model are in fact reflected in our data.

It is not a coincidence that the same set of data supported the two models under examination. It testifies to their internal consistency and derivative history: The identity model is the logical progeny of the test trial potentiating model; it incorporated all the latter's assumptions. Empirical verifications of such logic are always reassuring.

Figure 8.36 illustrates performance under each S-and-T sequence condition plotted as a function of the cycle, the total time, irrespective of the numbers of S and T trials experienced. To scrutinize both learning and retention processes occurring during the acquisition period from another perspective, we connected only data points within each four-cycle repetitive pattern, the smallest repetitive unit *common* to all three S-T conditions. If all the positive effects on performance had occurred uniquely on the S trial with no positive contribution from the T trial at all, Condition SSST should have been the best, followed by Condition TS (Anticipation), which differed little from Condition ST (Study-Test) and STTT in this order. This, however, proved not to be the case.

First, let us compare Conditions ST (Study-Test) and SSST with respect to each T that was common to both conditions: There were no significant differences between these two conditions, $F(2, 27) = .33$, $p < 0.20$, in spite of the fact that Condition SSST had 50% more S opportunities than Condition STST (study-test method). The results make better sense, if we grant that the positive effects on performance are not limited to the encoding processes of correct item (distance) information on the S trial and that the positive effects include those from retrieval processes occurring on the T trial.

After all, the correct response (exclusive of a lucky guess) is the joint product of successful encoding on S trials, successful storage during the retention interval, and successful retrieval on T trials (cf. Izawa, 1969). Any failure of one, or more, of these processes leads to the failure of the production of the correct response. Then, the relative strength of Condition STST as compared to Condition SSST is understandable, as the former enjoyed 50% more T (retrieval practice) trials than the latter, although the opposite held for S trials. A lack of differences between these two conditions may imply that the positive effects of Ts were almost as strong as those of S trials.

Let us pursue this point further. If, indeed, the positive effects on performance of T trials (retrieval practice) were equally as strong as those of S trials (encoding practice), suggested earlier from the Condition ST versus SSST comparison, we would expect little performance differences between Conditions SSST and STTT. Evaluated on the basis of each repetitive pattern of four cycles (Fig. 8.33, Cycles 5, 9, 13, . . . , and 25) our expectation seems borne out. There were no significant differences between these two conditions, or among all of the three S-T conditions including the ST (study-test) sequence. However, conditions interacted significantly with trials (stage of the acquisition period): An ANOVA based on the three S-T conditions revealed the interactions to be reliable at p of 0.01, $F(10, 135) = 2.60$.

Comparing Condition SSST versus ST seems to indicate that the test trial potentiating effect on the T trial appears as effective as the encoding effect on the S trial. That, however, was not the whole story; much more was involved. (See Fig. 8.36.) During the acquisition phase, performances over the three successive Ts within repetitive pattern of Condition STTT varied radically, but in general, errors increased substantially. Such error increments over consecutive tests did occur in other learning situations such as Duffy et al. (1975) and Hagman (1983). In case of verbal studies, however, results are mixed: Although similar increases in error were observed by Bregman and Wiener (1970), this was seldom the case with Izawa's paired-association learning situations (1966, 1967a, 1967b, 1968, 1969, 1970a, 1970b, 1971b, 1976, 1989 in press).

In motor learning of distance, the large increment in error over repetitive tests is in sharp contrast to the hypermnesia, performance improvements observed in pictorial or verbal materials in free (or forced) recall situations discussed by Roediger and Challis (Chap. 7 in this volume). They gave subjects much more time for response productions in an unrestricted order in which only one study opportunity was administered. The two learning situations might have differed too extensively in fundamental cognitive processes to be comparable. For one, the latter situation involved retrieval from preexperimentally acquired, long-term semantic memory. The former (motor learning) deals with episodic memory, newly learned behavior acquired for the first time in the controlled setting of a laboratory. These opposite effects of repetitive tests would seem to direct our attention to much needed future research.

For the moment, let us limit discussion to multi-trial motor and verbal paired-associate learning situations. Even here, a highly varied performance over the successive Ts per repetitive pattern, with no intervening S in motor learning, was observed as in previous findings (e.g., Hagman, 1983); these differ greatly from the remarkably stable performances on successive Ts in paired-associate learning situations. Izawa consistently demonstrated this in scores of studies. Such a contrasting difference may, in part, have come from the fact that subjective distinction between the correct and incorrect responses may not be as salient in Euclidean distance or location learning via the kinesthetic arm movement, as it is in verbal paired-associate learning. Say for example, one deviates 3 cm (error) from the correct response of a 15 cm Euclidean distance (length) on a T trial in motor learning. For a blindfolded subject, the degree of that error may not be as clear-cut in haptic learning, as it would be in verbal tasks.

This inherent ambiguity, coupled with the absence of feedback from the experimenter on consecutive Ts, may cause the subject to vacillate in his judgments about the correct lengths. Such active kinesthetic explorations may produce greater encoding power on the subsequent S trial, resulting in the powerful test trial potentiating effects demonstrated in Fig. 8.35.

The most intriguing positive effects of test trials were demonstrated by their long-term retention manifested in the delayed tests. See Fig. 8.36. There were no significant differences among the three S-and-T conditions as a unit, at the end of the acquisition period, and no significant retention loss occurred over the 3 minute retention interval. This is primarily due to the fact that three drastically different response patterns occurred from the end of the acquisition phase to the first delayed test, two conditions (ST and SSST) led to diminished performances, one (ST) lost significantly and the remaining condition (STTT) gained significantly. The overall end product of these retention phenomena represents an averaging out of responses over the 3 minute intervals; thus, the lack of significant across the board change.

Yet, when the two delayed tests were considered jointly, both differences among the three S-T conditions and interactions between conditions and delayed tests were highly significant, each $p < 0.001$. Most dramatic of all were the differences between Conditions SSST and STTT, $F(1, 18) = 34.1$, $p < 0.0001$. These outcomes can be attributed to extraordinarily large differences among three conditions on the second delayed test, given 24 hours following the acquisition phase: Condition STTT being the best (lowest in error) followed by Conditions ST and SSST in this order, again lined up neatly in accordance with the density of the test trials in the conditions.

Most noteworthy is the pattern the three S-and-T sequence conditions displayed with long-term retention processes that occurred from the first to the second delayed test, following the acquisition period, administered at 3 min and 24 hours respectively. Condition ST (study-test) resulted in significant retention loss over the 3 minute retention interval (until the first delayed test), but no further loss occurred, as measured 24 hours later. In the case of Condition SSST, which was benefitted by having the greatest number of learning (study, S) opportunities, no tangible forgetting occurred on relatively short-term bases such as the 3 min retention interval (Delayed Test 1). Yet the same SSST condition incurred a spectacular loss in the 24 hour retention interval following the training session, as seen in the far right entry of Fig. 8.36. It is quite ironic that the group that was provided with the most study opportunities exhibited the poorest long-term retention by far.

In glaring contrast, Condition STTT with the fewest opportunities for studying produced *improved* its performance on every delayed test. The STTT condition, which made for the poorest performance numerically (though insignificantly) at the end of the acquisition period, gained significantly over the 3 minute retention interval, and added further to its phenomenal gain during the 24 hour retention interval! This highly unusual phenomenon, an improvement in long-term retention, occurred in the condition with repetitive T trials without any intervening S trial within the four-cycle repetitive pattern; both Conditions ST and SSST, with two and three times more S trials, respectively, suffered from substantial long-term retention losses during either short or long delayed test intervals.

In addition to the test trial potentiating effect demonstrated during the acquisition period, the remarkable positive effect of unreinforced tests is in its impressive strength in long-term memory, (i.e., the long-term prevention of forgetting). When this capacity for long-term (24 hour) retention under Condition STTT is compared with the phenomenal loss under Condition SSST with the same delay, we come to appreciate the astounding differences in the processes occurring between S and T trials in motor learning. Notice also that such differences were detected only in the retention phase: When examined in the context of all cycles (total time), S and T trials appeared very similar in their positive effects on performance during the acquisition phase.

This intriguing long-term prophylactic effect against forgetting by the repetitive tests, as observed in Experiment 8, is not an isolated incident. It is replicable: Hagman observed the phenomenon also, along with other aspects of our major findings (also cf. Eysenck & Frith, 1977).

It may be tempting to attribute both test trial potentiating and long-term forgetting prophylaxis to the spacing between S trials. This interpretation, however, is not supported by either motor learning studies (Hagman, 1983,

Experiment 3) or verbal learning experiments (Izawa, 1967, 1971a, 1971b). The issue was specifically addressed by Izawa (1971a) in accounting for the spaced practice effects from the test trial potentiating model. Thus, in respect to motor learning, the test trial potentiating model appears to be the only one that accounts for both the potentiating and prophylactic effects found in one set of assumptions underlying this one model (for references of other models, see Izawa, 1989).

EXPERIMENT 9

By way of definition, Euclidean locations differ distinctly from Euclidean distances in the sense that the former are fixed at specific positions in real space, whereas the latter are not. In the laboratory setting, a Euclidean location is defined in terms of the movement stopping position, whereas a Euclidean distance refers to extent of movement independent of position in space. How does this difference impact our cognitive motor system? Are there similarities between the encoding of locations and that of distances?

We note, in this context, some instances in which unfilled and filled (interference producing) retention intervals have differential effects respectively on distance and location learning (e.g., Laabs, 1973). Because the retention interval is the major concern of our chapter throughout, it is imperative to investigate differences between anticipation and study-test methods in the domain of location learning, to examine in what ways the methods employed to present stimulus item information control the learning of location and distance. Do these effects differ for learning distance (Experiment 8) as compared to location (Experiment 9)?

On the other hand, both distance and location learning share numerous common characteristics prevalent in motor skill learning phenomena. In view of the alarming paucity of studies in this field, Experiment 9 was conducted on location learning, using the same design employed in Experiment 8 for distance learning; see Fig. 8.33.

We introduced an innovation. Unlike common location learning wherein a one-dimensional location is learned using only one hand (e.g., Hagman, 1983; Laabs, 1973), our subjects must coordinate the use of both hands in learning 4 two-dimensional Euclidean locations, on a standard architectural drawing board of 60.96×127 cm. Although this innovation necessarily induced complexity in both data analyses and interpretation, it is essential that the totality of the cognitive system be understood. This is necessary, in particular for purposes of application to, for example, industrial settings that require the use of both hands to optimize production. The four locations, identified as V, M. R, and J, are shown in Fig. 8.37. These are depicted for the Experimenter on the drawing board and constitute the targets blindfolded subjects seek to "hit."

Schematically presented, a "parallel bar" (shaded) used for architectural drawing shown in its lowest position in Fig. 8.37 allows vertical movements. A 30/60 right triangle (shown likewise, 14.4×25.4 cm) permits horizontal movements along the parallel bar with a total target area of 35.72 × 121.29 cm. Subjects place their left hand on a defined grip along the parallel bar slide, as the right hand is placed on a grip attached to the 30/60 right triangle. The apex of the triangle was pointed to the target. The left hand moved the parallel bar in coordination with the right hand that keeps the base of the 30/60 right triangle flush against the parallel bar.

For Experiment 9 (Fig. 8.33), another set of 40 right-handed students from the same subject pool at Tulane participated, 10 per condition. There were three starting points in Experiment 9: the center point (designated as 0, at the center, bottom edge of the drawing board Fig. 8.37), and two points, 30 cm to the left and right respectively (shown as − 30 cm and + 30 cm). One of them was selected randomly, from cycle to cycle, with the restriction that all starting points were used equally often both during the experiment's acquisition phase and during delayed test phase. All four locations, J, M, R, and V, were presented on each S or T trial in randomized order from cycle to cycle, as shown in Fig. 8.33. The four locations were presented one after another without returning to the starting point on each cycle. The sliding bar for each hand had separate grips for both experimenter and subject, so that the subject was guided without being touched during S trials. Five seconds were allowed for the execution of each movement per item. The intercycle interval was 10 seconds. All other procedures were the same as in Experiment 8. As the respective slide bars were manipulated, the subject was blindfolded and exposed to white noise in order to prevent the intrusion by both visual and acoustic cues.

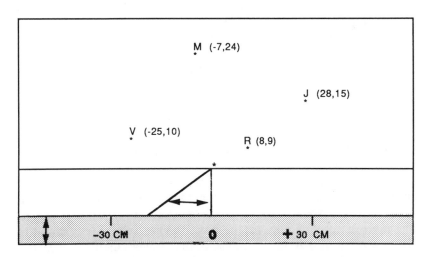

FIG. 8.37. The space and four locations utilized in the learning of two-dimensional Euclidean locations, Experiment 9.

Anticipation and Study-Test Methods Differ Little in the Learning of Euclidean Locations

Our ambition to investigate location learning from an innovative but complex perspective generated a problem concerning the response measure. A two-dimensional location, produced by two hands, necessarily involve deviations from the target in two dimensions: the horizontal one by the right hand, and the vertical one by the left hand. Consider also that there is more than sufficient evidence for heuristics for encoding pattern information through touch or movements (e.g., Book & Garling, 1981; Kosslyn, Pick, & Fariello, 1974; Lederman, Klatzky, & Barber, 1985; Rieser, Lockman, & Pick, 1980; Sherman, Croxton, & Smith, 1979). Experimental findings seem to indicate that the subjects use implicit spatial axes rather than a movement based heuristics in judging positions or locations. Some of the natural spatial axes seem to be horizontal and vertical axes (cf. Lederman, Klatzky, & Barber, 1985; Tversky, 1981). It appears, then, that consideration of vertical and horizontal deviations may have merits, keeping firmly in mind, however, that previous studies utilized either one finger, one hand, or one arm only, seldom requiring both hands concurrently to learn movement related responses, if ever.

See Fig. 8.38 to illustrate this procedure for a hypothetical target location L at Point (1, 1) and the subject's response L ' at Coordinate (3, 2.5). In this case, the response deviated from the target by + 2 cm on the horizontal and + 1.5 cm in the vertical dimension. The horizontal and vertical target-deviations (errors), however, are bound to give very different pictures. See the two upper panels of Fig. 8.39 drawn to illustrate this point for our four locations learned in Experiment 9.

Which of the two error measures best represents the two dimensional deviation from targets? Unlike previous studies, in this novel situation involving both hands a combined horizontal (the right hand maneuver) – vertical (the left hand maneuver) deviation appears to express the true extent of effort made by Response L ' for Target L, although there was no denial to the fact that each hand did contribute to the deviation in producing the response. Moreover, decomposing the response into two independent elements may not give us an accurate picture, may it be singly, or as a total sum of the two. The critical characteristics of the combined product of the response, made by coordinating both hands, does not seem to be adequately expressed.

See Fig. 8.38 for our hypothetical example. The combined contribution of both hands may be expressed by the shortest distance between the response location and the target: the length of the straight line between Points L and L' (the diagonal), 2.5 cm. We will analyze our data in terms of this measure because it makes better sense logically than the three measures we previously considered: horizontal or vertical deviations alone, or the summation of the two.

In dealing with deviations from the shortest straight line (errors) between the start (Response L') and Target L, we will not consider the direction of

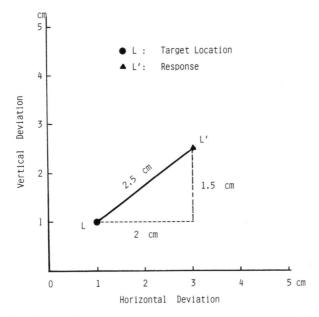

FIG. 8.38.   An illustration of error measures for two dimensional location responses.

deviations for two reasons. First, because we define locations by two dimensional coordinates and because the direction of a deviation is immaterial to our study. Although assignments of positive (+) or negative (−) deviations may be possible for the diagonal distance, the simple dichotomy of + or − either horizontally or vertically do not do justice for the same reason stated above. To divide the space into quarters by moving the origin to the target position, L, which may be labeled as + + , + − , − − and − + (in clockwise following the conventional two dimensional expression for the X- and Y- axes) would simply invite unnecessary complexity relative to what can be gained newly to our knowledge. Second, even if a fair dichotomy of + and − deviations could be found, the usage of such a measure is likely to overestimate subjects' response accuracy, because overshooting (+) deviations will be cancelled out by undershooting (−) deviations. Therefore, we will analyze our data with respect to the absolute deviations from the shortest distance between the target and the start, and refer to it simply as the *absolute error*.

When we examined our four locations in terms of total absolute deviations, the results produced are shown in the bottom panel of Fig. 8.39. As a matter of course, the picture of the absolute deviation measure, as defined above, is quite different from errors defined by either vertical or horizontal deviations, shown in the upper panels of Fig. 8.39.

Yet, error rates for the four individual locations in our set (analogous to individual pairs in verbal list) differed significantly, $ps < 0.01$, in accordance

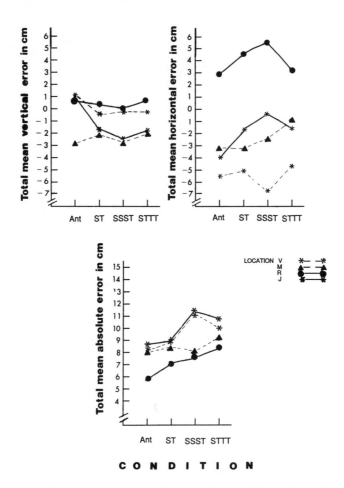

FIG. 8.39. Individual location differences demonstrable in terms of three error measures: vertical, horizontal, or absolute errors (see text for definitions), Experiment 9.

with the well known fact that individual target location differences are likely to be great (cf. Hagman, 1983). Another common characteristic was that none of the response measures in Fig. 8.39 showed reliable differences among the conditions, the major concern in Experiment 9. The curves stay nearly flat, with minor crossings. Differences in target locations did not influence error differences among conditions irrespective of error measure. The only other significance was location × trials: Early in the acquisition phase location differences were greater, but they diminished significantly toward the end.

It is of interest to note in Fig. 8.39 that (signed) response location differences were greatest when horizontal errors alone were considered (Fig. 8.39, upper right), whereas differences were smallest with absolute errors, closely followed by vertical errors. The motions that involve either hand traversing the body tended to underestimate, that is, fall short of the target (cf. Laabs, 1973). In the present study in every condition, Location V, which involved the most extensive crossing of the body by the right hand, gave rise to the greatest negative horizontal errors. In contrast, movements that do not involve crossing the body with either hand, tended to overshoot targets (cf. Laabs, 1973); Location R produced the most of these horizontal errors by overestimation of distance.

Overall, we also observed that simple vertical (up-down) movements tended to be easier to learn; Locations R and V, requiring the shortest vertical movement, display less overall vertical error than do other locations. One aspect of this finding is that the vertical locations closest to the subject seemed inherently less variable, because of that proximity and because the bounds were defined by the external dimensions of the board itself. The greater accuracy for vertical dimension may, in part, have stemmed from the fact that this operation did not require crossing the body. Only further investigations can determinate the relationships, if any, among errors, positions of targets on the board, and position relative to subject's body.

Although Hagman (1983) obtained basically the same results for both distance (Experiment 1) and location (Experiment 2) learning, Laabs (1973) obtained different results for these two types of motor learning. Experiment 9 differs from previous studies in which the subject used either preferred right hand or right arm to learn a single location. Our subjects were required to use both hands to learn and move among a set of 4 two-dimensional Euclidean locations.

Figure 8.40 gives data in terms of mean unsigned absolute errors (as defined earlier) for the four locations learned under anticipation and study-test methods. Overall, performance differences under the two methods varied little, $F(1, 18) = 0.58$. No significant differences were obtained for any of the following: (a) the acquisition period, (b) in long-term memory (two delayed tests considered jointly or separately), and (c) in retention loss between acquisition and any of the delayed tests.

A lack of performance differences between anticipation and study-test methods, although consistent with expectations raised by the identity model, does not accord with predictions from alternative models. This state of affairs in two-dimensional Euclidean location learning (both hands) seen here is similar to the data for one-dimensional (i.e., movement in one direction only) Euclidean distance learning (one hand) in previous Experiment 8.

As far as the study-test and anticipation methods are concerned, the only difference we observed between Experiments 8 and 9 was limited to the retention loss that occurred from the end of the acquisition period and the first delayed test given 3 minutes later. The retention loss was significant in distance learning, but not so in location learning. However, this was not directly relevant to the identity model that addresses only performance differences be-

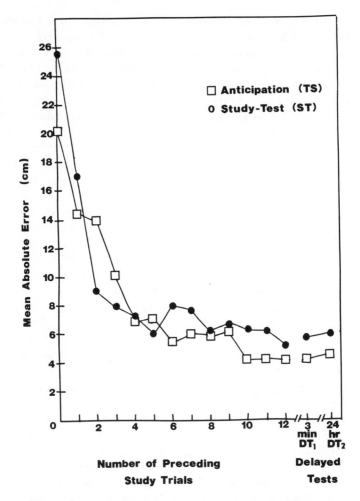

FIG. 8.40.   Comparisons of study-test and anticipation methods in both acquisition phase and long-term retention phase (delayed tests) in the learning of two-dimensional Euclidean locations, Experiment 9.

tween the anticipation and study-test methods. The two methods in question differed little, either during the acquisition period based on relatively short-term memory, or during the retention phase based on long-term memory on delayed tests. Nonsignificant outcomes in each of these phases align well with identity model expectations. Whether the forgetting between these two phases (acquisition and retention) is large (for distance learning), or small (for location learning), the extent of forgetting did not differ from one method to the other. Thus, the identity model is not challenged by these data.

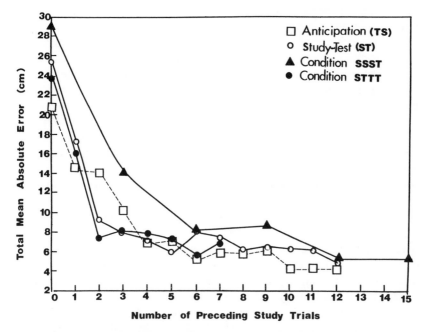

FIG. 8.41.   Performance comparisons of all four conditions (anticipation or TS, standard study-test or ST, SSST, and STTT) as a function of preceding study (S) trials in Euclidean location learning, Experiment 9.

Effects of Tests on Motor Learning of Euclidean Locations

In order to examine test trial potentiating effects on location learning in Experiment 9, Fig. 8.41 was prepared as a function of preceding S (study) trials for all four conditions: the anticipation (TS) condition plus three S-and-T conditions (ST, SSST, and STTT). Just as in the Euclidean distance learning situation in Experiment 8, the Euclidean location learning situation in Experiment 9 also produced large differences among conditions. The condition with most S trials (SSST) had the highest in error rate, followed by both study-test (ST) and anticipation (TS) conditions, and then by Condition STTT. However, this demonstration of test trial potentiating effects was observed very early in the acquisition phase for the current two-dimensional location learning (two-handed).

Early in learning, within the first one-third of the acquisition phase, virtually all conditions hit the floor or the plateau, and no improvement was brought about for the remaining two-thirds of the acquisition period; all curves stay flat. For this reason, overall differences among the conditions were statistically nonsignificant, although Condition SSST with the fewest Ts and most Ss was consistently highest in error; that trend was predictable from the test trial potentiating model.

The floor effect apparent here may be attributable to the development of some subjective stereotyped notion of the location, or the limit beyond which no improvement was achievable. It is worth noting that the magnitude of deviations in the absolute sense at the end of the acquisition period was in the order of 4-5 cm in the current location learning, whereas deviation for distance learning in Experiment 8 was far greater, 15 cm or more. In addition to qualitative and quantitative differences in cognitive motor encoding systems between location and distance learning, special circumstances generated by our current study must be considered: It is possible that the two-handed encoding of locations may have generated a greater amount of total information about the environment than one-dimensional distances encoded with one hand, and thus produced more accuracy (smaller deviations) in Experiment 9 than in Experiment 8.

Even the undeniable floor effect on error levels in Experiment 9, involving Euclidean location learning, could not entirely mask the test trial potentiating effect. When our analyses were limited to Conditions SSST and STTT, the former was consistently and reliably higher in target deviations than the latter, and the two curves never came close enough to cross each other: examined by tests following S_3 and S_6, the conditions differed significantly: $F(1, 18) = 4.54$, $p < 0.05$.

Figure 8.42 illustrates how learning or short-term forgetting took place within and between repetitive four-cycle patterns of S and T trials for Conditions ST, SSST, and STTT. Of particular interest are performances of successive Ts within the STTT pattern: No significant retention loss occurred in two-dimensional location learning. The virtually horizontal performance graph within these repetitive Ts with no intervening S resemble closely the verbal paired-associate learning situations discussed by Izawa (1966, 1967a, 1967b, 1968, 1969, 1970a, 1970b, 1971b, 1976, 1989), but is in sharp contrast to our distance learning data (Fig. 8.36) and Hagman's (1983) findings. In both of the latter cases, large retention losses were observed.

Only future investigations can tell whether this inconsistency may be attributed to radically different types of location learning (Hagman's Experiment 2 used a one-dimensional location via one hand, whereas Experiment 9 used 4 two-dimensional locations via both hands), or whether our current floor effect during the latter two-thirds of the acquisition period may have masked the otherwise demonstrable phenomena.

It is of considerable interest that performance on the delayed test in the three S-and-T sequence conditions show no significant forgetting during the 3 minute delay, or the 24 hour retention interval. It is remarkable that memory for Euclidean locations was impressively stable for as long as one full day when two-handed learning was involved. Similarly, it is noteworthy that there

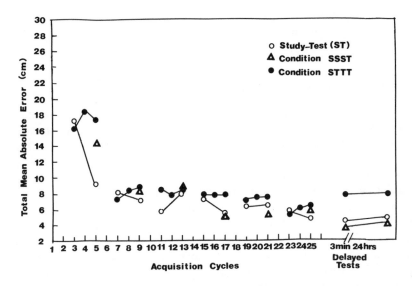

FIG. 8.42. Performances within repetitive pattern (4 cycle-unit) and long-term retention (delayed tests) of the three study(S)-and-test(T) sequence conditions in Euclidean location learning, Experiment 9.

were no statistical differences among the conditions for retention data (Fig. 8.42) in Experiment 9.

Both of these aspects are in sharp contrast with Experiment 8 (Fig. 8.36) and Hagman (1983, Fig. 2 and 3), where large and highly intriguing differences and retention losses occurred among the conditions, when either a one-dimensional distance or a location was learned, using one hand only. In these latter studies, the condition tested most often (STTT and STTTTT) demonstrated the poorest scores at the end of their respective acquisition periods, but showed the best results (lowest in error) for long-term memory (24 hour delayed test). Typically in these studies, staggering memory losses occurred during the 24 hour period that allowed for most frequent study (SSST or SSSSST).

However, significant improvement over a 24 hour retention interval was dramatically demonstrated with the learning of Euclidean distances in our Experiment 8 and Hagman's Experiment 1. But neither Hagman's Experiment 2, nor our Experiment 9 produced such improvements when Euclidean locations were to be learned. Performance stayed the same; neither forgetting nor improvements were observed at the end of the 24 hour retention interval.

CONCLUDING REMARKS

We attempted to assess the generality of both the test trial potentiating model (Izawa, 1971b) and the identity model (Izawa, 1985a) in the relatively less cultivated (i.e., underinvestigated) field of motor learning. The tasks involved acquisition of Euclidean distances (Experiment 8) and locations (Experiment 9), via the tactile sensory modality.

The Test Trial Potentiating Model

Unreinforced (not accompanied by immediate feedback) test trials were found to have two distinct, separable empirical functions in verbal learning earlier (Izawa, 1966, 1967a, 1967b, 1968, 1969, 1970a, 1970b, 1971b, 1976, 1989): a) test (T) trials potentiate subsequent study (S) trials by increasing the latter's encoding power, and (b) T trials prevent forgetting. Both the test trial potentiating effect and forgetting-prevention effect were demonstrated very clearly in Experiment 8 where one-dimensional Euclidean distances were learned one-handed as well as by Hagman (1983). These effects were less conspicuous in Experiment 9, the two-handed learning of two-dimensional Euclidean locations primarily because of the apparent floor effect that was manifested very early in the acquisition period. Thus, the positive effects of the test were clearly demonstrated with the tactile and kinesthetic learning of movements.

What is most remarkable is the benefit of the test trials for long-term memory retrieval under the 24 hour delayed test (cf. also Estes, 1979). The conditions with repetitive tests, Conditions STTT and STTTTT (respectively ours and Hagman's) completely prevented long term forgetting for both the 3 minute delayed test and the 24 hour delayed test, whereas other conditions with more S trials (also cf. ST, SSSSST; Hagman, 1983, Fig. 3) were heir to substantial forgetting over 1 day for the learning of locations. Furthermore, in the case of one-dimensional distance learning, Conditions STTT and STTTTT produced significant performance improvements. With other conditions, memory deteriorated overnight in glaring contrast to the remarkable improvements produced by Conditions STTT and STTTTT (see our Fig. 8.36 and Hagman's Fig. 1).

The above phenomenon, the improvement in long-term memory performance, may even require a more positive term than the prevention-of-forgetting effect, used previously. The prevention-of-forgetting effect implies that performance levels stayed the same, or at least no significant performance decrement occurred. It does not seem to suggest any positive increments to raise performance above earlier tests, especially from the end of the acquisition period. Apparently, repetitive tests do have an underlying capacity to facilitate recovery of whatever was lost subsequent to the last study trial. This recovery of long-term memory may be referred to as the long-term memory (LTM) retrieval-facilitation effect.

There were previous observations suggestive of the LTM retrieval-facilitation effect in verbal learning (e.g., Izawa, 1968); she administered two delayed tests; conditions involving repetitive tests invariably improved performance from

Delayed T_1 to Delayed T_2 (Izawa's Fig. 1 and 2, 1968). However, in the latter situations, two delayed tests were given one immediately after the other. Considering both the findings in verbal learning and the present results from motor learning, it is not clear whether the improvements on Delayed T_2 were small, because it was too close to Delayed T_1, or because one type of learning was linguistic whereas the other was kinesthetic. Similarly, it is mandatory to determine in which domain or types of learning materials the LTM retrieval-facilitation effect of tests is demonstrable. What about the extent of the delayed test retention interval? We seem to have a long list of future research agenda to identify different variables contributing to the long-term memory (LTM) retrieval-facilitation effects of the test, inclusive of the above.

So far, we have identified the positive effects of tests as (a) the potentiating effect, (b) the prevention-of-forgetting effect, and (c) the LTM retrieval-facilitation effect. These, however, must be accompanied by an assessment of their implications for theory. Qualitatively, the beneficial effects of the tests may come from the processes, uniquely involved in the active, subject-defined, self-generating response — in this case deciding when and where to stop movement (cf. Izawa, 1971b; Kelso, 1977; Summers, Levey, & Wrigley, 1981). These processes may not be present (or minimal at best) on the study (S) trial. If correct, the more such experiences on the repetitive tests, the better for the development of motor schemata for motor learning and verbal schemata for verbal learning.

In further pursuing the reasons for beneficial test effects, comparisons of the two experiments just described may be highly instructive; in particular, performance on successive Ts, within the four-cycle repetitive pattern unit and the LTM retrieval-facilitation effect. In Experiment 8 (distance learning), there were large overall performance decrements for three successive Ts within the four-cycle repetitive pattern unit in Condition STTT. Yet, the condition enjoyed the significant LTM retrieval-facilitation effect on delayed tests. Performance on the first delayed test was significantly better than the last test at the end of the acquisition period. We saw not only the absence of forgetting, which is usually true immediately after the acquisition period, but also the impressive *improvement* in LTM recall performance. Furthermore, between Delayed T_1 and Delayed T_2, yet another significant LTM *retention-enhancement* took place over a full day retention interval! Altogether during the 24 hour period from the end of the acquisition period to the second delayed test, a tremendous amount of retrieval-facilitation took place *without* any intervening study (S) trial whatsoever! This set of findings is not isolated. The same phenomena were observed by Hagman (1983, Experiment 1) as well.

However, no such LTM retrieval-facilitation effect was observed in Experiment 9, where two-handed learning of two-dimensional locations took place. Coincidentally, little forgetting took place over the three successive Ts within STTT, four-cycle repetitive unit. Conceivably, there could be a relationship between the short-term forgetting over the successive Ts and the long-term memory retrieval-facilitation effect. The greater short-term forgetting during the acquisition phase, the greater the LTM retrieval-facilitation during the retention phase.

This seemingly contradictory relationship is very difficult to deal with, given extant theoretical approaches. The only exception seems to be the approach derived from the Estes' stimulus sampling model (1955), from which both the test trial potentiating model and the identity model were developed. That is, the greater the performance loss on a short-term basis between S trials during the acquisition period, the more new encoding (conditioning) of new learning occurs on the subsequent S trial (on which new learning takes place exclusively, Izawa, 1969), thus the greater gross total acquisition. Therefore, over the delayed test retention interval, more of the conditioned (encoded) elements move to the available set to be sampled during the delayed tests, aided by the subjective maximization processes taking place during the delayed T trial per se (cf. Izawa, 1971b, 1989).

By contrast, beneficial effects of tests were minimal in Condition SSST. In general, the longer the retention interval, the greater the performance loss. The opposite is true of the LTM retrieval-facilitation effect observed in Condition STTT of the present experimental design where repetitive Ts were involved. Compilation of data from much better controlled conditions seems an acute requirement to advance theory.

Phenomenally, the LTM retrieval-facilitation effect, or the increment in performance on delayed Ts resembles the increased performance over successive Ts or hypermnesia with pictorial material (cf. Roediger & Challis, Chap. 7 in this volume). It is a worthwhile challenge to explore possible linkages between the two. Speaking of the pictorial materials, we are currently completing a study with such materials, to evaluate the effects of tests, from our vantage point. Preliminary examinations of data suggest support for the test trial potentiating model here also.

The Identity Model

Performance differences between anticipation and study-test methods are accounted for by short-term memory (STM) processes occurring in the inherently different retention intervals, under the whole list design (cf. Fig. 8.1), whereas basic events specified in Matrices S, T, r_I, r_S, r_T (Equations 3-7) are assumed to be identical for the two methods. Such short-term memory processes that may differentially control performance during the acquisition period may lead to either (a) a large advantage for the study-test method that enjoys the shorter mean S-T interval, or (b) small differences between the two methods on the basis of a very few critical items in STM falling into nonoverlap areas due to either many critical items belonging to the overlap area, not sufficient critical items being generated, or not remaining in STM if generated (Izawa, 1983, 1985b).

In the delayed test situations, however, it is safe to assume that performances are primarily based on the long-term memory components. If so, the identity model predicts small performance differences between anticipation and study-test procedures for the presentation of item information.

In the present experiments with motor learning of Euclidean distances (Experiment 8) and locations (Experiment 9), the whole list design (Fig. 8.1) was employed. Throughout both experiments, anticipation and study-test methods did not differ significantly during any of the acquisition phases, supporting the second prediction of the identity model for data greatly involved with short-term memory components. Similarly, again in support of the identity model, the performance levels for the delayed tests based on predominantly long-term memory components were very similar for both methods.

Intuitively, it seemed axiomatic that the benefits of immediate feedback with the anticipation method could be appreciable for kinesthetic information processing in learning distances and locations. However, the expected superiority of the anticipation method never materialized.

In a similar vein, similarity of results from the two methods did not support either the differential task model (Battig & Brackett, 1961) or the differential acquisition model (Kanak & Neuner, 1970); these predicted significantly superior performances with the study-test method.

From the standpoint of the encoding model (Barch & Levine, 1967), examined in Part 2, we must introduce the factor of difficulty. In a sense, Experiment 8 could be viewed as being easier for learners than Experiment 9, because the former involved only one-dimensional (horizontal) distance learning whereas the latter involved two-handed and two-dimensional location learning. If correct, Experiment 9 should provide a basis for superior performance for the anticipation method, whereas Experiment 8 should result in better performance for the study-test method. However, neither occurred.

Nonetheless, two-handed, two-dimensional location learning (Experiment 9) might in fact be easier; in some ways, the environment might provide more information concerning the attributes (horizontal and vertical locations) for an accurate response. The respective performance levels at the end of the acquisition period seem to be consonant with such a position. If correct, the encoding model would expect the superiority of the study-test method in Experiment 9, and the anticipation method to be more advantageous in Experiment 8, which could be considered as more difficult. These expectations, however, were not born out either. Thus, the nonsignificant performance differences within both Experiments 8 and 9 do not seem to support any of our alternatives; they support the identity model only.

In addition, our laboratory is currently in the process of compiling data from studies with pictorial materials to examine possible differences between study-test and anticipation methods. Preliminary analyses suggest outcomes favorable to the identity model.

In summary, Parts 1, 2, and 3 considered the identity model in terms of visual, auditory, and kinesthetic information processing systems respectively, and explored a large variety of learning materials including natural and artificial languages (linguistic materials inclusive of nonsense syllables and numbers), nonverbal materials such as Morse Code signals, Euclidean distances, and locations. The identity model holds up very well for all of the aforementioned situations; in addition it is entirely possible, perhaps likely, that it will also account for the learning of pictorial materials (preliminary analyses from ongoing investigations lend credence to that surmise).

Very detailed qualitative analyses under the sublist manipulation procedures, revealed that the model's failure rate, considering present, past, and unpublished studies, is cumulatively less than 5% or thereabouts under visual information processing (Part 1), whereas 0% deviation incurred, respectively, under auditory (Part 2) and tactile (Part 3) information processing; not a bad record at all in this genre of empirical science. Similarly, very conservative quantitative examinations of the identity model under a highly restrictive parameter estimation procedure also support the basic soundness of the identity model.

PART 3 REFERENCES

Adams, J. A. (1983). On the integration of the verbal and motor domains. In R. A. Magill (Ed.), *Memory and control of action* (pp. 3–15). Amsterdam: North-Holland.

Adams, J. A., & Dijkstra, S. (1966). Short-term memory for motor responses. *Journal of Experimental Psychology, 71*, 314–318.

Ammons, C. H. (1960). Temporary and permanent inhibitory effects associated with acquisition of a simple perceptual-motor skill. *Journal of General Psychology, 62*, 223–245.

Ammons, R. B., Farr, R. G., Block, E., Neumann, E., Dey, M., Marion, R., & Ammons, C. H. (1958). Long-term retention of perceptual-motor skills, *Journal of Experimental Psychology, 55*, 318–328.

Barch, A. M., & Levine, J. R. (1967). Presentation method in auditory identification learning. *Journal of Verbal Learning and Verbal Behavior, 6*, 282–288.

Battig, W. F., & Brackett, H. R. (1961). Comparison of anticipation and recall methods in paired-associate learning. *Psychological Reports, 9*, 59–65.

Book, A., & Garling, T. (1981). Maintenance of orientation during locomotion in unfamiliar environments. *Journal of Experimental Psychology: Human Perception and Performance, 7*, 902–915.

Bregman, A. S., & Wiener, J.R. (1970). Effects of test trials in paired-associate and free-recall learning. *Journal of Verbal Learning and Verbal Behavior, 9*, 689–698.

Conrad, R. (1964). Acoustic confusions in immediate memory. *British Journal of Psychology, 55*, 75–84.

Craft, J. L., & Hinrichs, J. V. (1971). Short-term retention of simple motor response: Similarity of prior and succeeding response. *Journal of Experimental Psychology, 87*, 297–302.

Duffy, T. M., Montague, W. E., Labbs, G. J., & Hillix, W. A. (1975). The effect of overt rehearsal on motor short-term memory. *Journal of Motor Behavior, 7*, 59–63.

Easton, R. D., & Moran, P. W. (1978). A quantitative confirmation of visual capture of curvature. *Journal of General Psychology, 98*, 105–112.

Estes, W. K. (1955). Statistical theory of spontaneous recovery and regression. *Psychological Review, 62*, 145–154.

Estes, W. K. (1979). Role of response availability in the effects of cued-recall tests on memory. *Journal of Experimental Psychology: Human Learning and Memory, 5*, 567–573.

Eysenck, H. J., & Frith, C. D. (1977). *Reminiscence, motivation and personality*. New York: Plenum.

Fishkin, S., Pishkin, V., & Stahl, M. (1975). Factors involved in visual capture. *Perceptual and Motor Skills, 40*, 427–434.

Fleishman, E. A., & Parker, J. F., Jr. (1962). Factors in the retention and relearning of perceptual-motor skills. *Journal of Experimental Psychology, 64*, 215–226.

Freides, D. (1974). Human information processing and sensory modality: Cross-modal functions, information complexity, memory and deficit. *Psychological Bulletin, 81*, 284–310.

Gibson, J. J. (1933). Adaptation, after-effect and contrast in the perception of curved lines. *Journal of Experimental Psychology, 16*, 1–31.

Gollin, E. S. (1960). Developmental studies of visual recognition of incomplete objects. *Perceptual Motor Skills, 11*, 289–298.

Goodnow, J. J. (1971). Matching auditory and visual series: Modality problem or translation problem? *Child Development, 42*, 1187–1201.

Hagman, J. D. (1983). Presentation and test trial effects on acquisition and retention of distance and location. *Journal of Experimental Psychology: Learning, Memory, and Cognition, 9*, 334–345.

Hall, A. D., & Newman, S. E. (1987). Braille learning: Relative importance of seven variables. *Applied Cognitive Psychology, 1*, 133–141.

Hatta, T., Yamamoto, M., & Mito, H. (1984). Functional hemisphere differences in auditory and tactile recognition in aged people. *The Japanese Journal of Psychology, 54*(6), 358–363.

Hay, J. C., Pick, H. L., Jr., & Ikeda, K. (1965). Visual capture produced by prism spectacles. *Psychonomic Science, 2*, 215–216.

Hellyer, S. (1962). Supplementary report: Frequency of stimulus presentation and short-term decrement in recall. *Journal of Experimental Psychology, 64*, 650.

Herman, L. M., & Bailey, D. R. (1970). Comparative effects of retroactive and proactive interference in motor short-term memory. *Journal of Experimental Psychology, 86*, 407–415.

Howard, I. P., & Templeton, W. B. (1966). *Human spatial orientation*. New York: Wiley.

Izawa, C. (1966). Reinforcement-test sequences in paired-associated learning. *Psychological Reports, 18*, 879–919.

Izawa, C. (1967a). Function of test trials in paired-associated learning. *Journal of Experimental Psychology, 75*, 194–209.

Izawa, C. (1967b). Mixed- versus unmixed-list designs in paired-associate learning. *Psychological Reports, 20*, 1191–1200.

Izawa, C. (1968). Effects of reinforcement, neutral and test trials upon paired-associate acquisition and retention. *Psychological Reports, 23*, 947–959.

Izawa, C. (1969). Comparison of reinforcement and test-trials in paired-associate learning. *Journal of Experimental Psychology, 81*, 600–603.

Izawa, C. (1970a). Optimal potentiating effects and forgetting-prevention effects of tests in paired-associate learning. *Journal of Experimental Psychology, 83*, 340–344.

Izawa, C. (1970b). Reinforcement-test-blank acquisition programming under the unmixed-list design in paired-associate learning. *Psychonomic Science, 19*, 75–77.

Izawa, C. (1971a). Massed and spaced practice in paired-associate learning: List versus item distributions. *Journal of Experimental Psychology, 89*, 10–21.

Izawa, C. (1971b). The test trial potentiating model. *Journal of Mathematical Psychology, 8*, 200–224.

Izawa, C. (1976). Vocalized and silent tests in paired-associate learning. *American Journal of Psychology, 89*, 681–693.

Izawa, C. (1985a). A test of the differences between anticipation and study-test methods of paired-associate learning. *Journal of Experimental Psychology: Learning, Memory, and Cognition, 11*, 165–184.

Izawa, C. (1985b). The identity model and factors controlling the superiority of study-test method over the anticipation method. *Journal of General Psychology, 112*, 65–78.

Izawa, C. (1989). A search for the control factors of the repetition effect. *Japanese Psychological Review, 31*(3).

Jones, B., & Connolly, K. (1970). Memory Effects in cross-modal matching. *Journal of Experimental Psychology, 7*, 218–220.

Kanak, N. J., & Neuner, S. D. (1970). Associative symmetry and item availability as a function of five methods of paired-associate acquisition. *Journal of Experimental Psychology, 86*, 288–295.

Keele, S. W., Pokorny, R. A., Corcos, D. M., & Ivry, R. (1985). Do perception and motor production share common timing mechanisms: A correlational analysis. *Acta Psychologica, 60*(2,3), 173–191.

Kelso, J. A. S. (1977). Planning and efferent components in the coding of movement. *Journal of Motor Behavior, 9*, 33–47.

Kinney, J. A., & Luria, S. M. (1970). Conflicting visual and tactual-kinesthetic stimulation. *Perception & Psychophysics, 8*, 189–192.

Kirman, J. H., & Kirman, N. F. (1985). A new tactile illusion: Temporal limits on the processing of spatiotemporal patterns. *The Journal of General Psychology, 112*(3), 243–259.

Kosslyn, S. M., Pick, H. L., Jr., & Fariello, G. R. (1974). Cognitive maps in children and men. *Child Development, 45*, 707–716.

Laabs, G. J. (1973). Retention characteristics of different reproduction cues in motor short-term memory. *Journal of Experimental Psychology, 100*, 168–177.

Lederman, S. J., & Abbott, S. G. (1981). Texture perception: Studies of intersensory organization using a discrepancy paradigm, and visual versus tactual psychophysics. *Journal of Experimental Psychology: Human Perception and Performance, 7*, 902–915.

Lederman, S. J., Klatzky, R. L., & Barber, P. O. (1985). Spatial and movement-based heuristics for encoding pattern information through touch. *Journal of Experimental Psychology: General, 114*, 33–49.

Lederman, S. J., Thorne, G., & Jones, B. (1986). Perception of texture by vision and touch: Multidimensionality and intersensory integration. *Journal of Experimental Psychology: Human Perception and Performance, 12*(2), 169–180.

Millar, S. (1972a). Effects of interpolated tasks on latency and accuracy of intramodal and cross-modal shape recognition by children. *Journal of Experimental Psychology, 96*, 170–175.

Millar, S. (1972b). The development of visual and kinesthetic judgments of distance. *British Journal of Psychology, 63*, 271–282.

Miller, E. A. (1972). Interaction of vision and touch in conflict and nonconflict form perception tasks. *Journal of Experimental Psychology, 96*, 114–123.

Morton, J. (1970). A functional model for memory. In D. A. Norman (Ed.), *Models of human memory* (pp. 203–254), New York: Academic Press.

Myers, A. K., Cotton, B., & Hilp, H. A. (1981). Matching of the rate of concurrent tone bursts and light flashes as a function of flash surround luminance. *Perception & Psychophysics, 30*, 33–38.

O'Connor, N., & Hermelin, B. (1972). Seeing and hearing in space and time. *Perception & Psychophysics, 11*, 46–48.

O'Connor, N., & Hermelin, B. (1978). *Seeing and hearing and space and time.* New York: Academic Press.

Pepper, R. L., & Herman, L. M. (1970). Decay and interference effects in the short-term retention of a discreet motor act. *Journal of Experimental Psychology Monograph, 83,* (2, Pt. 2), 1–18.

Peterson, L. R., & Peterson, M. J. (1959). Short-term retention of individual verbal items. *Journal of Experimental Psychology, 58*, 193–198.

Posner, M. I. (1967). Characteristics of visual and kinesthetic memory codes. *Journal of Experimental Psychology, 75,* 103–107.

Posner, M. I., & Konick, A. F. (1966). Short-term retention of visual and kinesthetic information. *Organizational Behavior and Human Performance, 1,* 71–88.

Rieser, J. J., Lockman, J. J., & Pick, H. L. (1980). The role of visual experience in knowledge of spatial layout. *Perception & Psychophysics, 28,* 185–190.

Rock, I., & Victor, J. (1964). Vision and touch: An experimentally created conflict between the two senses. *Science, 143,* 594–596.

Sherman, R. C., Croxton, J., & Smith, M. (1979). Movement and structure as determinants of spatial representations. *Journal of Nonverbal Behavior, 4,* 27–38.

Singer, G., & Day, R. H. (1969). Visual capture of haptically judged depth. *Perception & Psychophysics, 5,* 315–316.

Stelmach, G. E. (1970). Kinesthetic recall and information reduction activity. *Journal of Motor Behavior, 2,* 183–194.

Stelmach, G. E., & Barber, J. L. (1970). Interpolated activity in short term motor memory. *Perceptual and Motor Skills, 30,* 231–234.

Stelmach, G. E., & Walsh, M. F. (1972). Response biasing as a function of duration and extent of positioning acts. *Journal of Experimental Psychology, 92,* 354–359.

Summers, J. J., Levey, A. J., & Wrigley, W. J. (1981). The role of planning and efference in the recall of location and distance cues in short-term motor memory. *Journal of Motor Behavior, 13,* 65–76.

Teghtsoonian, R., & Teghtsoonian, M. (1970). Two varieties of perceived length. *Perception & Psychophysics, 8,* 389–392.

Turpin, B. A. M., & Stelmach, G. E. (1984). Repetition effects with kinesthetic and visual-kinesthetic stimuli. *Bulletin of the Psychonomic Society, 22(3),* 200–202.

Tversky, B. (1969). Pictorial and verbal encoding in a short-term memory task. *Perception & Psychophysics, 6,* 225–233.

Tversky, B. (1981). Distortions in memory for maps. *Cognitive Psychology, 13,* 407–433.

Walk, R. D., & Pick, H. L., Jr. (1981). *Intersensory perception and sensory integration.* New York: Plenum.

Walker, J. T., & Scott, K. (1981). Auditory-visual conflicts in the perceived duration of lights, tones, and gaps. *Journal of Experimental Psychology: Human Perception and Performance, 7,* 1327–1339.

Williams, H. L., Beaver, W. S., Spence, M. T., & Rundell, O. H. (1969). Digital and kinesthetic memory with interpolated information processing. *Journal of Experimental Psychology, 80,* 537–541.

Wrisberg, C. A. (1975). The serial-position effect in short-term motor retention. *Journal of Motor Behavior, 7,* 289–295.

Wrisberg, C. A., & Schmidt, R. A. (1975). A note on motor learning without post-response knowledge of results. *Journal of Motor Behavior, 7,* 221–225.

Zakay, D., & Shilo, E. (1985). The influence of temporal and spatial variation on tactile identification of letters. *The Journal of General Psychology, 112(2),* 147–152.

ACKNOWLEDGMENTS

Support for this chapter was provided, in part, by BRSG Grant S07 RR07040, awarded by the Biomedical Research Support Grant Program, Division of Research Resources, National Institute of Health and by a grant by the "Friends of Tulane in Japan."

We acknowledge with gratitude the reliable assistance rendered in collection and processing of data for Experiments 1 through 8 by Tulane students, Jesse Gonzales, John Ranseen, Mark Lampert, Gregory Boetje, Nancy Collins, Roxy Jarema, Dave Matson, Douglas Bell, Mike Lasen, Marc Switzer, Chris Dover, Tim Traunt, and John Baay, II. The unpublished data (Fig. 8.17) was collected by Ronald Cohen, also a student. This chapter could not have been possible without the keen interest and exemplary devotion of these students.

We also thank Larry Roth, Nobumasa Watari, and Gregory Meffert for important contributions to the preparation of our computer programs and assistance with analyses of the data. We deeply appreciate assistance rendered by Lynn Train, Hester Chang, Hima B. Narumanchi, and Rashmi S. Desai, a volunteer, for illustrations, data preparation and general assistance. Miss Mylene M. Montes deserves a special thanks for her valuable contributions in the final phase of manuscript preparation as a knowledgeable processor of words and a skilled reader of technical proof.

Special acknowledgments are due to Gregory Meffert, Elly S. Heliczer and James Izawa-Hayden, who voluntarily contributed their dependable services to the present effort solely because of their interest and concern.

The experiments that constitute the foundation of this chapter and the drafting of the chapter itself, benefitted in many essential ways from the willingness of all concerned to strive for excellence. For this, we remain most grateful.

9

On the Puzzling Relationship Between Environmental Context and Human Memory

Robert A. Bjork
Alan Richardson-Klavehn
University of California, Los Angeles

It would be hard to overstate the importance of understanding the profound influence of environmental context on human memory. Such influences appear in nearly all aspects of our everyday lives, and a full understanding of storage and retrieval processes in human memory awaits our ability to describe how such processes are influenced by environmental context (EC).

Anecdotal Evidence for EC-Dependent Memory

In an excellent recent chapter, Smith (1988) summarizes the kinds of anecdotal evidence that our episodic memories become attached to and can later be cued by environmental stimuli. Many of us have experienced, on returning to the town in which we grew up or to a school we attended, the flood of memories for events, pranks, names, colloquial expressions, and emotions that are resurrected by reinstating such environmental cues. In the case of immigrants returning to their country of origin, or soldiers returning to battlefields or prison camps, the effects can be especially profound, even after absences of 40 or 50 years. Language abilities come back, events are reconstructed, and powerful emotions return, often to an extent that is overwhelming.

As Smith (1988) points out, such long-term effects of reinstatement do not exhaust the kinds of effects of environmental context on memory. There are short-term effects as well. Failing to recognize a known person (e.g., the neighborhood butcher) when that person is encountered in an atypical context (e.g., the opera) is a situation familiar to most of us. Forgetting what one left one's office to do until one returns to one's office is another familiar case. Smith's compelling examples could easily be augmented by many more.

Those of us who have competed in some sport know well the perils of attempting to "improve" one's execution of some well-learned cognitive-motor skill. The environmental cues during a sports competition, including body-state variables such as stress, anxiety, and level of adrenalin, differ markedly from those present during practice. Unless one has highly overlearned the new technique—and managed to associate that technique with competition-type cues—actual competition will trigger the old form, or worse yet, something in between the old and the new form. Teachers who decide to reorganize a "canned" lecture on some topic often find themselves, in the actual lecture context, confused and tongue-tied in some netherland midway between the new organization and the old organization. In actual combat, military personnel trained in the operation of new equipment will often regress to motor behavior appropriate to the old equipment.

The preceding examples represent cases in which a change of context produces undesirable forgetting, but changing context can produce desirable forgetting as well. A sabbatical or vacation in a new setting can aid creativity. As Smith (1988) notes, an author who becomes "stale" on the job may become—by virtue of a move to a new environment—"freed from the hackneyed ideas one cannot escape in the old work setting" (p. 18). He also points out that environmental cues help compartmentalize our lives because "different personal roles are called upon . . . when one is at one's work place, one's home, a restaurant, a theater, a workout gym, a bank, a party, a doctor's office, a campground, or a place of worship" (p. 18). Contextual associations ensure that appropriate, and not inappropriate, material is retrieved from memory, and used to control behavior. The general dependency of proactive and retroactive interference on context overlap is a topic to which we return later.

Finally, if one considers mood state part of one's environmental context, another array of instances could be cited. The present cognitive therapy for depression, for example, views the patient as caught in a pathological deteriorating spiral. The patient's depressed state leads her/him to retrieve those memories consistent with that state, worsening the depression, which further restricts retrieval access, and so forth. The goal of the therapy is to break that cycle by reschematizing the patient's interpretation of his/her roles and relationships at home and at work.

Practical Importance of the Context-Memory Relationship

If human memory and performance is as dependent on environment context as the foregoing examples suggest, the practical importance of understanding that dependency is clear for areas such as political and social psychology, environmental psychology, education, artistic performance, sports, witness testimony, therapy, and manipulating one's own moods or creativity. As will become increasingly clear in this chapter, however, understanding the interplay of context and memory requires us to enumerate the different effective forms of context, internal and external, and to discover how those forms interact with different aspects of performance.

Theoretical Importance of the Context–Memory Relationship

One need look no further than the chapters in this volume, particularly those by Murdock, Nelson, and Shiffrin, to appreciate the importance of contextual factors in current models of memory. That context influences what is activated or available in memory, that generating or studying items somehow "connects" them to the current episodic context, and that recall probabilities are a function of strength of association to the current context are primitive assumptions in many theories.

Thirty or forty years ago the emphasis in explaining forgetting was on interference between different sets of learned materials; presently such interference mechanisms are deemphasized and the concept of context occupies the central explanatory role. For example, E. Bjork and R. Bjork (1988) contend that the retrieval failures that seem to be a fundamental weakness of human memory are in fact an adaptive feature of the system. Given that human long-term memory has such an astounding storage capacity, in terms of both amount and duration of storage (e.g., see the estimates in Landauer, 1986), it is adaptive that information becomes inaccessible with disuse and/or a change in context. Even highly overlearned material such as one's phone number or street address eventually becomes inaccessible when that information is no longer current. Such loss of retrieval access is adaptive because information that is nonretrievable, by virtue of its being out of date or irrelevant to the current context, is also noninterfering, which improves retrieval speed and accuracy for information that is current and relevant.

Integrated, Influential, and Incidental Context

A number of researchers have distinguished between those aspects of context that are related in a meaningful way to the to-be-remembered event or information of interest, and those aspects of context that are incidental to or independent of the target event or information. For example, Baddeley (1982) distinguishes *interactive* and *independent* forms of context, Eich (1985) distinguishes *integrated* and *isolated* aspects of context, and Hewitt (cited in Godden & Baddeley, 1980) distinguishes between *intrinsic* and *extrinsic* context. All of these distinctions capture the idea that contextual stimuli can either become explicitly associated with target stimuli at encoding or that they can be encoded in some sense independently of the target information. Here we wish to accommodate the additional possibility that contextual stimuli can influence the encoding of target material without necessarily becoming explicitly associated with that material at the time of encoding. For example, a context can influence a subject's interpretation of an ambiguous stimulus without the subject becoming aware of that influence. At the risk of adding to the proliferation of terms, we therefore make a threefold distinction between *integrated, influential*, and *incidental* aspects of context. Incidental context, in the sense in which we use it, is not only independent or isolated from the target information, but also does not influence the subject's interpretation of, or interaction with, the target material at encoding.

The reason the integrated/influential/incidental distinction is important is that the existence of sizeable effects on memory of integrated–influential aspects of context are not surprising, nor of much interest for present purposes. We know that cuing recall of a target event by reinstating a cue that was originally explicitly associated with that target at encoding will exceed uncued recall (e.g., Thomson & Tulving, 1970). Similarly, changing semantic context so as to activate different senses of a word at study and test is known to impair recall and recognition, in contrast to the case in which the same sense is activated on both occasions (e.g., Barclay, Bransford, Franks, McCarrell, & Nitsch, 1974; Light & Carter-Sobell, 1970). On the other hand, it is still an open question whether there are effects of incidental context on memory—a question that is currently subject to considerable debate (e.g., Fernandez & Glenberg, 1985).

There are two issues concerning incidental EC that must be distinguished. First, is incidental EC information encoded into the episodic memory trace corresponding to target information? Second, assuming EC information is encoded into the memory trace, what role, if any, does it play in the retrieval of target information?

Before proceeding further, it is worth noting that the prevalent view of EC as an incidental form of context may not always be easy to defend in practice. For example, Smith (1988) restricts his consideration of environmental context (EC) to those "external stimuli which are not implicitly or explicitly related to the learning material in any meaningful way" (p. 14), and he defines "EC-dependent memory" as "a class of phenomena in which cognitive processing is affected in subtle, profound, and sometimes important ways by the coincidental background EC in which the experiences are set" (p. 14). However, in a number of naturalistic examples, including some of those previously discussed, the relationship between the environmental cues and the target material could be interpreted as "meaningful" (i.e., integrated–influential). Consider the interesting story Smith recounts about his father returning to Austin, Texas "after 42 long years of forgetting." Among other things, his father recalled "in vivid detail . . . how an armadillo had climbed up the drainpipe one night and become his pet" (p. 13). Is the drainpipe in this case related in a meaningful way to the event being recalled? (In fact, Smith's father was looking at a parking lot, his former residence having

TABLE 9.1
Types of EC-Dependent Memory Phenomena

Manipulation of interest	Sequence of events	Phenomenon of interest
1. Physical reinstatement of study context at test	Learn List 1 (in Context A) Recall List 1 (in Context A or B)	AA > AB
2. Imaginal reinstatement of study context at test	Learn List 1 (in Context A) Recall List 1 (in Context B, with or without imagining A)	AB(A) > AB
3. Varied contexts across study sessions	Learn List 1 (in Context A) Learn List 2 (in Context A or B) Recall List 1 (in neutral context, N)	ABN > AAN
4. Varied contexts across study sessions	Learn List 1 (in Context A) Learn List 2 (in Context A or B) Recall Lists 1 and 2 (in neutral context, N)	ABN > AAN

been torn down. The example nonetheless illustrates that "meaningfulness" may be difficult to judge in practice.)

THE LABORATORY PHENOMENA OF INTEREST

Controlled experimentation dating back at least as far as the 1930s has revealed several important types of EC-dependent memory. Reinstatement (actual or imaginal) at test of the study context has been shown to enhance recall, and variation of study contexts across study sessions has been found to reduce interference between sets of learned materials and to enhance total recall. Those phenomena are outlined in Table 9.1 and are described briefly later. It is important to emphasize that we are focussing here on recall as the measure of memory performance; recognition performance does not show the same pattern of EC-dependency as that shown by recall (e.g., Godden & Baddeley, 1980; Smith, 1985, 1986; Smith, Glenberg, & Bjork, 1978).

Contextual Reinstatement at Test

Physical Reinstatement. In numerous published reports, material presented to subjects in some environment, A, has been better recalled when subjects were later tested in A than when they are tested in some different environment, B; that is AA > AB. The typical experiment in the literature, of which there are many (see Smith, 1988, Table 2.1), has examined the effect of reinstating room context on recall, but other types of EC manipulations have been employed (e.g., on land vs. underwater). The conditions under which physical reinstatement enhances performance are a matter of current debate, and are considered further later in this chapter.

Imaginal Reinstatement. In 1979 Smith showed that when study and test contexts differ subjects can enhance performance at test by mentally reinstating the study context. Since Smith's original report, there have been several other demonstrations of such imaginal reinstatement effects (Fisher, Geiselman, Holland, & MacKinnon, 1984; Frerk, Holcomb, Johnson, & Nelson, 1985; Smith, 1984).

Contextual Variation at Study

Reduction of Retroactive Interference. When a first list is learned in some context, A, the retroactive interference owing to the learning of a second list can be reduced if the second list is learned in a new context, B, compared to the case in which the new list is learned in A. In the general case, recall or relearning of the first list in some neutral context, N, will be better in the ABN case than in the AAN case. Such results first appeared in the 1950s (Bilodeau & Schlosberg, 1951; Greenspoon & Ranyard, 1957) and have since been replicated with several types of lists and several types of recall tests, together with additional experimental controls to rule out the possibility of certain artifacts (Coggins & Kanak, 1985; Eckert, Kanak, & Stevens, 1984; Kanak & Stevens, 1985). Some evidence for reduction of proactive interference due to context variation has also been provided (Dallett & Wilcox, 1968).

Enhanced Total Recall. Smith, Glenberg, and Bjork (1978) demonstrated that recall of a twice-studied list in a neutral context, N, was enhanced if the two study sessions took place in different environments A and B; that is, ABN > AAN. Glenberg (1979) obtained similar results, and Smith (1982) showed that the same effect held for unique lists as well as repeated lists. Subsequent studies using course materials (Chen, 1984; Smith & Rothkopf, 1984) as well as word lists (e.g., Smith, 1984) have obtained mixed results.

THE PUZZLE: PART I

Reinstatement Phenomena in the Laboratory and in the Real World

Although we tend to believe—based on our experiences and the kind of anec- dotes alluded to earlier—that being back in the context in which certain experiences took place helps the recall of those events in a big way, the laboratory evidence for physical reinstatement effects is inconsistent. The positive reports of physical reinstatement effects in the literature are offset by other reports (some published, but many only "word-of-mouth") of insignificant differences between same-room and different-room recall levels. The recent papers by Fernandez and Glenberg (1985) and Saufley, Otaka, and Bavaresco (1985) are particularly impressive in the number of comparisons that show nonsignificant differences. Additionally, Fernandez and Glenberg's Experiment 8 was a direct replication of Smith (1979, Experiment 1), using precisely the same materials and environmental contexts that were used in the original study, but more than twice the number of subjects. Fernandez and Glenberg failed to obtain a context effect despite statistical power of .94 to detect an effect of the size reported by Smith (1979). In view of the pervasive tendency to suppress publication of nonsignificant effects, these data suggest the possibility that a number of the significant effects of physical reinstatement in the literature represent Type I errors.

Possible Solutions to Part I of the Puzzle

Incidental EC-Dependent Memory Does Not Exist. As mentioned earlier, the question is not whether some environmental stimuli can cue memories, but whether environmental stimuli that are truly incidental—unrelated to the episode or learned material to be recalled—can aid later recall when they are reinstated. In the typical laboratory experiment the experimental task is unrelated to the environment (typically a room) in which the task is administered. In naturalistic examples, however, the contexts are not so clearly incidental. We are often recalling connected episodes, for example, in which some feature of the environment (e.g., a school flagpole) may have played a central role (e.g., in a high school prank).

Consider the following example from Smith (1988): "While working at my desk, I interrupted my work to go to the office for some file folders. Still thinking about my work, I trudged absent-mindedly to the office. Upon arriving at the office, I realized I had forgotten what I needed there. The file folders could not be remembered until I returned to my office" (p. 15). It could well be that on returning to his office Smith's file-folder memory was triggered by the materials that he wanted to file, which were possibly sitting in a prominent place. In that case, the to-be-filed materials seem like a meaningful rather than an incidental aspect of context. Eich (1985) showed that when subjects are asked to use interactive imagery to relate the to-be-remembered materials to objects in or features of the room environment at study there is a clear advantage of physically reinstating the study context at test.

Another potentially important difference between controlled experiments and naturalistic incidents is that in experiments we tell *all* subjects, whether they are tested in the study context or in a different context, to try to recall the study material. By contrast, in naturalistic cases a return to some original context can cue us to attempt to recall information associated with that context that we would not otherwise have attempted to recall. When we return to a school or town and interact with people we knew during the time that we spent there, the nature of those experiences induces us to attempt to recollect events, names, and facts from the past era. We are put in an appropriate retrieval mode, so to speak. It may well be that we *could* recollect that information as well outside the original context as we could in it, but we are not induced to try.

At the Flowerree Symposium in New Orleans in February 1987, for example, one of us (RAB), together with Richard Shiffrin and Judy Mahy-Shiffrin, attempted to recall a dinner we had eaten together some years earlier at L'Orangerie, an expensive restaurant in Beverly Hills. We were able to recall a number of details, including some of the dishes that we ate, where we sat, how the restaurant was decorated, that the restaurant was somewhat hot and cramped for such a luxurious place, and that Goldie Hawn was sitting at a table about 10 ft away. Could we have recalled more had we been back at L'Orangerie? Maybe we could have, but the point is that the appropriate comparison is not typically made in the case of naturalistic incidents that we label "EC-dependent" memory; there is no attempt to recall the target material in a context different from the context in which that material was initially encountered.

The possibility that physical reinstatement of environmental context aids recall only because it induces the rememberer to try to recall suggests that we come to believe that incidental context aids recall in a manner analogous to the way many people come to believe that they have psychic abilities. When we attend a school reunion, or return to an arena where we played some sport, to a country club where we worked as a teenager, or to a town in Europe where we spent a year in an education-abroad program, the process of recollecting triggered by our return is itself memorable and worthy of comment in a way that similar recollections out of context—as we are falling asleep, for example—are not. So we become believers.

That the typical layperson—and probably every novelist—believes in the power of environmental cues to aid recall there can be no doubt. Consider the following passage from Isaac Asimov's (1986) *Robots and Empire*, for example, in which Gladia—a central character in the book—returns to her home planet (Solaria) after an absence of 20 decades:

> Gladia stood on the soil of Solaria. She smelled the vegetation—not quite the odors of Aurora—and at once she crossed the gap of twenty decades.
>
> Nothing, she knew, could bring back associations in the way that odors could. Not sights, not sounds.
>
> Just that faint, unique smell brought back childhood—the freedom of run-

ning about, with a dozen robots watching her carefully—the excitement of seeing other children sometimes, coming to a halt, staring shyly, approaching one another a half-step at a time, reaching out to touch, and then a robot saying, "Enough, Miss Gladia," and being led away—looking over the shoulder at the other child, with whom there was another set of attendant robots in charge. (p. 127)

The assertion that smells are powerful cues in reinstating memories is one with which most people would agree. However, in two unpublished experiments carried out at UCLA by Stephen White and the first author, there has been no evidence whatsoever that reinstating incidental environmental odors aids recall of material studied in the presence of those odors.

Our Experiments Are Poor Simulations of the Real World. The typical controlled experiment on the effects of reinstating environmental context differs from the typical real-world anecdote in the nature of the material recalled, in the length of the interval between initial exposure to some type of material and retrieval of that material, and in the extent of the similarity between the context of initial exposure and the retrieval context in the case in which those contexts are different. In experiments, the typical recall target is some kind of relatively sterile verbal-learning list, the retention interval from study to test ranges from a few minutes to a few days, and the characteristics of the test context in the "different context" condition overlap in many respects with those of the study context (e.g., same campus, same building, same experiment, same experimenter, same fellow subjects). By contrast, in real-world anecdotes the recall target is often a social/behavioral event in one's life, the retention interval is years or decades, and the difference between the same and different contexts is enormous in terms of geographic location, physical features of the environment, nature of the social context, and so forth. Given these differences, experiments are usually weak simulations, at best, of real world cases. One could argue that context reinstatement effects are more likely to be observed when the target material is inaccessible under normal circumstances, as would occur at very long retention intervals, and when physical reinstatement of the original context re-presents environmental cues that differ greatly from those typically available.

It should be added that certain experimenters have gone to considerable lengths to make the same/different manipulation of EC a potent manipulation. One example is research by the second author that we report later. In the first of the recent papers reviving interest in EC effects, Smith et al. (1978) changed every dimension of room context that they could think of, including altering the appearance of the experimenter to such an extent that some subjects did not realize that the experimenter was the same person. In the work of Godden and Baddeley (1975, 1980) the subjects were student divers and the two contexts were on land versus underwater, which should be a potent difference. In terms of what can be done within the confines of a standard experimental room, however, Dallett and Wilcox (1968) may deserve the prize. To make their "box environment" different from their "drum environment" —as in *memory drum*—they concocted the following arrangement.

> In the box environment, *S* stood with his head inside a large box, his neck in a foam-rubber-padded U-shaped cutout in the floor of the box, with a curtain to eliminate peripheral stimuli behind him. The room was darkened, and the interior of the box lighted with flashing red and green lights. The inner dimensions of the box were about 3 ft. × 3 ft. at the end where *S*'s head was, and tapered to about 1 ft. × 2 ft. approximately 3½ ft. in front of *S*'s head. None of the walls were parallel. The inside of the box was painted white, with green and black lines added, converging to a false vanishing point which did not coincide with the perspective of the walls. Some of these painted lines were "connected" to black strings hung across the interior of the box. Half of one wall was covered by furry red patches made of a nylon bathmat. After constructing the box and using it, it seemed to the *E*s that a great deal of its effect came from the changing illumination; a red 40-w. bulb flashed at a rate of approximately 80/min, while a green bulb flashed at approximately 18/min. These were the only lights in the box. The *S*s generally agreed that the box was highly unusual, and on two occasions *S*s had to be excused because of nausea. (pp. 475–476)

The extremity of the contextual manipulations in the Godden and Baddeley and Dallett and Wilcox studies point up the possibility that some manipulations of EC may achieve their effects via changes in the physiological state of the subjects. Physiological and drug state-dependent effects must clearly be distinguished from the effects of interest here, namely those produced simply by a change in the location in which material is studied and tested.

THE PUZZLE: PART II

First-Order versus Second-Order Effects of Environmental Context

The second piece of the puzzle is that the other three categories of laboratory phenomena summarized in Table 9.1 (imaginal reinstatement at test and the two effects of context variation at study) are apparently more reliable than the basic physical-reinstatement effect. These three categories of effect seem to require the assumption that learned material is associated to its incidental environmental context. Curiously, then, effects that might be regarded as second-order consequences of associative processes tying material to incidental context seem more reliable than does an effect that would be expected to be

TABLE 9.2
Two Measures of Original-List Retention as a Function
of Whether Original and Interpolated Lists were Learned
in the Same or Different Contexts

	Measure of retention	
Original and interpolated contexts	CVCs recalled on Trial 1[a]	Trials to relearn
Same (Groups AAA, AAB, BBA, BBB)	2.63	8.46
Different (Groups ABA, ABB, BAA, BAB)	5.52	6.26

Note: After data presented in "Stimulus Conditions and Retroactive Inhibition" by J. Greenspoon and R. Ranyard, 1957, Journal of Experimental Psychology, 53, 55–59.
[a]Out of 10 possible.

a first-order consequence of such contextual–associative processes. The six tests of imaginal reinstatement and the eight tests of interference reduction owing to varied input contexts in the literature (see Smith, 1988, Tables 2.2 & 2.4) all yielded positive results, and 8 out of 13 tests of enhanced total recall owing to multiple input contexts (see Smith, 1988, Table 2.5) yielded positive results.

The data presented in Table 9.2 demonstrate how large such "second-order" effects can be. Greenspoon and Ranyard (1957) had subjects learn each of two successive lists of 10 nonsense syllables to a criterion of two successive errorless trials through the list (serial anticipation method). After the second list was learned, subjects relearned the first list—again to a criterion of two errorless trials. Two distinctive rooms (A & B) served as the learning contexts. Across subjects the List-1 and List-2 contexts were either the same or different and List 1 was relearned either in its original study context or in the other context. Combining these two manipulations resulted in eight conditions: AAA, AAB, ABA, ABB, BAA, BAB, BBA, and BBB.

The results in Table 9.2 are shown as a function of whether List 1 and List 2 were learned in the same or in different rooms. Two measures of List 1 retention are shown: The mean number of nonsense syllables recalled correctly on the first relearning trial, and the mean number of trials necessary to relearn List 1 to criterion. The data are averaged over cases in which original and relearning contexts for List 1 matched and mismatched. Looking at either measure in Table 9.2, the retroactive interference owing to List-2 learning was greatly reduced when List 1 and List 2 were learned in different rooms. We could cite equally impressive examples of enhanced total recall of material learned in different contexts (compared to material learned in a single context) and of imaginal reinstatement effects.

A Possible Solution to Both Pieces of the Puzzle

Both of the preceding solutions to the first part of the puzzle fail on the second part of the puzzle. They present reasons why we should not expect first-order physical reinstatement effects in the typical laboratory experiment, but neither explanation accounts for the fact that other types of EC effects are apparently reliable in controlled experiments. If learned material does not become associated to incidental environmental context, then those second-order effects (of imaginary reinstatement and of contextual variation during input) should not obtain. And if our laboratory manipulations of EC are too ineffective to reveal first-order (physical reinstatement) effects they should not reveal second-order effects either. We propose a hypothesis in this section that provides a potential solution to both parts of the puzzle.

The key assumption is that physical reinstatement will only be advantageous in situations in which subjects in the different-context condition either cannot or do not mentally reinstate the original context. We assume further that mental reinstatement is as good as physical reinstatement in facilitating recall (and might be even better for reasons we touch on later), and that in the typical laboratory experiment subjects can and do mentally reinstate the study context when they are in the different-context condition. It follows that EC effects in the typical physical reinstatement experiment (i.e., first-order EC effects) should be weak or nonexistent.

The advantage of context variation across study sessions in terms of retroactive interference reduction may then be explicable for the following reason. When subjects attempt to reinstate the List-1 study context mentally at test, any advantage of mental reinstatement that accrues to List 1 will be offset in the AAN case by increased interference from List 2, because both lists are associated with the context that is mentally reinstated. In the ABN case, by contrast, mental reinstatement of the List-1 context will not lead to reinstatement of the List-2 context, so that mental reinstatement does not carry the cost of increased List-2 interference. It might also be the case, however, that subjects *could* mentally reinstate the List-1 episode without reinstating List-2 learning if they tried, but that the three-session procedure in such experiments renders them (for some reason) unlikely to do so.

The advantage of context variation for total recall is explicable along similar lines. The to-be-remembered material is associated with more EC cues in the ABN case than in the AAN case. More retrieval cues are therefore available for mental reinstatement in the former case than in the latter case. The advantages of providing multiple retrieval routes to target material are well known (the *encoding variability* principle).

One can also account for the positive effects of imaginal reinstatement instructions. In the typical physical reinstatement experiment, any mental reinstatement strategy employed by subjects in the different-context condition will be largely of their own devising (although, as we note below, their likelihood of adopting such a strategy and the precise strategy employed might be influenced by demand characteristics). By contrast, in an imaginal reinstatement experiment the group of subjects instructed to reinstate are likely to receive precise instructions as to strategy. In Smith (1979, Experiment 2), for example, one reinstatement group was told to "write down the location of their list-learning room, and to list any 10 things they could remember seeing in that room . . . [and] . . . to take 2 min. to think about [the study room], what it looked like, what sounds and smells there were, where it was, and the way it made them feel" (p. 465). Those subjects were then told to "use their memory for [the study room] to help them recall the list and test words from the previous day" (p. 465). Subjects receiving mental reinstatement instructions may therefore adopt more varied and effective retrieval strategies than do subjects who mentally reinstate without receiving explicit instructions.

We argued earlier that subjects in the different-context condition in the typical first-order physical reinstatement experiment can and do mentally reinstate the study context, weakening or eliminating the context effect. This argument is plausible for two reasons. First, the relatively short retention intervals typically employed permit successful mental reinstatement. Second, whether subjects attempt to reinstate the study context at test might be influenced in subtle but profound ways by the recall instructions. Given that the experimenter in such experiments is not typically blind to experimental condition, some of the positive effects of physical and imaginal context reinstatement in the literature might be attributable to differing demand characteristics placed on subjects in the same- and different-context conditions.

Whether we actually obtain an effect of physically reinstating the study context at test should, therefore, depend on how difficult it is to mentally reinstate the study context, on the extent to which our instructions induce subjects to attempt such mental reinstatement, and on the distribution of mental-reinstatement ability in the population from which our sample is drawn. Consistent with this view, Smith (1979) showed that the advantage of physical reinstatement over mental reinstatement increases as mental reinstatement is rendered more difficult (by increasing the number of rooms previously encountered in the experiment, and in which the target list might have been studied).

WITHIN-SUBJECT MANIPULATIONS
OF EC MATCH/MISMATCH

Smith, Glenberg, and Bjork's (1978) Experiment 2

With respect to the issues raised in the preceding section, a design used by Smith, Glenberg, and Bjork (1978, Experiment 2) is of particular interest. In contrast to most other experiments in the literature, the effect of physically reinstating study context was tested within subjects. The experiment was carried out across 3 consecutive days. On Day 1 subjects studied a list of 45 word pairs in which the response word was a weak associate of the stimulus word. At the end of Day-1 training Smith and his colleagues tested cued recall of 15 of the 45 pairs in order to give a sense of closure to the subjects. On Day 2 all subjects were brought to a context that differed from their Day-1 context (if tested in context A on Day 1, they moved to context B on Day 2, and vice versa). In the Day-2 context they studied a second list of 45 word-word pairs. Fifteen of the pairs in List 2 shared a stimulus member with 15 of the pairs in List 1, but had a different response term (Common-Cue pairs). The remaining 30 pairs were unique to List 2 (Unique-Cue pairs). As for List 1, 15 of the List-2 pairs were tested at the end of training; for both List 1 and List 2 the stimulus terms (and response terms) of the tested pairs were unique to that list.

For the final Day-3 test subjects returned either to the context in which they had served on Day 1 or to the context in which they had served on Day 2 (there was also a condition in which they returned to a novel, neutral, context but that condition is not relevant here). They received a 45-item MMFR cued recall test, containing the stimulus terms of the 15 Common-Cue pairs, and the 30 stimulus terms from the Unique-Cue pairs that had not been tested on Day 1 or Day 2 (15 stimulus terms from List 1 and 15 from List 2).

The results of the Day-3 final test are shown in Fig. 9.1, with performance for Unique-Cue pairs plotted in the top panel and performance on the Common-Cue pairs plotted in the bottom panel. The context effect is clear, and similar for both types of pair: Physically reinstating either the Day-1 or the Day-2 context enhanced recall of the response terms studied in that context in comparison to recall of the response terms studied in the other context. In the Common-Cue case the context effect is superimposed on a recency effect, with Day-2 responses recalled better overall than Day-1 responses.

The particular within-subject design employed by Smith et al. (1978) has several major advantages. First of all, in contrast to a number of recent experiments in which there has been little or no effect of physical EC reinstatement, the effects in Fig. 9.1 are clear and sizeable. It is possible that the 3-day design employed by Smith et al., coupled with the cued-recall procedure, deterred subjects from mentally reinstating the "other" study context, that is, the context that differed from the context in which the Day-3 test took place. Second, the design removes certain concerns about differences in demand characteristics across same- and different-context conditions because each subject acts as her/his own control. Third, the design does not confound the manipulation of match between study and test contexts with a manipulation of old/novel context. With the standard between-subject context manipulation different-context subjects are tested in a context that they have not encountered before in the experiment, whereas same-context subjects are tested in a context that they have encountered before (for an exception, see Smith,

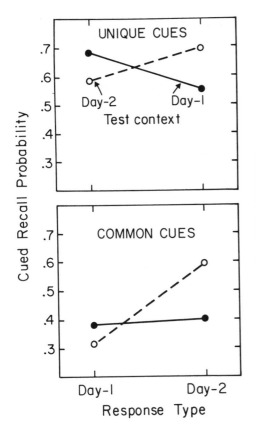

FIG. 9.1. Cued-recall proportions on Day 3 for cues that were unique to (top panel) or common to (bottom panel) Day-1 and Day-2 lists, as a function of whether the Day-3 test context matched the Day-1 or the Day-2 study context (after Smith et al., 1978, Experiment 2).

1979, Experiment 1). Finally, the within-subject design opens the possibility of correlating (across individual subjects) the size of the memory advantage of same- over different-context items with certain individual-difference variables.

Richardson-Klavehn's (1988) Experiment 1

In his doctoral dissertation, Richardson-Klavehn (1988) set out to perform an "improved" version of the Smith et al. experiment. The same Day-1, Day-2, and Day-3 conditions were employed, but there was an attempt to increase the strength of the contextual manipulation. The two contexts used on Day 1 and Day 2 were quite dramatically different (inside a cramped office without natural light on the seventh floor of an eight-story building vs. outdoors on a sunny foliage-surrounded patio). In addition, the interpersonal context was systematically varied across contexts. The experimenter was either a caucasian male or an Asian-Indian female, and, for a given subject, the other three subjects in the four-member group changed. The method of presentation of the to-be-remembered pairs also differed across contexts. Pairs were either presented to the subjects as a group in large green uppercase letters on large white cards, or they appeared in small individual booklets in lowercase black letters on a blue background.

An attempt was also made to increase the statistical power of the experiment over that of the Smith et al. (1978) experiment. The total number of subjects (across the four groups ABA, ABB, BAA, and BAB) was increased from 16 to 53. Additionally, the Day-3 test was changed from cued recall to free recall in view of the argument that free recall provides fewer explicit retrieval cues to the subject than does cued recall, increasing the probability that EC cues will be used (e.g., Eich, 1980; Smith, 1988). To permit a free recall test to be used, eight word-word pairs were studied on each day and no Day-1 and Day-2 pairs shared stimulus terms (that is, there were no Common-Cue pairs). In contrast to the intentional learning task used by Smith et al., an incidental learning task was used in which subjects generated sentences linking the two members of each word-word pair.

A further difference between Richardson-Klavehn (Experiment 1) and

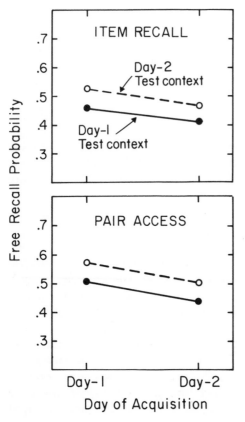

FIG. 9.2. Two measures of Day-3 free recall performance (proportion of individual items recalled, and proportion of pairs accessed) for Day-1 and Day-2 lists, as a function of whether the Day-3 test context matched the Day-1 or the Day-2 study context (after Richardson-Klavehn, 1988, Experiment 1).

Smith et al. (Experiment 2) was that a battery of 11 individual-difference tests was administered across the 3 hour-long experimental sessions. The battery included objective tests of spatial ability and field dependence, together with questionnaire measures of imagery vividness and control, use of imagery in spontaneous thought, tendency to become absorbed in current experiences, and tendency to "screen out" irrelevant environmental stimulation. The design of the experiment permitted the individual-difference measures to be correlated with a derived within-subject measure of context-dependency, namely the number of words recalled from the study context that matched the Day-3 test context minus the number of words recalled from the other (nonmatching) context.

The results of Richardson-Klavehn's Experiment 1 are shown in Fig. 9.2. Whether one looks at the proportion of individual words recalled (top panel), or the proportion of pairs for which one or both members of the pair was recalled (bottom panel), there is no indication whatsoever that recall was influenced by the match/mismatch of study and test contexts. Recall was somewhat better overall when the Day-3 test was administered in the Day-2 context, but that trend was equally evident for Day-1 and for Day-2 words, and apparently reflects nothing more than chance differences between subjects tested in their Day-1 context and subjects tested in their Day-2 context.

As subjects had been permitted to recall Day-1 and Day-2 words in any order they chose, it was possible that an output order measure might prove sensitive to EC match/mismatch (as in Smith, 1982, Experiment 3, for example). The output position of each word correctly recalled by a subject was expressed as a percentage of the total number of items (including intrusions) output by that subject. The mean of these percentile scores was computed separately for Day-1 and Day-2 words. Analyses using these mean output percentile scores showed that Day-1 words appeared, on average, earlier in output than did Day-2 words; however, there was no indication that the relative positions of Day-1 and Day-2 words in output changed as a function of Day-3 test context (Day-1 vs. Day-2).

The absence of any indication, however weak, of an overall context effect in Experiment 1 rendered the individual-difference measures of limited usefulness with respect to the original goals of the experiment: If some subjects were more sensitive to match between ECs at study and test than others were, the differences between means should still be in the direction expected under the hypothesis of a context effect. Any argument for the value of the individual difference measures would have to assume that context-sensitive subjects in the experiment were balanced by subjects who were negatively context-sensitive (i.e., subjects who consistently perform better under different-context than under same-context conditions).

Richardson-Klavehn's (1988) Experiment 2

The contrast between the clear effects obtained in Smith et al.'s Experiment 2 and the absence of effects in Richardson-Klavehn's Experiment 1 is perplexing. This difference in results could have resulted from a number of procedural differences between the studies, including number of to-be-remembered items (45 pairs/day vs. 8 pairs/day), orienting task (intentional learning vs. incidental learning), and test type (cued recall vs. free recall). In particular, it was considered possible that a cued recall test (as used by Smith et al.) was less likely than was a free recall test to induce the subjects to mentally reinstate the study context that was not physically reinstated at test. A cued recall test might induce subjects to search memory using the current cue-word as a probe, which might inhibit mental reinstatement and might, therefore, permit incidental context to influence that search. Richardson-Klavehn therefore repeated his experiment using the same study procedures and cued recall tests used by Smith et al. Appropriate numbers of Common-Cue and Unique-Cue pairs were generated from word-association norms according to the guidelines given by Smith et al., and study and test lists constructed exactly as in the original experiment.

The procedure in Richardson-Klavehn's Experiment 2 was exactly the same as the Smith et al. procedure—including a change in input modality (visual

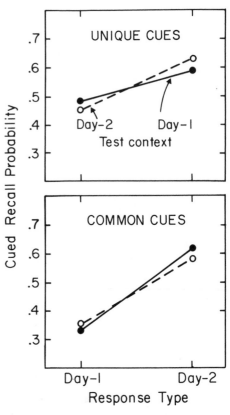

FIG. 9.3. Cued-recall proportions on Day 3 for cues that were unique to (top panel) or common to (bottom panel) Day-1 and Day-2 lists, as a function of whether the Day-3 test context matched the Day-1 or the Day-2 study context (after Richardson-Klavehn, 1988, Experiment 2).

to auditory, auditory to visual) from Day 1 to Day 2—except for the following differences: (a) The difference between Day-1 and Day-2 environments was larger in Richardson-Klavehn's experiment than in Smith et al.'s, both in terms of physical differences (the indoor and outdoor contexts were again used) and because experimenter and subject cohort changed systematically across contexts; (b) there were more subjects in Richardson-Klavehn's experiment than in the corresponding conditions of Smith et al.'s (a total of 57 vs. a total of 16); and (c) seven individual difference measures (a subset of those described earlier) were administered—three on Day 1, two on Day 2 and two on Day 3.

The results of Richardson-Klavehn's Experiment 2 are shown in Fig. 9.3, with performance for Unique-Cue pairs plotted in the top panel and performance on Common-Cue pairs plotted in the bottom panel. Overall performance was in the range obtained by Smith et al., but same-context words were not recalled more frequently than were different-context words. The small (statistically insignificant) trend in the direction of a context effect in the Unique-Cue data is perfectly offset by a small (insignificant) trend in the opposite direction in the Common-Cue data. One other difference in the results of the two experiments is that there was a recency effect for both Unique-Cue and Common-Cue pairs in the Richardson-Klavehn data (Day-2 responses being recalled better than Day-1 responses); by contrast, recency was present only for Common-Cue pairs in Smith et al.'s experiment.

WHEN IS RETRIEVAL AIDED BY THE PHYSICAL REINSTATEMENT OF INCIDENTAL ENVIRONMENTAL CONTEXT?

Given the inconsistency between the results shown in Fig. 9.1 and those shown in Figs. 9.2 and 9.3, and given the other failures to obtain advantages of physical context reinstatement in the literature, what is one to believe? Does physical reinstatement of incidental environmental context aid recall of material originally learned in that context or not? If physical reinstatement does aid recall, under what conditions does it do so?

One could attempt to argue that the reinstatement of *truly* incidental context *never* aids recall. The central assumption of such a position is that EC does not influence the form of a given episodic memory trace except when features of the EC were actively associated with the material learned (or the event that took place) in that environment, or when the EC influences the subject's interpretation of the learned material or event. By definition, then, the EC in these cases would be integrated or influential, not incidental. In that view, as mentioned earlier, reinstating incidental EC might trigger a recall effort that might not otherwise be attempted. Presumably, however, the same attempt to recall the target information in a different context would be as productive.

For a number of reasons, however, we question the tenability of the position that incidental EC never influences the form of the episodic memory trace. For example, this view cannot account for what we have termed the "second-order" effects of EC, and it seems at odds with the growing evidence that stimulus-driven processing, which is mostly or entirely automatic and independent of awareness, influences heavily the form of long-term memory representations.

Given that we assume that incidental aspects of environmental context *are* encoded as part of the episodic memory trace corresponding to the target material, how do we account for the repeated failures to find positive effects of physical reinstatement in controlled experiments? In the following, we summarize two interpretations of when physical reinstatement of EC should and should not aid recall.

The Outshining Hypothesis

Smith (1988; Smith & Vela, 1986) formulated an *Outshining Hypothesis*, the central tenet of which is that the effectiveness of EC cues depends on what other cues are available. The *outshining* label comes from a visual analogy: ". . . the idea that a heavenly body which is visible on a moonless night is more difficult to see when there is a full moon, and is completely outshone in the daytime by the sun" (p. 19). According to the analogy, EC cues are relatively weak retrieval cues in comparison to other types of retrieval cues (e.g., a copy cue or the stimulus member of a paired associate). EC cues will therefore influence retrieval processes only when more powerful cues are not available to guide retrieval.

The basic idea that EC cues become more important the fewer the other retrieval cues available has been stated by a number of other authors (e.g., Eich, 1980; Geiselman & Bjork, 1980; Smith et al., 1978; Spear, 1978). Smith elaborated the idea and applied it in a systematic fashion to a number of contextual phenomena. The strongest evidence in support of the hypothesis thus far is that recognition memory tests show little sensitivity to EC under conditions in which recall shows reliable effects of EC match/mismatch (e.g., Godden & Baddeley, 1980; Smith et al., 1978). The hypothesis accounts for these findings in a natural way: The copy cue provided on a typical recognition test overrides (outshines) EC cues. If the value of the copy cue is decreased by inducing shallow (poor) encoding at input, or by altering physical form of the copy cue between study and test, recognition should show positive effects of EC reinstatement. Smith (1985, 1986) reported finding EC-dependent recognition under such conditions.

It is our view that there is considerable merit to the outshining hypothesis, but that it is not a sufficient explanation of the pattern of effects and non-effects of EC match/mismatch. Among the findings not explained by the hypothesis are the following:

1. As reviewed earlier, there have been a number of failures to find EC effects in free recall (e.g., Richardson-Klavehn's Experiment 1—see Fig. 9.2), including a failure to replicate a published report (Fernandez & Glenberg, 1985, Experiment 8). According to the outshining principle, however, free recall tests should be maximally sensitive to EC reinstatement because those tests provide little to the subject in the way of external retrieval cues.

2. The outshining hypothesis cannot explain why Richardson-Klavehn's Experiment 2 failed to replicate the substantial effects in Smith et al.'s Experiment 2. Although, according to the hypothesis, the cued recall test used in these experiments is not the most EC-sensitive test that could have been used, the encoding procedures and test cues were precisely the same in the two experiments.

3. The positive effects of EC variation during study (in terms of reduced interference and enhanced total recall) seem reliable—apparently more reliable than is the effect of physical EC reinstatement. The outshining principle does not address this difference between the first- and second-order effects of EC.

A Mental Reinstatement Hypothesis

According to the outshining principle, the physical reinstatement of EC cues will aid performance only if such cues are not "outshone" by other cues at the time of test. In order to account for the failures to find effects of EC reinstatement on recall measures, we believe it is necessary to make the additional assumption that physical reinstatement of EC cues will benefit performance only when those EC cues cannot (or typically would not) be reinstated mentally at the time of test.

In laboratory experiments, of course, subjects who are tested in a context different from that used for original learning are normally given exactly the same recall instructions and recall time as the subjects who are tested in the original learning context (assuming that the possible subtle differences in demand characteristics across conditions, alluded to earlier, are avoided). The recall instructions given to different-context subjects in an episodic memory task—to recall material encountered earlier at a particular time and place— essentially constitute instructions to mentally reinstate the study context. Given that all subjects receive the same instructions, the ability of different-context subjects to mentally reinstate the study context weakens or eliminates the context effect.

Thus, only in those situations in which imaginal reinstatement is difficult or impossible should we expect reliable effects of physical reinstatement. Such situations can be brought about experimentally (e.g., as in Smith's 1979 Experiment 3, referred to earlier), but may also occur naturally, particularly in those real-world situations that involve long retention intervals.

Judgment concerning the truth of the mental reinstatement hypothesis must necessarily await explicit experimental testing. The current virtue of the hypothesis, however, is that it provides an integrated framework within which the unreliability of first-order (physical reinstatement) EC effects and the reliability of second-order (imaginal reinstatement, interference reduction, and enhanced total recall) EC effects can be naturally accommodated.

Memory and Metamemory Effects of EC Reinstatement

In our view, given that both outshining and mental reinstatement do not occur, physically reinstating EC cues can affect cognitive processing in two ways. To distinguish these effects, we describe one as a memory effect, and the other as a metamemory effect.

Memory. The memory effect is straightforward. We *do* think that EC cues are encoded as part of episodic memory traces, so physically reinstating those cues should aid access to the target episode of interest (subject to the caveats given earlier). The effectiveness of such cues will vary greatly depending on the extent to which those cues were available to, and processed by, the subject's sensory organs at encoding (the *functional* contextual cues as opposed to the *nominal* physical contextual cues—see Geiselman & Bjork, 1980), and on the extent to which those cues are unique to the episode in question. If many episodes take place in the presence of the same EC cues, the effectiveness of those cues will be diminished *(cue-overload—*see Watkins & Watkins, 1975). The reduction of interference between sets of learned materials that occurs when those materials are learned in different contexts (compared to when they are learned in the same context) can be viewed as an enhancement of the ability of the EC cues to specify target material uniquely, increasing the signal-to-noise ratio of the retrieval operation.

Metamemory. The metamemory effect is an effect on the subject's control processes. Physically reinstating EC cues may trigger a person to attempt to recall a prior event, or material learned earlier, whereas without such reinstatement no attempt would have been made to recall the target event or material. In certain situations, being in the context of original learning for an extended time period may result in more active, extensive, and temporally extended attempts at recollection than would be attempted in a different context, were such attempts made at all. The "triggering effect" of environmental cues that we note here bears some similarities to the notion of *retrieval mode* put forward by Tulving (1983, Chap. 9). In Tulving's view a necessary precondition for the effectiveness of stimuli as cues for the recall of personal experiences is that the memory system be in retrieval mode (because the majority of potential retrieval cues do not elicit episodic memories unless the subject is instructed to retrieve memories connected with those stimuli). Our concept of the metamemory effects of environmental cues differs from Tulving's retrieval mode notion in that we postulate that reinstatement of environmental cues (and not just recall instructions) can have the effect of inducing a subject to attempt to remember events that occurred in the presence of those cues.

Interpreting the Effects and Non-Effects, Anecdotal and Experimental, of Reinstating Incidental EC Cues

One implication of the explanations we offer here is that the conditions under which physical reinstatement of incidental EC cues will aid memory is quite restricted. What are we to make, then, of the numerous anecdotes that seem so convincing, and of the numerous positive effects reported in the literature?

Naturalistic Examples.   We believe that the naturalistic examples reflect both genuine and nongenuine effects of reinstating incidental context. There are straightforward reasons to treat some anecdotes as genuine examples: Some of the examples satisfy the preconditions for the effectiveness of reinstatement that we set forth earlier. The long retention intervals (years, decades) common to many cases would make mental reinstatement difficult or impossible. In many cases the EC cues were unique to the episode in question, and there would usually not be any explicit "test" procedure that might provide cues that would outshine the EC cues.

As mentioned earlier, however, we also believe that there are two reasons why many such examples are fallacious—as far as being demonstrations that recall is aided by the physical reinstatement of *incidental* cues: (a) In real-world cases the reinstated context typically contains environmental stimuli that were integrated with target material at encoding, or which influenced the interpretation of that material when it was encoded; and (b) the anecdotes do not typically include the appropriate different-context comparison, in which the subject is to try to recall target information when in an EC different to that in which original learning took place. The memories "reinstated" by a return to some context might be just as accessible in a different context were something to cue the person to attempt to access those memories as actively and extensively as they are likely to do when in the original context.

Published Results.   With respect to the positive effects of physical reinstatement in controlled laboratory experiments, we make three points:

1. Given the editorial policies of major journals, many failures to find effects of context reinstatement may never have appeared in print. It is therefore possible that some published examples of positive effects of incidental context represent Type I errors.

2. In certain cases manipulations that were nominally of incidental context may actually have constituted manipulations of influential context. Subjects may, for example, have used environmental stimuli as "pegs" to anchor

learned items at encoding, a technique similar to that of the method of loci. It is plausible that this type of encoding strategy is sometimes adopted spontaneously because subjects learn of such techniques in psychology classes. Alternatively, subtle cues given by the experimenter might induce the subjects to focus attention on environmental stimuli during encoding of target material.

3. Certain of the positive results reported may have been a consequence of the recall instructions given by the experimenter. As these experiments do not typically use single-blind testing (in which the experimenter is unaware of the subject's experimental condition), the experimenter may sometimes be more enthusiastic and motivating in the same-context condition than in the different-context condition. Even in the case of the within-subjects designs discussed earlier, which would seem to be free of differential biasing, our experience indicates that the instructions to subjects at test must be very carefully worded. If they are not, subjects tested in a particular context can assume that they are only to recall material learned in that context, and not material learned in the other context. Recall of different-context words would then reflect intrusion errors on the part of the subject. In free-recall experiments of the within-subject type, subjects could assume that they are to begin recall with words learned in the test context, causing output interference for different-context items. Output order analyses of Richardson-Klavehn's (1988) Experiment 1 data revealed no indication that such interference was occurring, but it must be noted that this experiment did not obtain a positive context effect.

Implications for Models of Memory

As we noted at the outset, context-dependent forgetting is a primitive assumption in many current memory models. This assumption is not often submitted to critical analysis, even though the value of such memory models as explanations of remembering and forgetting is largely predicated on its truth. The literature reviewed here suggests that our reliance on context change as the major factor explaining forgetting needs to be seriously questioned. We have argued that the range of situations under which changing incidental EC will negatively affect performance (i.e., produce forgetting) is limited, owing to the roles of outshining and mental reinstatement. Tying general explanations of forgetting to changes in incidental EC would therefore not appear to be advisable, even if EC cues are encoded and later influence retrieval under some conditions. It might be argued that changes in integral and influential context are primarily responsible for forgetting; however, this argument lacks plausibility. It is clear that large amounts of forgetting occur in situations in which no obvious changes in integral or influential context have occurred. For example, an item on a recognition test, unless highly ambiguous in meaning, is likely to be interpreted semantically in the same way as it was interpreted at study. Yet a subject might still fail to recognize that item. Change in physiological context is another often-invoked candidate in explanations of forgetting. Again, the idea that this type of context is subject to changes within an experimental session that are extreme enough to produce forgetting is simply implausible.

Based on the evidence reviewed above concerning the role of contextual variation in reducing interference, it seems that theoretical explanations of forgetting need to focus not on contextual change, but on the interference that occurs between items that are encoded in similar contexts. In other words, we need to develop theories that deal in a systematic manner with the problems of interference that preoccupied researchers in an earlier era. As proposed by those earlier researchers (e.g., Bilodeau & Schlosberg, 1951; McGovern, 1964), contextual factors probably play an important role in modulating interference processes. However, as noted by Bjork (1989), in the brain-metaphor-influenced theoretical environment of the late 1980s, it is perhaps finally appropriate to reintroduce the additional notion of active retrieval inhibition into our explanations of forgetting and remembering.

INCIDENTAL EC CUES IN PERSPECTIVE: TOWARD A TAXONOMY

We have restricted our focus here to contexts of a particular type (incidental environmental context) and to effects on memory measured in a particular way (recall). In terms of the possible types of contextual features that might be reinstated, however, and in terms of the possible measures of memory that might show an influence of such reinstatement, that restriction is severe. In this final section, in an attempt to lend some organization to the entire space defined by the various types of contexts and types of measures, we propose a three-dimensional taxonomy.

In describing our taxonomy, we use the word "target" to refer to information presented in some original context, the memory representation of which is then assessed with or without some aspect or aspects of that context being reinstated at test. The three dimensions in our taxonomy are *Type of Context, Context-Target Relationship*, and *Type of Processing* demanded by the test used to assess memory.

Type of Context

The first dimension refers to the distinction between *intraitem and extraitem* aspects of context (Geiselman & Bjork, 1980). Intraitem context refers to the various features of the stimulus bundle when the target is presented in the original context. Examples are modality of presentation, language, voicing, typeface, and so forth. Extraitem context denotes those aspects of the environment that are "outside" the stimulus bundle. Room cues, body-state cues (including physiological state and drug state), mood, background noises, other list items, the cue-member of a cue-target pair, and so forth are all examples of extraitem aspects of context.

Context-Target Relationship

The second dimension refers to the relationship between the aspect of context that is of interest and the target item as encoded. As we argued above, that relationship can be *integral, influential,* or *incidental.* Given typical encoding processes, examples of intraitem contextual features that are integral to the encoded representation of the target might be the language in which a to-be-remembered sentence is spoken, the melody accompanying to-be-remembered lyrics, and several different features of a to-be-remembered face. Examples of integral extra item context might be the stimulus member of a highly integrable S-R pair (e.g., *sour grapes*), or a feature of an environment with which the subject specifically associated a to-be-remembered word at encoding (as in the method of loci).

Influential context refers to intraitem or extraitem aspects of context that are not integral to the target as encoded, but nonetheless influence the form of the encoding. Intraitem aspects of context such as voicing or script may not end up as integral to the memory trace of the target but they may influence the encoding of the target. For example, consider the possible differential impact of male versus female speaker on the encoding of the homophone *bow* (weapon vs. piece of clothing). Experimental evidence suggests that sex of speaker also affects the connotative meaning of nonhomophonic words (e.g., Geiselman & Bellezza, 1977; Geiselman & Crawley, 1983). Extraitem aspects of context can exert similar influences on encoding. Smith et al. (1978) point out that the homographs *knot* and *bow* would both be interpreted very differently in the context of a ship and in the context of a gift shop. Certain drug states, such as that induced by marijuana, are thought to influence the form of encoded target material. Similar influences could clearly occur in the case of mood changes. Even time of day has been found to influence semantic memory retrieval processes (e.g., Tilley & Warren, 1983), suggesting that time of day could influence episodic encoding. These types of influences can occur at least sometimes without the awareness of the subject; for example, in Tulving's famous experiments (e.g., Tulving & Thomson, 1973), a subject would sometimes fail to recognize the response-word (e.g., *COLD*) of a previously studied pair (*ground-COLD*) on a recognition test even though he/she had generated that response alternative him/herself in response to an associated word (*hot*). In other experiments targets and biasing contexts were not attentionally encoded (e.g., they were presented on the unattended channel in a dichotic listening task—see Eich, 1984), but the context nonetheless influenced subjects' subsequent interpretation of the target.

Finally, incidental context is defined by exclusion to refer to those aspects of context that are not integral or influential. We have given a number of examples in this chapter of extra item cues that would typically be incidental, such as room cues, ambient temperature (over a reasonable range), and so forth. Intraitem contextual cues that would frequently be incidental are print color, print case (upper and lower), intensity of a visual or auditory target over the normal range, and so forth.

Type of Processing at Test

The third dimension in our taxonomy refers to the nature of the processing demanded by the test that is used to assess memory. We presume, following Jacoby (1983) and Roediger and Blaxton (1987), that two types of test processing can be distinguished: *Data-driven processing* and *conceptually driven processing*. In data-driven tests the subject is required to operate on perceptual information provided by the experimenter. For example, the subject might be required to identify a rapidly flashed word (perceptual identification), supply deleted letters to complete a word (fragment completion), or spell an auditorily presented homophone. In conceptually driven tests the subject must engage in constructive, semantically based processing in order to perform the task. A typical example of such a test is free recall. Recognition memory tests involve a blend of data-driven and conceptually driven processing: The subject operates on perceptual data provided by the experimenter, but must usually reconstruct the study episode in order to perform successfully.

The differential sensitivity of different memory tests to manipulations of elaboration at study and of match between perceptual and linguistic contexts at study and test can also be used to classify memory tests as data-driven or conceptually driven (e.g., Jacoby, 1983; Roediger & Blaxton, 1987; see following discussion). By contrast, we classify memory tests as data-driven or conceptually driven based on criteria of type of test cues and task requirements. We prefer the latter method of classification for the purpose of constructing a taxonomy of forms of context because it avoids certain problems of circularity when it comes to determining the forms of context to which each type of memory measure is sensitive.

Blaxton (1985) and Roediger and Blaxton (1987) point out that data-driven tests typically differ from conceptually driven tests with respect to whether the subject is required to display explicit knowledge concerning some prior episode. In the terms used by Johnson and Hasher (1987) and Richardson-Klavehn and Bjork (1988), data-driven tests are generally *indirect* tests of memory whereas conceptually driven tests are generally *direct* tests of memory. In indirect tests, the subject is simply required to engage in some cognitive activity, the instructions refer only to the task at hand, and the effect of a prior episode is assessed by comparing performance with relevant prior experience to performance without such experience (a control condition). In tests of perceptual identification or fragment completion, for example, some test items have been studied prior to their appearance on the test, whereas other items have not been studied. The measures of interest reflect a change in performance (typically a facilitation) caused by prior exposure to the test stimuli. It is particularly appropriate, therefore, to refer to such measures as *indirect* because the measure of the effect of an episode that is obtained is usually derived from a comparison of at least two data points.

As indirect memory tests involve no reference to a prior episode on the part of the experimenter, they are particularly well-suited to reveal effects of a prior episode that are expressed in performance without the subject consciously remembering the episode that caused the behavioral change. An outstanding example of such *memory without awareness* (Jacoby & Witherspoon, 1982) is the human global anterograde amnesic syndrome. Amnesics are, by definition, people who experience profound difficulty remembering information encountered subsequent to the onset of the amnesia—notably information concerning personal experiences. Despite this deficit, amnesics will often behave exactly like normal control subjects if their memory is assessed using an indirect test, such as fragment completion (for summaries, see Richardson-Klavehn & Bjork, 1988 and Shimamura, 1986). Of course, the fact that indirect tests *can* reveal the effect of an episode when a subject is not making conscious reference to that episode does not imply that normal subjects never make such conscious reference in performing indirect tests.

In contrast to indirect tests, the instructions in direct memory tests refer explicitly or directly to some prior episode in the personal history of the subject, and the subject must give evidence of knowledge concerning the episode in order to achieve success at the task. A normal subject is therefore typically in some sense made consciously "aware of the episode" in question by the task instructions; there is, however, considerable latitude with respect to the mental processes that can be involved in direct tests. Subjects might experience mental states similar to those that they experienced during the episode in question (reexperiencing the episode); on the other hand, they might achieve success by using semantic-conceptual knowledge to reconstruct what most likely occurred, or could simply guess correctly (e.g., as in forced-choice recognition). Performance on direct tests typically reflects a blend of these different mental processes.

Although direct tests are typically conceptually driven and indirect tests are typically data-driven, Blaxton (1985) and Roediger and Blaxton (1987) correctly point out that the conceptually driven/data-driven and direct/indirect dichotomies are not logically coextensive. Direct tests can be data-driven, such as when a subject is given a word (such as *CHOPPER*) as a cue to recall a graphemically similar word (such as *COPPER*) that was presented during some prior episode (*graphemically cued recall*). On the other hand, indirect tests can be conceptually driven: Retrieving the answer to a general knowledge question (e.g., "What metal makes up 10% of yellow gold?"), which does not require knowledge of a prior episode, clearly involves semantically based constructive processing.

One might expect that the direct/indirect distinction would be important with respect to a taxonomy of forms of context. Direct measures, after all, require retrieval of information about prior episodes, whereas indirect measures do not. One could therefore entertain the hypothesis that reinstatement of prior episodic context would matter only for direct measures, and not for indirect measures. That hypothesis, however, is false. As documented by Richardson-Klavehn and Bjork (1988) and Roediger and Blaxton (1987), the data-driven/conceptually driven distinction performs better than does the direct/indirect distinction in helping to clarify the pattern of contextual effects on memory. Regardless of direct/indirect status, data-driven tests are not sensitive to manipulations of elaboration of processing at study, but are sensitive to the match between study and test language, modality, typeface, and so forth. Conceptually driven tests, on the other hand, uniformly benefit from increasing the amount of elaborative processing accorded to study items, but are relatively not sensitive to factors such as language and modality—in fact, performance can actually be better when the perceptual data at study and test do not match than when they do match. For example, recognition memory for an item presented in verbal form at test (e.g., *CART*) is better when that item was studied as a picture or generated in response to a cue (*horse-???*) than when that item was presented in verbal form at study. The reverse pattern holds for data-driven tests: Performance in perceptual identification and fragment completion is enhanced more by prior study of an item in verbal form than by prior generation of that item, or study of that item in pictorial form (e.g., Blaxton, 1985; Jacoby, 1983; Roediger & Blaxton, 1987; Roediger & Weldon, 1987; Weldon & Roediger, 1987; Winnick & Daniel, 1970).

Concluding Comments

Combining the three dimensions of the taxonomy ($2 \times 3 \times 2$) yields 12 cases in which physical reinstatement might or might not enhance performance. For some of those cases, as we pointed out earlier, the research literature provides a fairly clear answer. When the context-target relationship is *integral*, for example, physical reinstatement aids performance whatever the type of context (intra- or extraitem) or the type of processing (data-driven or conceptually driven). By contrast, the status (with respect to effects/noneffects) of a number of the cells in the taxonomy is currently unclear. It is not the purpose of this chapter to address all of these cases; here we have been concerned largely with one problematic cell—the effects of incidental extra item context on performance on a conceptually driven memory test (recall). We have tried to emphasize the importance of the distinction between integral, influential, and incidental context in the analysis of this issue. The data-driven/conceptually driven distinction, although not introduced in our analysis, is also important with respect to the effects of incidental EC: Thus far there is little evidence that data-driven tests such as perceptual identification are sensitive to manipulations of incidental EC. Speaking more generally, our taxonomy demonstrates that "context" cannot be treated as a unitary construct (as it often is, particularly in theoretical models of memory): Whether reinstating context affects memory will depend on an interaction of the form of context in question and the way that memory is measured.

ACKNOWLEDGMENTS

The preparation of this chapter and the original research reported herein were supported, in part, by Grant 3186 from the Committee on Research, University of California, to the first author. The second author is deeply indebted to Amina Memon for numerous helpful suggestions, for assistance in preparing experimental materials and scoring data, and for serving as an experimenter in Experiment 1 of Richardson-Klavehn (1988); and also to Greta Mathews for serving as an experimenter in Experiment 2 of Richardson-Klavehn (1988).

REFERENCES

Asimov, I. (1986). *Robots and empire.* New York: Ballantine.

Baddeley, A. D. (1982). Domains of recollection. *Psychological Review, 89,* 708–729.

Barclay, J. R., Bransford, J. D., Franks, J. J., McCarrell, N. S., & Nitsch, K. (1974). Comprehension and semantic flexibility. *Journal of Verbal Learning and Verbal Behavior, 13,* 471–481.

Bilodeau, I. M., & Schlosberg, H. (1951). Similarity in stimulating conditions as a variable in retroactive inhibition. *Journal of Experimental Psychology, 41,* 199–204.

Bjork, E. L., & Bjork, R. A. (1988). On the adaptive aspects of retrieval failure in autobiographical memory. In M. M. Gruneberg, P. E. Morris, & R. N. Sykes (Eds.), *Practical aspects of memory II.* London: Wiley.

Bjork, R. A. (1989). Retrieval inhibition as an adaptive mechanism in human memory. In H. L. Roediger & F. I. M. Craik (Eds.), *Varieties of memory and consciousness: Essays in honour of Endel Tulving.* Hillsdale, NJ: Lawrence Erlbaum Associates.

Blaxton, T. A. (1984). *Investigating dissociations among memory measures: Support for a transfer-appropriate processing framework.* Unpublished doctoral dissertation, Purdue University, West Lafayette, IN.

Chen, M. (1984). *Effects of number of study environments on exam performance.* Unpublished master's thesis, Texas A & M University, College Station, TX.

Coggins, K. A., & Kanak, N. J. (1985). *Environmental context effects on the learning of a second list.* Paper presented at the Annual Meeting of the Southwestern Psychological Association, Austin, TX.

Dallett, K., & Wilcox, S. G. (1968). Contextual stimuli and proactive inhibition. *Journal of Experimental Psychology, 78,* 475–480.

Eckert, E., Kanak, N. J., & Stevens, R. (1984). Memory for frequency as a function of the environmental context. *Bulletin of the Psychonomic Society, 22,* 507–510.

Eich, E. (1980). The cue-dependent nature of state-dependent retrieval. *Memory & Cognition, 8*, 157–173.

Eich, E. (1984). Memory for unattended events: Remembering with and without awareness. *Memory & Cognition, 12*, 105–111.

Eich, E. (1985). Context, memory, and integrated item/context imagery. *Journal of Experimental Psychology: Learning, Memory, and Cognition, 11*, 764–770.

Fernandez, A., & Glenberg, A. M. (1985). Changing environmental context does not reliably affect memory. *Memory & Cognition, 13*, 333–345.

Fisher, R. P., Geiselman, R. E., Holland, H. L., & MacKinnon, D. P. (1984). Hypnotic and cognitive interviews to enhance the memory of eyewitnesses to crime. *International Journal of Investigative and Forensic Hypnosis, 7*, 28–31.

Frerk, N., Holcomb, L., Johnson, S., & Nelson, T. (1985). *Context-dependent learning in a classroom situation.* Unpublished manuscript, Gustavus Adolphus College, St. Peter, MN.

Geiselman, R. E., & Bellezza, F. S. (1977). Incidental retention of speaker's voice. *Memory & Cognition, 5*, 658–665.

Geiselman, R. E., & Bjork, R. A. (1980). Primary versus secondary rehearsal in imagined voices: Differential effects on recognition. *Cognitive Psychology, 12*, 188–205.

Geiselman, R. E., & Crawley, J. M. (1983). Incidental processing of speaker characteristics: Voice as connnotative information. *Journal of Verbal Learning and Verbal Behavior, 22*, 15–23.

Glenberg, A. M. (1979). Component levels theory of the effects of spacing on recall and recognition. *Memory & Cognition, 2*, 95–112.

Godden, D. R., & Baddeley, A. D. (1975). Context-dependent memory in two natural environments: On land and underwater. *British Journal of Psychology, 66*, 325–331.

Godden, D. R., & Baddeley, A. D. (1980). When does context influence recognition memory? *British Journal of Psychology, 71*, 99–104.

Greenspoon, J., & Ranyard, R. (1957). Stimulus conditions and retroactive inhibition. *Journal of Experimental Psychology, 53*, 55–59.

Jacoby, L. L. (1983). Remembering the data: Analyzing interactive processes in reading. *Journal of Verbal Learning and Verbal Behavior, 22*, 485–508.

Jacoby, L. L., & Witherspoon, D. (1982). Remembering without awareness. *Canadian Journal of Psychology, 36*, 300–324.

Johnson, M. K., & Hasher, L. (1987). Human learning and memory. *Annual Review of Psychology, 38*, 631–668.

Kanak, N. J., & Stevens, R. (1985). *Field independence-dependence in learning and retention and environmental context.* Paper presented at the Annual Meeting of the Southwestern Psychological Association, Austin, TX.

Landauer, T. K. (1986). How much do people remember? Some estimates of the quantity of learned information in long-term memory. *Cognitive Science, 10*, 477–493.

Light, L. L., & Carter-Sobell, L. (1970). Effects of changed semantic context on recognition memory. *Journal of Verbal Learning and Verbal Behavior, 9*, 1–11.

McGovern, J. B. (1964). Extinction of associations in four transfer paradigms. *Psychological Monographs, 78 (16, Whole No. 593)*, 1–21.

Richardson-Klavehn, A. (1988). *Effects of incidental environmental context on human memory: Elusive or nonexistent?* Unpublished doctoral dissertation, University of California, Los Angeles.

Richardson-Klavehn, A., & Bjork, R. A. (1988). Measures of memory. *Annual Review of Psychology, 39*, 475–543.

Roediger, H. L., & Blaxton, T. A. (1987). Retrieval modes produce dissociations in memory for surface information. In D. S. Gorfein & R. R. Hoffman (Eds.), *Memory and cognitive processes: The Ebbinghaus Centennial Conference.* Hillsdale, NJ: Lawrence Erlbaum Associates.

Roediger, H. L., & Weldon, M. S. (1987). Reversing the picture superiority effect. In M. A.

McDaniel & M. Pressley (Eds.), *Imagery and related mnemonic processes: Theory, individual differences, and applications*. New York: Springer.

Saufley, W. H., Otaka, S. R., & Bavaresco, J. L. (1985). Context effects: Classroom tests and context independence. *Memory & Cognition, 13*, 522–528.

Shimamura, A. P. (1986). Priming effects in amnesia: Evidence for a dissociable memory function. *Quarterly Journal of Experimental Psychology, 38A*, 619–644.

Smith, S. M. (1979). Remembering in and out of context. *Journal of Experimental Psychology: Human Learning and Memory, 5*, 460–471.

Smith, S. M. (1982). Enhancement of recall using multiple environmental contexts during learning. *Memory & Cognition, 10*, 405–412.

Smith, S. M. (1984). A comparison of two techniques for reducing context-dependent forgetting. *Memory & Cognition, 12*, 477–482.

Smith, S. M. (1985). Environmental context and recognition memory reconsidered. *Bulletin of the Psychonomic Society, 23*, 173–176.

Smith, S. M. (1986). Environmental context-dependent recognition memory using a short-term memory task for input. *Memory & Cognition, 14*, 347–354.

Smith, S. M. (1988). Environmental context-dependent memory. In D. M. Thomson & G. M. Davies (Eds.), *Memory in context: Context in memory*. New York: Wiley.

Smith, S. M., Glenberg, A. M., & Bjork, R. A. (1978). Environmental context and human memory. *Memory & Cognition, 6*, 342–353.

Smith, S. M., & Rothkopf, E. Z. (1984). Contextual enrichment and distribution of practice in the classroom. *Cognition and Instruction, 1*, 341–358.

Smith, S. M., & Vela, E. (1986). *Outshining: The relative effectiveness of cues*. Paper presented at the Annual Meeting of the Psychonomic Society, New Orleans, LA.

Spear, N. E. (1978). *The processing of memories: Forgetting and retention*. Hillsdale, NJ: Lawrence Erlbaum Associates.

Thomson, D. M., & Tulving, E. (1970). Associative encoding and retrieval: Weak and strong cues. *Journal of Experimental Psychology, 86*, 255–262.

Tilley, A., & Warren, P. (1983). Retrieval from semantic memory at different times of day. *Journal of Experimental Psychology: Learning, Memory, and Cognition, 9*, 718–724.

Tulving, E. (1983). *Elements of episodic memory*. New York: Oxford University Press.

Tulving, E., & Thomson, D. M. (1973). Encoding specificity and retrieval processes in episodic memory. *Psychological Review, 80*, 352–373.

Watkins, O. C., & Watkins, M. J. (1975). Build-up of proactive inhibition as a cue-overload effect. *Journal of Experimental Psychology: Human Learning and Memory, 1*, 442–425.

Weldon, M. S., & Roediger, H. L. (1987). Altering retrieval demands reverses the picture superiority effect. *Memory & Cognition, 15*, 269–280.

Winnick, W. A., & Daniel, S. A. (1970). Two kinds of response priming in tachistoscopic word recognition. *Journal of Experimental Psychology, 84*, 74–81.

10

Prototypes, Schemata, and the Form of Human Knowledge: The Cognition of Abstraction

Robert L. Solso
University of Nevada - Reno

Nothing is more revealing than movement.
—Martha Graham

The question "What is the source and structure of human knowledge?" is as old as the history of mankind. The answer is still incomplete, but some fresh new ways have recently been formulated by cognitive psychologists which suggest that real progress has been made in this endeavor. Although no definitive, universally accepted solution has been put forth to the riddle of the form of human knowledge, there does exist a body of data that has identified some of its essential properties. The "form of human knowledge" is beginning to take shape and, in this chapter, part of that information will be systematized under the rubric of prototypes and schemata.

This chapter is organized around four principle segments. In the first section a selected review of the history of human knowledge is presented. The second section contains a report of the theoretical and empirical issues involved in structural knowledge with particular attention to schemata. In the third section a review of recent developments in this field is offered plus a proposed model of "dance grammar." This section also includes a speculative notion which suggests that the source and structure of human knowledge may be traced to the evolution of the skeletal-muscular system. This "muscle-bound" idea is called the Muscle Abstraction Principle (MAP). And in the final section, cognitive psychology is related to what is nebulously referred to as "the real world."

THE FORM OF HUMAN KNOWLEDGE: PAST AND PRESENT

All serious investigations of the nature of human knowledge soon run into a double dichotomous conundrum: The first puzzle is, "Is knowledge innate or acquired? and the second is, "Is knowledge represented isomorphically (i.e., in the same form) with the elements of the 'external' physical world or are the elements represented in the human mind metaphorically?" The arguments are orthogonal and thus we can characterize the primitive components of the study of knowledge as conforming to a 2 × 2 matrix. These themes and interactions were part of the initial efforts by Greek philosophers to account for the source and form of knowledge.

Early Theories of Knowledge

Neither time nor space are sufficient to give more than a brief, highly selective, historical review of the early theories of knowledge. First consider the conclusion reached by Socrates and the method of inquiry used in his attempt to answer the question of whether knowledge is innate or acquired. In the frequently cited *Meno*, Socrates interrogates a young slave about his knowledge of geometry. Through a method of questioning that bears his name, Socrates is able to extract simple information about a square, but then the lad falters. Socrates persists in asking questions, until the young man finally discovers that he actually "knows" quite a lot of the geometry of a square. The philosopher concludes that within the uneducated boy, knowledge of geometry lay dormant, just waiting to be released.

One can argue with both the method[1] and the conclusion. Yet, no matter how rudimentary the effort, the exchange between Socrates and the slave boy represents a good starting point for the development of the nature and origin of human knowledge and understanding.

Like ripples in a pond, theories and hypotheses about the nature of knowledge continued to spread its circle through Western intellectual thought from Descartes through the analytic concepts of Locke, Kant, Berkeley, and Hume. During the latter half of this century a new wave of hypotheses about the nature of human knowledge has been formed, largely through studies of cognitive science aided by a dazzling array of computers and other instruments that existed only in the science fiction of an earlier age. Although progress in the understanding of human knowledge has taken many different forms, this paper will concentrate on the development of abstract memory representations with the possibility that cognitive schemata may have been patterned after motor abstractions.

Schema Theory—Bartlett.   The modern study of the structure of human knowledge can be traced to Sir Frederic Bartlett who, in his remarkable book *Remembering: A Study in Experimental and Social Psychology* (1932) and in his less frequently cited but important later book *Thinking* (1958), laid

---

[1]Some would contend that Socrates shaped the slave boy's responses by positively reinforcing responses that appeared to demonstrate knowledge of geometry and ignored other responses.

out the basic principles of schema theory upon which most modern theories are based.[2]

A schema, as defined by Bartlett, is "an active organization of past reactions, or past experiences, which must always be supposed to be operating in any well adapted organic response." In another section, schemata were described as "masses of organized past experiences." In an excellent review and interpretation of Bartlett's theory, Brewer and Nakamura (1984) contended that Bartlett thought of schemata as real entities, that is schemata exist and schema theory attempts to describe them. This interpretation of schema theory is consistent with the theories of many contemporary cognitive psychologists. A notable exception is a recent, provocative article by Hintzman (1986).

Bartlett's view of schemata offered an impression of the way knowledge is represented that differed significantly from the philosophic tradition of his 19th century compatriots, namely the British Empiricists—Hobbes, Berkeley, and James Mill. For Bartlett, schemata were composed of "old knowledge" that was organized (a term used frequently throughout Bartlett's writing) in thematic patterns, such as in the gist of a story. Knowledge is not represented in terms of a collection of specific mental images (a view generally espoused by the aforementioned British Empiricists) but as a collection of organized patterns of information.

Furthermore, Bartlett was not content with the development of a limited philosophic issue, but thought that schemata permeated most forms of cognition. For example, he wrote of the organization of symmetrical visual figures, rules, stories, and motor responses. In one often cited passage, he suggested that after a tennis player has developed some knowledge about kinesthetic movements (such as a tennis stroke) then making a new stroke is not "something absolutely new, and . . . never merely a repeat (of) something old." As people have experiences with things—be they paragraphs of a story, see-

---

[2]As early as 1918 and 1926, Dr. Henry Head, a neurophysiologist, to whom Bartlett gave ample credit, developed a schema hypothesis in which schemata were thought to be physiological phenomena. In order to clarify the history of this concept I have quoted Bartlett extensively.

During the later stages of the war [World War I] . . . Sir Henry Head was carrying out his experimental work with aphasic patients . . . We met frequently, and it became his habit to read over to me the chapters of his projected book as they were written. I cannot pretend that I contributed much to them, but it is quite certain that from his reading of these chapters . . . I got the clue which I wanted for putting into order my own different collection of detailed experimental results. . . . He considered that he had irrefutable experimental evidence that past responses continued to have a direct functional significance on the shaping of present behaviour, not as stored individual traces of reaction, but as organized response groups to which he gave the name of 'schemata.' That I might take over and use 'schemata' as a chief clue to reduce to order what often seemed to me to be the tangled mass of my own results, was not, at any time, a suggestion made by Head to me, and unfortunately, owing to his rapidly failing health, I was never able to discuss that matter properly with him. It was an importation from one field of experiment into another one. (Bartlett 1958, p. 146)

ing a tennis ball in flight, or repetition of rules such as one might encounter in learning the conventional modes of one's culture—they form abstract generic cognitive representations or schemata.

Although schema theories have multiplied throughout the past 20 years and each new theorist usually invokes the name of Bartlett, that was not always the case. Originally, Bartlett's work did not impress American psychologists, who were infatuated with behaviorism. (See Brewer & Nakamura, 1984, for more details on this topic.) As the cognitive movement began to gain momentum, however, more American psychologists began to consider Bartlett's important work.

RECENT THEORIES AND DATA: SCHEMATA AND PROTOTYPES

Schemata, Prototypes, and Exemplars

For some time cognitive psychologists have used a variety of terms that all, more or less, refer to memories based on impressions of a class of sensory experiences. We identify correctly, say, a salmon as a type of fish, not because we recognize a specific salmon as being associated with fish, but because we have formed in memory the defining and characteristic features of the category of fish and recognize a specific salmon as being enough like the other members *or* close enough to the epitome of the class to call it a "fish." Some of the many items that have been incorrectly used interchangeably, include prototypes, schemata, abstract memory representations, pseudomemories, schema abstractions, blended memories, generic memory systems, schemata-abstractions, frames, beta structures, schema-like concepts, knowledge units, exemplars, and concept formation. In an effort to "clean up" the usage of three of these terms (schemata, prototypes, and exemplars) the following definitions are offered:

> *Schemata:* A hypothetical memory structure that includes knowledge about a class of information and the rules that govern the use of that knowledge.
> *Prototypes:* A memory representation of a class of information that represents the epitome of a group of sensory impression.
> *Exemplars:* Members of a class of sensory stimuli.

The distinction between prototypes and exemplars is similar to the classical distinction between form and matter. A prototype is the form or organization of elements whereas exemplars contain the elements themselves. Schemata include both exemplars and prototypes but, in addition, contain the rules of organization and inter- and intra-relationships.

Even though schema theory deals with abstraction of information, it also deals with very tangible and real human events. Consider the following example from everyday life. In viewing a theatrical event such as the opera *Carmen*, one senses the elements of the opera (e.g., the notes played by the orchestra, the words sung by the singers, and the visual components of the scene) that are organized into prototypes (e.g., thematic musical patterns, the substance of the story, and a general impression of the scenery). The opera schema embodies all of these elements acting together. It not only governs their formation, but also relates these memory components to one's world knowledge thereby giving a richer and fuller meaning to the experience. The same opera may be put on by a different producer, a different opera company with different singers and staging, and may even be sung in a different language. Though the elements are different, our modal experience (i.e., the essence of Carmen) is easily recognized.

To continue with our example, Bizet's *Carmen* is far more than a story about gypsies, thieves, cigarette-girls, smugglers, and bullfighters; it is more than arias, songs, choruses, duets, and recitatives; it is more than sets of canteena, brightly colored dresses and costumes, a square in Seville, and a smuggler's hide-out; it is more than a corps of dancers, the seductive Carmen sashaying across the stage, or the strutting of bullfighters. It is, of course, all of these elements and yet it is none of them. It is all elements acting together so that we perceive people endowed with strong and realistic emotions, with passionate feelings acting in violent ways. And, if the performance is skillful and the viewers are significantly receptive, it may stir a sympathetic emotional reaction in its audience that is understood because it is akin to other deeply felt experiences and, yet, is different.

Furthermore, and to me this is one of the most intriguing aspects of the human mind, if we experience a thematically similar event based on *Carmen*, such as the film *Carmen Jones* performed by an all black cast of several years ago, or a ballet, or an abstract painting, or a "rock" arrangement, or (in keeping with the festive New Orleans atmosphere) as a theme for a Mardi Gras party, or even the mundane experiences of one's daily life, not only can we recognize the basic infrastructure in the media, but if we are very discerning we can divine the quintessence of *Carmen*. And what is the "quintessence" of *Carmen* for you may not be the quintessence for me because of our basically nonidentical knowledge structure and its resulting schemata.

Each of us develops a singular framework in which information about the world and the laws that govern the relationships among information is contained. A large part of these permanent impressions and their relationships is organized around a central idiosyncratic theme commonly referred to as one's "personality." This dominant theme colors the way reality is perceived and yet we still do not know the details of the formation of or aberrations in personality makeup. (It seems that students of clinical psychology might find fertile ideas in the cognitive literature on schemata for their theories of abnormality.) Consider the different perspectives on the impressions gathered by the conductor of an opera, or the prompter, or the person in charge of props, or the music critic for the *New York Times*, or the mother of a bit player, or the young boy who is experiencing the opera for the first time.

The examples are as endless as are the kinds of people. And, it is about time that we use the collected wisdom about the way humans gather information about our world, incorporate that information into higher order structures and use these very tangible (albeit highly personalistic) structures in understanding "reality." Although some would maintain that "art is not a thing, it is a feeling," it would seem in light of our current understanding of the deeper structures of human cognition that a more accurate assessment would be "art is not a thing, it is a schema."

RECENT DEVELOPMENTS IN SCHEMA RESEARCH

The modern period of American empirical research on schemata (à la Bartlett) is far more pedestrian than ogling the passionate Carmen or pitying the blindly jealous Don Jose. For the most part, much of the scientific investigation into abstract memory representations did not deal with schemata but with the arrangment and coding of exemplars, concept formation, and prototype formation. Recently, however, several American psychologists have used the schemata concept as a cornerstone of their theories. We now turn to some of the research in that area.

Research Results

The study of prototypes (and schemata indirectly) was introduced into the New World by Posner and his coworkers (Posner, Goldsmith, & Welton, 1967; Posner & Keele, 1968, 1970) over 2 decades ago and has germinated several hundred research projects. Curiously embedded in these early empirical studies lay the seeds of several major theoretical issues that still remain unsettled today as well as the principal methodology for studying prototype formation. The issues and techniques will be briefly described here.

Abstraction of Prototype: Prototype as a Mean.   In a seminal study by Posner, Goldsmith, and Welton (1967), a prototype figure was formed by arranging nine dots in a pattern (e.g., a triangle). From this basic pattern, a series of exemplar patterns were formed by means of offsetting one or more of the dots. The derived figures ranged in distortion from slight to extreme. In a typical experiment, subjects were asked to sort 12 different distorted patterns (which were formed from three different prototypes) into one of three categories. The subjects never saw the prototype nor were they told that the distortions were derived from a central pattern. Once the subjects had learned to classify the distorted patterns, they were given a second batch of figures to classify. Some of these figures were derived from the prototype in the same way as the original set, some were "old" figures, and one of the figures was the prototype. The subjects classified the "old" patterns with an accuracy of about 87%, had a bit more difficulty with the new distortions, which yielded an accuracy rate of about 75%, but the prototype was classified as "well" as the old patterns. From these data Posner argued that subjects formed a prototype on the basis of abstracted information derived from the patterns that are distortions of the prototype. Mathematically, one could conceptualize the prototype as an abstract value, such as the mean of a series of numbers, which represents the series.

Abstraction of Prototype: Prototype as a Mode.   Studies by Franks and Bransford (1971), using sentences; and Newman (1977) and Solso and McCarthy (1981b), using faces; and Solso and Raynis (1979), using line figures, also presented evidence for memory abstraction. However, they identified the underlying cognitive principle to be the frequency with which subjects experience features of the prototype.

In one of our first experiments, McCarthy and I constructed a "prototype"

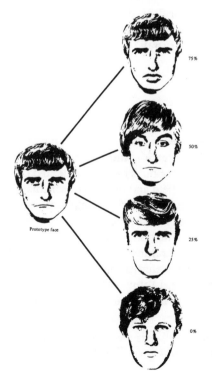

FIG. 10.1. Examples of prototype face and exemplar faces used in Solso and McCarthy (1981a).

face from a series of templates of an "Identikit," a face identification device used in police work. From this face, which was randomly composed, exemplar faces were derived that resembled the prototype face in terms of the number of features in common with the prototype face (see Fig. 10.1). Thus, from a prototype face made up of four main features (hair, eyes, nose plus chin, and mouth) a similar face could be derived that shared 50% of the features, that is two of the four features (say the mouth and hair). Participants in this experiment were given 10 exemplar faces to study briefly and then were given a second series of faces, which included some "new" faces, some "old" faces, and the prototype. They were than asked to give their confidence ratings as to whether the face was "old" or "new." As shown in Fig. 10.2 the prototype was judged overwhelmingly as an "old" item with the greatest confidence ratings. A second experiment was conducted that was identical to the above experiment except that recognition was delayed by 6 weeks.[3] As shown in Fig. 10.2, the results were nearly identical to the immediate recognition condition. In yet another experiment using the same material with subjects from USSR, Solso found that Soviet students' data were nearly identical to those of American students. This experiment has been replicated numerous times with highly reliable results. Clearly, the phenomenon is robust and transcends national boundaries. We refer to the phenomenon of falsely recognizing a stimulus as a previously experienced item with greater confidence than ascribed to an actually perceived item as "pseudomemory." In these experiments, the prototype is thought to be derived on the basis of the most frequently experienced features, which is mathematically similar to the modal representation of a set of information.

The Breadth of Prototype-Schema Experiments

Few ventures in modern cognitive psychology have captured the interest of so many different specialists than the rediscovered subject of abstract memory representations and the laws that govern their creation and relationship with other cognitive processes. Whereas several recent books have documented the results of many hundreds of experiments in this field and theories of schemata, those efforts will not be repeated here. However, a selected sample of these studies are presented both to give the reader an idea of the nature of current thinking and to build a logical foundation for the latter part of this chapter.

In a recent computer-assisted search of the literature on schemata, schema, prototypes, and abstract memory representation (terms that, unfortunately, are loosely used in the psychological literature), I found that in the 20 years since the seminal work of Posner et al. (1967) more than 300 articles have

---

[3]Recently, we have looked at prototype formation in very short term memory. In a preliminary study, Solso, Heck, and Mearns (1987) found that prototype formation of numbers could develop in less than ten seconds.

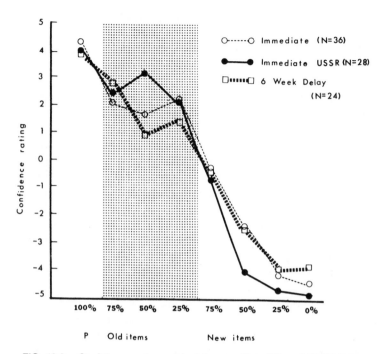

FIG. 10.2.   Confidence ratings of facial recognition. US and USSR Data.

dealt with these themes. (And, it is my impression that this number significantly underestimates the actual number of papers published worldwide.) From this long list of papers, it was possible to collect most of the articles or abstracts. These papers were sorted into two broad categories with approximately the same number of studies in each: One group was primarily theoretical in nature and the other, while not necessarily atheoretical, emphasizes the use of schema-prototype methodology/theory to enhance our understanding of other cognitive phenomena. Examples of theoretical articles include the work of Hintzman (1986), Homa (Homa, Sterling, & Treppel, 1981), Knapp and Anderson (1984), Medin (Medin & Schaffer, 1978; Medin & Smith, 1981, and Medin & Wattenmaker, 1987), and others.

The second group is more or less concerned with the use of the methodology of schema-prototype research as a means of resolving issues in visual memory (e.g., Franks & Bransford 1971, Reed, 1972), language processing (e.g., Kintsch & van Dijk, 1978), motor reactions (e.g., Schmidt, 1982a, 1982b), music (e.g., Welker, 1982), mathematics (e.g., Mayer, 1982), cognitive representations of the natural environment (e.g., Paradice, 1981), political affairs (e.g., Fiske, 1986), personal relationships (e.g., Ginsburg, 1987), and so forth, with specialized groups such as professional dancers (Solso, Ament, Kuraishy, & Mearns, 1986), elderly subjects (e.g., Hess & Slaughter, 1986), cross-cultural subjects (e.g., Cole & Scribner, 1974), infants (e.g., Cohen &

Strauss, 1979), and personality and psychiatric types (e.g., Cantor & Mischel, 1979), and as a means of organizing concepts in personality and social psychology (e.g., Wyer & Srull, 1984). We consider some of the second group of studies with particular emphasis on those done by the author.

Prototype Formation Among Elderly Subjects. As an example of both the versatility and utility of prototype experiments, consider a recent experiment conducted by Gabriel and Kuraishy in our Nevada laboratories (see Solso, Gabriel, & Kuraishy, 1987). Our study was motivated by an interest in the possible cognitive differences between elderly subjects and college students (the predominant population for prototype studies). The specific cognitive phenomenon under inquiry was prototype formation of two classes of stimuli: faces and numbers.

The first experiment was a replication of the earlier mentioned prototype experiment in which Identikit faces were used, and the second experiment replicated the technique developed by Solso and McCarthy (1981a) in which numerical prototypes were employed. This second methodology consisted of selecting a three-digit number as a prototype number (e.g., 386) and then generating a series of exemplar numbers that repeated each digit of the prototype in the same position, but did not contain a combination of the numbers in the prototype. For example, the numbers 371, 482, and 246 would qualify as exemplar numbers as they each repeat one of the numbers of the prototype in its original position and yet do not contain any two numbers of the prototype. A series of 15 exemplars were developed and shown to elderly subjects (median age = 74). After a few minutes the subjects were shown some "old" numbers, some "new" numbers, and the prototype number and were asked to judge each number on the same dimensions. Confidence ratings were also collected.

We found that elderly subjects performed almost identically to younger subjects (see Fig. 10.2) on the facial recognition task. Several features of these results are worth comment. There is a general belief that intellectual ability declines with age and, in fact, many types of cognitive abilities do. However, at least one type of ability—the ability to form abstractions of a class of exemplars—for a specific kind of information (facial memory) shows no appreciable diminution among elderly subjects. In addition, elderly subjects were successful in distinguishing between previously seen faces and unseen faces, with the exception of the prototype face. These findings by themselves are interesting but they are even more interesting when we consider them in connection with the data from the numerical part of the experiment.

When elderly subjects were given the numerical portion of the experiment they were, in general, able to distinguish between the old items and the new items and their confidence ratings were similar to the college age control group. However, they differed significantly on their evaluation of the prototype item. Although the control group falsely recognized the prototype number as an "old" item and rated their evaluation positively, the elderly group neither false alarmed nor hit on the prototype numbers. Their overall scores fell in between. It appears that the ability to abstract information from one class of stimuli (facial information) remains intact for elderly subjects but that for another class (numerical information) that ability diminishes. Why this occurs is still unresolved; however, part of the answer may be in interest and experience.

Language and Schemata. Since Bartlett's notion that stories are coded and remembered by means of schemata, several contemporary researchers have proposed ideas that further add to our understanding of the functional properties of memory for narrative compositions. Most notable among this contemporary work is that of Bower (1976a, 1976b), Bower, Black, and Turner (1979), Just and Carpenter (1987), Kintsch and van Dijk (1978), Mandler and Johnson (1977), Mervis and Rosch (1981), Minsky (1975), Rumelhart (1975), Schank and Abelson (1977), Thorndyke (1977), and van Dijk and Kintsch (1983). We focus on Kintsch and van Dijk's model of story abstraction.

The model of comprehension developed by Kintsch and van Dijk allows researchers interested in the structure of stories to make very precise predictions about the memorability of specific types of information. The technique developed by the authors is consistent with modern scientific methodology in psychology as contrasted with the subjective method used earlier in the important work of Bartlett.

In one test of the theory, Kintsch and van Dijk (1978) asked subjects to read a semitechnical report. Following the reading of the report one third of the subjects were immediately asked to recall and write a summary of the report. Another third of the subjects were tested after one month, and the final third after three months. It is noted that this part of the procedure is similar to the experiment conducted by Bartlett. Recall accounts and summaries were organized into propositions and analyzed with specific predictions made by the model. Several important conclusions were made by the authors about text comprehension and memory. As indicated by the data gathered over three different time periods, it appears that subjects lost more and more of the specific details of the report over time but retained the gist of the story with about the same degree of fidelity throughout a 3-month period—a finding consistent with the protocol analysis of Bartlett. Additionally, it seems that the analysis of written material, such as books, stories, and technical reports, is organized in a way that is susceptible to careful empirical study of propositions that may tell us more about the way text material is organized and how the human mind records and stores in memory written material.

A correlated way to look at stories is to think of narrative information as being structured in the form of a hierarchy in which the most important ideas are supported by less important statements. From an informal perspective we certainly seem to think of stories in a structured way, if not in terms of a hierarchy. If asked to tell what a story is about, for example *The Grapes of Wrath*, we may try to find a sentence or two that embodies the essence of the book. When asked to expand our interpretation of the story, we may, without consciously dissecting the book into its components, nevertheless discuss the theme, the setting, and the way it turned out. In addition, this pattern of cognition seems to apply to a wide class of episodes—from relating a casual happening to telling someone about a lecture. Furthermore, this proclivity seems to occur very early in life as has been aptly demonstrated by J. Mandler and her work with story grammar among children.

These results, as well as many more, seem to represent real progress in the attempt to answer the question of how narrative knowledge is represented in the human mind. Also, these theories suggest a mega-theory that is capacious enough to account for a wide range of human thought and actions. A mega-theory of the abstraction of information may embody other modalities such as motor performance. Measurable progress has been made in motor acquisition and the cognition of abstraction, a subject to which we now turn.

Motor Schemata.   One puzzle that may have a solution in schemata theory is the question of how complex motor activities, such as the rapid fingering of a violin throughout a complicated musical passage, or the deftness of a professional basketball player as he moves both ball and himself in graceful harmony, or the beauty of a ballerina performing an intricate procedure, might be understood in light of the physiological limitations of the sensory-cognitive-motor system. Recently, one of my colleagues, a physiological psychologist, ruefully told me that it is "impossible" for a human to play an integrated musical piece because the time required for the firing of neurons, to the selection of responses, to the execution of notes, and then the performance of another cycle requires more time than the human system is able to handle. Of course, people can, and therefore we must search for other mechanisms that explain this talent.

For an explanation of how the human can process intricate patterns of activities we again return to the seminal thoughts of Bartlett, who introduced the concept of schemata in the following passage. "Suppose I am making a stroke in a quick game, such as tennis or cricket . . . The stroke is literally manufactured out of the living visual and postural 'schemata' of the movement and their interrelations." In addition to accounting for athletic ability, schema theory also provides a rationale for human musical ability. Recently, the concept of motor schemata and related hierarchical systems as a means of explaining both the diversity and unity of motor responses has been an integral part of the writings of Kelso (1982), Pew (1984), Rosenbaum, Inhoff, and Gordon (1984), Schmidt (1982a, 1982b), and Solso (1988) among others.

Motor schema, as contrasted with the experiments on visual prototypes (e.g., Posner, Goldsmith, & Welton, 1967; Posner & Keele, 1968; and Solso & McCarthy, 1981b), involve both a spatial image and a temporal concept. With repeated kinesthetic experiences with patterns derived from a prototype pattern (or "mother" pattern, as we sometimes refer to it in our laboratory) we hypothesize that subjects form a motor schema that resembles the prototype. In order to specify precisely what a motor schema is, we define it as an internalized representation of a class of motor movements in which the most frequently experienced movements are integrated into a composite pattern. In general, the contribution of each movement to the development of the composite pattern or prototype is hypothesized to contribute to the abstracted composite figure in direct proportion to the frequency with which the movement is experienced. Exceptions to this rule may be found in particularly novel, idiosyncratic, traumatic, or emotionally laden movements.

Several years ago, Raynis and I became interested in this topic and did an experiment in which prototype formation for kinesthetically presented geometric figures was demonstrated (see Solso & Raynis, 1979). The basic paradigm involved the development of a "base" geometric figure from which exemplar items could be derived. Exemplar geometric figures were scaled in terms of their similarity to the base figure. Blindfolded college students were asked to try to remember the feeling they experienced as their hand was led through the series of exemplar motions. The subjects practiced the movements until they could successfully reproduce them. Then, after a short recess, each subject was asked to differentiate "new" from "old" kinesthetically presented geometric figures and to assign a confidence rating to each evaluation. It was no surprise to find that most subjects could identify clearly the old from the new patterns as shown in Fig. 10.3. We also anticipated that the subjects would erroneously identify the prototype (or base) figure as an "old" item. We were not prepared to find that the confidence with which subjects rated this new item as an old item would be greater than the actual old items. As in the Solso and McCarthy (1981b) experiment with faces, we found evidence of pseudo-memory. The tendency to falsely recognize a kinesthetically acquired geometric prototype is a very powerful matter.

These experimental results have caused me to consider other topics in motor learning and, as discussed in some detail in a later section, to think about the ecological realities involved in the evolution of the central nervous system and skeletal–musculature system of vertebrate animals. Undoubtedly, the two developed in a complementary fashion, for example, the cognitive proficiency for tool making and prehensile facility evolved concurrently. The appreciation of the coincidental evolution of cognitive ingenuity and physiological skills caused me to search for a single principle that might lead to a unified theory of cognitive–physiological development. One intermediate stage in this theory building required that we collect some additional data on how our earlier results of prototype formation might fare with specialized groups, especially as related to cognitive-Kinesthetic performance.

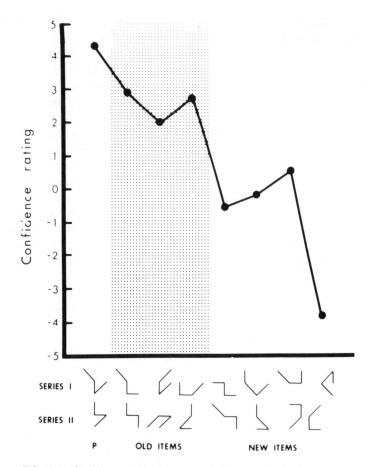

FIG. 10.3.   Confidence ratings for geometric figures presented kinesthetically.

Toward a Theory of Dance Grammar.   Recently we (Solso, Ament, Kuraishy, & Mearns, 1986) extended these findings by looking at kinesthetically formed prototypes among specialized samples, notably professional dancers. Following observations made by Chase and Simon (1973a, 1973b) of chess masters, class A players, and novice players, it appears that people with specialized knowledge code information in their specific field differently than do nonspecialists.

Students of dance learn certain themes in the course of their training, such as "centering," movements around a central point, organization of "steps," gestures, expressions of a feeling, and rhythm. They learn to express a "story" through controlled movements. It is plausible to think of the actions of dancers in terms of surface characteristics and deeper structures analogous to "story grammars" that are similar, in form, to the cognitive representations demonstrated by workers in structural linguistics and story schemata. The acquisition of new steps may be a form of a transformational process in which more enduring patterns, or prototypes, remain unchanged but are manifest in motor sequences that appear to be original routines.

Thoughts on Motor Abstractions as the Source of Cognitive Abstractions. At an even more fundamental level I would like to suggest that "dance grammar" may be a singular instance of a much more profound and universal feature of human (and animal) reality. It is possible that at the core of kinesthetic *and* psychological processes there exists an innate motor aptitude that, in keeping with modern theories in structural linguistics, reading, and artificial intelligence, could be called "kinesthetic competence." It appears that kinesthetic competence emerges without the intervention of training or learning. An activity, such as walking in the child, occurs naturally at more or less the same time, in all of the diverse cultures of the world and as far as can be estimated, throughout many centuries. The same can be said for the emergence of similar activities in other animals.

The Motor Abstraction Principle (MAP). Complex body actions may be governed by a set of genetically determined universal rules that are engaged at appropriate maturational periods. Throughout the long evolution of species, a symbiotic development of both cognitive and physiological attributes occurred. It is hypothesized that as genetically determined rules of motor performance evolved, corollary rules, which govern cognitive abstraction, evolved simultaneously.

Such an hypothesis suggests that during the very early evolution of creatures, motor systems emerged as means of survival. The appearance of primitive muscles allowed the organism to make simple responses. However, with the emergence of even slightly more complex muscles systems the organism was not only capable of making rudimentary reactions but also assemblies of action were possible; indeed necessary. It is suggested that these assemblies were organized generalized response structures which were rule governed. During this period of our evolutionary history, only the most simple of nervous systems was in place. Certainly, the development of the human brain as we now know it occurred much later.

It is postulated that as man's central nervous system became more and more sophisticated, a means of storing quiescent motor activity into higher order abstractions and rules which govern them, or schemata, was already well established. Much later in the evolutionary history of organisms, other forms of abstractions were modeled after these rudimentary patterns of storing and regulating potential motor activities. It is suggested that "natural" language abstraction, musical abstraction, and a wide class of *cognitive* affairs, were fashioned after and built upon a neurological apparatus originally designed to handle motor abstractions. Thus, the "revolutionary" theories of modern psycholinguists, personality theorists, developmental psychologists, and musicians, which embodied concepts as deep structure and ideas about the nature of linguistic, personality and musical syntax, may be concepts that reflect a larger principle of abstraction whose geniuses can be traced to the evolution of locomotion, emotional reactions, gesticulation, and digestive processes along with other primitive attributes.

In the case of language development and abstraction, we have adequate reason to believe that spoken language preceded written language. and spoken language is expressed through a series of complex muscle actions. Even music is expressed through muscle operations. It does not necessarily follow that the cognitive abstraction of language and music originate from kinesthetic abstraction simply because both music and spoken language rely on muscle contraction and relaxation as their main means of expression. However, as we also have adequate reason to believe that muscle development antedated cognition (as we commonly use that term) it is suggested that during the earliest evolution of a primitive nervous system, simple response patterns were organized into larger clusters of actions and that that initial "wiring" of the organism's central nervous system served as an archetype for other developments within the same system. That system, as we now know it, is the predominant means used to store vast amounts of useful information in meaningful schemata.

If this thesis is valid, then it would seem that the vigorous study of the structure of motor actions and the abstraction of kinesthetic acts may tell us a great deal about the *cognitive* nature of the species. Whereas our endeavor is in its infancy, it is difficult, at this time, to do much more than identify the simple parameters of a theory of motor abstraction and a more manageable system, a schema theory of dance.

Dance Schema.   It is difficult to watch classic ballet or any form of dance in which a story is being told without finding correlates with language. A dancer may perform a series of steps and body movements that, when isolated, are relatively meaningless—as a sentence drawn out of context from a story— but when integrated into the entire production forms an important and meaningful element. These "sentences" of dance are combined with other "sentences" to make paragraphs and stories.

A good portion of a dancer's life is taken up with repetitious activities designed to build stamina and to learn the rudiments of technique which are reminiscent of exemplars in the cognitive laboratory. The latter component is of interest to us in our work on developing a theory of dance grammar, which is thought to be an important ingredient in a comprehensive theory of the representation of knowledge. Much of technical training in dance focuses on mastering a few basic patterns of motion. From these patterns, variations and embellishments are added. What may appear to be a simple stretching exercise or a rotation procedure may become an integral part of a "turn" and a "turn" may be a component in a dance routine that may be a part of the dance story or dance schema. In order to perform a complex pattern, one must perfect a limited number of simple patterns.

The elementary ingredients of dance movements include meter, tempo, step or movement, and phrasing. These parts are combined in extended phrases called "basic dance sequences" and "the dance." A brief definition of these concepts follows:

Meter: The way beats are organized into groups. This concept is the same concept in dance as in music. A meter of 3/4 indicates three quarter notes (or beats) per measure with each quarter note representing one beat. "Three-quarter time" is easily recognized as a classic waltz meter.

Tempo: The relative rapidity or rate of movement. The notion is difficult to describe verbally and, in actual practice, tempo is frequently set by a metronome. In general, dancers consider a tempo of 60 (60 beats per minute) to be a medium tempo, 120 fast and 30 slow. This subjective evaluation interacts with complexity of the dance and emotional expression being conveyed.

Steps or movements: The basic units of motion a dancer makes.

Phrasing: The grouping of two or more movements so they act as a unit. Phrasing may also include accented counts.

Basic Dance Sequence: The combination of phrases into a short dance episode. The episode may involve several phrases.

The Dance: A narrative story expressed in movement. Certain of these elements seem to correspond to linguistic elements. The approximate parallels are shown in the following:

Dance		Language
Step or movement	~	Word
Phrasing	~	Clause
Basic Dance Sequence	~	Sentence
The Dance	~	Story

Dance Notation. A short time ago choreographers began to record dance movements through a system called Labanotation. This notation system is a written form that, through a series of rather complex symbols, identifies what each part of the body does and where it moves in a dance sequence. It includes phrasing, counts, and tempo. The purpose of Labanotation is to provide a documentation of each movement in a dance so it can be replicated. Although it is doubtful that the originator consciously planned a system that might correspond to linguistic rules, there are some remarkably similar concepts between the two. Labanotation is a type of dance language that reflects an underlying reality that may have common features with the structural components of natural language.

Research Implications. If the underlying cognitive processes of dance grammar are structurally similar to natural language grammar, then we would ex-

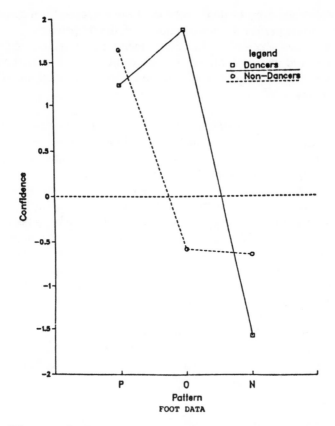

FIG. 10.4. Confidence ratings for geometric patterns (P = Prototype, O = Old Items, N = New Items) presented kinesthetically to dancers and non-dancers.

pect similar results in a whole range of experiments to be done on kinesthetic acquisition and transformation.

One suggested line of research is the parsing of dance movements vis-à-vis language parsing. Another series of experiments might engage the now standard techniques of story analysis in exploring the intricacies of dance. One study may measure the longitudinal effects of differential "forgetting" of dance components in a way similar to measuring these effects on stories by Bartlett and Kintsch and van Dijk. Almost no work has been reported on the transformational processes in dance and that topic may richly enhance our knowledge of the underlying cognitive mechanisms involved in dance grammar and kinesthetic acquisition. Yet another approach to the issue is to examine motor prototypes of dancers, a topic on which some data has been collected and to which we now turn.

Research Results.   In a first step to provide evidence for the hypothesis that involved kinesthetic activities engage a type of abstraction process we (Solso et al., 1986) selected a group of highly trained professional dancers who were performing at a local casino (Bally's Grand in Reno) for a motor learning task. The experimental design was similar to the previously mentioned kinesthetic experiment (Solso & Raynis, 1979) except, in addition to hand movements, we also examined patterns of motor responses made by tracing the foot of a dancer through a series of exemplar motions. Following acquisition of exemplars the dancers were asked to evaluate, by means of confidence ratings, new patterns, old patterns, and the prototype pattern from which the original exemplar items and been derived.

As shown in Fig. 10.4, our results indicated, in general, that professional dancers tended to form abstract representations from kinesthetically presented exemplars, that is, they gave a "false alarm" to the prototype figure. However, our data did not show that they rated the prototype figure as an "old item" with greater confidence than did a control group of nonprofessionals. The dancers did differentiate between old figures and new figures (with the exception of the prototype) better than the control group, which is understandable in light of the years of experience professional dancers have with motor activities and learning. At this time we cannot conclude that training enhances the abstraction process but, on the other hand, the converse has not been demonstrated. This work is continuing with patterns of motor behavior that more closely resemble dance movements.

The results obtained in both the earlier study with motor abstraction among college students and this latter experiment with professional dancers encourage us to think that we may be on the right course in our effort to find an important link between "dance grammar" and natural language grammar. At the very least, these experiments have shown clearly that both students and professional dancers tend to store an abstract internal representation of a class of motor exemplars commonly called a prototype.

Toward a "Mega-Theory" of Cognition

In the beginning of this chapter a brief review of the long history of the nature and form of knowledge was discussed. Through a series of studies on schemata and prototypes with a wide range of subjects—college students (both American and Russian), professional dancers, river rafters, children, elderly subjects—and with a broad class of experimental material—digits, faces, stories, geometric forms, kinesthetic movements, music—it is becoming increasingly clear that information gleaned from the "external" world is represented cognitively as an abstraction. One reason for this tendency, which seems to be a predominant component of human information processing, is the limited capacity for storage of information. This limitation seems to be due to the narrow perceptual apparatus and restricted capacity to store information so apparent in man and other animals.

Our efforts will continue to develop a "mega-theory" of cognition that will be capacious enough to embody a vast amount of the cognitive activities of humankind. An important first step in building a larger model is finding a connection between what appear to be two diverse patterns of human activity: natural language processing and abstraction, and body movements (especially dance) and abstraction. In addition to the epistemological issues addressed in these studies there are other more common problems that may be solved by cognitive psychologists.

APPLIED COGNITIVE PSYCHOLOGY

In this final section we draw on a theme from Lev Vygotsky, the brilliant Russian scholar, in what to some may seem to be a surprising source for the idea expressed. Normally, we associate Vygotsky with the development of abstract theories of the mind that deal with "mega-issues" and grand principles of human action. However, Vygotsky thought that scientific psychology was much more than the investigation of abstract theoretical models of the mind. Psychology must become "partial" not "impartial," which I interpret as a plea for psychologists to become "involved" in the problems of humankind rather than a repudiation of the objective analysis of the mental life of the species. Psychologists should be thinkers, but they also should be "doers." "I am for practicing psychologists, for practical work, and so in the broad sense for boldness and the advance of our branch of science into life" (Vygotsky, 1978).

Today we use the term "ecological validity" to represent the use of knowledge to understand the "real world." In addition to Vygotsky in Russia, Bartlett in England and Neisser (see especially Neisser, 1987) and George Miller in America, have appealed to psychologists not to confine their attention to the exclusive study of laboratory endeavors, but should direct some effort to the examination of events that happen in the ordinary life of ordinary people.

Almost 20 years ago, when out of a seething mix of functional psychologists, psycholinguists, computer specialists, and psychophysicists, along with others, who gave birth to modern cognitive science, George Miller (1970), then President of the American Psychological Association, expressed the idea that scientific psychology is potentially one of the most revolutionary exercises ever conceived by the human mind. Unfortunately, since Miller's passionate appeal, we have been unsuccessful in "giving psychology away" whereas, during the same time, we have been eminently successful in developing enigmatic models of the mind.

Most important among the matters crying out for our attention are questions dealing with how everyday experiences are stored and abstracted in memory, how children learn to read, what is the nature of personality, what are the dynamics of negotiations—such as the important talks between the Soviets and Americans on arms reduction—what specific cognitive differences exist in the thinking of psychotic patients, whether the cognitive activities of elderly people are fundamentally different from younger people, what is learned in motor tasks, how motor information is stored and used in making complex kinesthetic reactions, what cognitive differences exist between exceptional people—such as talented musicians, artists, and athletes—and others, what are the components of intelligence and creativity and whether we can encourage the development of these components and, perhaps most important of all, what is the source of knowledge. The list could go on, but the main point is that many of the problems encountered by mankind and the puzzling mysteries of the human mind, may, just may, be within the ken of this new breed of psychologists.

Because the rewards are so important, I would appeal to my theoretically inclined colleagues, who have been endowed with exceptional intellect, privileged educational opportunities, and a stable and facilitating political environment in which to work, not to abandon their influential theoretical work, but to tithe a portion of their talent to real issues that affect real people as we travel through time and space together.

ACKNOWLEDGMENTS

Part of the research cited in this paper was done while the author was supported through a Fulbright Award and the National Academy of Sciences. I acknowledge this support with thanks. Nancy Benjamin read an earlier version of this paper and made many helpful editorial comments for which I thank her.

REFERENCES

Bartlett, F. (1932). *A study in experimental and social psychology*. Cambridge: Cambridge University Press.

Bartlett, F. (1958). *Thinking: An experimental and social study*. New York: Basic Books.

Bower, G. H. (1976a, September). *Comprehending and recalling stories*. Division 3 Presidential Address presented at the annual meeting of the American Psychological Association, Washington, DC.

Bower, G. H. (1976b). Experiments on story understanding and recall. *Quarterly Journal of Experimental Psychology, 28*, 511–534.

Bower, G. H., Black, J. B., & Turner, T. (1979). Scripts in memory for text. *Cognitive Psychology, 1*, 331–350.

Brewer, W. F., & Nakamura, G. V. (1984). The nature and functions of schemas. In R. S. Wyer, Jr. & R. K. Srull (Eds.), *Handbook of social cognition* (Vol. 1, pp. 263–298). Hillsdale, NJ: Lawrence Erlbaum Associates.

Cantor, N., & Mischel, W. (1979). Prototypes in person perception. In L. Berkowitz (Ed.), *Advances in experimental social psychology*, (Vol. 12, pp. 3–25). New York: Academic Press.

Chase, W. G., & Simon, H. A. (1973a). The mind's eye in chess. In W. G. Chase (Ed.), *Visual information processing*. New York: Academic Press.

Chase, W. G., & Simon, H. A. (1973b). Perception in chess. *Cognitive psychology, 4*, 55–81.

Cohen, L. B., & Strauss, M. S. (1979). Concept acquisition in the human infant. *Child Development, 50*, 419–424.

Cole, M., & Scribner, S. (1974). *Culture and thought*. New York: Wiley.

Fiske, S. T. (1986). Schema-based versus piecemeal politics: A patchwork quilt, but not a blanket, of evidence. In R. R. Lau & D. O. Sears, *Political cognition*. Hillsdale, NJ: Lawrence Erlbaum Associates.

Franks, J., & Bransford, J. D. (1971). Abstraction of visual patterns. *Journal of Experimental Psychology, 90*, 65–74.

Ginsburg, G. P. (1987). Rules, scripts and prototypes in personal relationships. In S. Duck (Ed.), *Handbook of research in personal relationships*. Chichester, U.K.: Wiley.

Head, H. (1918). Sensation and the cerebral cortex. *Brain, 41*, 57–253.

Head, H. (1926). *Aphasia and kindred disorders of speech*. Cambridge, England: Cambridge University Press.

Hess, T. M., & Slaughter, S. J. (1986). Aging effects on prototype abstraction and concept identification. *Journal of Gerontology, 41*, 214, 221.

Hintzman, D. L. (1986). "Schema Abstraction" in a Multiple-Trace Memory Model. *Psychological Review, 93*, 411–428.

Homa, D., Sterling, S., & Treppel, L. (1981). Limitations of exemplar-based generalization and the abstraction of categorical information. *Journal of Experimental Psychology: Human Learning and Memory, 7*, 418–439.

Just, M. A., & Carpenter, P. A. (1987). *The psychology of reading and language comprehension*, Newton, MA: Allyn & Bacon.

Kelso, J. A. S. (1982). The precess approach to understanding human motor behavior: An introduction. In J. A. S. Kelso (Ed.), *Human motor behavior*, Hillsdale, NJ: Lawrence Erlbaum Associates.

Kintsch, W., & van Dijk, T. A. (1978). Toward a model of text comprehension and production. *Psychological Review, 85*, 363–394.

Knapp, G., & Anderson, J. A. (1984). Theory of categorization based on Distributed Memory Storage. *Journal of Experimental Psychology: Learning Memory and Cognition. 10*, 616–617.

Mandler, J. M., & Johnson, N. S. (1977). Remembrance of things passed: Story structure and recall, *Cognitive Psychology, 9*, 111–151.

Mayer, R. E. (1982). Memory of algebra story problems. *Journal of Educational Psychology, 74*, 199–216.

Medin, D. L., & Schaffer, M. M. (1978). Context theory of classification learning. *Psychological Review, 85*, 207–238.

Medin, D. L., & Smith, E. E. (1981). Strategies and classification learning. *Journal of Experimental Psychology: Human Learning and Memory, 7*, 241–253.

Medin, D. L., & Wattenmaker, W. D. (1987). Category cohesiveness, theories, and cognitive archeology. In U. Neisser (Ed.), *Concepts and conceptual development: Ecological and intellectual factors in categorization*. Cambridge: Cambridge University Press.

Mervis, C. B., & Rosch, E. (1981). Categorization of natural objects. *Annual Review of Psychology, 32*, 89–115.

Miller, G. A. (1970). Psychology as a means of promoting human welfare. *American Psychologist.* 1063–1075.

Minsky, M. A. (1975). Framework for representing knowledge. In P. H. Winston (Ed.), *The psychology of computer vision*. New York: McGraw-Hill.

Neisser, U. (Ed.) (1987). *Concepts and conceptual development: Ecological and intellectual factors in categorization.* (Emory Symposia in Cognition 1). Cambridge, England: Cambridge University Press.

Newman, P. G. (1977). Visual prototype formation with discontinuous representation of dimensions of variability. *Memory & Cognition, 5,* 187–197.

Paradice, W. E. J. (1981). *Cognitive representations of the natural environment.* Unpublished doctoral dissertation, University of Idaho, Moscow, ID.

Pew, R. W. (1984). A distributed processing view of human motor control In W. Prinz & A. F. Sanders (Eds.), *Cognition and motor processes.* New York: Springer-Verlag.

Posner, M. I., Goldsmith, R., & Welton, K. E., Jr. (1967). Perceived distance and the classification of distorted patterns. *Journal of Experimental Psychology, 73,* 28–38.

Posner, M. I., & Keele, S. W. (1968). On the genesis of abstract ideas. *Journal of Experimental Psychology, 77, 353*-363.

Posner, M. I., & Keele, S. W. (1970). Retention of abstract ideas. *Jounral of Experimental Psychology, 83,* 304–308.

Reed, S. K. (1972). Pattern recognition and categorization. *Cognitive Psychology, 3,* 382–407.

Rosenbaum, S. A., Inhoff, A. W., & Gordon, A. M. (1984). Choosing between movement sequences: A hierarchical editor model. *Journal of Experimental Psychology: General, 113,* 372–393.

Rumelhart, D. E. (1975). Notes on a schema for stories. In D. G. Bobrow & A. Collins (Eds.), *Representation and understanding.* New York: Academic Press.

Schank, R., & Abelson, R. (1977). *Scripts, plants, goals and understanding: An inquiry into human knowledge structures.* Hillsdale, NJ: Lawrence Erlbaum Associates.

Schmidt, R. A. (1982a). A schema theory of discrete motor skill learning. *Psychological Review, 82,* 225–260.

Schmidt, R. A. (1982b). The schema concept. In J. A. S. Kelso (Ed.), *Human motor behavior.* Hillsdale, NJ: Lawrence Erlbaum Associates.

Solso, R. L. (1988). *Cognitive psychology* (2nd ed.). Newton, MA: Allyn & Bacon.

Solso, R. L., Gabriel M., & Kuraishy F. (1987). *Faces and numbers: Deferential prototype formation among elderly subjects.* Unpublished manuscript. University of Nevada-Reno, Reno, NV.

Solso, R. L., Ament, P., Kuraishy, F., & Mearns, C. (1986, November). Prototype formation of various classes. Paper presented at the 27th meeting of Psychonomic Society, New Orleans.

Solso, R. L., & McCarthy, J. E. (1981a). Prototype formation: Central tendency model vs attribute frequency model. *Bulletin of the Psychonomic Society, 17,* 10–11.

Solso, R. L., & McCarthy, J. E. (1981b). Prototype Formation of Faces: A case of pseudomemory. *British Journal of Psychology, 72,* 499–503.

Solso, R. L., & Raynis, S. A. (1979). Prototype Formation from imaged, kinesthetically, and visually presented geometric figures. *Journal of Experimental Psychology: Human Perception and Performance, 5,* 701–712.

Solso, R. L., Heck, M., & Mearns, C. (1987, November). Prototype formation in very short term memory (VSTM). Paper presented at the Annual Meeting of the Psychonomic Society, Seattle, WA.

Thorndyke, P. W. (1977). Cognitive structures in comprehension and memory of narrative discourse. *Cognitive Psychology, 9,* 77–110.

van Dijk, T. A., & Kintsch, W. (1983). *Strategies of discourse comprehension.* New York: Academic Press.

Vygotsky, L. S. (1978). *Mind in society.* (Edited by M. Cole, V. John-Steiner, S. Scribner, & E. Souberman.) Cambridge, MA: Harvard University Press.

Welker, R. L. (1982). Abstraction of themes from melodic variations. *Journal of Experimental Psychology: Human Perception and Performance, 8,* 435–447.

Wyer, R. S., & Srull, T. K. (Eds.). (1984). *Handbook of social cognition* (Vol. 1). Hillsdale, NJ: Lawrence Erlbaum Associates.

11

Implicitly Activated Knowledge and Memory

Douglas L. Nelson
University of South Florida

When an individual makes a commitment to participate in a psychological experiment, he or she begins an episode that involves coming at a particular time to a particular place, meeting a stranger and, on the basis of instructions from that stranger, engaging in some sort of mental activity. This episode is compacted in time and it can vary in importance to the individual. Although it is a rare experience for most, participating in an experiment represents another episode that is squeezed in between other experiences, for example breakfast routine, an hour of reading, discussing a pending exam with another student, and so forth (Tulving, 1983). If the experiment is a memory experiment, the subject is frequently confronted with familiar words that must be learned or encoded, followed by testing or retrieval. As with other more routine episodes, the participant brings a wealth of prior knowledge to the situation. The purpose of this chapter is to describe the influence of one aspect of that prior knowledge on memory performance: word knowledge.

Word knowledge, for present purposes, refers to connections between related words. It is the knowledge that FREEZE is what happens when heat is removed from water, that FREEZE is meaningfully associated to cold, ice, thaw, and so forth, and that it sounds like PLEASE and like FREEDOM. This knowledge is acquired through incidental and formal learning and is the result of hundreds of experiences that are distributed over many different contexts. Through such experiences words become connected and, depending on the conditions and the amount of practice, these connections vary in relative strength and number. On hearing or seeing a familiar word its connections to related concepts are implicitly activated (e.g., Collins & Loftus, 1975; Underwood, 1965). Such activation is crucial to comprehension and action because it provides the basic means for accessing experience related to the current stimulus. Given that this process is basic for achieving everyday discourse, it seems reasonable to assume that it operates during laboratory experiments on memory as well. However, despite the reasonableness of this assumption, relatively little is known about the influence of the activation of related concepts on memory for the stimulus that is directly experienced. Although the concept of implicit activation is widely accepted, current theories of memory generally ignore the potential effect that such activation might have on memory for words presented by the experimenter. The implication of this neglect is that most researchers assume that the activation of related concepts has little or no effect on memory for words that are directly experienced.

The thesis of this chapter is that implicitly activated concepts frequently influence memory for encoded information. Our approach involves the presentation of familiar words that are known to be preconnected to few or to many related concepts. In some experiments these words are presented as prompts or retrieval cues for other studied words. In these cases, cue set size is varied. In other experiments, these words are presented as the items to be remembered and, in these cases, target set size is varied. Although there are important exceptions, this research has indicated that words connected to larger numbers of related concepts are not as effective as cues and are not as likely to be remembered as targets. The assumption is that implicitly activated concepts can interfere with memory performance. For both phonemically and meaningfully related concepts, cues that define larger sets of related entities are not as likely to be effective as those that define smaller sets. This is called the cue set size effect. In addition, targets that activate larger sets of phonemically or meaningfully related items are not as likely to be recalled in the presence of retrieval cues. This is called the target set size effect. For each type of effect, however, there are exceptions to this general pattern and these exceptions help explain the set size findings.

The specific purpose of this chapter is to describe what we have learned in the past 10 years about both cue and target set size effects. The first section summarizes the assumptions of the sensory–semantic model, which has served as our working hypothesis, and the second section summarizes the major findings.

SENSORY–SEMANTIC MODEL

The sensory–semantic model is described by assumptions about the structure of prior knowledge, about encoding processes that involve this knowledge, and about retrieval of this encoded information at later points in time. Each of these assumptions will be considered in turn.

Structural Assumptions

We assume that a complex stimulus like a familiar word has multiple representations in memory that encode it as a visual, phonological, and meaningful entity. Each of these representations can be reduced to finer levels of analysis (e.g., the phonological pattern can be reduced to phonemes and phonemes can be reduced to features). However, because our tasks typically involve the presentation of words under perceptually clear conditions, the model focuses on structure at the word level. Following the network approach, we assume that each type of information about a word is represented in a different domain (e.g., Collins & Loftus, 1975). Prior knowledge consists of connections formed between domains and within domains. Between-domain connections refer to interconnections between visual, phonological, and meaningful entries corresponding to a single word, and within-domain connections refer to connections to related entries within a given domain of information. The visual presentation of a familiar word can activate processes that lead to its naming and that lead to the recovery of its meaning. In addition, this presentation can lead to the activation of other words that look and sound like it and still other words that are meaningfully related to it.

Although separable effects can be demonstrated (e.g., Nelson, Brooks, & Bordon, 1974; Raser, 1972), we classify visual and phonological features together for our purposes and refer to them as sensory or nonsemantic features to distinguish them from meaning or semantic features. Given that attention is explicitly directed to the sensory attributes relevant to rhyme (e.g., /ēz/), the presentation of a word activates its rhyme-related entities (e.g., FREEZE activates PLEASE, SNEEZE, and so forth). For meaning features, we have incorporated the distinction between extensive and intensive meaning (Johnson-Laird, Herrmann, & Chaffin, 1984). Extensive relations concern the meaning referent(s) to the real world, and intensive relations refer to connections between an extensive referent and its associated meanings. For example, the presentation of FREEZE activates an extensive meaning, for example, liquid to solid state by heat loss, and this meaning then activates related entities like COLD, ICE, and so forth.

We assume that related entries within any domain of information vary in relative strength and number. This assumption is operationalized through the use of controlled association norms. Words, names of common categories, pictures, beginning stems (e.g., /frē/), ending stems (e.g., /ēz/), or word fragments (e.g., F_E_ZE are presented to large groups of subjects (n = 100-250) who are asked to write the first word that comes to mind. Some may be asked to write the first meaningful associate or the first category instance, and others may be asked to write the first word that sounds like the cue, that rhymes with it, or that completes the fragment. Single rather than multiple responses are used to avoid problems associated with response chaining and retrieval inhibition and because the first response provides a superior measure of set size (Joelson & Herrmann, 1978). Following tradition, the probability of any given word is used to estimate the relative strength of that word in relation to its cue. The number of different but appropriate words is used to estimate set size (see Nelson & Friedrich, 1980; Nelson & McEvoy, 1979b for details).

Both types of counts are illustrated in Table 11.1 for rhyme and meaning. Note that the sound /ēz/ produces a relatively large number of rhymes compared to the sound /ûrst/, and that one of the weaker items given by only 2% of the subjects is FREEZE. The word FREEZE in turn produces a relatively large set of meaningfully related associates. Hence, FREEZE would be classed as belonging to a large rhyme set and as having a large associative meaning set. Other items, like THIRST, have small sets in each of these domains of information, and still others have small sets in one domain and large sets in the other. Hundreds of items have been normed with this procedure and can be cross-referenced in both phonemic and meaning domains. Our assumption is that the mental structures measured by the controlled association procedures are the same structures that can become important in various episodic tasks.

In these tasks a single study trial on a list of words is followed by a single test trial. List words (or targets) and retrieval cues are obtained from the controlled association norms and target set size, cue set size or cue-to-target strength are varied or controlled. During the study phase, the targets are presented under intentional or incidental encoding orientations at a fixed rate of presentation that is usually set at 3s per item. The length of this study

TABLE 11.1
Examples of Normatively Defined Rhyme- and Meaning Sets

/ûrst/ (Set Size = 5)		/ēz/ (Set Size = 21)		Thirst (Set Size = 6)		Freeze (Set Size = 15)	
Response	(Xi)	Response	(Xi)	Response	(Xi)	Response	(Xi)
First	.33	Please	.27	Water	.31	Cold	.46
Burst	.28	Sneeze	.12	Drink	.30	Ice	.14
Hearst	.21	Breeze	.11	Hunger	.17	Thaw	.06
Worst	.05	Tease	.08	Quench	.10	Frozen	.04
Thirst	.02	Bees	.07	Dry	.07	Winter	.02
		Squeeze	.07	Coke	.01	Snow	.02
		Peas	.05			Defrost	.02
		Knees	.03			Dry	.02
		Fees	.02			Food	.02
		Seize	.02			Solid	.01
		Fleas	.02			Burn	.01
		Freeze	.02			Melt	.01
		Sleaze	.02			Frostbite	.01
		Trees	.02			Refrigerator	.01
		Ease	.01			Stop	.01
		Appease	.01				
		Cheese	.01				
		Chinese	.01				
		Disease	.01				
		Pees	.01				
		Tees	.01				

list is usually set at 24 words. During this phase, contextual information that biases the encoding of the target can be absent or present. When absent, each target is presented individually. When present, subjects are told to attend to the relationship between the contextual information and the target. Following either type of study presentation, memory for the targets is tested. This test usually follows immediately and is usually self-paced. In cued recall, separate cues are presented for each target. These cues can be extralist cues that were absent during the study phase, or they can consist of intralist cues that were present during the study phase. In recognition, the targets themselves are presented as cues under either perceptually clear or perceptually ambiguous conditions.

Encoding Assumptions

These assumptions characterize some of the mental events that can occur when familiar words are encountered during a hypothetical study trial. We assume that the mental representation of each word becomes connected to the representation of the episode and to the representations of other items in the list (Anderson & Bower, 1974; Smith, Glenberg, & Bjork, 1978). Given that the words of the study list are not directly related, both word-to-episode and word-to-word connections are assumed to be episodic because they occur in a particular time and place while the subject exists in a particular state of being (Tulving, 1983). However, we assume that this unique episodic experience is not isolated from the subject's prior knowledge. The presentation of a familiar word activates related concepts (Collins & Loftus, 1975; Hillinger, 1980; Meyer, Schvaneveldt, & Ruddy, 1975; Underwood, 1965), and these related concepts can become incorporated into the representation of the episodic experience. The primary purpose of the encoding assumptions is to describe how and when various types of concepts become incorporated.

According to the first of three encoding assumptions, we assume that the presentation of a familiar word can activate local networks or neighborhoods of related concepts that have not been physically presented in the task. Consistent with other models, we assume that weaker (more distant) concepts receive less activation than stronger concepts, and that the activation of related concepts is inversely related to their number (e.g., Anderson, 1983; Ratcliff & McKoon, 1981). According to the second assumption, the activation of these concepts during the experimental episode strengthens their connection to the target and connects them to the episode. In addition to encoding the visual, phonological, and meaning entries that uniquely characterize each target, we assume that the activation of related entries in any domain during the encoding experience attaches them to that experience. Note that this assumption differs from our earlier premise (Nelson, 1981; Nelson, Bajo, & Casanueva, 1985). We had assumed that the activation of related concepts weakened the encoding of the target in proportion to the number of activated concepts. We no longer think that this assumption is viable (Nelson, Canas, & Bajo, 1987), and currently assume that the activation of related concepts connects them to the episode without weakening the encoding of the target representation.

According to the third assumption, the activation and encoding of related concepts is responsive to contextual information. We assume that the presentation of the target leads to the activation of *its* visual, phonological and meaning characteristics no matter what the context (Nelson, 1979). However, the encoding of *related concepts* is presumed to be highly sensitive to contextual information present during the study trial. In the absence of specific contextual information (e.g., the word FREEZE presented alone), we assume that the encoding of sensory features is limited to the target but that there is a general activation and encoding of meaning-related concepts. The initiation of this activation and the activation itself are presumed to be completely automatic and, therefore, fragile and easily disrupted. In contrast, in the presence of rhyme-related context (e.g., *TEASE* FREEZE), the encoding of related concepts in both domains is presumed to be relatively broad. As when context is absent, the meaning of the target is unspecified and there is a general activation and encoding of meaningfully related concepts. Furthermore, the context draws attention to rhyme, which is a necessary prerequisite for activating rhyme-related concepts. To initiate the activation of rhyme-related concepts subjects must directly attend to rhyme and this attention reflects the action of a control process. Finally, when meaningfully related context words are present during study (e.g., *REFRIGERATOR* FREEZE), the encoding of related concepts in both domains is relatively confined. In this case, the meaning of the target is specified and the context word does not draw attention to rhyme or to any other sensory attributes of the words.

These three encoding assumptions describe the conditions that determine when various types of related entities become encoded and, therefore, they indicate when various types of target set size will affect memory performance. However, not all encoded information is equally important for all retention tests (e.g., Jenkins, 1979). As the model is now constituted, we assume that the encoding of related concepts leaves word-to-episode and word-to-word connections unaffected. Targets having larger and smaller sets of a given type are equally well connected to the episode and to each other. One implication of this assumption is that retention tests that rely primarily on these connections will not show target set size effects. These effects should be manifested only when the testing conditions lead to the recovery of the full breadth of the episodic encoding but require production of the specific target.

Retrieval Assumptions

One problem for the retrieval assumptions is to explain when and how memory performance will be affected by the encoding of related concepts during the study trial. Another problem for the retrieval assumptions is to explain cue set size effects that arise when extralist cues and certain types of intralist cues are presented in cued recall tests. These assumptions must also be able to account for encoding specificity effects associated with cue switching from study to test (Tulving & Thomson, 1973). Finally, the retrieval assumptions must be able to explain how and why set size effects vary with the nature of the retention test. What is needed is a retrieval model that can accommodate a wide variety of findings.

We begin with the assumption that different retention tests are sensitive to different aspects of the memory representation established during study (Gillund & Shiffrin, 1984; Jacoby, 1983). Different retention tests provide qualitatively different types of information and make qualitatively different demands on what was encoded. In free recall and recognition we assume that performance is highly dependent on word-to-episode and on word-to-word connections (e.g., Gillund & Shiffrin, 1984; Raaijmakers & Shiffrin, 1981). Connections from the target to its related concepts play little or no role. In contrast, for cued recall, the experimenter presents a cue for each target that provides only partial information, for example, some of its letters, part of its sound, or an aspect of its meaning. Connections from these cues to related concepts are critical for performance and engender a search process that is qualitatively different from search processes involved in free recall and recognition.

In the most recent formulation of the model, we assume that the probability of successful cued recall is dependent on the product of three successfully completed phases. Each of these phases is presumably influenced by different independent variables. In the first phase, we assume that the test cue activates a search set of related entries within the domain of information specified in the cue. A rhyme cue activates a rhyme set, an assonant cue activates a set of entries sharing the same initial letters, and a meaning cue activates a set of meaningfully related words. The presumption is that access to a particular domain is controlled so that all possible connections with the cue are not functionally activated. When a rhyming word is represented it does not functionally activate its meaningfully related associates and when a meaning-related word is presented it does not functionally activate its rhymes (Nelson, McEvoy, & Friedrich, 1982; also see Shiffrin, 1970). At this point in the retrieval process, the activated entries exist only in the domain of information specified in the cue. These entries are not the encoded targets. Given that the set of entries defined by the cue includes an entry that overlaps in all phoneme positions with the target, this entry is not the episodically encoded version of the target. This cue-defined entry simply has the same name as the encoded target. Similarly, given that one of the cue-defined entries overlaps semantically with the target, this entry is not necessarily identical to the episodically encoded version of target meaning. These entries exist only in relation to their cues and other conditions that prevail during the retention test.

The activation of these domain-specific, cue-defined entries provides a search set for a goal-directed retrieval process. The goal of this process is to produce the studied target. In this initial phase, the probability of sampling the entry that overlaps with the target is primarily determined by characteristics of the test cues. These characteristic include cue set size, cue-to-target strength (both pre- and post-study trial strength), level of the cue (instance or category), and number of test cues presented. Manipulations of these characteristics influence cue effectiveness by varying the amount of retrieval inhibition present in the recall situation (Nelson et al., 1982, Raaijmakers & Shiffrin, 1981; Roediger, 1974; Rundus, 1973; Watkins, 1975).

During the second phase of the retrieval process, entries sampled in the initial phase act as internally produced retrieval cues for recovering the episodic encoding of the target. This encoding includes the representation of the target as well as related concepts linked to it during study. In this phase, concern is with the probability of activating the post-study trial connection between the cue-defined entry sampled in the initial phase and the episodic encoding of the target. Any manipulation that influences this probability affects the chances of successful recall. Manipulations of the presence of context words are critical in this phase. For example, presenting context words with their targets during study can facilitate this phase when these context words also serve as test cues. Context words can inhibit this phase if they are changed from study to test (Tulving & Thomson, 1973).

Given that the cue-defined entry is sampled and that it successfully reactivates the episodic representation, the final phase of the retrieval process involves target recovery. Episodically encoded information recovered during the second phase must be unpacked. The entry that corresponds to the target must be produced as a single response. The probability of sampling this entry is primarily determined by what has been encoded about the target during the study episode. To the extent that this encoding includes related concepts, the chances of sampling the target are reduced. It is during this phase that target set size effects become apparent. These effects are produced by the same sampling process that produces cue set size effects. Entries in the encoded set are sampled on a probabilistic basis and, the more potential targets there are, the greater the retrieval inhibition. This interference can arise from within the sensory, the semantic, or from both domains depending only on what types of related concepts were encoded along with the target during study.

MAJOR FINDINGS

Sampling the Cue-Defined Entry

According to the initial retrieval assumption, an extralist test cue provides domain-specific access to a set of entries defined by the cue. The likelihood of sampling an entry that overlaps in name or meaning with the target is re-

TABLE 11.2
Probability of Correct Recall as a Function of Type of Cue and
Category Size

	Type of Test Cue				
Category Size	Associatively Related Words	Taxonomic Category Names	Rhyming Words	Word Endings	Mean
Small	.51	.80	.44	.82	.64
Large	.43	.67	.38	.70	.54

Note: From Nelson & McEvoy, 1979b, Experiment 2

duced by variables that increase the likelihood of sampling nontarget entries. In some of our earliest work, the nature of the test cue was varied and crossed with cue-defined set size (Nelson & McEvoy, 1979b). Guessing probabilities were equated at each level of set size by equalizing normatively defined cue-to-target strength for each cue. The question was whether extralist cues would be less effective when they defined larger sets. Given targets of equivalent pre-experimental strength, would *FREEZE* which defines a set of 15 related concepts be a less effective cue that *THIRST* which defines a set of 6 related concepts?

As shown in Table 11.2, names of taxonomic categories, meaningfully related associates, word ending stems, and rhyming words were used. In all cases, extralist cues that defined larger sets were less effective than those defining smaller sets. Such set size effects have been consistently obtained for all types of extralist cues, including pictures (Nelson & Castano, 1984), word beginning stems (Nelson & McEvoy, 1984), word fragments (Nelson, Canas, Bajo, & Keelean, 1987), and even whole words when presented under perceptually difficult conditions (Nelson, McEvoy, & Bajo, 1984). Figure 11.1 shows the category size manipulation for finer gradations of set size for both ending stems and meaningfully related associates (Nelson & McEvoy, 1980). These data were based on 28-item lists with different targets used for each type of cue. Increases in category size produced approximately linear declines in the probability of cued recall and, for every concept estimated to be in the set, the probability of recall decreased by about 1%. Furthermore, for ending stems, it took an average of 71 ms longer to recover correct targets from large compared to small sets. For word fragment cues this difference averaged 227 ms (Nelson, McEvoy, & Bajo, 1988). Not only are targets less likely to be recovered from larger sets, but, given that they are recovered, it appears to take longer.

The cue set size findings indicate that extralist cues serve to access their local neighborhoods of related concepts, and that these neighborhoods are searched in order to recover target information. The larger the set, the less the chances are of recovering any recently experienced entry. Set size, however, is not the only determinant of recovery. The likelihood of success in the ini-

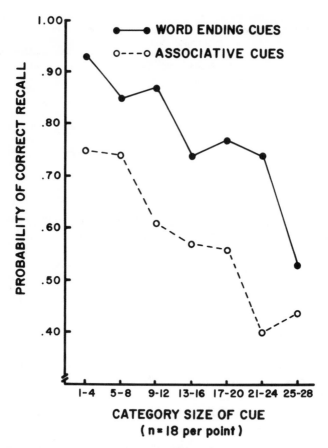

FIG. 11.1.   Probability of correct recall for extralist word ending and associative cues as a function of set size.

tial retrieval phase is determined by any variable that influences the characteristics of the test cue and its relation to both the target and other nontargets in the set. For example, for both sensory and semantic cues, the likelihood of cued recall varies with the pre-experimental strength of the cue-to-target relationship. Weaker cues are not as effective as stronger cues even though the target has recently been studied in the experimental context (Bahrick, 1970; Nelson & Castano, 1984; Nelson & McEvoy, 1979b; Nelson et al., 1982). In addition, for both types of cues, instance cues are not as effective as category cues, that is, *HAWK* is not as effective as *BIRD of PREY* as a cue for VULTURE, and *TEASE* is not as effective as *EEZE* as a cue for FREEZE (Nelson & McEvoy, 1984; Nelson et al., 1982). Finally, for both types of cues, increasing the number of weak instances in the presented test cue reduces the likelihood of recall (Nelson et al., 1982; Roediger, 1974).

These finding indicate that larger sets, weaker cues, instance cues, and multiple cues are all associated with a lowered likelihood of cued recall. Interestingly, none of these variables interact. Cue set size effects are as apparent with strong as with weak cues, with category as with instance cues, and with multiple as with single cues. None of these variables constrain or expand the breadth of the search that is defined by the normative cue. For example, presenting the dual cue *SQUEEZE BREEZE* defines the /ēz/ category as well as either cue alone. Of course, this will not invariably be true for all dual cues. Providing the dual cue *SQUEEZE* (rhyme): *ICE* (meaning) places constraints on the possible targets that go beyond those placed by either individual cue. The probability that subjects will produce the target should approach unity even when the subjects have not experienced a study phase (Rubin & Wallace, 1986). The relevant set has been redefined in this situation.

One implication of these considerations is that, unless a variable redefines the set, it will have no influence on the magnitude of the cue set size effect. Variables that affect performance without affecting the magnitude of this effect have their influence on some other phase of retrieval. For instance, reductions in study time or test time decrease recall without affecting the magnitude of the cue set size effect (Nelson & McEvoy, 1979b). Less effective encoding strategies produce lowered levels of recall, but equivalent effects of cue set size (Nelson et al, 1985). Similarly, changing modality of presentation from study to test (Nelson & McEvoy, 1979a), recall tests that encourage generation-recognition as a retrieval strategy (Nelson & McEvoy, 1979a), and recall tests that are implicit rather than explicit in nature (Nelson, Canas, Bajo, & Keelean, 1987), all reduce recall probability without affecting the magnitude of the cue set size effect. These variables fail to change the effect because they have no influence on the breadth of relevant targets defined by the cue.

The general implication of these findings is that cue set size effects will be obtained whenever retention tests provide partial information about each studied target. What is critical is that testing conditions encourage searching the domain of information specified by the test cue. Whenever such a search is initiated in any task, prior knowledge will influence episodic performance. In data-driven tasks like fragment completion and perceptual identification (e.g., Jacoby & Dallas, 1981; Roediger & Blaxton, 1987), size effects are linked to the sensory features of the cues. Providing that the normatively defined sets are of comparable size, fragment cues like F_E_Z_ produce set size effects that are equivalent to those obtained for ending stem cues in cued recall (Nelson, Canas, Bajo, & Keelean, 1987). Like cued recall with word stems, the fragment completion task involves a search through entries that share letters–sounds with the test cue. Similarly, in perceptual identification under bright target/patterned mask conditions, set size effects are comparable to those found in cued recall when ending stem are provided as cues. Set size effects are also found in this task when the targets themselves are presented as cues (Nelson et al., 1984). Finally, similar effects of set size have also been found in experiments on auditory recognition (Luce, 1986).

The presence of nonsemantic set size effects in perceptual identification tasks indicates that search through nonsemantic knowledge represents an important component process. Perceptual identification, fragment completion and recall cued with word stems all rely on this process because the test stimuli in these tasks provide some but not all of the sensory features of their targets. When all of the letter–sound information is provided under perceptually clear conditions, as in standard tests of recognition, sensory set size effects should not be and are not found (Nelson, Canas, Casanueva, & Castano, 1985). The targets are presented as test cues and they provide complete sensory information so that nonsemantic search is not required. Similarly, meaning set size effects are also not typically found in the recognition task (Canas & Nelson, 1986; Nelson, Canas, & Bajo, 1987; Nelson, Canas, Casanueva, & Castano, 1985). Once again, the test cue consists of the target itself and this cue provides complete information on its extensive and intensive meaning. There is no need to search through concepts that are meaningfully related. In recognition, then, the probability of sampling the cue-defined entry corresponding to the target is at or near unity in both domains of information. An exception occurs when the testing conditions confuse the system such as when the recognition test includes both targets and extralist cues and subjects must randomly switch between them. In this situation, subjects sometimes treat targets as extralist cues and meaning set size effects arise (Nelson, Canas, & Bajo, 1987).

These cue set size findings indicate that, regardless of the nature of the retention test, when test cues provide only partial information or when they are treated as if they provide only partial information, this information serves to direct search through prior knowledge for relevant information. The success of this search is determined by the likelihood of sampling the cue-defined entry that corresponds to the target in sound or meaning. The likelihood of sampling this entry is determined by the number of competing entries in the cue-defined set, the relative cue-to-target entry strength, and the number and level of the cues. All of these variables are effective and important because they control the likelihood of recovering nontargets. The recovery of nontargets produces retrieval inhibition that blocks recovery of the target entry and produces recall failure (e.g., Nelson et al., 1982; Raaijmakers & Shiffrin, 1981). Hence, the probability of sampling the target entry in the initial phase of cued recall depends on the likelihood of encountering retrieval inhibition that arises in the search through prior knowledge networks defined by the test cue.

Cuing the Episodic Encoding of the Target

In the second phase, cue-defined entries recovered in the initial search phase serve as internally generated cues for accessing the episodic encoding of the target. This encoding theoretically includes information about the name and meaning of the target as well as related concepts in these domains that may have been encoded during study. When many meaning or rhyme-related concepts have been encoded, many related concepts are recovered. The assumption is that the recovery of the episodic encoding of the target entry in a particular domain automatically activates information encoded with it in that domain during study. Furthermore, depending on the nature of the retention test, information recovered in one domain can be used to recover information encoded in another domain. In other words, recovering the name for the target can activate its episodically encoded meaning including, if any, meaning-related concepts. Recovering the meaning of the target can activate its episodically encoded name and, if any, rhyme-related concepts.

One implication of the episodic encoding assumption is that *target* set size effects should be independent of the information provided in the test cue. For example, rhyme set size of the targets should influence recall probability even when the test cues are meaningfully related to these targets. Meaning set size effects should be apparent in cued recall even when prompting is with rhyme cues. As long as the study trial conditions are appropriate for producing target set size effects of a particular type, these effects are apparent for cues from either domain. Target set size effects are independent of whether the test cue provides sensory or semantic information. This finding has now been replicated many times (e.g., Nelson, Bajo, & Canas, 1987; Nelson, Bajo, & Casanueva, 1985; Nelson & Friedrich, 1980).

Another implication of the episodic encoding assumption is that the link between the cue-defined entry and the episodic encoding is critical to cued recall performance. To strengthen this connection, the cues used at test can be presented as study context words, as in *REFRIGERATOR* FREEZE. These cues qualify as intralist rather than extralist cues. The encoding of the cue and its target in the experimental context can now be direct. Given *REFRIGERATOR* as the test cue, the cue-defined entry corresponding to the meaning of FREEZE is more likely to be sampled in the initial phase compared to when *REFRIGERATOR* is presented as an extralist cue. In fact, the meaning set size of intralist context cues has little or no effect on recall (Nelson & Castano, 1984; Nelson & McEvoy, 1979b).

Presenting test cues as context words should also facilitate the second phase. The cue-defined entry corresponding to FREEZE should be a more effective internal cue for recovering the episodic encoding of FREEZE. Recall for intralist meaning cues is substantially better than that obtained for extralist meaning cues (Nelson & Castano, 1984; Nelson & McEvoy, 1979b). Some of this improvement can be attributed to more successful sampling of the cue-defined entry, but some of it also presumably due to the strengthening of the connection between the cue and the target. Finally, the recovery of the episodic encoding of the target can be disrupted by changing the study context words at test, a manipulation that produces encoding specificity effects

(Tulving & Thomson, 1973). After studying *REFRIGERATOR* FREEZE, the effectiveness of the extralist cue *THAW* is reduced. Sampling the entry of FREEZE related to *THAW* should be unaffected. But, when cues change, this alternation reduces the likelihood of recovering the link to the episodic representation of the target. The thaw meaning of freeze is different from the "refrigerator" meaning of freeze. Note that this analysis implies that cue set size effects and encoding specificity effects should occur independently. This expectation, unfortunately, has not been tested with meaning cues.

When the study context words share sensory features with their targets (e.g., when the cues *TEASE*, /ēz/, FREEDOM, or /frē/ appear with FREEZE), the model predicts that sampling the cue-defined entry and retrieving the episodic encoding should be facilitated. However, the effects are small and the results are mixed. Several experiments show that juxtaposing sensory cues with their targets during study facilitates recall (Nelson & Castano, 1984; Nelson & McEvoy, 1979b), and one study shows no consistent benefits (Nelson & McEvoy, 1984). When effects are obtained, they tend to be greater when the context units are rhyming words as compared to word stems, but even with rhymes the effects are much smaller than those found with meaning-related context words. These reduced effects of practice may arise because the rhyme connections are initially weaker than the meaning connections.

Alternatively, according to the encoding assumptions of the model, focusing on sensory information is what is required to activate related concepts in the sensory domain. The focus on a pair of rhyming words implicitly activates other rhyme-related words, and they are likely to interfere with recall. Unlike meaning set size effects that are eliminated when pairs of related words are presented, rhyme set size effects are still apparent when rhyme test cues are present during study as context words (Nelson & McEvoy, 1979b, 1984; Nelson & Castano, 1984). Benefits that accrue from presenting the test cue during study may be reduced for rhyme cues because of the interference stemming from the encoding of implicitly activated rhymes. Finally, although the benefits derived from study presentation are small, the costs of switching cues at test are great. Encoding specificity effects are found for sensory cues (Nelson & McEvoy, 1984). For example, relative to studying FREEZE alone, studying *FREE* FREEZE reduces the effectiveness of *EEZE* as a retrieval cue. Once again, this alteration in the cue reduces the likelihood of recovering the episodic representation. Interestingly, as predicted from the model, cue set size effects are independent of these encoding specificity effects.

Recovering the Target

The third phase of retrieval involves recovering the target from the episodic encoding and, during this phase, target set size effects are evident. The cued recall task requires the production of a single word, the presented target, even though a number of related concepts may have become connected to the

TABLE 11.3
Meaning Set Size and Encoding Orientation

Meaning Set Size of Target	Encoding Orientation			
	Intentional	Pleasantness	Concreteness	Associates
Small	.73	.85	.87	.82
Large	.66	.80	.79	.73

Note: From Nelson, Bajo, & Casanueva, 1985, Experiment 1

episode during study. Note that the encoding assumptions prescribe when various types of related concepts can become encoded during study and, therefore, they determine when interference will be observed during target recovery. Target set size effects are not produced at test because all close associates of the target are invariably activated (Nelson et al., 1982).

In our first experiments on target set size, subjects studied a list of 24 words, with half defining normatively large associative sets and half defining normatively smaller sets (Nelson & Friedrich, 1980). Subjects were given intentional learning instructions and, at test, recall was cued with extralist cues that, for different groups, were either meaning- or rhyme-related to their targets. Care was taken to equate both cue set size and strength to avoid confounding cue with target set size factors. The results of this study showed that target words with larger sets were not as likely to be recalled no matter what type of cue was given. As shown in Table 11.3, other work has shown that this result is uninfluenced by intent to learn (Nelson, Bajo, & Casanueva, 1985). As shown in Table 11.4, the effect is observed even when the targets are encoded in the presence of rhyme context words (Nelson, Bajo, & Canas, 1987). In this experiment, subjects were intentionally oriented and told to remember the words or they were incidentally oriented and asked to rate the rhyme pairs on how well they rhymed. As can be seen, no matter how they were oriented, words with larger meaning sets were not recalled as well as those with smaller sets.

These findings indicate that the probability of sampling the target from an encoded meaning set is affected by the size of the set regardless of encoding orientation. However, other studies have shown that even minor disruptions eliminate this effect (Nelson, Bajo, & Casanueva, 1985). When subjects are taken from the room for just 3 minutes of multiplication problems prior to testing, meaning set size effects are no longer obtained. These effects appear to be very fragile. In addition, meaning set size effects are not found at all when targets are encoded in the presence of meaningfully related context words (Nelson & Castano, 1984; Nelson & Friedrich, 1980; Nelson & McEvoy, 1979b). Recall of targets with larger sets is just as good as the recall of targets with smaller sets. When a specific meaning of the target is indicated by the context, meaning-related concepts are presumably

TABLE 11.4
Meaning Set Size and Encoding Orientation

Meaning Set Size of Target	Encoding Orientation	
	Intentional	Incidental
Small	.64	.62
Large	.53	.40

Note: From Nelson, Bajo, & Canas, 1987, Experiment 2

not encoded and, therefore, no interference with the target recovery process is observed.

Research with rhyme indicates that the rhyme set size of the target also influences recall provided that rhyme is emphasized during study. Given such an emphasis, words that are members of larger rhyme sets are not as likely to be recalled regardless of whether recall is prompted with meaning-related words or with other rhymes (Nelson & Friedrich, 1980). The emphasis on rhyme during study is critical. Rhyme set size of the target has no effect in the absence of the biasing rhyme context. The effect is completely dependent on encoding orientation. In one experiment, subjects were presented with meaningfully related rhyme pairs, for example, *SNEEZE* FREEZE, and their encoding orientation toward these pairs was manipulated. Subjects given intentional learning instructions showed the usual rhyme set size result and, in contrast, those asked to rate the pairs on meaning relatedness showed no effect (Nelson, Bajo, & Canas, 1987). Not only must rhyme context be present during study, subjects must actively attend to rhyme for the effect to emerge. Furthermore, and also in contrast to meaning, once subjects attend to rhyme, the detrimental effects of large rhyme sets are found after distractions to other tasks and long delays (Nelson, Bajo, & Canas, 1987).

These findings indicate that familiar words having larger meaning-related or rhyme-related sets are generally not as likely to be recalled. Results indicating that both types of set size effects are dependent on the study trial context but not on the domain of information provided in the test cue indicate that encoding processes are important. Moreover, differential effects of encoding orientation and test disruption indicate that automatic and controlled processing play different roles in the two types of effects. Meaning set size effects are found regardless of encoding orientation and they are fragile; rhyme set size effects are very sensitive to orientation and, once induced, they are relatively robust. One implication of these findings is that the encoding of meaning-related concepts is initiated by an automatic process and, in contrast, the encoding of rhyme-related concepts is initiated by consciously controlled activities (Shiffrin & Schneider, 1977). Meaning is attended through long-practiced habit; rhyme is attended through instruction. The initial orientation to these two domains clearly appears to differ but, once attention is fixed, related concepts in the relevant domain are presumed to be automatically activated. Meaning set size effects are so fragile in the experimental context because their encoding is completely automatic and controlled only by meaningfully related contextual information. Rhyme set size effects are more robust because subjects must selectively attend to rhyme to initiate the encoding of rhyme-related concepts. Rhyme then becomes part of what is consciously remembered about the episode.

Finally, the encoding assumptions indicate when interference can occur during testing. The problem of how related concepts interfere is solved by using the same principal that served to explain cue set size effects: retrieval inhibition. With target set size effects, the assumption is that the inhibition is produced by searching encoded sets instead of cue-defined sets. Presumably, related concepts that were encoded during the study trial interfere with target recovery whenever the testing conditions require search of the encoded set. Such search is particularly likely when the test cue is a member of that set but is not the target itself. As with cue set size, the larger the set, the greater the chances are of recovering a related concept in place of the target entry.

ACKNOWLEDGMENTS

This research was supported by grant NIMH 16360 to the author. Special thanks are offered to Cathy McEvoy for her help with this work.

REFERENCES

Anderson, J. R. (1983). A spreading activation theory of memory. *Journal of Verbal Learning and Verbal Behavior, 22*, 261–295.

Anderson, J. R., & Bower, G. H. (1974). A propositional theory of memory. *Memory & Cognition, 2*, 406–412.

Bahrick, H. P. (1970). A two-phase model for prompted recall. *Psychological Review, 77*, 215–222.

Canas, J., & Nelson, D. L. (1986). Recognition and environmental context: The effect of testing by phone. *Bulletin of the Psychonomic Society, 24*, 407–409.

Collins, A. M., & Loftus, E. F. (1975). A spreading activation theory of semantic processing. *Psychological Review, 82*, 407–428.

Gillund, G., & Shiffrin, R. M. (1984). A retrieval model for both recognition and recall. *Psychological Review, 91*, 1–67.

Hillinger, M. L. (1980). Priming effects with phonemically similar words: The encoding-bias hypothesis reconsidered. *Memory & Cognition, 8*, 115–123.

Jacoby, L. L. (1983). Perceptual enhancement: Persistent effects of an experience. *Journal of Experimental Psychology: Learning Memory and Cognition, 9*, 21–38.

Jacoby, L. L., & Dallas, M. (1981). On the relationship between autobiographical memory and perceptual learning. *Journal of Experimental Psychology: General, 110*, 306–340.

Jenkins, J. J. (1979). Four points to remember: A tetrahedral model of memory experiments. In L. S. Cermak & F. I. M. Craik (Eds.), *Levels of processing in human memory* (pp. 429–446). Hillsdale, NJ: Lawrence Erlbaum Associates.

Joelson, J. M., & Herrmann, D. J. (1978). Properties of categories in semantic memory. *American Journal of Psychology, 91*, 101–114.

Johnson-Laird, P. N., Herrmann, D. J., & Chaffin, R. (1984). Only connections: A critique of semantic networks. *Psychological Bulletin, 96*, 292–315.

Luce, P. A. (1986). *Neighborhoods of words in the mental lexicon.* Unpublished doctoral dissertation, Indiana University, Bloomington, IN.

Meyer, D. E., Schvaneveldt, R. W., & Ruddy, M. E. (1975). Loci of contextual effects on visual word recognition. In P. M. A. Rabbitt & S. Dornic (Eds.), *Attention and performance V* (pp. 98–118). London: Academic Press.

Nelson, D. L. (1979). Remembering pictures and words: Appearance, significance and name. In L. S. Cermak & F. I. M. Craik (Eds.), *Levels of processing in human memory* (pp. 45–76). Hillsdale, NJ: Lawrence Erlbaum Associates.

Nelson, D. L. (1981). Many are called but few are chosen: The influence of context on the effects of category size. In G. H. Bower (Ed.), *The psychology of learning and motivation: Advances in research and theory* (Vol. 15). New York: Academic Press.

Nelson, D. L., Bajo, M. T., & Canas, J. (1987). Prior knowledge and memory: The episodic encoding of implicitly activated associates and rhymes. *Journal of Experimental Psychology: Learning Memory and Cognition, 13*, 54–63.

Nelson, D. L., Bajo, M. T., & Casanueva, D. M. (1985). Prior knowledge: The influence of natural category size as a function of intention and interval. *Journal of Experimental Psychology: Learning, Memory and Cognition, 11*, 94–105.

Nelson, D. L., Brooks, D. H., & Borden, R. C. (1974). The effects of formal similarity: Phonetic, graphic or both? *Journal of Experimental Psychology, 103*, 91–96.

Nelson, D. L., Canas, J., & Bajo, M. T. (1987). The effects of natural category size on memory for episodic encodings. *Memory & Cognition, 15*, 133–140.

Nelson, D. L., Canas, J., Bajo, M. T., & Keelean, P. (1987). Comparing word fragment completion and cued-recall with letter cues. *Journal of Experimental Psychology: Learning Memory and Recognition, 13*, 542–552.

Nelson, D. L., Canas, J., Casanueva, D., & Castano, D. (1985). Prior knowledge and recognition. *American Journal of Psychology, 98*, 379–397.

Nelson, D. L., & Castano, D. (1984). Mental representations for pictures and words: Same or different? *American Journal of Psychology, 97*, 1–15.

Nelson, D. L., & Friedrich, M. A. (1980). Encoding and cuing sounds and senses. *Journal of Experimental Psychology: Human Learning and Memory, 6*, 717–731.

Nelson, D. L, & McEvoy, C. L. (1979a). Effects of retention interval and modality on sensory and semantic trace information. *Memory & Cognition, 7*, 257–262.

Nelson, D. L., & McEvoy, C. L. (1979b). Encoding context and set size. *Journal of Experimental Psychology: Human Learning and Memory, 5*, 292–314.

Nelson, D. L., & McEvoy, C. L. (1980). Cue set size effects with extralist associates and endings. Unpublished raw data.

Nelson, D. L., & McEvoy, C. L. (1984). Word fragments as retrieval cues: Letter generation or search through nonsemantic memory? *American Journal of Psychology, 97*, 17–36.

Nelson, D. L., McEvoy, C. L., & Bajo, M. T. (1984). Retrieval processes in perceptual recognition and cued recall: The influence of category size. *Memory and Cognition, 12*, 498–506.

Nelson, D. L., McEvoy, C. L., & Bajo, M. T. (1988). Lexical and semantic search in cued recall, fragment completion, perceptual identification and recognition. *American Journal of Psychology, 101*, 465–480.

Nelson, D. L., McEvoy, C. L., & Friedrich, M. A. (1982). Extralist cuing and retrieval inhibition. *Journal of Experimental Psychology: Learning, Memory, and Cognition, 8*, 89–105.

Raaijmakers, J. G. W., & Shiffrin, R. M. (1981). Search of associative memory. *Psychological Review, 1981, 88*, 93–134.

Raser, G. A. (1972). False recognition as a function of encoding dimension and lag. *Journal of Experimental Psychology, 93*, 333–337.

Ratcliff, R., & McKoon, G. (1981). Does activation really spread? *Psychological Review, 88*, 454–462.

Roediger, H. L. (1974). Inhibiting effects of recall. *Memory & Cognition, 2*, 261–269.

Roediger, H. L., & Blaxton, T. A. (1987). Retrieval modes produce dissociations in memory for surface information. In D. S. Gorfein & R. R. Hoffman (Eds.), *Memory and cognitive processes: The Ebbinghaus Centennial Conference*. Hillsdale, NJ: Lawrence Erlbaum Associates.

Rubin, D. C., & Wallace, W. T. (1986, November). *Rhyme and reason: Integral properties of words*. Paper presented at the meeting of the Psychonomic Society, New Orleans.

Rundus, D. (1973). Negative effects of using list items as recall cues. *Journal of Verbal Learning and Verbal Behavior, 12*, 43–50.

Shiffrin, R. M. (1970). Memory search. In D. A. Norman (Ed.), *Models of human memory* (pp. 375–447). New York: Academic Press.

Shiffrin, R. M., & Schneider, W. (1977). Controlled and automatic information processing: II. Perceptual learning, automatic attending, and a general theory. *Psychological Review, 84*, 127–190.

Smith, S. M., Glenberg, A. M., & Bjork, R. A. (1978). Environmental context and human memory. *Memory & Cognition, 6*, 342–353.

Tulving, E. (1983). *Elements of episodic memory*. New York: Oxford Press.

Tulving, E., & Thomson, D. M. (1973). Encoding specificity and retrieval processes in episodic memory. *Psychological Review, 80*, 352–373.

Underwood, B. J. (1965). False recognition produced by implicit verbal responses. *Journal of Experimental Psychology, 70*, 122–129.

Watkins, M. J. (1975). Inhibition in recall with extralist "cues." *Journal of Verbal Learning and Verbal Behavior, 14*, 294–303.

12

The Role of Spatial Frequency and Visual Detail in the Recognition of Patterns and Words

John Theios
Paul C. Amrhein
University of Wisconsin-Madison

Recently, a number of psychologists have been investigating differences in the cognitive processing of pictorial and lexical stimuli. It has been reported that in a concept verification task pictorial stimuli tend to be verified faster than lexical stimuli (Pellegrino, Rosinski, Chiesi, & Siegel, 1977; Potter & Faulconer, 1975; Rosch, 1975; and Smith & Magee, 1980). These data have been interpreted to suggest that pictorial stimuli access meaning faster than lexical stimuli. Snodgrass and McCullough (1986) questioned the validity of this interpretation and suggested that the results are due to greater *visual* dissimilarity between pictorial categories than between lexical categories. Snodgrass and McCullough showed that the difference reverses itself when they increase visual similarity between pictorial categories and decrease visual similarity within pictorial categories.

Visual similarity differences are not the only problem with the research literature on picture-word processing. Curiously, few psychologists have investigated the difference in picture-word processing time in terms of the psychophysical functions that underlie visual processing. This gap in the literature is significant, because visual memory must be constrained by the perceptual properties of the visual system. It is surprising to note that most picture-word processing experiments have used large pictures and small words as their stimuli. Physiologically, large pictures are initially processed by a greater number of receptor cells, and this inequality may lead to differences in perceptual discriminability and differences in processing time. Theios and Amrhein (1989) presented data that showed that visual processing time is inversely related to stimulus size, but there are no differences in picture and word processing times when the two types of stimuli are equated in size. They concluded that one must equate all the physical parameters of lexical and

389

pictorial stimuli if one is going to make valid inferences about human information processing based on recognition times for pictures and words.

There is very little psychophysical evidence that shows how parameters such as spatial frequency affect word and picture recognition. Part of the reason why few picture-word experiments have deliberately manipulated spatial frequency is because it is not readily apparent how spatial frequency is determined for pictures and words. Spatial frequency is typically defined as the number of intensity changes (contours) occurring across a given area of the retina. This definition is easily applied to "one-dimensional" stimuli such as sine wave and square wave gratings, but the definition is not easily applied to other, aperiodic stimuli. Square wave gratings can be described by Fourier analysis as the sum of a harmonic series of sine waves, differing in spatial frequency, phase, and amplitude. The Fourier analysis of words and pictures, however, would involve the irregular sum of many sine waves differing in spatial orientation as well as phase, amplitude, and spatial frequency. Determining the two-dimensional spectra of these aperiodic patterns at horizontal, vertical, and oblique orientations requires the use of a two-dimensional fast Fourier transform (e.g., see Gervais, Harvey, & Roberts, 1984). There is another approach to this methodological problem. Rather than attempt to determine the exact spatial frequency spectra of words and pictures, we have elected instead to investigate the effects of relative changes in visual detail on the recognition of patterns and words.

To understand the effects of spatial frequency we need to consider the physiological factors that underlie visual processing. First, the human visual system is maximally sensitive to frequencies in the range from 2 to 5 cycles per degree (c/deg). Stimuli comprising frequencies beyond this range need to be presented at higher brightness contrast levels in order to be discriminated. Second, there exist separate classes of cells, or channels, in the visual system that respond optimally to different spatial frequency ranges (cf. Breitmeyer, 1984; Breitmeyer & Ganz, 1976; Coltheart, 1980). Channels that are maximally sensitive to intermediate spatial frequencies and show an attenuated response to low spatial frequencies are called sustained channels. Channels that are maximally sensitive to low spatial frequencies and show an attenuated response to intermediate and high spatial frequencies are called transient channels. Sustained neurons in the visual system are characterized by small receptive field diameters, high spatial resolution, long response latencies, and slow impulse conduction. Transient neurons are characterized by large receptive field diameters, low spatial resolution, brief response latencies, and fast impulse conduction (Breitmeyer, 1984; Coltheart, 1980). Although these mechanisms may operate on ranges of frequencies that functionally overlap, these differences in response time are particularly evident in experiments that manipulate spatial frequency. Breitmeyer (1975) showed that reaction times are about 40 msec longer for high spatial frequency stimuli than low spatial frequency stimuli. Vassilev and Mitov (1976) and Harwerth and Levi (1978) reported similar results. Harwerth and Levi (1978) argued that this increase in RT was due to the difference in receptive field size for neurons in a single processing channel and to the reduced perceived brightness contrast associated with high spatial frequency stimuli. Other investigators have questioned this explanation. Vassilev and Mitov (1976) argued that the increase in reaction times demonstrated a response latency difference between two separate and distinct channels. In a later study, Vassilev and Strashimirov (1979) demonstrated that the increase in reaction time was not due solely to a change in brightness contrast sensitivity in the visual system. By presenting sinusoidal gratings at various suprathreshold levels, rather than equating stimuli on the basis of physical contrast, Vassilev and Strashimirov showed that visually evoked responses for high frequency stimuli increased in latency across all levels of brightness contrast. Regarding the hypothesis of contrast reduction, Georgeson and Sullivan (1975) showed that humans do not experience perceived contrast differences when high spatial frequency stimuli are presented at suprathreshold levels.

One can conclude several things from these data on visual processing. First, transient neurons in the visual system respond faster to suprathreshold stimuli than sustained neurons (Breitmeyer, 1984). Second, if one accepts the assumption that sustained and transient channels are frequency specific, one can conclude that high spatial frequency information takes longer to be perceived than low spatial frequency information. Therefore, high spatial frequency information in the distal stimulus must be presented for a longer duration than low frequency information if the two types of information are to be equally perceptible to the observer.

One way to operationally measure the effects of visual detail on visual recognition of lexical and pictorial stimuli is to employ a backward masking paradigm. This procedure allows the experimenter to control the duration of the stimulus processing. This control is necessary because presenting a stimulus for a very brief duration (i.e., less than 250 msec) typically results in processing persistence after the stimulus has been terminated (Coltheart, 1980; DiLollo, 1980; Turvey, 1973). Therefore, one cannot assume that the time it takes to process a stimulus is determined only by the duration of its presentation. In a backward masking paradigm, a target stimulus is presented for a very brief duration, followed by the onset of a masking stimulus. In this chapter we refer to the time between the onset of the target and the onset of the mask as the stimulus-mask onset asynchrony (SOA).

One type of mask frequently used to obscure the visual processing of a preceding target stimulus is a white flash mask (e.g., Baxt, 1871; Sperling, 1960). A white flash mask is a brightly illuminated uniform field that effectively reduces the perception of a target. Explanations as to why the white flash is effective generally assume that the sensory responses evoked by the target perceptually integrate with the flash. Because the white flash is usually much brighter than the target, the flash reduces the brightness contrast of the target (Breitmeyer, 1984; Eriksen, 1980). Another type of mask used in backward masking paradigms is the structure mask (Turvey, 1973). Structure masks comprise features similar to those found in the target stimuli. Structure masks are maximally effective when they share the same features as the targets (Eriksen, 1980). They are less effective if they are not featurally similar to the target.

Not surprisingly, spatial frequency of the stimulus seems to determine masking effectiveness. Green (1981a), using a white flash as a backward mask, tested this effect by presenting target gratings that varied in spatial frequency. The data showed that low spatial frequency gratings (i.e., 1.0 c/deg) were detected at shorter target-mask SOAs than high spatial frequency gratings (i.e., 7.8 c/deg). When the threshold curves for these stimuli were compared, Green found that the amount of backward masking for the low frequency gratings was 50% when the target-mask SOA was 20 msec; the function for the high frequency gratings did not reach 50% accuracy until SOAs of 40 msec. These backward masking results demonstrated a 20 msec advantage in processing time for low spatial frequency stimuli, consistent with the reaction time data of Breitmeyer (1975).

Like the work presented by Green (1981a), the present experiment attempted to investigate the temporal processing characteristics of the visual system. A backward masking paradigm was used to examine the effects of visual detail on word and pattern (grating) recognition times. This experiment incorporated three levels of visual detail for words and three levels of spatial frequency for gratings, and combined these target stimuli with three types of masks. It was assumed that all the masks would interfere with the recognition of the target stimuli if target and mask were presented within a 100 msec SOA (Coltheart, 1980). Based on the notion that featural similarity determines masking efficacy (Breitmeyer, 1984; Eriksen, 1980), it was assumed that a pattern mask, comprising vertical, horizontal, and diagonal lines like those used for the gratings, would more effectively mask processing of a pattern stimulus. It was also assumed that a lexical mask, comprising letters similar to those used for the word stimuli, would more effectively mask the processing of a word stimulus. Therefore, it was hypothesized that masks sharing features similar to targets would be more effective in obscuring target recognition and would produce longer recognition times. Following this logic, it was expected that the white flash mask would be neutral with respect to pattern and word targets. Basesd on the findings that low spatial frequencies are processed faster than high spatial frequencies (Breitmeyer, 1975; Green, 1981a, 1981b; Vassilev & Mitov, 1976; Vassilev & Strashimirov, 1979), it was hypothesized that for both words and patterns high spatial frequency stimuli would require a longer presentation period for correct recognition, across all masking conditions.

METHOD

Observers

Eighteen observers, ranging in age from 18 to 49 years, participated in the experiment. Fifteen observers were undergraduate students at the University of Wisconsin-Madison who received course credit for their participation. The other observers were graduate students and a faculty member at the University. All observers were native speakers of English and had normal or corrected-to-normal vision. Eight observers were female and 10 observers were male.

Materials and Design

Two stimulus concepts were chosen to be investigated, the concepts of horizontal and vertical. The experiment manipulated the visual detail and spatial frequency components of word and pattern stimuli. The words used were HORIZONTAL and VERTICAL and the patterns used were corresponding horizontal and vertical rectangular gratings. Words and gratings were printed with either predominantly thin, medium, or thick, feature components.[1] Twelve target and three mask cards, 14.6 cm in width × 23.5 cm in height, were used in the experiment. Six of the 12 target cards contained a rectangular wave grating, centered on the target card. The other 6 target cards contained a word stimulus, centered in the same position. Three of the gratings were composed of solid black horizontal lines printed on a white background. All horizontal gratings subtended a visual angle of 5 °× 39 ′. The low spatial frequency horizontal grating was composed of two rows of seven line segments aligned horizontally. Each line segment was 1.43 cm in length × .48 cm in width and subtended a visual angle of 35 ′ 13 ″ × 2 ′ 12 ″. This grating is characterized by a fundamental spatial frequency of 2.3 cycles per degree of visual angle. The medium spatial frequency horizontal grating was composed of three rows of seven line segments, aligned horizontally. Each line segment was 1.43 cm × .32 cm and subtended a visual angle of 35 ′ 13 ″ × 8 ′ 49 ″. This grating is characterized by a fundamental spatial frequency of 3.85 cycles per degree of visual angle. The high spatial frequency horizontal grating was composed of five rows of seven line segments, aligned horizontally. Each line segment was 1.43 cm × .08 cm and subtended a visual angle of 35 ′ 13 ″× 2 ′ 12 ″. This grating is characterized by a fundamental spatial frequency of 6.92 cycles per degree. Three of the six gratings were composed of solid black vertical lines printed on a white background. All vertical gratings subtended a visual angle of 4 ° 54 ′ × 39 ′. The low spatial frequency grid was composed of 14 vertically aligned line segments equal in size to the line segments printed on the low spatial frequency horizontal stimulus card. The vertically aligned line segments alternated at a rate of 2.76 cycles per degree. The medium spatial frequency vertical grid was composed of 18 line

---

[1]Because of the irregular feature characteristics of letters in a word, we were not able to exactly equate the spatial frequencies of the word and pattern stimuli. However, we did vary the relative spatial frequencies of stimulus words by presenting the word stimuli at three levels of visual detail. We did this by equating the line-widths of the letters in our words to the line-widths of the low, medium, and high spatial frequency gratings and roughly equating the widths of the white spaces in the gratings to the widths of the white spaces in our three types of words. When referring to the three types of stimuli, we used the labels low, medium, and high spatial frequency for both patterns and words for purposes of clarity and convenience of communication.

segments, equal in size to the line segments printed on the medium spatial frequency horizontal stimulus card, alternating at 3.57 cycles per degree. Likewise, the high spatial frequency vertical grid was composed of 36 line segments, equal in size to the line segments in the corresponding horizontal grid, alternating at a rate of 7.34 cycles per degree.

The six word-stimulus cards contained the word HORIZONTAL or VERTICAL. All words were printed in simple block (Helvetica, sans serif) capital letters. Each letter was 1.43 cm in height and 1.24 cm wide, subtending a visual angle of approximately 39 '. The stimulus word HORIZONTAL appeared on three cards, and corresponding to the horizontal grids, subtended a visual angle of 5 ° 39 '. The low visual detail horizontal word stimulus was composed of letters printed in solid black lines, approximately the same thickness as the line segments used in the low spatial frequency grids. The medium visual detail horizontal word stimulus contained the word HORIZONTAL printed in black outlined letters. The thickness of the letter outlines approximated the width of the line segments used for the medium spatial frequency grids. The high visual detail horizontal word stimulus again contained the same size letters and spacing as the other horizontal word stimuli. However, for this stimulus, the word HORIZONTAL was printed in a three-line font. A letter printed in this font can be described as an outlined letter with a black stripe down the center, following the curvature of each letter feature. These thin black lines were approximately the same width as the line segments used in the high spatial frequency grid stimuli. The word VERTICAL also appeared once on three separate stimulus cards. Like their grid counterparts, all vertical word stimuli subtended a visual angle of 4 ° 54 ' × 39 '. These three word stimuli were printed in the same three letter fonts used for the horizontal word stimuli: wide solid black lines, medium black outline, and three thin stripes. Again, the widths of the one, two, or three lines defining a letter in the low, medium, and high visual detail word conditions corresponded to the line segment widths for the low, medium, and high spatial frequency vertical grid stimuli.

Three types of visual masks were presented in this experiment. The lexical mask was the sentence: WHAT IS THE DIRECTION. It was printed in solid black letters identical to those used in the low visual detail word conditions. The words were arranged in two rows so that the mask subtended a visual angle of 5 ° 15 ' × 1 19 '. The pattern mask was a screen composed of vertical, horizontal, and diagonal lines, the same thickness as the lines used for the medium spatial frequency conditions. This mask subtended a visual angle of 5 ° 33 ' × 1 19 '. The third mask card used was a blank white card presented at a luminance level of 72.8 cd/m^2. The target stimuli were presented at an average luminance level of 1.25 cd/m^2. The structure masks were presented at an average luminance of 1.50 cd/m^2. The contrast level for all stimuli was approximately .90. A fixation stimulus was also used in this experiment. It was a small white fixation dot, subtending a visual angle of 8 ' 49 ", centered on a dark grey card, presented at a luminance level of .12 cd/m^2. Examples of the target and mask stimuli are reproduced in Fig. 12.1.

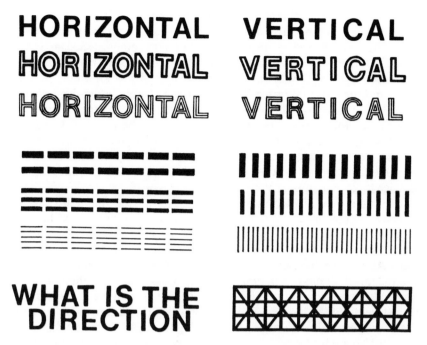

FIG. 12.1.   A representation of the 12 target stimuli and two structure masks. The top row shows the word stimuli used in the low visual detail condition. The second and third rows show the words used in the medium and high visual detail conditions, respectively. The fourth, fifth, and sixth rows depict the grid stimuli used in the low, medium, and high spatial frequency conditions, respectively. The lower left two rows show the lexical mask, and the pattern screen mask is depicted at the lower right of the figure.

A completely within-subjects experimental design was used. All of the 12 target stimuli were factorially combined with the three masks to produce a series of 36 trial conditions. Each condition was presented once at each of the 10 levels of stimulus-mask onset asynchrony (SOA). The 10 SOA durations ranged from 10 to 100 msec, increasing at 10 msec intervals.

Procedure

Each observer was tested individually during one experimental session that lasted approximately 1 hour. A three-channel Scientific Prototype model 320GA tachistoscope was used to control the presentation of a fixation field, a target stimulus field, and a mask field. All trials were conducted in a dimly illuminated room ($.063$ cd/m^2). Before the start of the trials, the observer was shown the 12 target stimulus cards and was told to respond with the word "horizontal" or "vertical" when he/she recognized the appropriate stimulus. The observer was instructed to say the word "nothing" when he/she was not certain of the identification of the stimulus (i.e., guessing was not encouraged).

The start of each trial sequence began with a verbal "ready" signal from the experimenter, who then activated the tachistoscope. A fixation dot appeared for 1,000 msec, followed by the presentation of a randomly selected target stimulus. The target stimulus appeared for an exposure duration corresponding to the chosen level of SOA. It was immediately followed by a masking stimulus, which appeared for 1,000 msec. When the trial was over, the viewing field went dark. The observer verbally reported her response to the experimenter, who recorded whether the response was correct. Prior to the actual trials, each observer was given one practice trial. The purpose of the practice was to acquaint the observer with the general procedure; therefore, the practice trial followed the same sequence as that used for the test trials, with the exception that the practice target stimulus was presented for 1,000 msec.

The trials were divided into three sets. During the first 120 trials, the observer was presented with only one type of mask. During the next 120 trials, the observer was presented with the second mask, and so on. The order in which the masks were selected was determined by a method of block randomization for each observer. This experiment used a method of limits, such that the target stimulus durations were organized in an ascending order. For every given mask condition, the observer was first shown the 12 target stimuli at the briefest SOA, 10 msec. The order in which the 12 cards were presented was quasi-randomly determined by shuffling the deck. After being presented with all 12 stimuli, the experimenter then reshuffled the stimulus cards and presented each card for 20 msec. This procedure of increasing the SOA by 10 msec was continued until the observer correctly identified all 12 stimuli for a given presentation duration (achieved by 100 msec).

RESULTS

This experiment addressed three questions:

1. All other things equal, is there a difference in the exposure duration at which lexical stimuli and analogical stimuli are first perceived?
2. Does spatial frequency (visual detail) of the stimulus affect the exposure duration necessary for target recognition?
3. How does type of mask affect recognition performance?

An overall, within-subjects, factorial analysis of variance was performed on the data from the experiment. No observer made a correct response at the 10 msec SOA and all observers were 100% correct at the 100 msec SOA. Thus, these two end conditions were not included in the analyses of variance. Subjects are a random effect and the fully-crossed fixed effects are Type of Stimulus (word or grid), Spatial Frequency of the Stimulus (high, medium, or low), Type of Mask (lexical, pattern, or flash), SOA (20, 30, 40, 50, 60, 70, 80, and 90 msec), and Items (horizontal or vertical). Given the power of this experiment, differences as little as 2% in accuracy could be significant at the .05 level of confidence. Because it is doubtful that 2% differences in accuracy are scientifically meaningful, we adopt a .01 level of confidence to guard against Type I decision errors.

There was no significant main effect due to Items [$F(1, 17) = .22, p > .64$]. The only significant interaction involving Items was the Mask by Item interaction [$F(2, 34) = 6.75, p = .003$]. The interaction was such that there was no difference between horizontal and vertical items with the lexical or pattern masks; but with the flash mask, vertical stimuli were more accurately reported than were horizontal stimuli (.54 vs. .49, respectively). It is doubtful whether this is a meaningful difference. In all subsequent analyses, we have collapsed over the horizontal and vertical items. There was no significant overall accuracy difference between word and grid stimuli (.63 and .64, respectively). There was a significant overall accuracy effect due to Spatial Frequency, low = .68, medium = .65, and high = .57 [$F(2, 34) = 44.14, p < .00001$]. Figure 12.2 presents the accuracy data for each spatial frequency as a function of SOA. The horizontal axis in Fig. 12.2 shows the SOA between the target and mask. The vertical axis shows the proportion of correct responses for the three levels of spatial frequency, low, medium, and high. The top solid line represents the proportion of correct responses for low spatial frequency stimuli. This line shows that low frequency stimuli are correctly identified 50% of the time

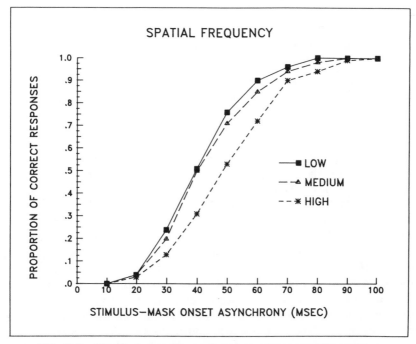

FIG. 12.2.   Report accuracy (proportion of correct responses) as a function of spatial frequency and stimulus-mask onset asynchrony (SOA).

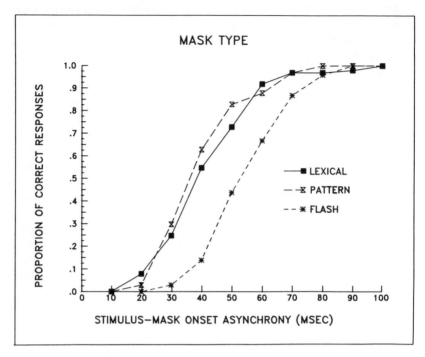

FIG. 12.3.   Report accuracy (proportion of correct responses) as a function of type of mask (lexical, pattern, or white flash) and stimulus-mask onset
asynchrony (SOA).

at SOAs of 40 msec. Similarly, medium spatial frequency stimuli are correctly
identified 49% of the time at 40 msec SOAs. However, high spatial frequency
stimuli required about a 50 msec presentation time before they were identified with the same accuracy. In general, the low and medium spatial frequency slopes are characteristically the same; but, the high spatial frequency
slope is shallower. Because the backward masking functions all start at zero
and end at unity, there is, of course, a highly significant effect due to SOA
$[F(7, 119) = 390, p < .00001]$ and a significant Spatial Frequency by SOA interaction $[F(14, 238) = 6.06, p < .0001]$.

Type of mask significantly affected overall response accuracy: Pattern = .70,
lexical = .68, and white flash = .51, $[F(2, 34) = 38.42, p < .00001]$. There was
no significant difference between the lexical mask and pattern mask in overall
accuracy $[F(1, 17) = 1.24, p > .28]$. The overall effects of the three mask conditions are shown in Fig. 12.3. The abscissa represents the SOA between the
target and mask stimulus. The ordinate represents the proportion of correct
responses, collapsed across all other conditions. The solid line and long-dashed
line represent the data for the lexical and pattern masks. In general, these
two masks are represented by the same psychophysical function, and show
that as SOA increases, masking effectiveness decreases. The short-dash line

represents the function for the white flash mask; although this function also shows that the efficacy of masking is reduced at longer SOAs, the slope of the white flash mask function is much shallower. This is reasonable as the light of the white flash mask was almost 50 times more intense as that of the structure masks.

Structure Masks

Because the two structure masks yield data characteristically different than the white flash mask, we here consider the data from just the two structure mask conditions. There was a significant main effect of spatial frequency of the target stimulus on recognition accuracy; low = .72, medium = .72, and high = .64 [$F(2,34) = 25.92$, $p < .00001$]. Of course there was no significant difference between the low and medium spatial frequencies. With the structure masks there was no significant difference in overall accuracy between word and grid stimuli, .69 and .70, respectively. There was no significant main effect in accuracy using a lexical mask versus a pattern mask, .68 versus .70, respectively. There was however, a significant interaction between Type of Mask (lexical or pattern) and Type of Stimulus (word or grid) [$F(1, 17) = 21.25$,

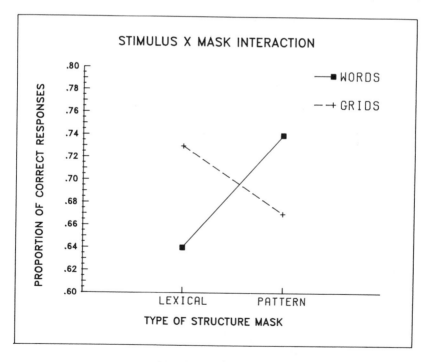

FIG. 12.4.   Interaction of type of stimulus and type of structure mask: Report accuracy (proportion of correct responses) as a function of type of stimulus (word or grid) and type of structure mask (lexical or pattern).

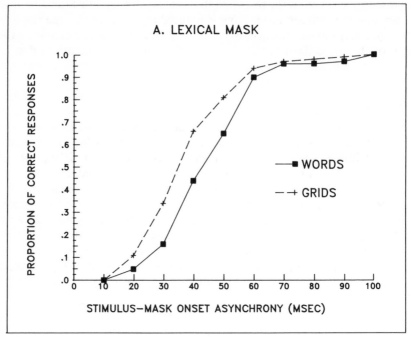

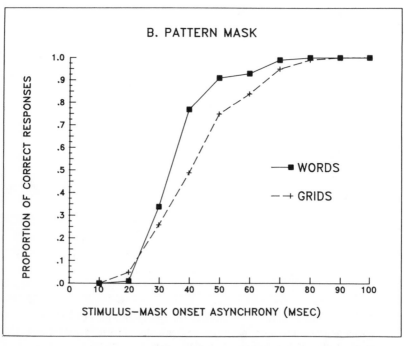

Figure 12.5 (*continued*)

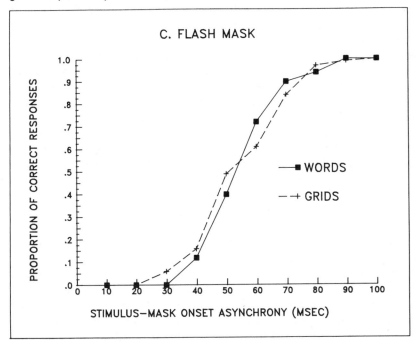

C. FLASH MASK

PROPORTION OF CORRECT RESPONSES

STIMULUS–MASK ONSET ASYNCHRONY (MSEC)

■ WORDS
-+ GRIDS

FIG. 12.5.   (A) Lexical Mask: Report accuracy (proportion of correct responses) for word and grid stimuli as a function of stimulus-mask onset asynchrony (SOA) using the lexical, sentence mask. (B) Pattern Mask: Report accuracy (proportion of correct responses) for word and grid stimuli as a function of SOA using the pattern, screen mask. (C) White Flash Mask: Report accuracy (proportion of correct responses) for word and grid stimuli as a function of SOA using the white flash mask.

$p = .0002$]. The interaction is represented graphically in Fig. 12.4. Relative to a pattern mask, a lexical mask resulted in a 14% decrease in accuracy of reporting a word stimulus. Analogously, relative to a lexical mask, a pattern mask resulted in an 8% decrease in accuracy of reporting a grid stimulus. The interaction as a function of SOA can be dramatically seen in Fig. 12.5a and 12.5b. Figure 12.5c shows the data from the white flash mask condition.

White Flash Mask

We here consider the data from the white flash mask condition. Conceptually, the white flash mask should be neutral with respect to the two kinds of target stimuli, words and grids. It should primarily affect peripheral processing rather than central processing (Turvey, 1973). In addition, performance in the white flash mask condition was poorer than that in the structure mask conditions due to the fact that the luminance of the flash mask was much brighter than that of the structure masks. With the white flash mask there was no significant difference between word stimuli and grid stimuli, .51 and .52, respectively. These three results can be seen in Fig. 12.5c. With the white flash mask there was a significant main effect of spatial frequency of the target stimulus on recognition accuracy, low = .58, medium = .52, and high = .43 [$F(2, 34) = 34.75$, $p < .00001$]. There was, of course, a highly significant main effect of SOA [$F(7, 119) = 202$, $p < .00001$]. In addition, there was a significant main effect of items (the concepts of horizontal and vertical direction) [$F(1, 17) = 10.16$, $p = .005$]. For some reason, with the white flash mask the vertical stimuli [both grids (.54) and words (.54)] were more easily recognized than were the horizontal stimuli [both grids (.49) and words (.49)]. The two-way interaction of SOA with Spatial Frequency was significant [$F(14, 238) = 4.40$, $p < .00001$]. This is to be expected, however, since there was a significant main effect due to Spatial Frequency and the SOA curves each start at zero and end at unity.

The only unexpected interaction was that between stimulus type (word or grid) and spatial frequency [$F(2, 34) = 6.92$, $p = .003$]. The interaction is such that grid stimuli are recognized about 4% more accurately than words on the low and medium frequency trials, but word stimuli are recognized about 7% more accurately than grids on the high frequency trials. The interaction is represented graphically in Fig. 12.6. Our feeling is that our "high-frequency," three-thin-line letter font was beginning to be integrated by the visual system into one-wide-line, lower frequency letters, leading to a slightly improved performance on the word stimuli in the high-frequency white-flash mask condition. Curiously, this interaction was not present in the structure mask conditions.

False alarm errors, or those instances in which observers reported the incorrect directional response, occurred less than 1% of the time across all conditions. These errors were not analyzed separately by condition.

DISCUSSION

Processing of Words and Analogical Patterns

First of all, it should go without saying that investigators wishing to study the cognitive processing of different classes of stimuli such as pictures and words, should equate the stimuli as to overall size (cf. Theios & Amrhein, 1989). This control insures that the obtained processing time differences are not due to the "sensory front end" of the visual information processing system by insuring that the same input channels initially process both classes of stimuli. For example, at the first level of sensory processing it is desirable that the same receptor cells be involved in processing the different classes of stimuli. Otherwise, obtained processing time differences may be due to differences in early sensory processing rather than due to differences in later, higher-level cognitive processing. Unfortunately most cognitive psychologists

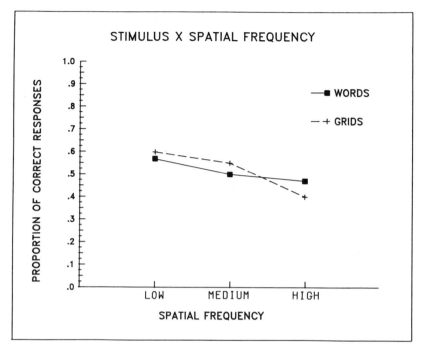

FIG. 12.6.   Interaction of stimulus type and spatial frequency when the white flash mask is used: Report accuracy (proportion of correct responses) as a function of spatial frequency for word and grid stimuli.

investigating differences in picture and word processing have not equated the two classes of stimuli for overall size. Typically, large pictures are compared with small words.

Even when the two different classes of stimuli are equated for overall size, some care should be taken to insure that the two classes of stimuli are roughly equated as to fundamental spatial frequency. By their very nature, words tend to be high frequency stimuli and pictorial stimuli of the type traditionally used by experimental psychologists tend to be fairly low in spatial frequency (e.g., simple line drawings). Thus, cognitive psychologists investigating picture and word processing should attempt to equate the two classes of stimuli as to their visual detail (or spatial frequency) as different receptor systems may mediate the processing of high and low spatial frequencies (Breitmeyer, 1975, 1984; Breitmeyer & Ganz, 1976; Coltheart, 1980). When it is impossible to equate lexical and pictorial stimuli as to spatial frequency, at least two widely differing levels of visual detail should be used in each of the two differing stimulus classes. To manipulate visual detail in the present experiment, for example, we varied line width of words and patterns, and we used three different widths of line. Overall, we found no significant differences in processing accuracy between words and patterns of the same overall size and line width.

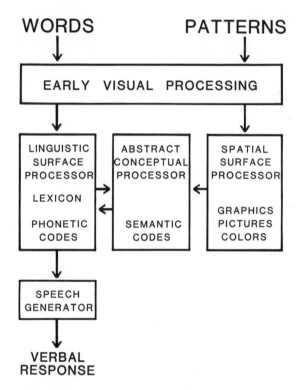

FIG. 12.7.   Flow diagram of that portion of the Theios and Amrhein (1989) theory of lexical and pictorial processing relevant to the tachistoscopic recognition of words and patterns.

The results of our experiment may be understood with reference to the theory for picture and word processing proposed by Theios (1984); and Theios and Amrhein (1983, 1989). The theory is represented graphically in Fig. 12.7. Briefly, the theory assumes that the *early visual processing system* deals with brightness contrasts and contours (i.e., raw analogical images) and is roughly equivalent to the iconic storage system postulated by Sperling (1960) and Averbach and Coriell (1961). Two surface processing systems operate on the information from the early visual processing system. One is the *graphical surface processing system* that performs computations on analogical images that will be used to determine the meanings of pictorial stimuli. This system could quite possibly be situated in the right hemisphere of the brain (cf. Springer & Deutsch, 1981). The other system is the *linguistic surface processing system* that is highly specialized to automatically find referents of lexical stimuli in what linguists call the "mental lexicon." These referents have to do only with *surface* aspects of words, such as their image, orthography, and sound (cf. Theios & Muise, 1977) and not their semantic aspects. This system is quite possibly located in the left hemisphere of the brain (cf. Gazzaniga, 1970).

The graphical and lexical surface processing systems operate as "interfaces" between the early visual processing system and an *abstract conceptual processing system* that actually computes and stores the meanings of stimuli. The abstract conceptual processor is in essence the long-term semantic memory system postulated by numerous psychologists. Its coding is neither linguistic nor imagistic in nature, but abstract, unrelated to the input modality of the stimulus (cf. Potter, 1979; Seymour, 1973; Snodgrass, 1984; Theios & Amrhein, 1989).

With regard to the present experiment, the white flash mask will have its effect primarily on the early visual processing system that essentially treats words as it does any other visual image. Therefore, there should be no significant difference between the backward masking functions of lexical and pictorial stimuli (patterns) equated for size and spatial frequency. The neutral white flash mask most likely just decreases brightness contrast of the proximal stimulus (Breitmeyer, 1984, p. 51; Eriksen, 1966; Thompson, 1966). In our experiment we found no significant differences in the backward masking functions of words and patterns using a white flash mask.

Theoretically, with structure masks, the result should be different. According to the theoretical model in Fig. 12.7, when a pattern or pictorial stimulus is used with a lexical mask the graphical surface processing system will have begun decoding the pattern stimulus when the lexical mask arrives at the early visual processing system. After some initial processing, the lexical mask will be shunted to the linguistic surface processing system. Thus, there will be parallel processing of the pattern stimulus and the lexical mask by different subsystems of the brain.

On the other hand, when a pattern mask is used with a pattern stimulus, there will be "traffic" problems. After the pattern mask has been processed by the early visual processing system it will be shunted to the graphically surface processing system, which is already engaged in attempting to decode the target pattern. Thus, in the graphical surface processing system, there will be competition for processing resources, integration or confusion of the two images, and perhaps even replacement of the first image by the second. According to the theoretical model of Fig. 12.7, performance on a pattern or pictorial stimulus will be poorer with a pattern or pictorial mask than with a lexical mask.

A similar situation holds in the case of a pattern or pictorial mask used with a word stimulus. The linguistic surface processing system will have begun decoding the word when the masking pattern arrives at the early visual processing system. After some initial processing, the pattern mask will be shunted to the graphical surface processing system. Thus, there will be parallel processing of the lexical stimulus and the pattern mask by different subsystems of the brain. On the other hand, if a lexical mask (say, a sentence) is used with a word stimulus, things are different. After the lexical mask has been processed by the early visual processing system it will be shunted to the linguistic surface processing system, which is already engaged in attempting to decode the target word. Thus, in the linguistic surface processing system, there will be competition for processing resources, integration or confusion of the two linguistic messages, and perhaps even replacement of the first message by the second. Therefore, according to the theoretical model in Fig. 12.7, performance on a word stimulus will be poorer with a lexical mask than with a pattern or pictorial mask. This interaction between target stimulus type (word or pattern) and mask type (lexical or pattern) is exactly what we obtained in our experiment (see Fig. 12.4 and 12.5).

Spatial Frequency and Backward Masking

The results of this experiment confirmed the hypothesis that the spatial frequency of a stimulus affects its recognition. In general, the experiment showed that observers were able to recognize low and medium spatial frequency stimuli at shorter SOAs than higher spatial frequency stimuli. These effects were consistent for both word and grid stimuli.

The findings suggest that the physical properties of a stimulus constrain the manner in which it is processed by the visual recognition system. High spatial frequency stimuli require a longer presentation period than low or medium spatial frequency stimuli before they can be correctly identified. These operational differences can be attributed to different processing mechanisms in the visual system, and can be explained by one of several sustained-transient models of visual processing (cf. Breitmeyer, 1984; Breitmeyer & Ganz, 1976; Green, 1981b). Interpreting these results on the basis of a physiological model requires several assumptions. First, one must assume that the visual system contains multiple channels each of which operate optimally at a specific range of spatial frequencies; and second, one must assume that these channels respond with different latencies (cf. Breitmeyer, 1984; Breitmeyer & Ganz, 1976; Coltheart, 1980). Based on these assumptions, one can predict that high spatial frequency information will be processed with a longer latency than low spatial frequency information.

The findings of this experiment have strong implications for experiments that use a backward masking paradigm. The data from the white flash mask conditions showed that the effectiveness of the mask decreased monotonically as a function of SOA. Overall, the white flash mask affected the perception of high spatial frequency stimuli the most, whereas it had a lesser effect on the perception of medium and low spatial frequency stimuli. Presumably much of the masking due to the white flash occurred at peripheral levels of processing (Eriksen, 1980; Turvey, 1973; also see Breitmeyer, 1984, pp. 51–58 for a review). Likewise, the amount of masking by the pattern and lexical masks decreased monotonically with SOA. The structure masks were also most effective in obscuring the perception of high frequency stimuli. The spatial frequency results of this experiment for both words and gratings replicated the findings of Green (1981a) who used only gratings.

SUMMARY AND CONCLUSIONS

1. There was no significant difference between the backward masking functions of word and pattern stimuli when they are matched in size and spatial frequency.
2. The minimum visual processing time necessary for recognition of word and pattern stimuli was an increasing function of spatial frequency of the stimulus.
3. Pattern masks were more effective than lexical masks in masking pattern stimuli. Similarly, lexical masks were more effective than pattern masks in masking words.
4. A white flash mask was equally effective in masking both pattern and word stimuli.
5. These results imply that researchers investigating the cognitive processing of different classes of visual stimuli such as pictures and words should control and equate, to the greatest extent possible, all physical parameters of both sets of stimuli.
6. At a minimum, researchers should attempt to equate as much as possible the overall size and the general level of visual detail of pictorial and lexical stimuli.

ACKNOWLEDGMENTS

This research was supported by funds from the Wisconsin Alumni Research Foundation awarded by the University of Wisconsin-Madison Graduate School Research Committee (Projects 161069, 170769, 190682) to John Theios.

REFERENCES

Averbach, E., & Coriell, A. S. (1961). Short-term memory in vision. *Bell System Technical Journal, 40*, 309–328.

Baxt, N. (1871). Uber die Zeit welche notig ist damit ein Gesichtseindruck zum Bewusstsein kommit und uber die Grosse der bewussten Wahrnehmung bei einem Gesichtseindrucke von gegebener Dauer [On the time that is necessary in order for a visual impression to attain consciousness and on the extent of conscious perception of a visual impression of given duration]. *Pfluger's Arch. gesammte Physiology, 4*, 325–336.

Breitmeyer, B. G. (1975). Simple reaction time as a measure of the temporal response properties of transient and sustained channels. *Vision Research, 15*, 1411–1412.

Breitmeyer, B. G. (1984). *Visual Masking: An integrative approach.* New York: Oxford University Press.

Breitmeyer, B. G., & Ganz, L. (1976). Implications of sustained and transient channels for theories of visual pattern masking, saccadic suppression, and information processing. *Psychological Review, 83,* 1-36.

Coltheart, M. (1980). Iconic memory and visible persistence. *Perception & Psychophysics, 27,* 183-228.

DiLollo, V. (1980). Temporal integration in visual memory. *Journal of Experimental Psychology: General, 109,* 75-97.

Eriksen, C. W. (1966). Temporal luminance summation effects in backward and forward masking. *Perception & Psychophysics, 1,* 87-92.

Eriksen, C. W. (1980). The use of a visual mask may seriously confound your experiment. *Perception & Psychophysics, 28,* 89-92.

Gazzaniga, M. S. (1970). *The bisected brain.* New York: Appleton.

Georgeson, M. A., & Sullivan, G. D. (1975). Contrast constancy: Debluring in human vision by spatial frequency channels. *Journal of Physiology, 252,* 627-656.

Gervais, M. J., Harvey, L. O., & Roberts, J. O. (1984). Identification confusions among letters of the alphabet. *Journal of Experimental Psychology: Human Perception and Performance, 10,* 655-666.

Green, M. (1981a). Spatial frequency effects in masking by light. *Vision Research, 21,* 861-866.

Green, M. (1981b). Psychophysical relationships among mechanisms sensitive to pattern, motion and flicker. *Vision Research, 21,* 971-983.

Harwerth, R. S., & Levi, D. M. (1978). Reaction time as a measure of supra-threshold grating detection. *Vision Research, 18,* 1579-1586.

Pellegrino, J. W., Rosinski, R. R., Chiesi, H. L., & Siegel, A. (1977). Picture-word differences in decision latency: An analysis of single and dual memory models. *Memory & Cognition, 5,* 383-396.

Potter, M. C. (1979). Mundane symbolism: The relations among objects, names, and ideas. In N. R. Smith & M. B. Franklin (Eds.), *Symbolic functioning in childhood.* Hillsdale, NJ: Lawrence Erlbaum Associates.

Potter, M. C., & Faulconer, B. A. (1975). Time to understand pictures and words. *Nature, 253,* 437-438.

Rosch, E. (1975). Cognitive representations of semantic categories. *Journal of Experimental Psychology: General, 104,* 192-233.

Seymour, P. H. K. (1973). A model for reading, naming and comparison. *British Journal of Psychology, 64,* 35-49.

Smith, M. C., & Magee, L. E. (1980). Tracing the time course of picture-word processing. *Journal of Experimental Psychology: General, 109,* 373-392.

Snodgrass, J. G. (1984). Concepts and their surface representations. *Journal of Verbal Learning and Verbal Behavior, 23,* 3-22.

Snodgrass, J. G., & McCullough, B. (1986). The role of visual similarity in picture categorization. *Journal of Experimental Psychology: Learning, Memory and Cognition, 21,* 147-154.

Sperling, G. (1960). The information available in brief visual presentations. *Psychological Monographs, 74* (Whole No. 498), 1-29.

Springer, S. P., & Deutsch, G. (1981). *Left brain, right brain.* San Francisco: W. H. Freeman.

Theios, J. (1984). A theory of visual and cognitive processing of pictures and words. *XXIII International Congress of Psychology, Abstracts Volume II.* Mexico City: Editorial Trillas, 18.

Theios, J., & Amrhein, P. C. (1983). A model for the processing of successively presented pictures and words. *Bulletin of the Psychonomic Society, 21,* 352. (Abstract No. 197)

Theios, J., & Amrhein, P. C. (1989). A theoretical analysis of the cognitive processing of lexical and pictorial stimuli: Reading, naming, and visual and conceptual comparisons. *Psychological Review, 96,* 5-24.

Theios, J., & Muise, J. G. (1977). The word identification process in reading. In N. J. Castellan, D. B. Pisoni, & G. R. Potts (Eds.), *Cognitive theory* (Vol. 2, pp. 289–327). Hillsdale, NJ: Lawrence Erlbaum Associates.

Thompson, J. H. (1966). What happens to the stimulus in backward masking? *Journal of Experimental Psychology, 71*, 580–586.

Turvey, M. T. (1973). On peripheral and central processes in vision: Inferences from an information-processing analysis of masking with patterned stimuli. *Psychological Review, 80*, 1–52.

Vassilev, A., & Mitov, D. (1976). Perception time and spatial frequency. *Vision Research, 16*, 89–92.

Vassilev, A., & Strashimirov, D. (1979). On the latency of human visually evoked response to sinusoidal gratings. *Vision Research, 19*, 843–845.

Postscript

CLOSING REMARKS OF THE 1987 FLOWERREE
MARDI GRAS SYMPOSIUM ON COGNITION

All of our participants have now completed their presentations. The only regrettable fact is that even the most challenging and trenchant symposia must end. Thanks are due to all those who took the time to attend—from early morning to late afternoon for these 2 days. The audience has made this symposium an unprecedented success. Again, the greatest gratitude goes to the Flowerrees and the Psychology Department for their marvelous support. We were most honored by the presence of Mr. and Mrs. Flowerree on February 23, 1987, their first opportunity to visit at symposium time.

As with any venture of this nature, the hard core of its success depends on the quality of the speakers. It is our hope that they enjoyed participating in this Flowerree Mardi Gras Symposium on Cognition and now better comprehend something of the emerging trends reflected in the important work we have been privileged to hear about. We close now, in the expectation that they continue to mold tomorrow's cognitive psychology in important ways, and that all of us shall meet again soon to discuss our newest contributions. Until then, farewell and Godspeed! Thank you very much. Happy Mardi Gras!
(We closed the Symposium with many Mardi Gras
"throws" to confer Good Luck on all who attended.)

February 24, 1987
* * *
It was truly a privilege to witness, for the 2 days, presentations of the newest research products from the leading laboratories in psychology. It was all the more pleasant to do so in the convivial atmosphere of Mardi Gras,

411

our local specialty. It is this editor's hope that many of our readers will participate in and share the excitement of our next Flowerree Mardi Gras Symposium on Cognition. At that time, we will include many other issues of critical importance to cognitive psychology.

OTHER ACKNOWLEDGMENTS

In addition to our sincere thanks for the warm generosity of Mr. and Mrs. Flowerree, and to the Department of Psychology at Tulane, as well as the speakers and the audience, we must also acknowledge our great appreciation for the very essential assistance rendered by so many persons in the psychology department; without them, there would have been no symposium. In particular, the helpfulness of our students' services was indispensible for the smooth running of this event. In addition to my thanks to Professor Jeffrey Lockman for his help, my heartfelt gratitude goes to Gregory Beatty, Hester Chang, Theresa Constant, James Crounin, Margie Harbeson, Brad Hall, Larry Roth, C. Ned Silver, Mike Sparks, Nobumasa Watari, and Odette F. Woitschek, who volunteered much of their energy and made certain that our notables were able to arrive at various places on time witout undue stress.

Many thanks to Kathy Koesterer, Lynn Train, and Kathleen A. Oliver who provided reliable assistance in preparations of indices by operating the word-processors, as well as doing proofreading and other essential work that was so necessary in the completion of this volume. Their efforts were both critical and effective! What more can one ask? Furthermore, the volume's completion was greatly facilitated by the effective professionalism of John Eagleson, production editor; we are deeply indebted to him.

Chizuko Izawa
December, 1987

Author Index

Subject Index